A History of

The [illegible] y

BY

THE HON. J. W. FORTESCUE

SECOND PART CONTINUED—FROM THE RENEWAL OF WAR TO THE EVACUATION OF RIO DE LA PLATA

VOL. V

1803–1807

The Naval & Military Press Ltd

Published by
The Naval & Military Press Ltd
Unit 10, Ridgewood Industrial Park,
Uckfield, East Sussex,
TN22 5QE England
Tel: +44 (0) 1825 749494
Fax: +44 (0) 1825 765701

www.naval-military-press.com

A
HISTORY OF THE BRITISH ARMY

PREFATORY NOTE

In order to save space, no authorities have been quoted in the text for statements concerning the recruiting, strength, and establishment of the Army, or concerning the Militia and Volunteers at large; such authorities being set forth at length in the author's supplementary volume, *The County Lieutenancies and the Army, 1803–1814* (Macmillan, 1909).

Since it has become necessary in the present volume frequently to designate French and occasionally other foreign Regiments by their numbers, such numbers are printed in the text in Arabic numerals, to distinguish them from the British Regiments, whose numbers are printed in full. Thus "the Thirty-first" signifies a British Regiment; but "the 31st" a French or other foreign Regiment.

CONTENTS

BOOK XIII

CHAPTER I

The East Indies

CHAPTER II

The East Indies

CHAPTER III

The East Indies

CHAPTER IV

The East Indies

CHAPTER V

Ceylon

CHAPTER VI

England

The West Indies

CHAPTER VII

ENGLAND

CHAPTER VIII

England

THE WEST INDIES

THE MEDITERRANEAN

THE WEST INDIES

CHAPTER IX

THE MEDITERRANEAN

EXPEDITION TO THE ELBE

CHAPTER X

England

Cape of Good Hope

South America

Europe

CHAPTER XI

The Mediterranean

CHAPTER XII

South America

CHAPTER XIII

South America

MAPS AND PLANS

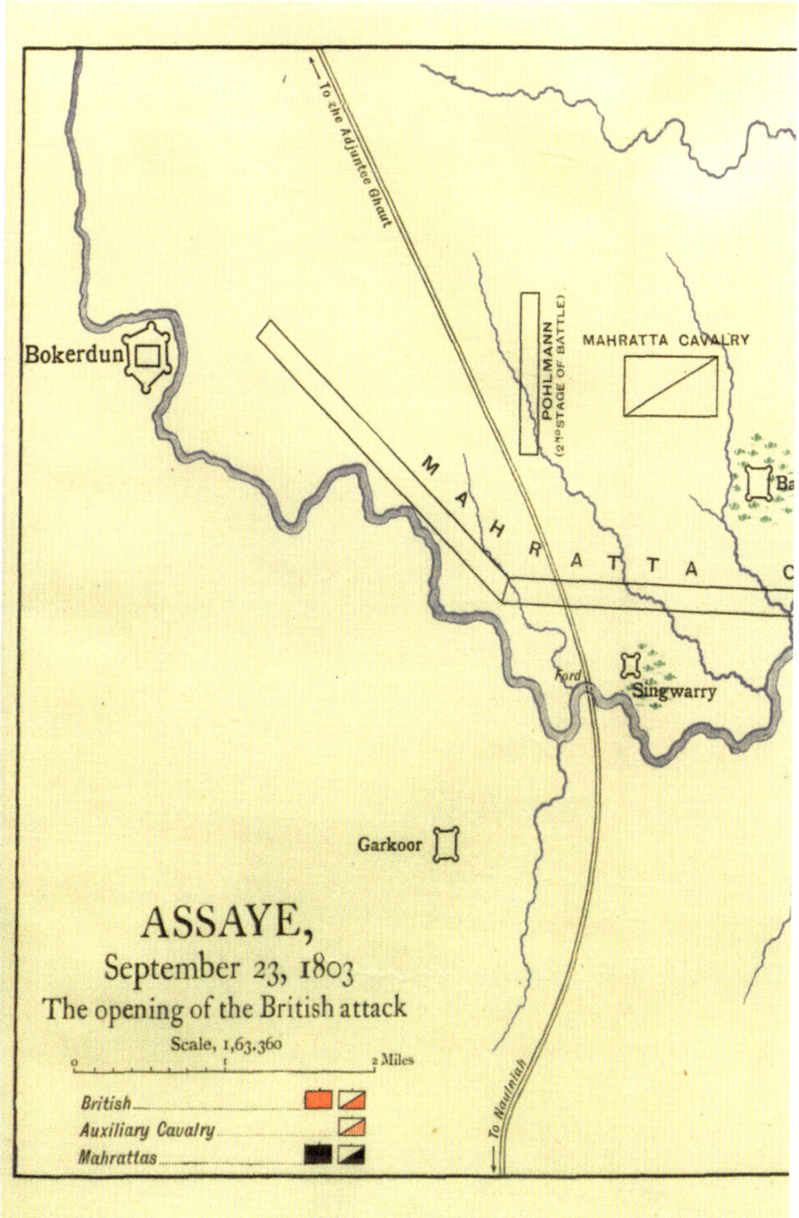

To the Adjuntee Ghaut
Bokerdun
POHLMANN
(2ND STAGE OF BATTLE)
MAHRATTA CAVALRY
MAHRATTA
Ford
Singwarry
Garkoor
To Naulniah
ASSAYE,
September 23, 1803
The opening of the British attack
Scale, 1,63.360
0
1
2 Miles
British
Auxiliary Cavalry
Mahrattas

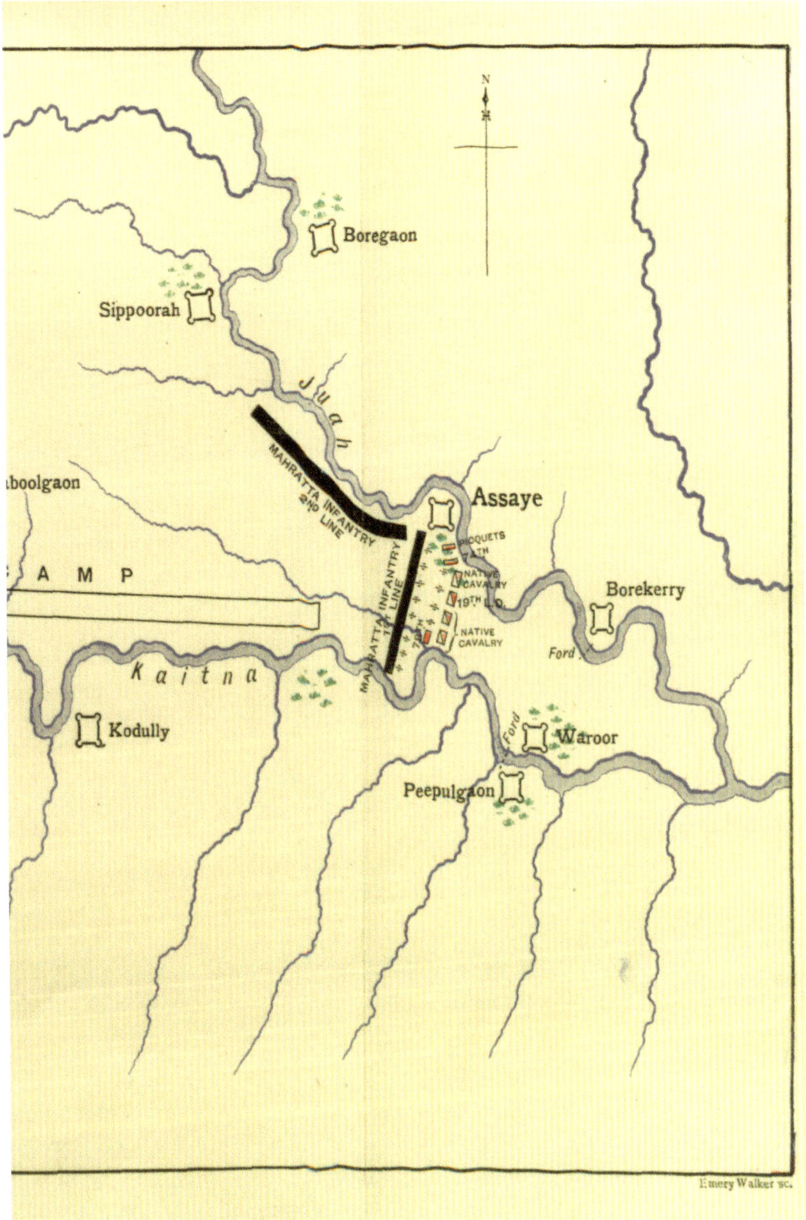

N
Boregaon
Sippoorah
Juah
MAHRATTA INFANTRY 2ND LINE
aboolgaon
Assaye
PICQUETS
74TH
NATIVE CAVALRY
19TH L.D.
78TH
NATIVE CAVALRY
MAHRATTA INFANTRY 1ST LINE
C A M P
Borekerry
Ford
Kaitna
Kodully
Ford
Waroor
Peepulgaon
Emery Walker sc.

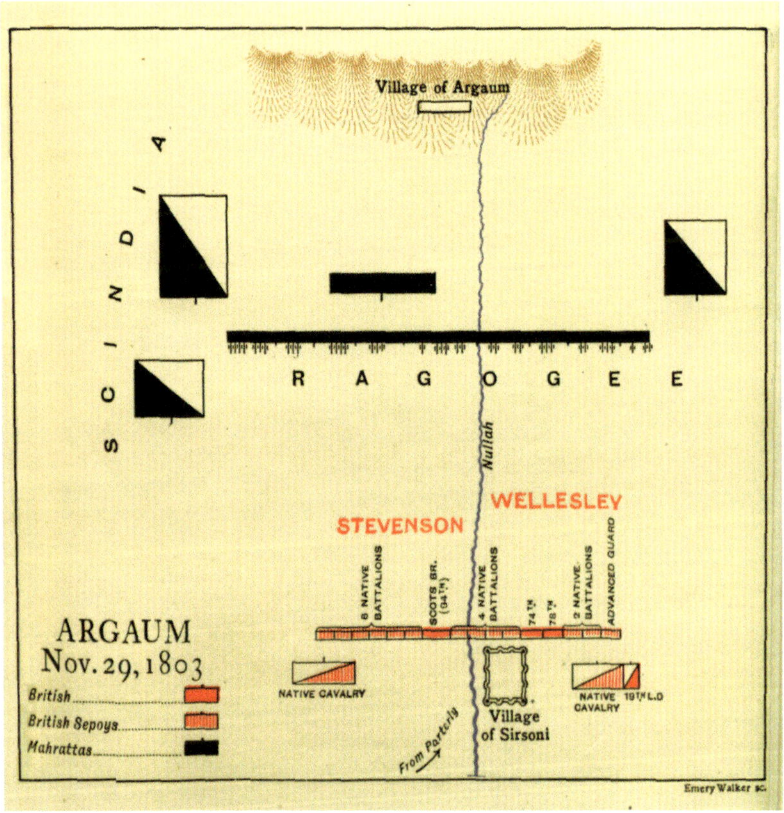

Village of Argaum
S C I N D I A
R A G O G E E
Nullah
WELLESLEY
STEVENSON
6 NATIVE BATTALIONS
SCOTS BR. (94TH)
4 NATIVE BATTALIONS
74TH
78TH
2 NATIVE BATTALIONS
ADVANCED GUARD
NATIVE CAVALRY
NATIVE CAVALRY
19TH L.D
Village of Sirsoni
From Parterly
ARGAUM
Nov. 29, 1803
British
British Sepoys
Mahrattas
Emery Walker sc.

Mota
Labada
STEVENSON
DEC. 12
NORTH GATE
Breached and taken by assault DEC.14-15
N.W.GATE
GATE
GATE
Escaladed
DEC. 15
Gawilghur
SOUTH GATE
WELLESLEY
DEC. 9
Sources of the Poorna and
Chandrabhaga

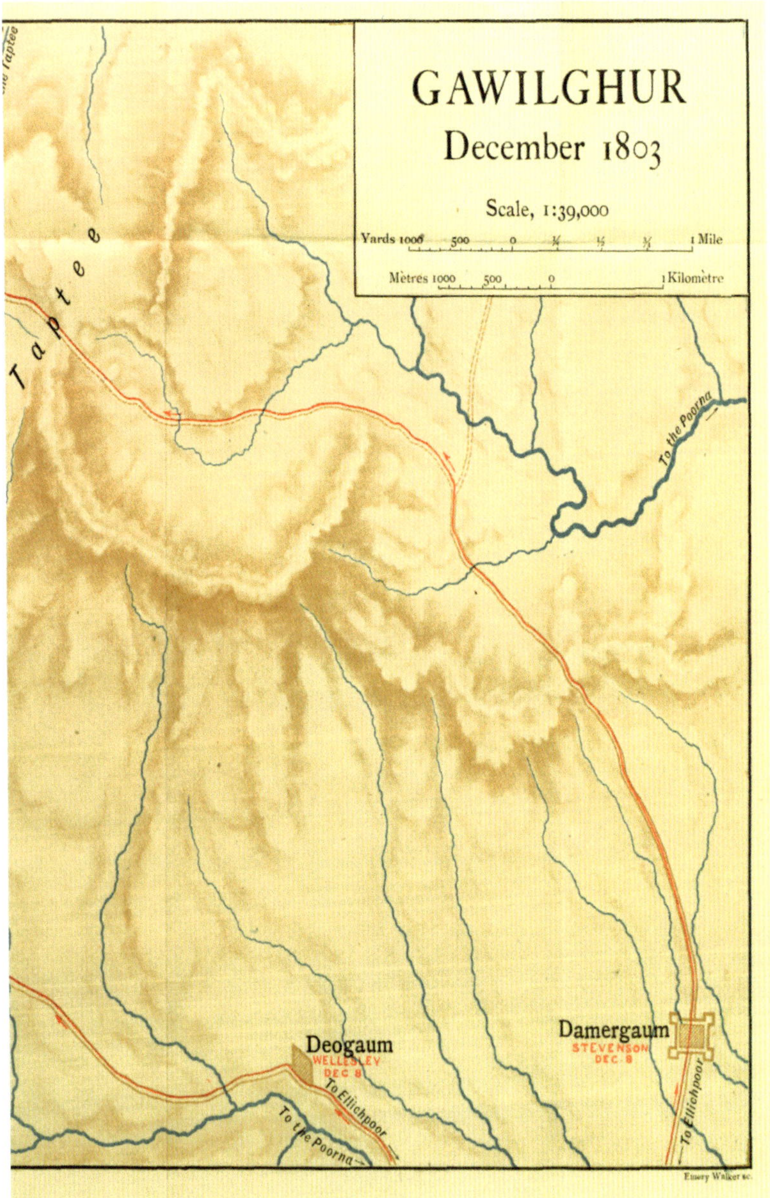
GAWILGHUR
December 1803
Scale, 1:39,000
Yards 1000 500 0 ¼ ½ ¾ 1 Mile
Mètres 1000 500 0 1 Kilomètre
Taptee
To the Poorna
Deogaum
WELLESLEY
DEC 8
To Ellichpoor
To the Poorna
Damergaum
STEVENSON
DEC 8
To Ellichpoor
Emery Walker sc.

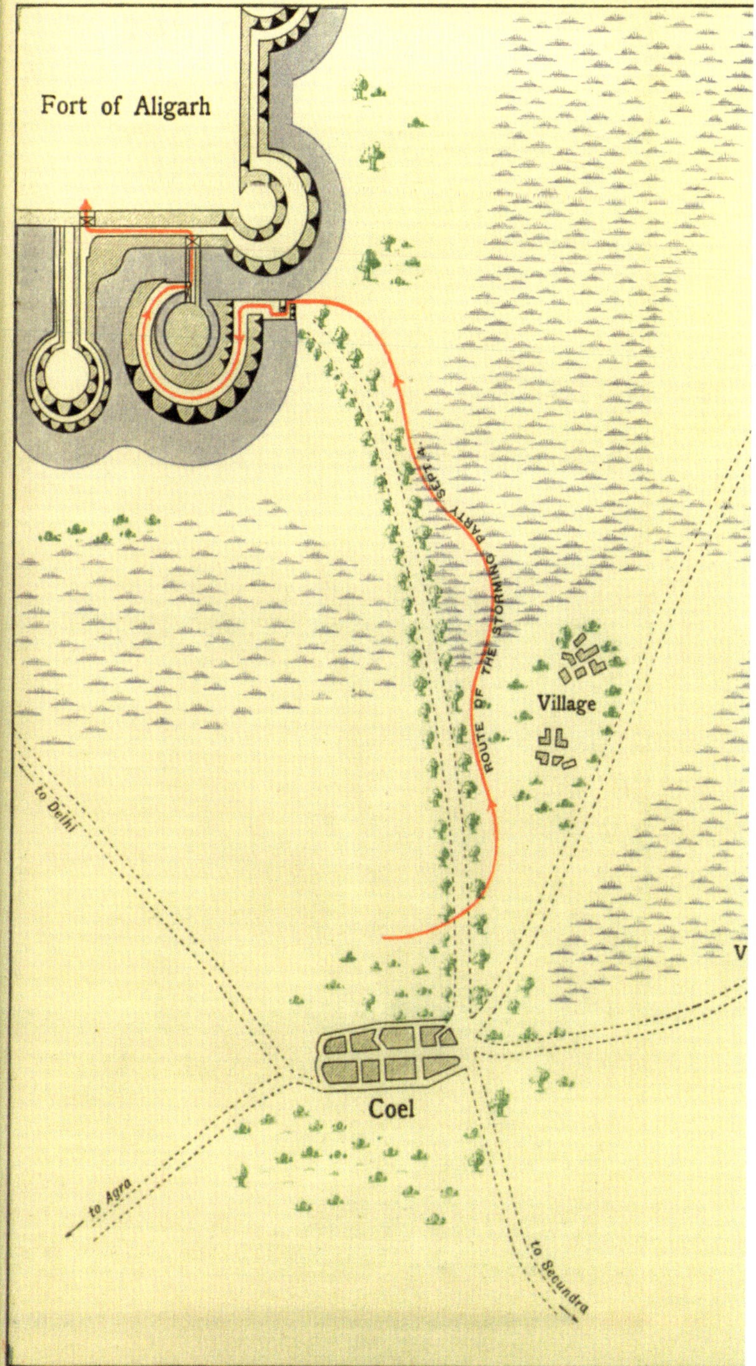
Fort of Aligarh
ROUTE OF THE STORMING PARTY SEPT. 4.
Village
to Delhi
Coel
to Agra
to Secundra

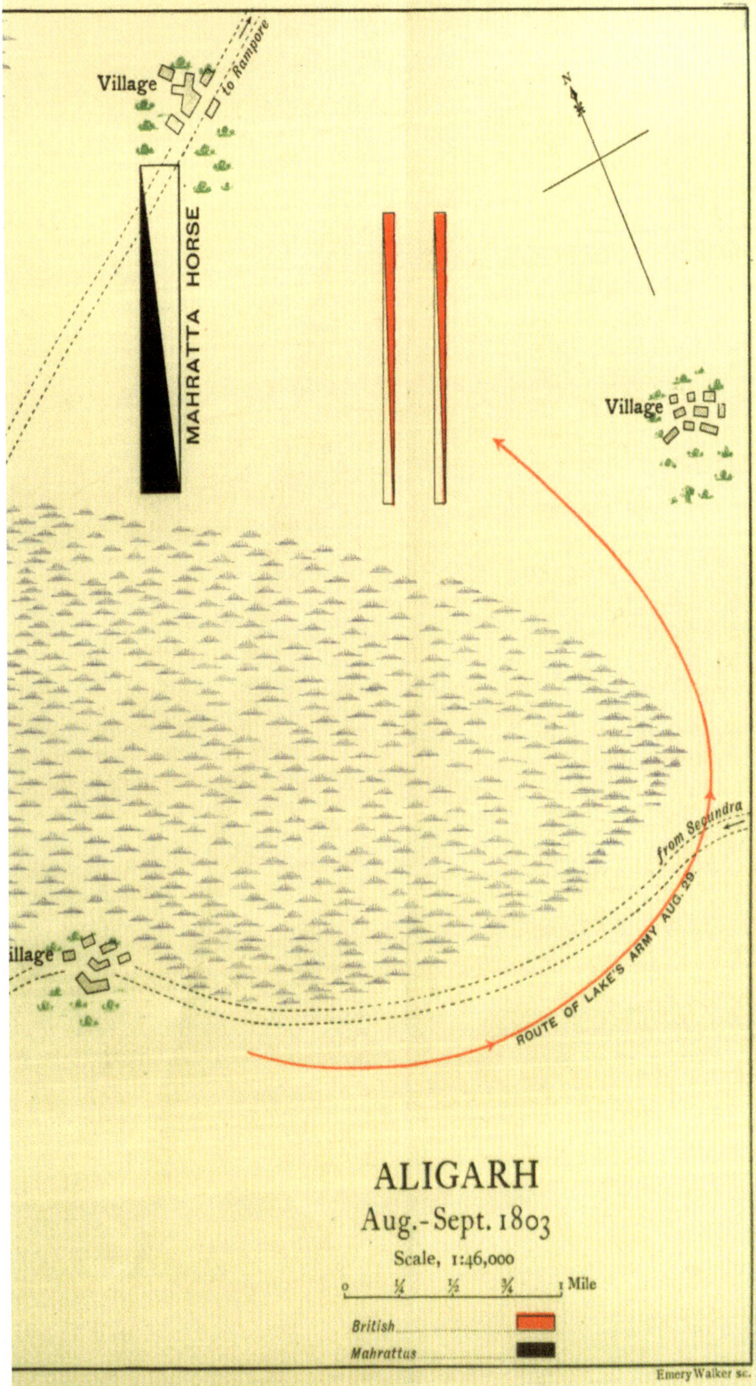
Village
to Rampore
N
MAHRATTA HORSE
Village
Village
from Secundra
ROUTE OF LAKE'S ARMY AUG. 29.
ALIGARH
Aug.-Sept. 1803
Scale, 1:46,000
0 ¼ ½ ¾ 1 Mile
British
Mahrattas
Emery Walker sc.

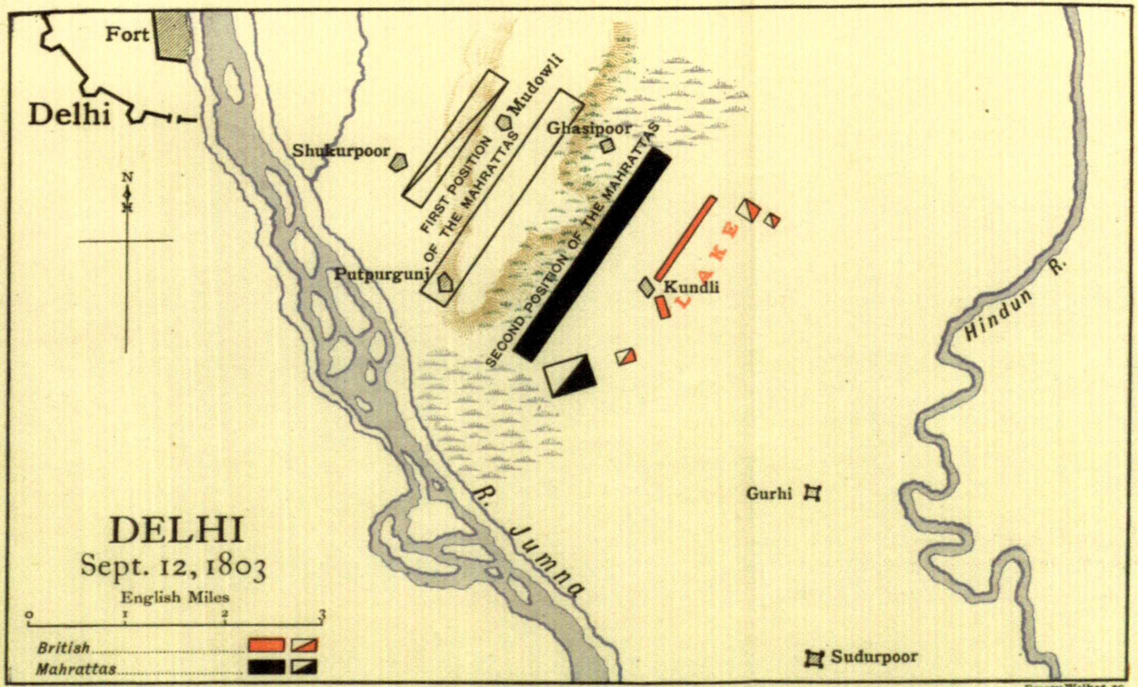
DELHI
Sept. 12, 1803
English Miles
0
1
2
3
British
Mahrattas
Delhi
Fort
Shukurpoor
Mudowli
Ghasipoor
FIRST POSITION OF THE MAHRATTAS
SECOND POSITION OF THE MAHRATTAS
Putpurgunj
Kundli
LAKE
N
R. Jumna
Hindun R.
Gurhi
Sudurpoor
Emery Walker sc.

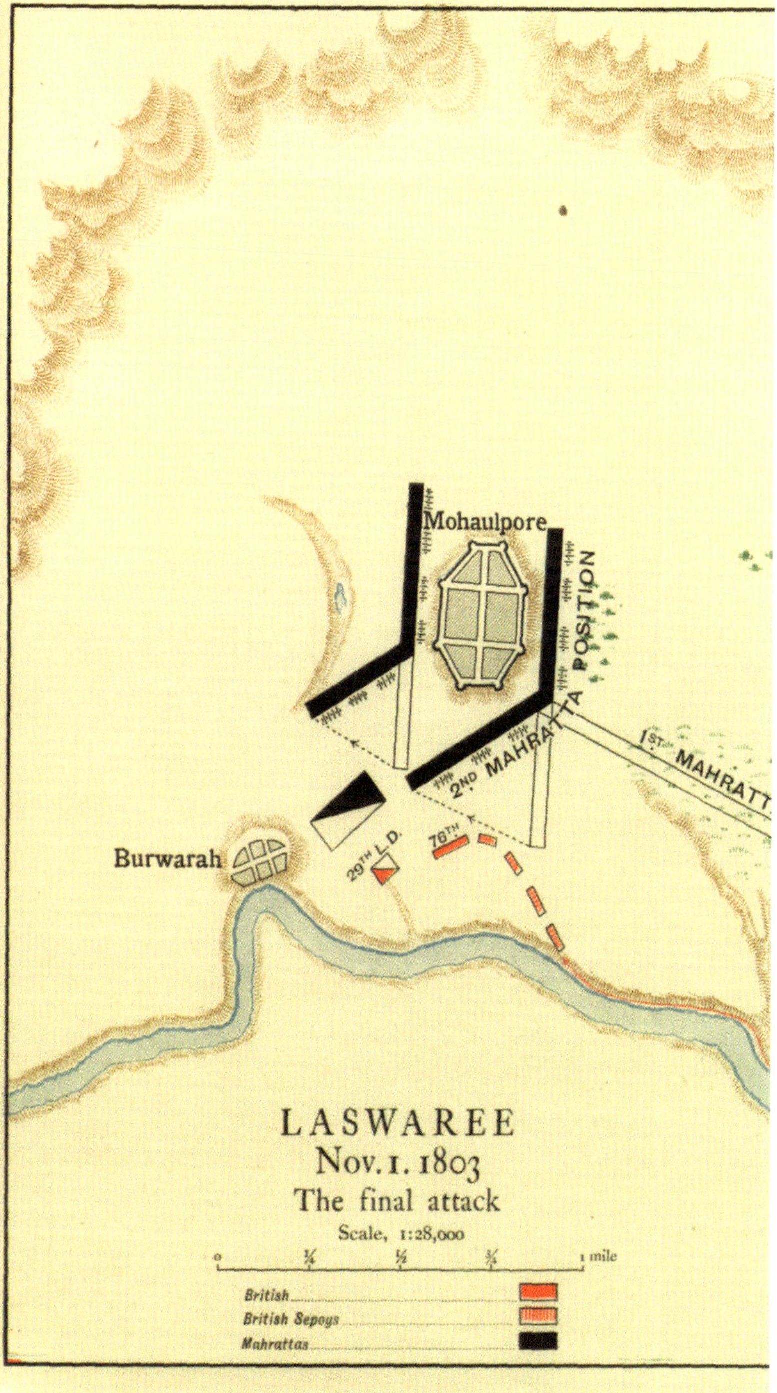

LASWAREE
Nov. 1. 1803
The final attack

Scale, 1:28,000

N
27TH L.D.
6TH N.C.
Sajepoorah
1ST BRIGADE
2ND & 4TH N.C.
SITE OF MACAN'S ATTACK
A POSITION
Singrah
ADVANCE OF BRITISH INFANTRY
Laswaree
Hussowly
Moopery
from Futtehpoor
Emery Walker sc.

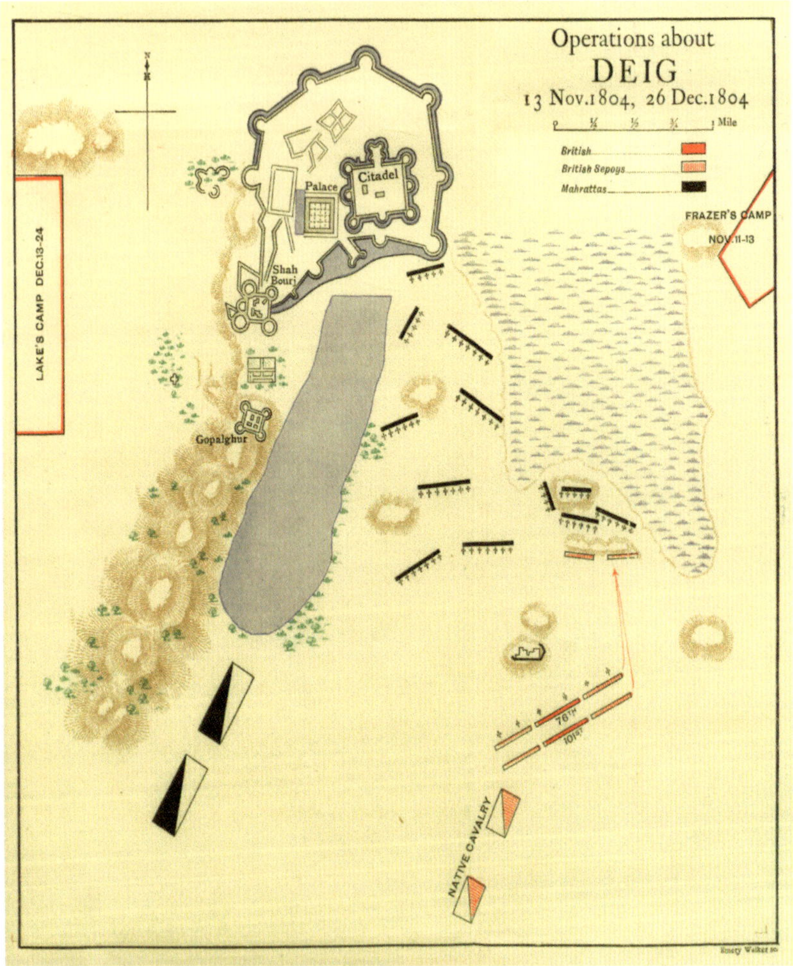

Operations about
DEIG
13 Nov. 1804, 26 Dec. 1804
Mile
British
British Sepoys
Mahrattas
Citadel
Palace
Shah Bourj
Gopalghur
LAKE'S CAMP DEC.13-24
FRAZER'S CAMP NOV. 11-13
76TH
101ST
NATIVE CAVALRY

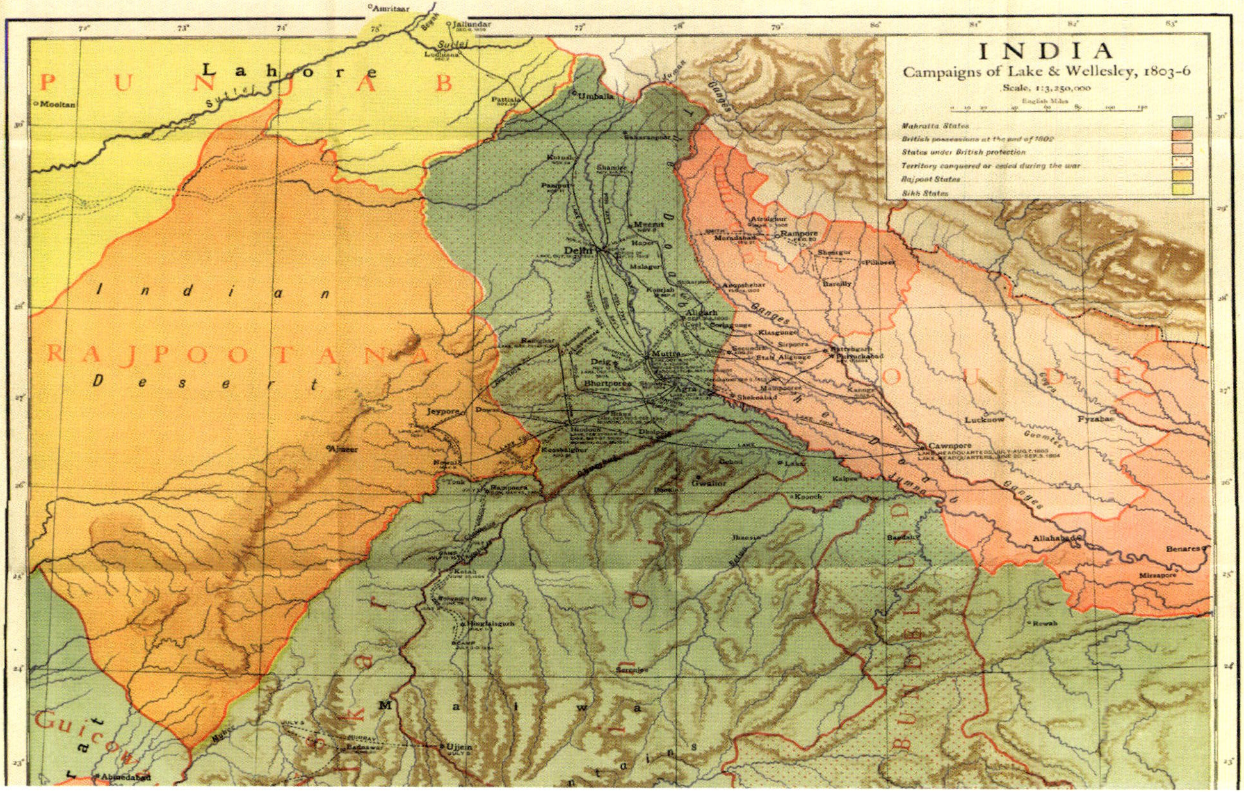

INDIA
Campaigns of Lake & Wellesley, 1803-6
Scale, 1:3,250,000
English Miles
Mahratta States
British possessions at the end of 1802
States under British protection
Territory conquered or ceded during the war
Rajpoot States
Sikh States
PUNJAB
Lahore
RAJPOOTANA
Indian Desert
OUDE
BUNDELCUND
Malwa
Delhi
Agra
Cawnpore
Lucknow
Allahabad
Benares
Gwalior
Jeypore
Ujjein
Ganges
Jumna
Sutlej

Gulf of Cambay
Baroda
Baroach
Surat
Songhur
Indore
Hosingabad
Nerbudda
Taptee
Satpura Hills
Asseerghur
Burhanpore
Deogaum
Damergaum
Ellichpoor
Argaum
Parterly
Akola
Nagpore
Wurda
Berar
Ragogee Bhonsla
Adjunta
Adjunta Ghaut
Assaye
Jafferabad
Naulniah
Wakud
Aurungabad
Bodnapoor
Jalnapoor
Toka
Partoor
Rackisbaum
Patree
Godavery
Nizams Dominions
Chandore
Bassein
Dongaur
Salsette I.
Bombay
Campoly
Shore Ghaut
Choule
Khandalla
Ahmednugger
Poona
Little Shore Ghaut
Eckluss
Satara
Beejapore
Kistna
Kolapore
Belgaum
Darwar
Goa
Curwar
Concan
Western Ghauts
Peishwa's Dominions
Hyderabad
Bhima
Moodgul
Copal
Tumbudra
Bellary
Gooty
Hurryhur
Mysore
Eastern Ghauts
Carnatic
Cuddapah
Nellore
Pennar
Ongola
Guntoor
Masulipatam
Mouths of the Kistna
Mouths of the Godavery
Condore
Rajamundry
Northern Sirkars
73°
74°
75°
76°
77°
78°
79°
80°
81°
82°
22°
21°
20°
19°
18°
17°
16°
15°
Emery Walker sc.

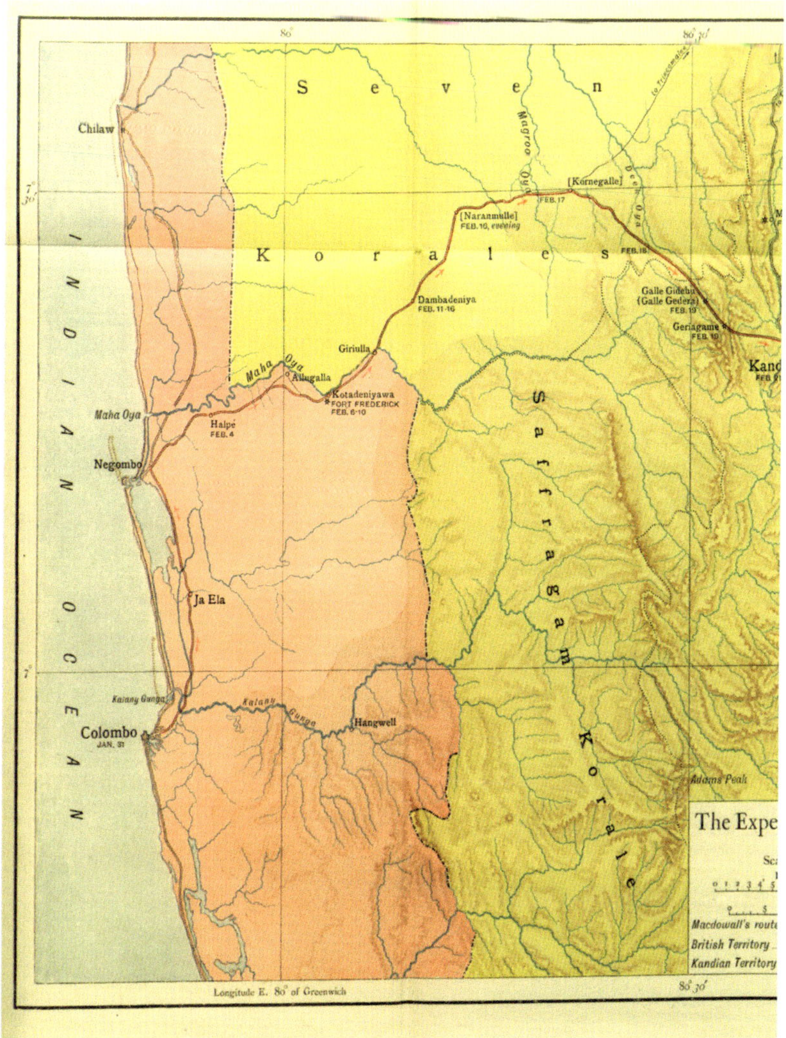

Seven Korales
Saffragam Korale
INDIAN OCEAN
Chilaw
[Kornegalle]
FEB. 17
[Naranmulle]
FEB. 16, evening
FEB. 18
Magroo Oya
Dambadeniya
FEB. 11-16
Giriulla
Maha Oya
Allugalla
Kotadeniyawa
FORT FREDERICK
FEB. 6-10
Halpe
FEB. 4
Negombo
Ja Ela
Kalany Ganga
Colombo
JAN. 31
Hangwell
Adams Peak
British Territory
Kandian Territory
80°
80° 30'
7° 30'
7°
Longitude E. 80° of Greenwich

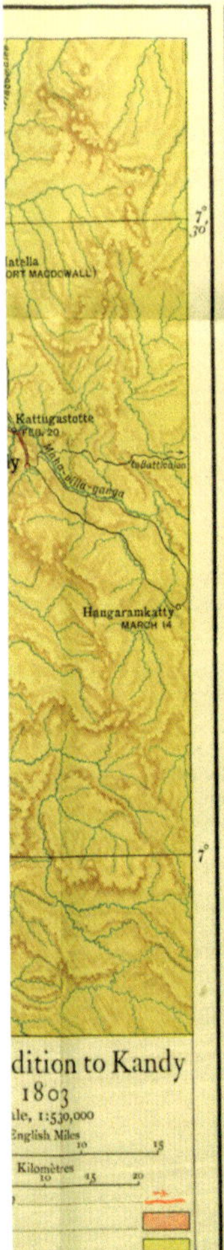

Kattugastotte
Maha-villa-ganga
Hangaramkatty
MARCH 14
dition to Kandy
1803
ale, 1:530,000
English Miles
Kilomètres

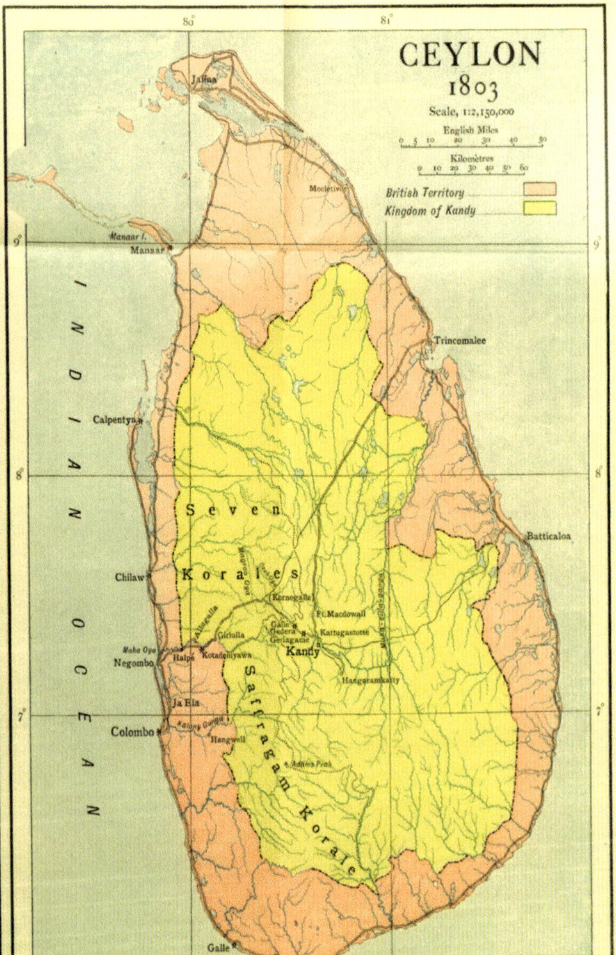

CEYLON
1803
Scale, 1:2,150,000
English Miles
Kilomètres
British Territory
Kingdom of Kandy
INDIAN OCEAN
Jaffna
Moeletivo
Manaar I.
Manaar
Trincomalee
Calpentyn
Seven Korales
Batticaloa
Chilaw
Kornegalle
Ft. Macdowall
Giriulla
Kattugastotte
Kandy
Maha Oya
Negombo
Halpe
Kotadeniyawa
Hangaramkatty
Saffragam Korale
Ja Ela
Colombo
Hangwell
Galle
Matura
Dondra Hd.
81° Longitude E. of Greenwich
Emery Walker sc.

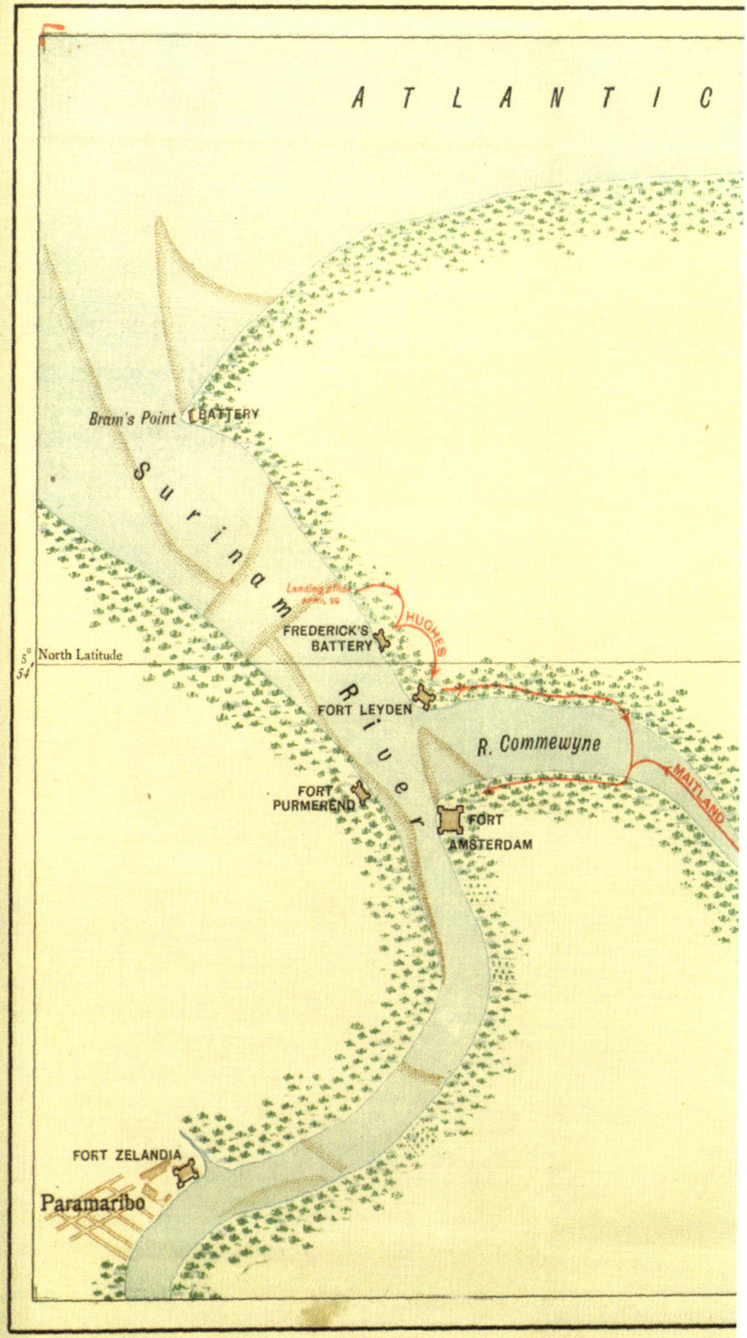
ATLANTIC
Bram's Point
BATTERY
Surinam River
Landing place
HUGHES
FREDERICK'S BATTERY
5° 54' North Latitude
FORT LEYDEN
R. Commewyne
MAITLAND
FORT PURMEREND
FORT AMSTERDAM
FORT ZELANDIA
Paramaribo

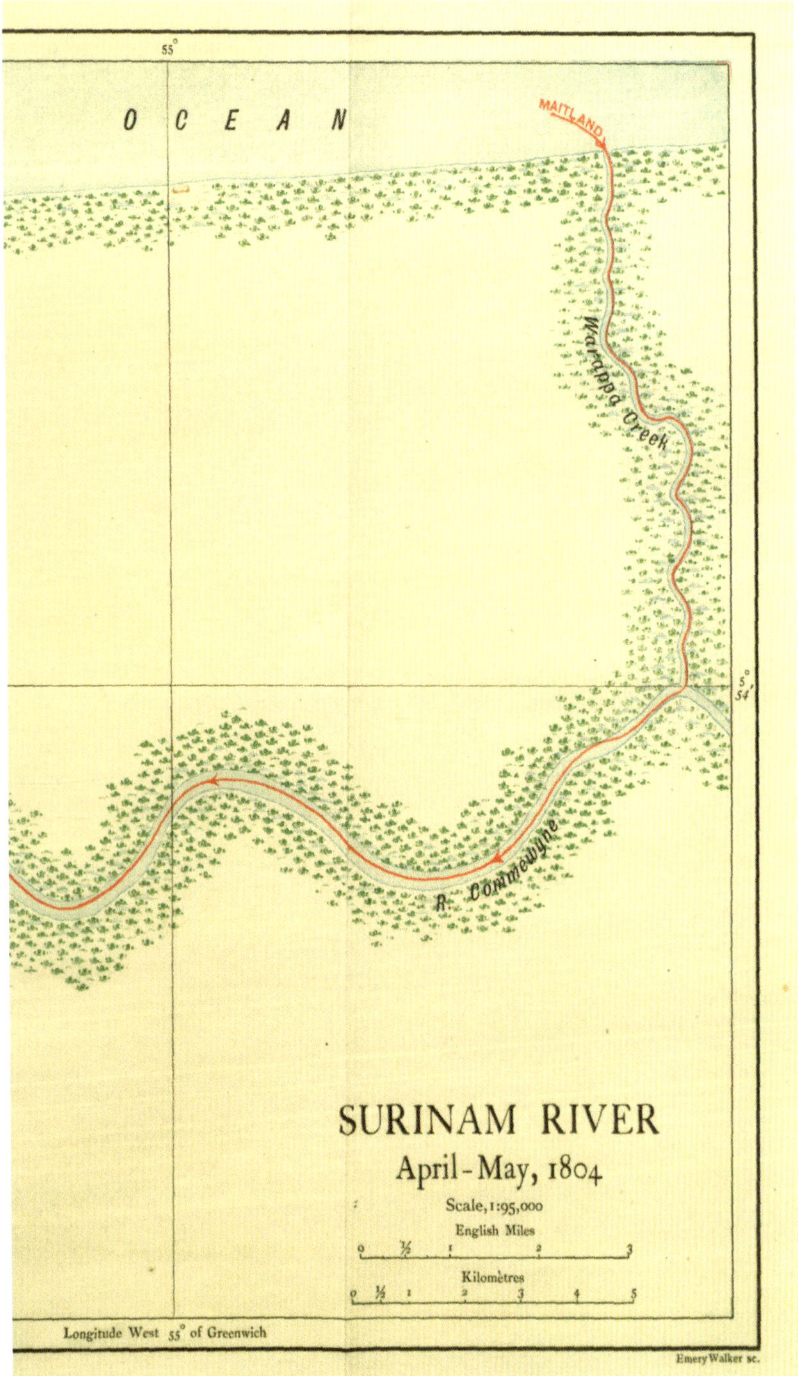
55°
OCEAN
MAITLAND
Warappa Creek
5° 54′
R. Commewyne
SURINAM RIVER
April - May, 1804
Scale, 1:95,000
English Miles
0 ½ 1 2 3
Kilomètres
0 ½ 1 2 3 4 5
Longitude West 55° of Greenwich
Emery Walker sc.

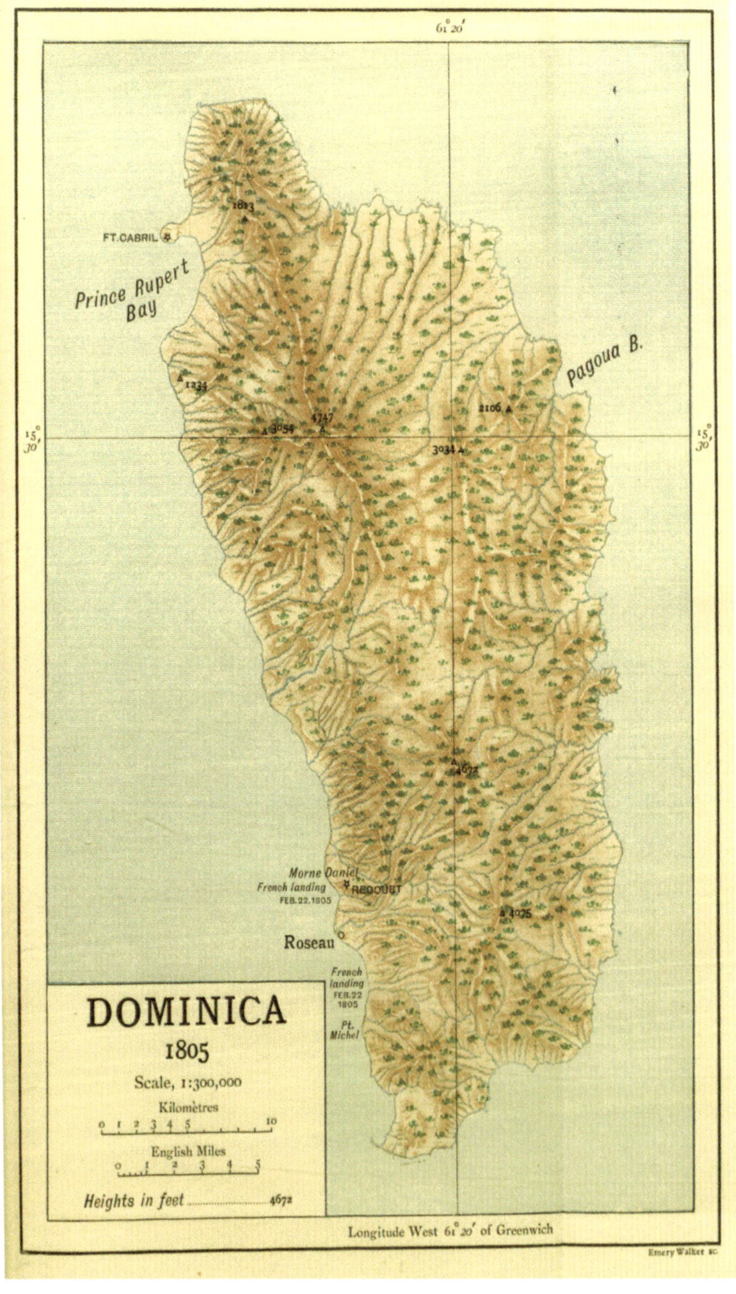
DOMINICA
1805
Scale, 1:300,000
Kilomètres
0 1 2 3 4 5 10
English Miles
0 1 2 3 4 5
Heights in feet 4672
Prince Rupert Bay
FT. CABRIL
Pagoua B.
Morne Daniel
French landing FEB. 22. 1805
REDOUBT
Roseau
French landing FEB. 22 1805
Pt. Michel
61° 20′
15° 30′
Longitude West 61° 20′ of Greenwich
Emery Walker sc.

Environs of
MAIDA
Contours at intervals of 20 metres
St. Euphemia
Bay of St. Euphemia
R. Lamato
French Camp
San Pietro di Maida
Maida
Ancona
The Marches
Abruzzi
Pescara
Sulmona
ADRIATIC SEA
Molise
Capitinata
Pontecorvo
Sessa
Gaeta
Gulf of Gaeta
Terra di Lavoro
Capua
Benevento
Principato Ultra
Principato Citra
Naples
Ischia
Capri
Basilicata
Bari
Otranto
Matera
Tarento
Brindisi
Policastro
Cas. of Roseta
Gulf of Tarento
TYRRHENIAN SEA
PAPAL STATES

SOUTHERN ITALY AND SICILY
Scale, 1:2,000,000
English Miles
Kilometres
CAPRI
October, 1808
Scale, 1:72,500
English Miles
Contours at intervals of 20 metres
MAIDA
4 July, 1806
Scale, 1:50,000
Scale of 1 mile
Contours at intervals of 10 metres
FRENCH CAMP
COLE
OSWALD
ACLAND
KEMPT
DIGONET
PEYRI
COMPERE
R. Lamato
To Maida
SICILY
Calabria
THE TWO SICILIES
MEDITERRANEAN SEA
Lipari Isles
Gulf of Policastro
Palermo
Trapani
Marsala
Mazzara
Castro Giovanni
Girgenti
Terranova
Syracuse
Agosta
Catania
R. Giaretta
Mt. Etna
Taormina
Milazzo
Messina
S. Placido
Faro Pt
Scilla
Pezzo
Reggio
Palmi
Tropea
Monteleone
G. of St. Euphemia
Maida
St. Euphemia
Nicastro
Amantea
Cosenza
Catanzaro
Cotrone
R. Crati
C. Passaro
Malta
Valetta
Capri
Anacapri
Marina Grande
Porto Tragara
Punta Tragara
Grotta Verde
Limbo
Damecuta
Monte Solaro
Longitude East 16° of Greenwich
14°
18°
36°
38°
Emery Walker sc.

Skagerack
Cattegat
Jutland
DENMARK
Schleswig
Holstein
Fünen
Zealand
Anholt
The Sound
Gottenburg
Elsinore
Helsingborg
Kronborg
Scania
SW
Copenhagen
Roskilde
Amager
Saltholm
Malmö
Kiöge
Kiöge Bay
Möen
Rügen
Stralsund
Swedish Pomerania
Kiel
To Oldenburg
Cuxhaven (To Hamburg)
Elbe
Weser
OLDENBURG
Glückstadt
Lübeck
Stade
Bremerlehe
Hamburg
MECKLENBURG SCHWERIN
MECKLENBURG STRELITZ
Strelitz
Schwerin
Lauenburg
Lüneburg
Blumenthal
Bremen
HANOVER (Brunswick-Lüneburg)
To Brunswick-Wolfenbüttel
Verden
Hoya
Nienburg
Minden
LIPPE
Hanover
Aller
Leine
Pom
Stettin
Oder
P R
Branden
Berlin
Brandenburg
Potsdam
Longitude East 14° of Greenwich
Hameln
Hildesheim

NORTH GERMANY
AND DENMARK
Scale, 1:2,000,000
English Miles
0 10 20 30 40 50 100
Kilomètres
0 10 20 30 40 50 100
16°
18°
20°
22°
56°
54°
E D E N
Gothland
Baltic
Sea
RUSSIA
Memel
Tilsit
Bornholm
(To Denmark)
Königsberg
Friedland
Eylau
Braunsberg
Frische Haff
Passarge
Dantzic
Vistula
East
Wormditt
Heilsberg
Guttstadt
Colberg
West
Prussia
Allenstein
Osterode
Prussia
Graudenz
Gilgenburg
New
East
Prussia
Thorn
Pultusk
Warsaw
U S S I A
b u r g
South Prussia
Posen
Emery Walker, sc.

From Saldanha Bay
Melkbosch Pt.
Robben I.
Table Bay
Lion's Rump
Cape Town
Salt R.
Salt River
Table Mountain
Scale, 1:950,000
English Miles
Wynberg
Muizenberg
Simon's B.
Simonstown
False Bay
Olifants R.
Roggeveld Mountains
Nieuwveld Mountains
Great Kar
Berg R.
Saldanha Bay
Zwarte Bergen
Olifants R.
Little Karroo
Breede R.
Robben I.
Table B.
Cape Town
Stellenbosch
Simon's B.
Simonstown
HOTTENTOT'S HOLLAND
False Bay
Mossel Bay
Gouritz R.
C. Agulhas
Longit

24°
26°
28°
30°
32°
34°
Orange R.
Caledon R.
Sneeuwberg
Graaf Reinet
Sundays R.
Groote R.
Gt. Kei R.
Gt. Fish R.
Algoa Bay
Gamtoos R.
CAPE COLONY
Scale, 1:3,500,000
English Miles
0 10 20 30 40 50 100 150
Longitude East 24° of Greenwich
Emery Walker

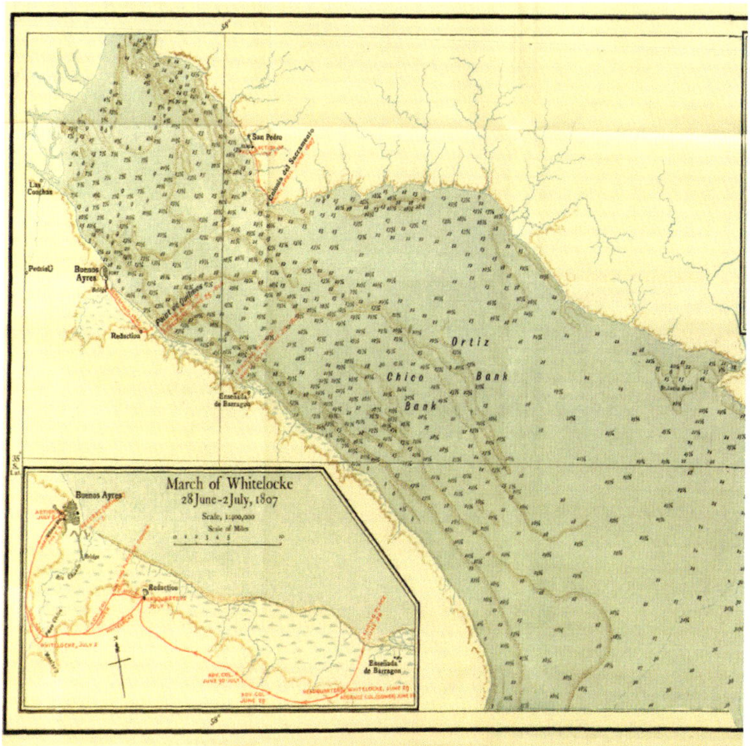
March of Whitelocke
28 June-2 July, 1807
Scale of Miles
Buenos Ayres
Redaction
Ensenada de Barragon
Bridge
San Pedro
Colonia del Sacramento
Las Conchas
Ortiz
Bank
Chico
Bank

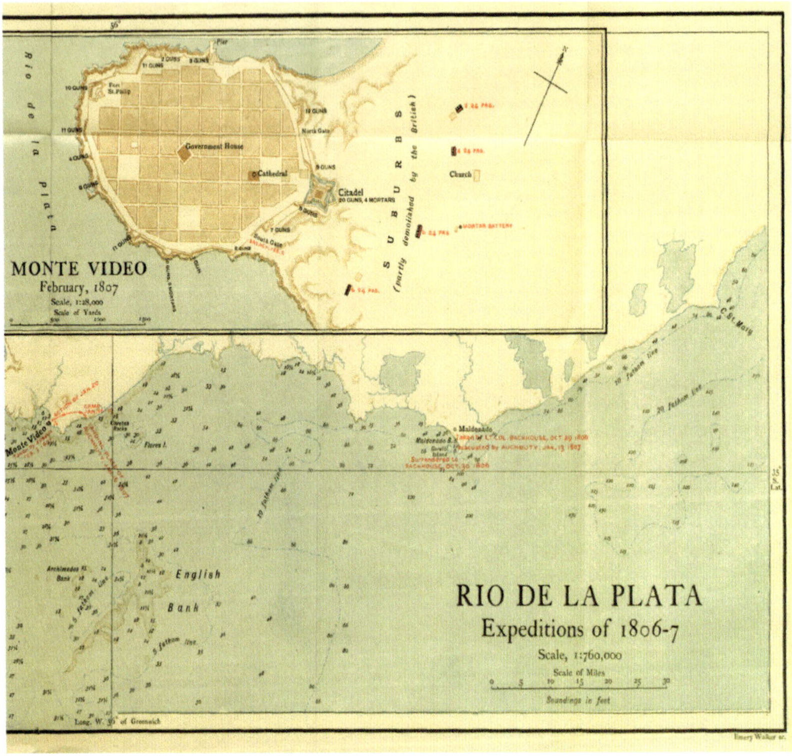
MONTE VIDEO
February, 1807
Scale, 1:28,000
Scale of Yards
Rio de la Plata
Government House
Cathedral
Citadel
20 GUNS, 4 MORTARS
North Gate
South Gate
Church
SUBURBS
(partly demolished by the British)
MORTAR BATTERY
English
Bank
Archimedes Bank
Flores I.
Maldonado
C. St. Mary
RIO DE LA PLATA
Expeditions of 1806-7
Scale, 1:760,000
Scale of Miles
Soundings in feet
Long. W. 56° of Greenwich
Emery Walker sc.

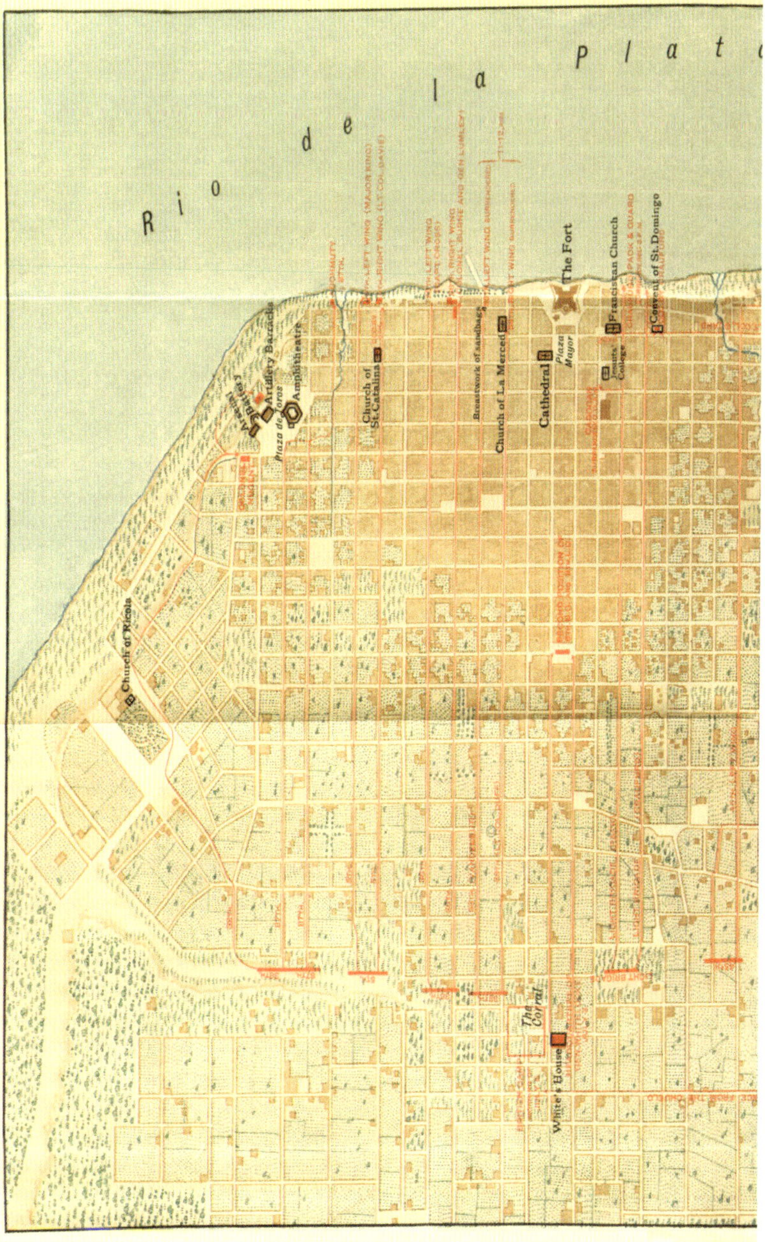

Rio de la Plata
Arsenal
Battery
Artillery Barracks
Plaza de Toros
Amphitheatre
Church of St. Catalina
Breastwork of sandbags
Church of La Merced
Cathedral
Plaza Mayor
The Fort
Jesuits College
Franciscan Church
Convent of St. Domingo
Church of Ricola
The Corral
White's House

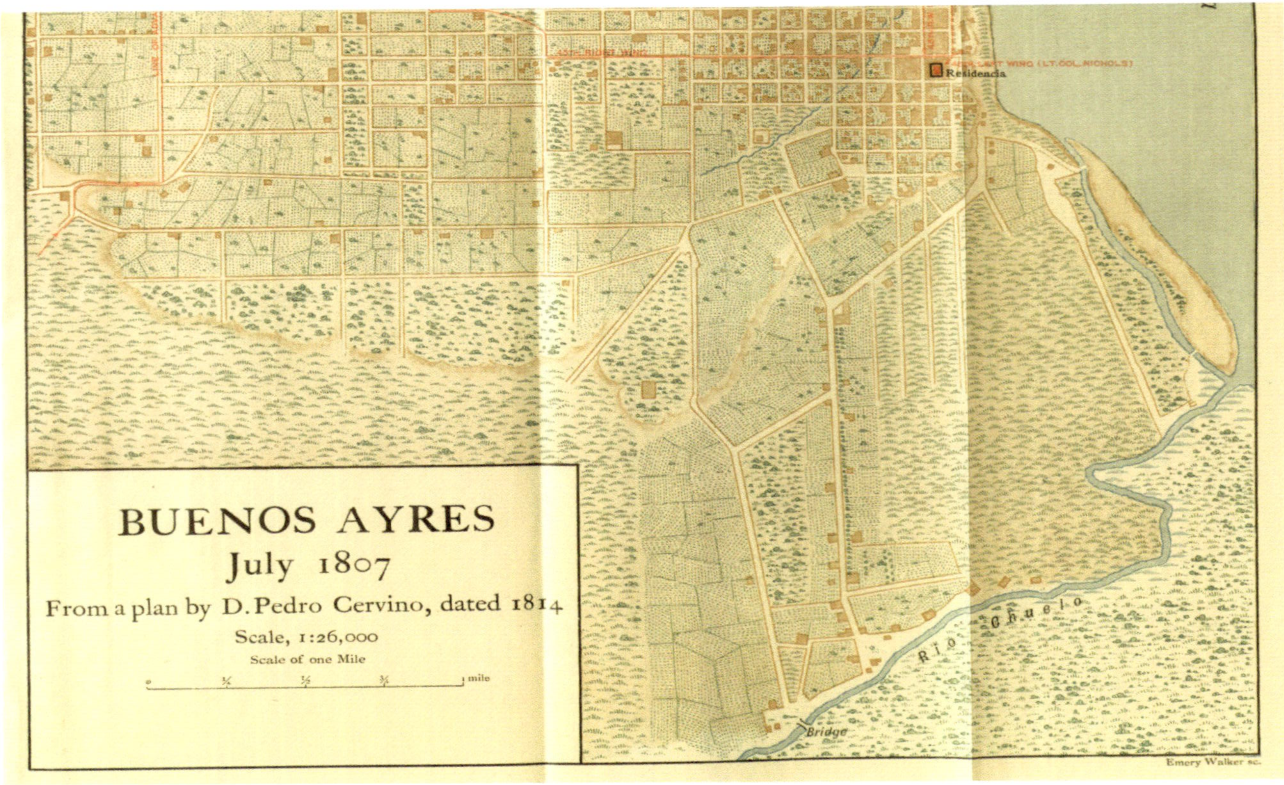
Residencia
Rio Chuelo
Bridge
BUENOS AYRES
July 1807
From a plan by D. Pedro Cervino, dated 1814
Scale, 1:26,000
Scale of one Mile
0
¼
½
¾
1 mile
Emery Walker sc.

EUROPE
from the Peace of Tilsit, July 1807,
to the War with Austria, 1809.
Scale, 1:19,000,000
English Miles
0 50 100 200 300 400
BRITISH ISLES
IRELAND
SCOTLAND
WALES
ENGLAND
London
North Sea
Atlantic Ocean
English Channel
Channel Islands
NORWAY
SWEDEN
Stockholm
Christiania
Skagerrack
DENMARK
Copenhagen
Baltic
Heligoland
SWEDISH POMERANIA
POMERANIA
PRUSSIA
Berlin
BRANDENBURG
GRAND DUCHY OF WARSAW
SAXONY
Dresden
HOLLAND
Amsterdam
HANOVER
BOHEMIA
AUSTRIAN EMPIRE
Vienna
HUNGARY
BAVARIA
Munich
TYROL
SALZBURG
Paris
Orleans
Bay of Biscay
FRANCE
Lyons
Bordeaux
Toulouse
Strassburg
HELVETIA
SAVOY
PIEDMONT
Turin
Milan
Venice
Genoa
LUCCA
TUSCANY
Florence
PAPAL STATES
Rome
Corsica
SARDINIA
Adriatic Sea
BOSNIA
Naples
KINGDOM OF THE TWO SICILIES
SICILY
Palermo
Malta
Ionian Islands
SPAIN
Madrid
PORTUGAL
Lisbon
Oporto
ANDORRA
Barcelona
Balearic Islands
Mallorca
Minorca
Gibraltar
Mediterranean
MOROCCO
ALGIERS
TUNIS
AFRICA
TRIPO
Meridian 0° of Greenwich
Longitude East

Boundary of France 1792
France at the end of 1802
Acquisitions 1803-7
Kingdom of Italy directly ruled by Napoleon
Dependent States
Kingdom of Sardinia
Sweden
Confederation of the Rhine under the protection of Napoleon, signed at Paris, July 1806.
Boundary of Confederation
Bavaria, Württemberg, Baden, Berg,
H.D. Hesse-Darmstadt, N.U. Nassau-Usingen,
N.W. Nassau-Weilberg, SLM. Salm-Salm,
S.K. Salm-Kryburg, H.H. Hohenz,-Hechingen,
H.S. Hohenz.-Sigmaringen, AR. Aremberg,
IS. Isenberg, LCH. Lichtenstein, LN. Leyen.
July 12
WBG. Würzburg, September 15
Kingdom of Saxony, December 11
5 Dukes of Saxony, " 15
(THUR. Thuringian States)
ANH. Anhalt (3), R. Reuss (4), LP. Lippe (2),
SCHW. Schwarzburg (2), W. Waldeck (1).
April 18, 1807
Westphalia, November 15
Mecklenburg-Strelitz, February 17, 1808
Mecklenburg-Schwerin, March 22
Oldenburg, October 14
B.F. = Black Forest
FINLAND (to Russia 1809)
St. Petersburg
G. of Finland
Riga
Moscow
Borodino
RUSSIA
Tilsit
Friedland
E. PRUSSIA
NEW E. PRUSSIA
WEST GALICIA
Cracow
TRANSYLVANIA
MOLDAVIA
WALLACHIA
Belgrade
SERVIA
Odessa
CRIMEA
Black Sea
Constantinople
Bosphorus
TURKISH EMPIRE
ASIA MINOR
Smyrna
MOREA
Rhodes
Crete
Cyprus
SYRIA
Levant Sea
Acre
Jaffa
Jerusalem
El Arish
Damietta
Rosetta
Aboukir
Alexandria
Mansourah
Ramanieh
Cairo
Suez
EGYPT
of Greenwich
Emery Walker sc.

BOOK XIII

CHAPTER I

IN Europe the Treaty of Amiens brought at least a truce; but east and west, in India and the Antilles, it brought not peace but the sword. The First Consul had gained what he sought—a short breathing-space upon honourable terms. The boundaries of France had been enlarged eastward to the Rhine, and northward to the Dutch frontier. Holland itself, under the name of the Batavian Republic, was subservient to her; and the greater part of Northern Italy was either actually French territory or dominated by French influence. The French Republic within her new limits now counted a population of forty million souls; and with all these vast acquisitions in Europe she still retained the Colonial Empire of the Monarchy. Her East Indian settlements were, under the Treaty, to be restored; in the West Indies Martinique and Tobago were to be again hers, as also was St. Domingo if she could obtain possession of it. Finally, at her head was the man who, after twice raising her from deep depression to dazzling glory, had restored law and order, confidence and credit, and, still insatiable in energy and ambition, was maturing his designs for the conquest of a great empire over sea. 1802.

The conquest of his dreams was that of India, and, as a means to that end, of Egypt. Nelson had turned his first expedition to the valley of the Nile into a disaster, and Sidney Smith and Abercromby had deepened the disaster into a humiliation. His vaunting letter to Tippoo from Cairo had also received a

1802. crushing answer in the storming of Seringapatam and the overthrow of Hyder Ali's dynasty in Mysore. But still the man clung to his vision of the tricolour flying supreme in the Mediterranean, and of French domination substituted for English in India. Thus it was in September 1802 he sent General Sebastiani to Algiers, Egypt, Syria, and the Ionian Islands with orders to take note of every military detail, and to sound the disposi-
1803. tion of the natives. In January 1803 Sebastiani returned with a bombastic report that the capture of Egypt would be child's play, and that the Ionian Islands were only waiting for an opportunity to declare themselves French. Meanwhile, to undermine still further British power in the East, Bonaparte had appointed in June 1802 two even more formidable agents. The first was Cavaignac, an old member of the Convention, who was charged with a mission to the Imaum of Muscat. The second was General Decaen, who bitterly hated the English, and thirsted for the chance of meeting them in the field. In title Decaen was merely Commander-in-Chief of the small French force in the East Indies, entrusted with the special duty of receiving back the captured French settlements from the British; and the troops that were to accompany him were no more than a garrison for those settlements, little exceeding one thousand men.[1] But the Consul's secret instructions showed designs of far wider extent. While acting always with carefully simulated gentleness and simplicity, Decaen was to inquire as to the strength and disposition of the British forces, and as to the natives that were most impatient of British rule. He was to think out in every detail the best method of carrying on a war of several campaigns in India, even without command of the sea; and, above all, he was to find a suitable base, with a port which could be defended against a hostile fleet. "Your mission" (so ended the document) "is, for military and political purposes, one of observation . . . but the First Consul, if you faith-

[1] *Corres. de Napoléon*, 6208, Letter to Decrès, 25th July 1802.

fully fulfil his instructions, may perhaps be able to put you in a position to gain the great glory which prolongs the memory of men beyond the lapse of centuries." 1803.

The date of these secret instructions was the 15th of January 1803, and in them occurs the expression, "unless war breaks out before the end of September 1804," which, elucidated by parallel passages in Napoleon's correspondence, shows that he was reckoning upon that time, and no earlier, for the renewal of hostilities. Evidently he counted upon choosing his own moment for aggression, with such a man as Addington in charge of England; but even if he had reckoned truly herein, which, as events were to prove, he did not, he overlooked the presence in India of Lord Wellesley and his brother Arthur. The destruction of Tippoo Sahib's power in Mysore had at last brought the British and the Mahrattas face to face; and no man of any foresight could doubt that before long there would be a desperate struggle between them for the mastery of India. The refusal of the Mahrattas to take their share in the partition of Mysore had sufficiently shown their jealousy and unfriendly feeling over the British successes in that province; and, divided though they were among themselves, they had begun to realise generally that their chances of supremacy were lost unless they could drive the British from the country. But this was not all. The French officer, Perron, though nominally no more than a commander in Scindia's service, was actually his vicegerent in the north, and, while holding the deposed Emperor Shah Alum in durance, used the imperial name to dignify and strengthen his own authority. So great was his power and so wide its range that he had already seen visions of an independent sovereignty, and he was known to have corresponded with the French Directory with the object of obtaining the support of the Republic. Thus Wellesley was threatened with a resurrection of French rivalry in India, and that not

1803. under the feeble direction of Bourbon kings, but under the active and indefatigable impulse of Bonaparte. To the British Viceroy, therefore, the power of the Mahrattas signified the power of France. Apart from France he was willing to live at peace with them, if by any chance a central authority could be established strong enough to bind the entire Mahratta Confederacy to fulfil a friendly treaty. Then the British dominions would be delivered from continual anarchy upon their frontiers. But while Perron and his compatriots remained in Scindia's service, there could be no trust and no security.

Nevertheless Wellesley's first essay was towards curbing the unruly Mahratta chiefs by restoring the authority of the Peishwa. Since 1798 internal dissensions had brought the whole Confederacy into confusion. In that year a family dispute had driven Scindia into collision with the Rajah of Kolapore, who was already at war with the Peishwa, Baji Rao; whereupon Scindia's rival, Jeswunt Rao Holkar, seized the opportunity to ravage his territory. Perron was fully engaged with the menace of an Afghan invasion in the north, so was unable to help his master; and Scindia and the Peishwa together had much ado to check the advance of the Rajah of Kolapore upon Poona. In the midst of the troubles, however, Scindia fell at variance with the Peishwa, first over the property of the latter's chief minister, Nana Farnavese, who died in March 1800; and secondly, over the permission granted by Baji Rao for British troops to follow Doondia Wao into Mahratta Territory. Meanwhile Holkar's depredations became so serious that Scindia found himself obliged to repair to Malwa to check them. In July 1801 Holkar won two decided successes, and, though completely defeated at Indore in October, soon recovered himself and advanced upon Poona. The combined armies of Scindia and the Peishwa strove to repel him, but were utterly routed before the city itself on the 25th of October 1802. Baji Rao thereupon fled to the coast, taking refuge in

a British ship, which conveyed him to Bassein; and 1803.
there on the 31st of December he signed a treaty whereby he threw himself upon the protection of the British Government, and concluded with it an offensive and defensive alliance. Scindia likewise invoked British help to save the Mahratta Confederacy from entire dissolution; and hence Wellesley found himself virtually the arbiter of the fortunes of the descendants of Sivajee. But, as he himself said, a principal object of the treaty was to prevent the sovereign power of the Mahratta States, or the power of any great branch of the Mahratta Empire, from passing into the hands of France.[1]

The treaty of Bassein was accepted by the Peishwa in all sincerity, for the unhappy man felt a genuine liking for the British, and was as loth to be a tool of Scindia as of Holkar. Wellesley, therefore, lost no time in assembling a powerful force at Hurryhur on the northern border of Mysore, with the double object of parrying any invasion by hostile Mahrattas and of escorting the Peishwa to his capital at Poona. In Feb.
taking this step he desired and expected a peaceful solution of all difficulties.[2] Scindia was the chief whose views were most likely to be adverse to the treaty, and whose hostility was most to be apprehended; and when in March Perron asked leave to pass through British territory to Calcutta in order to embark for Europe, Wellesley heaved a sigh of relief. For it seemed as though at least one dangerous element of strife, interested alike in Scindia's and Bonaparte's ascendancy, might be quietly eliminated.

Nor was the promise of a peaceful end to all troubles belied upon the march of the army from Hurryhur. Arthur Wellesley had wisely been appointed to command it, and the fame of his recent campaign against Doondia Wao was sufficient to ensure him at least a fearful deference. But the young General knew already that if deference was to be turned to friendship in an

[1] *Wellesley Desp.* iii. 109. [2] *Ibid.* iii. 29, 49.

1803. alien territory, his force must never be a burden upon the inhabitants. There must be no excesses, no plunder, no marauding, but strict discipline and, as a first means to that end, an efficient system of supply. It was this last which occupied his attention from the first moment when he was ordered to move to Hurryhur. "The only mode," he wrote, "by which we can inspire either our allies or our enemies with respect for our operations will be to show them that the army can move with ease and celerity at all times and in all situations." His letters of this period teem with calculations as to supplies and the cattle that are to draw them; and the famous draft-bullocks of Mysore, which had been taken after Tippoo's death into the Company's service, figure prominently as one of the chief factors in his army's efficiency. There was every prospect of difficulty, for the rainfall in the country adjoining the Western Ghauts had been scanty during the previous season. Forage was hardly obtainable; the crops had failed; the stricken districts were face to face with famine; even water was wanting in many tanks and streams where generally it had been abundant. Yet all these obstacles were overcome by his unflagging industry. All superfluous baggage was ruthlessly cut off, and the march from Seringapatam to Hurryhur was accomplished without injury or fatigue to the cattle; whereas the bullocks of other detachments, under commanders of higher rank, fell down in hundreds. Finally, when on the 12th of March he crossed the Toombuddra into Mahratta territory, he was received as a friend and a deliverer, and joined by all the local chieftains on his march to Poona.[1]

Jeswunt Rao Holkar, who was still in possession of the Mahratta capital, retired upon the news of his advance; but Arthur Wellesley continued to move steadily northward, and by the 1st of April had crossed the Kistna at Erroor, with his cattle still in perfect condition

[1] *Wellington Desp.* i. 374, 407; *Supplementary Despatches*, iv. 1-10, 17-22, 26-32, 41-43.

despite the length of his march. At the same time 1803.
Colonel Stevenson with the subsidiary forces of the Nizam was marching westward from Hyderabad to join him; and on the 15th of April the two forces April 15.
opened communication with each other at Ecklaus on the Neera River, some eighty miles east and south of their destination. By that time Holkar had reached Chandore, nearly twice that distance to north of Poona, leaving only Amrut Rao, a pretender to the Mahratta throne, with fifteen hundred men to hold the city; and Wellesley, judging it unnecessary to lead a large force against so paltry an enemy, decided to extend Stevenson's troops over a wider front for convenience of forage. Three days later came intelligence that Amrut Rao was preparing to burn and plunder Poona, whereupon Wellesley started with his cavalry on the morning of the 19th, and though delayed for six hours April 19.
by the difficulty of getting his light guns through the Little Bhore Ghaut, rode into the Peishwa's capital on the morning of the 20th, having traversed sixty miles April 20.
in thirty-two hours. Amrut Rao withdrew in haste at the news of his approach; the inhabitants, who had been driven from their homes by Holkar, hurried back to welcome the British General; the British infantry arrived to increase their confidence on the 22nd; April 22.
and on the 13th of May Baji Rao was escorted into May 13.
the city and reseated with great ceremony upon the throne.[1]

So far all had gone well. The Peishwa had been reinstated, but it remained to be seen whether his authority could be re-established; and various symptoms indicated that the prospect was not altogether promising. In the first place, Perron had not left India, as had been expected; and in the second, Wellesley, on the 30th May 30.
of May, had received despatches from the British Government forbidding him to restore the French and Dutch possessions in India until further orders, all stipulations of the Treaty of Amiens notwith-

[1] *Wellington Desp.* i. 457, 493, 505.

1803. standing.[1] This pointed to the near prospect of a renewal of hostilities with France, an event which was not likely to foster a pacific disposition in Scindia. Nevertheless, despite the untowardness of the outlook, the Viceroy did not seek to precipitate a war before the French could take part in it. Long and dreary negotiations followed for week upon week after the occupation of Poona. Scindia had admitted that the Treaty of Bassein was not injurious to him, nor to any of the Mahratta feudatory chieftains; but he none the less insisted that Ragogee Bhonsla, the Rajah of Berar, should join him to discuss the question. The place of meeting was to be on the frontier of the Nizam's dominions; and, as the Rajah was to bring with him as escort the whole of his army, the pretended consultation became in reality a serious menace to a faithful ally of the British. Scindia, in fact, told Colonel Collins, the British resident, that upon the Rajah's arrival he would inform him whether the issue were to be peace or war; but still Lord Wellesley forbore to take offence. The armies of the two chieftains duly effected their junction near the Ajunta Ghaut, on the Nizam's north-western boundary, on the 3rd of June; but several days passed, and still no decision
June 12. was announced to Collins. On the 12th of June he demanded his dismissal, but consented to stay upon being pressed by Scindia;[2] and after this the Mahratta chiefs continued to play the game of procrastination for two whole months, Collins frequently threatening to take his leave, and as frequently postponing his departure. The time thus gained was employed by them in endeavouring to persuade Holkar to join them in war against the British; and their motive was so transparent as to be secret to no one. Arthur Wellesley in wrath wrote repeated letters to Collins to cut the negotiations short, but without effect. Reiterated representations were made to Scindia and his ally to withdraw their troops, but were utterly thrown away

[1] *Wellesley Desp.* iii. 84. [2] *Wellington Desp.* ii. 28.

upon them ; and the negotiations dragged on and on 1803.
through June and July, as though they would have no ending.

Throughout this period of suspense Arthur Wellesley waited with almost feverish impatience. He had laid all his plans with the express object of fighting the Mahrattas during the rainy season, when the rivers would be high ; and he had many months before ordered the preparation of boats and pontoons, which would enable him to pass these rivers at any time and place, whereas his enemies would be dependent on fords which, in time of flood, would be impracticable. With this advantage and with his transport efficiently organised, he felt confident of success. Scindia might fight pitched battles and Holkar might pursue the more dangerous guerilla warfare which was traditional with the Mahrattas, but the young General was prepared to cope with either. British infantry would be too much even for Perron's best battalions ; and the Mysore bullocks would enable him to follow Holkar so swiftly that, even though he were not overtaken, that wily chieftain would find little time for mischief, and would see his following dwindle daily from sheer lack of plunder.

Two circumstances, for a time, reconciled Arthur Wellesley to some delay in June, namely the loss of a great number of bullocks from bad forage and exposure,[1] and the failure of the authorities at Bombay to produce the boats for which he had asked. This latter was, in fact, the beginning of a long series of differences with the Governor of Bombay, Mr. Duncan, who for some reason was singularly obstructive to the whole of the General's arrangements. Recognising the difficulty of acting from a base five hundred miles distant at Seringapatam, Arthur Wellesley had, as early as January, procured the formation of a large depôt on the coast, which should be at once within easy reach of Bombay by water and close to the mouth of the Ghaut that

[1] *Wellington Desp.* ii. 15, 18, 38.

1803. leads to Poona; but he could obtain no cattle to draw the supplies from the depôt to his camp; and the army was in great straits for food. Duncan had promised him a number of bullocks by the end of May; but not one of them had arrived. He had undertaken to send up pontoons, but contrived to despatch them in weather which broke down all the carriages after one march. Very early Wellesley, giving up the Governor of Bombay in despair, sought for an advanced base of his own making. His eye fell upon the fortress of Ahmednuggur, just twenty miles north of his camp; and inquiry soon showed that he had seen aright. "It is full of everything we want"; he wrote on the 16th of June, "the property of this country is lodged there. The capture of that place will retrieve our immediate distresses and will give everybody spirits." From that day forward information as to Ahmednuggur was eagerly gathered; and the General fully decided that the capture of the fort must be the first operation of the war, if war there should be.[1] But the favourable months kept slipping away without the slightest apparent approach to a decision, and at last in the July. middle of July Arthur Wellesley's patience gave way. Collins was still pressing Scindia to withdraw his army to Hindostan; but Scindia showed not a sign of yielding. "We ought," wrote the General, in effect, "to have insisted on his retiring in May. Since that time six valuable weeks have elapsed. We have gained nothing; on the contrary, we have consumed our resources. Holkar is still north of the Taptee and, even if his intentions be hostile to us, cannot join Scindia for some time. The swelling of the rivers still protects our frontier and exposes that of the enemy. Every day's delay deprives us of this advantage, and therefore no time should be lost." An amusingly insolent rejoinder of the Mahratta chiefs to a reiterated request for the withdrawal of their armies at last brought matters to a crisis. On the 3rd of August Collins quitted Scindia's

[1] *Wellington Desp.* ii. 10, 27, 36, 39, 40, 47, 97.

camp, and the fate of the Mahratta Empire was committed to the hazard of war. 1803. Aug. 3.

The Viceroy's plans for the campaign had for some time been matured, and he had resolved to carry the war into every part of the enemy's dominions. The principal forces to be faced were the joint armies of Scindia and of the Rajah of Berar in the Deccan, and the main army of Scindia commanded by Perron in the north. The former, which still lay about the Ajunta Ghaut, numbered in all about fifty thousand men with one hundred and ninety guns: of this force thirty-eight thousand were cavalry, ten thousand five hundred regular infantry, and a thousand rocket-men and match-lock-men. In the north Perron, who had fixed his headquarters at Coel, about fifty miles north of Agra, was at the head of about thirty-five thousand men, including from sixteen to twenty thousand horse, with a very large and well-appointed train of artillery.

To oppose these hosts there were formed two principal armies: the northern under General Gerard Lake, the hero of Linselles in 1793 and the obedient tool of Dublin Castle in 1798; the southern under Arthur Wellesley. Lake's headquarters were at Cawnpore, and the troops under his immediate command numbered ten thousand five hundred men, including three regiments of British cavalry and one battalion of British infantry. In addition to this force, between three and four thousand men were assembled near Allahabad for the invasion of Bundelcund; about two thousand more were collected at Mirzapore to cover the city and province of Benares, while other detachments guarded the frontier from Mirzapore over three hundred miles eastward and southward to Midnapore.

Arthur Wellesley's charge was the greater and more onerous. First, on the eastern coast a force of close upon five thousand men, including about six hundred European troops, was assembled at Ganjam under Lieutenant-colonel Harcourt to invade the province of Cuttack and the possessions of the Rajah of Berar.

1803. This column was to act independently. Secondly, on the west there were in Guzerat and Surat nearly three thousand British and nearly four thousand native infantry, affording, after all garrisons had been provided for, a field-force of rather more than four thousand men.[1] This was parted into two divisions, each about two thousand strong, the first being posted north of the Nerbudda at Baroda, and the second south of the Taptee between Surat and Songhur. Arthur Wellesley had particularly insisted upon the importance of Songhur itself, which lies fifty miles to eastward of Surat and commands a Ghaut which leads down to that city.[2] Both divisions were designed to operate eastward against Holkar, if he should declare war, and in any case to capture Baroach and the possessions of Scindia in their vicinity. Both were placed, at Arthur Wellesley's request, under the command of Colonel John Murray, and he had reason to regret his choice both then and later. For this was the Murray who, having done good service as Baird's Quartermaster-general in Egypt, was destined in the Peninsula to wreck Wellesley's plans at the passage of the Douro, and to bring himself to disgrace at Tarragona.

Thirdly, there was the army under Arthur Wellesley's personal command, just over eleven thousand strong, including over sixteen hundred Europeans, but exclusive of some five thousand Mysore and Mahratta horse. In addition to this force, and forming almost a part of it, was the Hyderabad contingent under Colonel Stevenson, numbering over nine thousand men, of whom nine hundred were Europeans. Wellesley's headquarters at the outbreak of the war were at Walkee, eight miles south of Ahmednuggur,[3] towards which fortress he had for some days past been slowly

[1] H.M. 65th, 86th, and Royal Artillery 1677
Two battalions each of the 1st and 6th Bombay N.I. . 2604

[2] *Wellington Desp.* ii. 156-159.

[3] Six miles is the distance named by himself (*Well. Desp.* ii. 173). Grant Duff, *Hist. of the Mahrattas*, iii. 168, gives the figure at eight miles, which seems more correct.

advancing, as the sands of the long negotiation gradually ran out. Stevenson was still guarding the various passes on the northern frontier of the Nizam's dominions about Aurungabad. As a reserve for Arthur Wellesley a force of over eight thousand men, together with large quantities of supplies, had been assembled at Moodgul, a little to the south of the River Kistna, under General Stuart; but the arrival of new garrisons for the French settlements had caused Stuart himself to return to Madras, and a part of his troops to be sent down to the Carnatic. The reserve was thus reduced to about four thousand men, of whom over twelve hundred were Europeans, and the remainder natives. In all, the British force assembled in India numbered, including the garrisons at Poona and Hyderabad, nearly fifty thousand men.[1] 1803.

[1] WELLESLEY'S ARMY—

Cavalry.	H.M. 19th Dragoons	384	
	4th, 5th, 7th Madras N.C.	1347	
			1731
Artillery			173
	Lascars and Pioneers		1010
Infantry.	H.M. 74th and 78th	1368	
	1/2nd, 1 and 2/3rd, 1/8th, 2/12th, 2/18th Madras N.I.	5631	
			6999
			9913
	Add ⅛ for Officers, Sergeants, etc.		1240
	Total		11,153

STEVENSON'S ARMY—

Cavalry.	3rd and 6th N.C.		909
Artillery		120	
	Lascars and Pioneers	488	
			608
Infantry.	H.M. Scotch Brigade (94th)	778	
	1/6th, 2/7th, 2/9th, 1 and 2/11th	6113	
			6891
			8408
	Add ⅛ for Officers, Sergeants, etc.		1051
	Total		9459

1803. Aug. 6. On the 6th of August Arthur Wellesley received the news of the final rupture with Scindia; but foul Aug. 8. weather made the roads impassable until the 8th, on which day he moved northward, pursuant to his long-cherished design, upon Ahmednuggur. This stronghold consisted, as usual, of a *pettah*, or fortified native town, and a fort proper, the two being about half a mile apart. The pettah, which was very large, was surrounded by a strong wall, without a ditch, but very neatly built, and rounded off at the top so that it was hardly broad enough for a man to stand upon. It had twelve gates, without detached works, also some forty bastions at intervals of about a hundred yards from each other, of which eight were large enough to mount two guns, and the rest were loopholed. Within were many high buildings with narrow streets and mud walls shutting off various enclosures, all of which contributed to make a formidable defence; and the garrison consisted of one thousand of Scindia's regular infantry with five small field-guns, and one thousand Arabs; the whole being under the command of three French officers. Altogether its capture to an ordinary man would have seemed no easy matter.

The General had already selected the leaders of his storming parties; and on arriving before the *pettah*, the walls of which were seen to be crowded with men, he halted at long cannon-shot, reconnoitred the place, and directed an escalade to be attempted at three different points. According to the rule then observed in all marches in India, the advanced guard was composed of one half-company from each battalion of infantry, forming the picquets coming on duty under the field-officer of the day; and to this body, reinforced by the flank-companies of the Seventy-eighth, was entrusted the left attack. The right column was composed of the flank companies of the Seventy-fourth and a battalion of Sepoys[1] under Captain Vesey, and the centre column of the battalion-companies of the

[1] 1/3rd Madras N.I.

Seventy-fourth and another battalion of Sepoys,[1] 1803.
under Lieutenant-colonel Wallace. The left column, Aug. 8.
commanded by Colonel Harness, reached the walls first, planted its ladders, and strove with the utmost gallantry to force its way into the town; but the men were hurled down as fast as they ascended, and after ten minutes abandoned the attempt, the Seventy-eighth having lost six officers killed and some fifty men killed and wounded. Vesey's men were delayed by an elephant from the artillery-train, which took fright and ran down through the middle of them, scattering them in all directions. They soon re-formed, however, and planted their two ladders at a re-entering angle formed by one of the bastions, when there was such a rush to be foremost that one of the ladders was broken down. The men, however, swarmed up the other, and the flank-companies of the Seventy-fourth, with about two hundred more, had surmounted the wall when the only remaining ladder was smashed by a cannon-shot, and Vesey was left alone with three hundred men. Without hesitation his party swept the enemy out of the streets adjoining the wall, until they reached a gate which had been marked out as the point of assault for the central column. Heavy firing announced that Wallace had already begun his attack; the gate was opened to admit his troops; and the two parties uniting soon drove the whole garrison out of the town with very heavy loss. Few of the enemy reached the fort, the bulk of them flying in other directions; and by three o'clock in the afternoon the British were in comfortable possession of Ahmednuggur at a cost of about one hundred and twenty killed and wounded.

The effect of this attack was great. "These English are a strange people and their General a wonderful man," wrote a Mahratta chief from Wellesley's camp after the action. "They came here in the morning, looked at the pettah-wall, walked over it, killed all the garrison, and returned to breakfast." On the following Aug. 9.

[1] 1/8th Madras N.I.

1803. day the General reconnoitred the fort; and on the same evening seized a favourable spot, on which during the night he constructed a battery of four eighteen-
Aug. 10. pounders. At daylight of the 10th these opened fire with great effect, breaching two contiguous bastions, insomuch that the native commandant presently begged for a cessation that he might arrange terms of surrender. Wellesley answered that he should continue to fire until he should have taken the fort or received its submission, and proceeded to batter the walls until on the evening of the 11th the enemy's hostages for the
Aug. 12. capitulation arrived. On the morning of the 12th the commandant marched out with his private property and his garrison of fourteen hundred men; and Arthur Wellesley had gained what he needed. The capture of Ahmednuggur gave him a fortress which covered Poona and the Nizam's western frontier, which cut Scindia off from the southern chiefs and controlled all his territory south of the Godavery, and which, most important of all, provided him with a good advanced base with abundance of supplies and stores from which to pursue his campaign.

This, though now forgotten, was a remarkable feat of arms, the fall of the fort being undoubtedly due to the moral effect produced by the escalade of the town. The fort was pronounced, not only by Wellesley himself but by his officers also, to be nearly, if not quite the strongest, that they had ever seen in the plains of India.[1] It was nearly circular in form, well built of solid stone, with bastions sixty feet high at short intervals, each mounting three or four guns, and the whole surrounded by a wide dry ditch. The glacis was so high that it covered about thirty feet of the walls, but, being of abrupt slope, enabled besiegers to find shelter close to the place when once the guns had been dismounted. This was the defect of the stronghold; but none the less it had

[1] It must, however, be remarked that one of his engineer officers describes it as a place of no great strength. *Twelve Years' Military Adventure*, p. 133.

proved too formidable even for Holkar at the zenith of his power. Wellesley mastered both fort and pettah in three days at a cost of seventy-nine Europeans and sixty-two natives killed and wounded.[1] 1803.

The General halted four days at Ahmednuggur to arrange the details for the protection and administration of the captured territory. Meanwhile a report came that Holkar was on the march to join Scindia; and, as though to confirm it, a party of irregular horse passed the Ajunta hills, apparently to make a raid upon the Nizam's dominions. Stevenson, as is not uncommon with a general who has a wide front to watch, became uneasy and irresolute, being anxious for his convoys and communications. First he moved back, then he moved forward, forming elaborate plans for shielding from attack the supplies that were on their way to him. Wellesley could hardly suppress his impatience. "Keep your infantry in a central situation and let your supplies collect on them," he wrote; "move forward yourself with the cavalry and one battalion, and dash at the first enemy that comes into your neighbourhood. You will either cut them up or drive them off. . . . A long defensive war will ruin us. . . . By any other plan than that above proposed we shall lose our supplies, do what we will." Poor Stevenson endeavoured to mend his ways, but still could not refrain from a slight movement rearward which brought his young chief's hand down upon him once more. "Depend upon it that no straggling horse will venture to your rear so long as you can keep the enemy in check and your detachment well in advance. Dash at the first fellows that make their appearance, and the campaign will be our own."[2] The chase of Doondia Wao had not been thrown away upon Arthur Wellesley.

Meanwhile by the 17th of August his cavalry had reached the Godavery; and on the following day he Aug. 17.

[1] The foregoing account is based on *Well. Desp.* ii. 193, 204, 313, and Welsh's *Military Reminiscences in the East Indies*, ii. 155-165.

[2] *Well. Desp.* ii. 208, 210, 219.

1803. was on march with his infantry to join them. The river, being swollen by the rains, was very wide, and the troops crossed in wicker boats made by themselves in the jungle, and covered with bullock-skins. On the
Aug. 24. 24th Wellesley's headquarters were at Toka, about
Aug. 29. fifty miles north of Ahmednuggur, and on the 29th he reached Aurungabad. The difficulties of the campaign seemed to increase with every step. The country through which he passed was completely exhausted and depopulated; vast numbers of bullocks had died of starvation and exposure; and though there were supplies enough for the troops, and the army itself was, as Wellesley said, "in excellent marching trim," yet the provision of food for the followers appeared to be impossible.[1]

Meanwhile Scindia and the Rajah of Berar, after drawing Stevenson as far east as Jafferabad by a feint in that direction, doubled back to westward, entered
Aug. 23-24. the Nizam's territory by the pass of Ajunta with their cavalry only, and seemed to be pushing forward rapidly towards the Godavery. Though Arthur Wellesley had matured all arrangements for repelling them if they should succeed in crossing that river,
Aug. 30. he immediately made one march to the eastward from Aurungabad, and then turned southward, so as to cover at once the advance of his supplies from Hyderabad and the Kistna, and to press closely upon the enemy if they should continue their advance.
Sept. 2. By the 2nd of September he had reached Rackisbaum on the Godavery; and on the same day Stevenson, who had hurried back to westward, assaulted and took the fort of Jalnapore, an isolated possession of Scindia some sixty miles east of Aurungabad. The enemy by that time had reached Partoor, about forty miles east and north of Rackisbaum, where they halted during
Sept. 3-4. the 3rd and 4th to await the arrival of some of Scindia's regular infantry. Wellesley and Stevenson likewise
Sept. 5-6. remained stationary on those days; but on the 5th and

[1] *Well. Desp.* ii. 235, 245.

6th Wellesley, finding that the Godavery was, by a most unusual accident, fordable, made two marches eastward so as to start level with the Mahrattas in case of a race to Hyderabad. At the same time, being satisfied that nothing could save the Nizam's territory from a raid except a counter-raid of the British upon Berar, he determined at all risks to send Stevenson north-eastward by way of Ellichpoor to attack the Rajah's fort of Gawilghur, and if possible to plunder Nagpoor. As to himself he felt confident enough, for his transport was now in such perfect order and his cattle and horses in such excellent condition, that a march of twenty-three miles in a day was an easy matter.[1] 1803.

Scindia and Ragogee, however, by no means enjoyed the vicinity of Arthur Wellesley on the Godavery. "They appear to be very much afraid of this division, and very little so of Colonel Stevenson's," wrote Wellesley; and accordingly on the night of the 6th Sept. 6. they broke up their camp and returned to the Ajunta Ghaut. Stevenson had unfortunately moved westward on the 5th from Jalnapore, which would have been an ideal position from which to intercept them; and though on the 6th and again on the 9th he surprised Sept. 9. and dispersed two parties of the enemy's horse, yet he did them little real harm. In fact he was still nervous, and wrote letters to Wellesley alleging doubts as to the sufficiency of his army for the raid into Berar, which brought upon him at least one very unpleasant reply. During the ensuing days both Generals were tied fast to their stations by the need for keeping open a passage for their convoys and supplies; but Wellesley comforted himself by the thought that Scindia, by bringing up his infantry and artillery, would be less difficult to overtake and more easily brought to action. The infantry duly joined the Mahratta army at Ajunta to the number of sixteen battalions, and on the 21st Sept. 21. the entire force of the enemy was assembled between Bokerdun and Jafferabad. Meanwhile on the 16th

[1] *Well. Desp.* ii. 273-277.

1803. Sept. 20. Wellesley moved eastward up the Godavery to meet his convoy, and turning northward on the 20th met Stevenson in consultation at Budnapore, a little to the west of Jalnapore, on the 21st. They then arranged to march upon the enemy, Stevenson taking the western route and Wellesley the eastern round the hills between Budnapore and Jalnapore, and on the evening of the 24th to attack him with their united forces.[1]

Beyond all question this division of the army was a most dangerous manœuvre, for it left the Mahratta leaders free by a small lateral movement to throw the whole of their force upon either moiety of the British. Wellesley, indeed, was so keenly alive to its faultiness after the event that he was careful to defend it, before it was attacked, when reporting it to a friend who was also a military critic. His excuse then was that he thought it necessary thus to separate his force into two parts, first to avoid delay in passing through defiles, and secondly to ensure that while he was advancing northward by one road, the enemy should not slip past him by the other. The real truth probably was that, knowing Scindia to be afraid of him, he did not hesitate to take even the most perilous liberties.

Sept. 23. On the 23rd Wellesley, on reaching Naulniah, some twenty miles north of Jalnapore, learned that the Mahratta chiefs had moved off in the morning with their cavalry, but that the infantry had not yet marched, and was still lying within six miles of his proposed encampment. Thereupon, though Stevenson was still out of reach, he sent word to him that he meant to attack at once; and, having secured his baggage at Naulniah, marched forward without further delay. Riding on with his staff and the cavalry only, he came, at about one o'clock of the afternoon, in sight not of the infantry alone but of the entire army of Scindia and Ragogee, encamped upon a peninsula formed by the rivers Kaitna in their front, and Juah in their rear. The Kaitna was impassable except by certain fords; the

[1] *Well. Desp.* ii. 284, 289, 295.

Juah was of smaller volume, but had very steep banks; 1803.
and the ground along both rivers was much broken by Sept. 23.
ravines. The enemy was in great force, for the whole of the peninsula was swarming with men. The cavalry, numbering twenty or thirty thousand, formed the right of the hostile army about the village of Bokerdun; and their encampment extended to eastward till it met that of the infantry, which prolonged the line to the village of Assaye. Among these last, as Wellesley knew, were sixteen regular battalions, amounting in all to more than ten thousand men; namely, the brigade of Pohlmann, a German, six thousand men; that of Dupont, two thousand five hundred men; and four auxiliary battalions of the Begum Somroo,[1] numbering yet two thousand more. With them was a certain proportion of European officers, though many, especially the English, had been enticed away by a proclamation which had been issued by the Viceroy at the beginning of the war, offering to all Europeans and British subjects the same pay as they received from Scindia. Besides these regular troops there was a mob of irregular infantry belonging to both of the Mahratta chiefs, and a good force of regular artillerymen with over one hundred guns. Altogether the host must have counted from forty to fifty thousand men.

Wellesley was in an extremely awkward situation. He had laid it down as a principle that the Mahrattas must never be attacked in a position of their own choice, nor on the other hand suffered to attack the British, no matter how strongly the defenders might be entrenched; but that they must always be allowed to get into motion, whether for advance or retreat, and must then be assailed while in the disorder of march.[2] His information had led him to expect that part of the Mahratta army would have been already withdrawn to

[1] The widow of the French officer, mentioned in vol. iii. 64.

[2] *Well. Desp.* ii. 403-404. The letter to Stevenson in which these maxims are laid down is dated Oct. 12, 1803, or more than seven weeks after the action; but it is evident that the plan had been thought out beforehand.

1803. Sept. 23. some distance, and that the rest would be moving off to join them. Yet there was the whole of it united, ready, and, as usual, well posted; for Wellesley freely acknowledged that the positions chosen by the Mahrattas were always "confoundedly strong and difficult of access." His own force consisted of two battalions of British and five of native infantry, the Nineteenth Light Dragoons and three regiments of native cavalry, a battalion of pioneers, and something fewer than five hundred artillerymen, of whom one-third were Europeans. In all he could put in line about seven thousand of all ranks,[1] with but fourteen cannon besides the eight light pieces attached to the cavalry and known as "galloper-guns." Stevenson, whom he had originally intended to join with him in the attack, was ten or twelve miles away. If he attempted to retire to Naulniah to await him, he would certainly be followed and surrounded by the enemy's cavalry, harassed until nightfall, and obliged either to risk the loss of his baggage or to weaken his attack on the following day by detaching a large baggage-guard. On the other hand, if he assailed the

[1] *Return of rank and file*:—

19th L.D.	313	rank and file.
4th N.C., 5th N.C., 7th N.C.	1145	" "
European Artillery	154	" "
Gun Lascars	323	" "
H.M. 74th	500	" "
H.M. 78th	670	" "
1/2nd N.I., 1/4th N.I., 1/8th N.I., 1/10th N.I., 2/12th N.I.	3014	
1st battalion Pioneers	605	
	6724	
Add one-eighth for officers and N.C.O.	800	
Total	7524	
Deduct for baggage-guard say	500	
Final Total	7024	

The bulk of the 2nd N.I. (750) reinforced the baggage-guard.

Mahrattas at once near the junction of the Kaitna 1803.
and the Juah, their straitened position would forbid Sept. 23.
them to take advantage of their enormous preponderance in numbers, and he could use the two streams for the protection of his flanks. Of course the defeat of his own force in such a narrow tongue of land would mean its certain annihilation.

That risk he was prepared to take; but there remained still the difficulty that the only ford known to his guides was commanded by the Mahratta artillery, and that consequently the forcing of the passage would be extremely hazardous. Sweeping the line of the banks with his glass, he noticed at some distance to his right the two villages of Peepulgaon and Waroor close together on opposite sides of the Kaitna, and, in spite of the denial of his guides, concluded that there must be a ford between them. A staff-officer was despatched to ascertain the truth; and during this delay the Mahrattas struck their tents and formed a single line of battle behind the Kaitna, with the cavalry on their right and the infantry on their left. Moreover, two large bodies of horse actually crossed the river to make closer observation, but kept at a safe distance when they found Wellesley's twelve hundred sabres ready to meet them. In due time the staff-officer came galloping back with the news that the General was correct in his conjecture about the ford; and orders were sent to the infantry, which had been carefully kept out of the enemy's sight, to diverge to their right and march upon Peepulgaon. The regular cavalry covered the rear of the battalions during the movement, and formed behind them for the passage of the river. Wellesley left his irregular horse, part of it Mysorean and part of it from the Peishwa's army, to keep in check the enemy on the south of the Kaitna. He was told, just at this critical moment, that the Peishwa's troops intended to turn against him; but he took no notice, rightly judging that they would await the issue of the action before they changed sides.

1803. Sept. 23. As the British infantry drew near to the river the enemy's guns opened fire, but with little effect. Strange to say, no attempt was made to dispute the passage of the ford; but the crossing took some time, for there were difficulties in dragging the guns through the water; and the Mahrattas used the opportunity to bring down a battery close to the bank on their own side of the river. As the head of the British column began to ascend from the ford to the peninsula this battery immediately poured upon it a heavy and continuous fire, which caused great loss. The head of Wellesley's orderly dragoon was carried away by a cannon-shot; the dead body remained in the saddle; and the whole of the staff was scattered by the plunging of the terrified horse until at length the ghastly burden fell to the ground. However, the column filed on, and Wellesley, leaving one of his staff-officers to watch the enemy's movements, busied himself with the formation of his order of battle.

Still fully persuaded that he was sure of falling on the Mahrattas' flank, he drew up his force in three lines. The first line from right to left consisted of the picquets, two native battalions, and the Seventy-eighth; the second line, of the Seventy-fourth and two native battalions, and the third of the cavalry, which played the part of a reserve. These dispositions had been nearly, if not quite, completed behind a slight ridge which concealed them from the enemy, when the staff-officer came galloping back with the news that the Mahrattas were changing position to their left, a manœuvre of which Wellesley had believed them to be incapable. The information was, however, correct; and the evolution, though performed unscientifically, went forward with perfect order and precision. The Mahratta regiments did not break into column, but each battalion moved off in line to the new alignment; so that while in motion they presented the appearance of an echelon of battalions with the left in advance. It was, however, but half of the hostile infantry which moved in this direction, the second Mahratta line retiring to the Juah, and there taking up a position parallel to the river, with its left resting upon the village of Assaye.[1] 1803. Sept. 23.

Wellesley, of course, was little concerned as yet with this second line ; but on hearing of the enemy's change of position, and perceiving that the space between the two rivers became wider immediately before him, he at once, and rightly, became anxious for his flanks, and prepared to extend his own front. With this object he ordered the picquets, which formed the right of his first line, to take ground to the right, so as to make room for the two native battalions of his second line on their left. At the same time he commanded the Seventy-fourth to incline to its right hand, and to form on the right of the picquets, and directed the cavalry to file up to the Juah for the purpose of protecting his right flank. Strict injunctions were given to Colonel Orrock, the officer in command of the picquets, that he was on no account to advance upon the village of Assaye nor to approach too closely to it.

The troops were about to enter upon this movement when the Mahratta line brought forward guns and opened a most destructive fire. The native bullock-drivers with the British artillery at once became unsteady ; not a few teams were severely maltreated, and several cannon, which had been advanced to answer the enemy's fire, were disabled. Moreover, since the enemy's echelon had advanced from its left, the first of its battalions to come into action were, of course, those opposed to the British right, which was precisely the quarter where the alterations in the line of battle

[1] I venture to differ at this point from Colonel Biddulph, who makes this movement to the Juah occur in the middle of the action. I base my opinion on *Notes relative to the late Transactions*, pp. 61-62, Wellington's memorandum on the battle (*Desp.* ii. 323), read in conjunction with the map in the *Notes*, and on the account given in *Wellington Suppl. Desp.* iv. 185-190, *note*. But I confess that it is with diffidence that I dissent from the view of so high an authority. The subject is strangely difficult and obscure.

1803. Sept. 23. were going forward. In a very short time the fire of the Mahratta guns became so terrible that no troops could long endure it; and Wellesley gave the word to advance, ordering the battalions of the second line to fall into their appointed places during the movement. Even then the picquets were slow in moving off, and Wellesley sent an impatient message to ask the cause. Orrock's reply was that his battalion-guns were disabled. "Then tell him to get on without them," rejoined the General; and presently the advance began.

Thereupon the enemy's cannonade redoubled in violence. Within a front of less than a mile one hundred pieces, admirably trained and very rapidly served, poured a tempest of shot upon the British ranks. The storm was severest in the centre, where the Sepoy battalions, unable to face it, swerved to their left and crowded in upon the Seventy-eighth. However, the greater part of them advanced rapidly and in good order under Wellesley's personal leadership upon the enemy's right wing, and, without pausing to fire, forced it back without difficulty; for the Mahratta infantry stood only so long as their artillery continued to play, whereas the gunners stuck to their guns most gallantly to the last, and were actually bayonetted in the act of loading their pieces. But even so this infantry was thrust back rather than beaten off; and the enemy's centre, being still untouched, presently closed in towards the Juah, while one compact division, six thousand strong, under the command of Pohlmann,[1] retired in fair order direct to its rear, that is to say westward, for some distance, when it halted and faced about. So far, therefore, all that had been accomplished was the capture of the guns on the right wing of the Mahrattas.

And meanwhile at the other extremity of Wellesley's line matters had gone disastrously wrong. Colonel Orrock, at the head of the picquets, for some reason,

[1] I suspect Pohlmann's brigade to have formed part of a second line immediately in rear of the troops which faced Wellesley.

forgot alike the object of his oblique movement to the right and Wellesley's explicit order to keep clear of Assaye. Possibly he was afraid that his men might give way if he attempted to alter the direction, for they had lost a third of their numbers before they fired a shot; or possibly he was himself so dazed by the fire that he could do nothing but lead on in the same direction that he had originally taken. But, be that as it may, it is certain that he continued to edge away to his right, widening the gap already made in Wellesley's centre by the swerving of the Sepoys already described, and that the hapless Seventy-fourth, trying in vain to take its appointed place upon his right, followed inevitably in his wake. Advancing straight upon Assaye, the two unfortunate corps were exposed to a terrific fire of musketry and artillery; and, though the Seventy-fourth carried the picquets forward for some way, yet at length the trial was too severe for the native troops. The picquets broke and ran back with confusion on to the Seventy-fourth, which happened at the time to be in difficult ground among cactus hedges; and while the British regiment stood alone, exposed to the concentrated fire of the enemy's left wing, a body of Mahratta horse came galloping round the village of Assaye and swooped upon its right flank, cutting the white soldiers down as only Eastern horsemen can cut, with all the terror and havoc of the sword.

1803. Sept. 23.

Yet still this glorious band, though reduced from a battalion to one strong company, "clung round its colours, undaunted and unbroken"; and it was not destined to be utterly swept away. Colonel Maxwell, who commanded the brigade of cavalry, was watching for the moment to act, and ordered the Nineteenth Light Dragoons and the Fourth Native Cavalry to advance. The two regiments, therefore, galloped forward amid the cheers of the wounded men of the Seventy-fourth, swept the Mahratta cavalry before them, and bore down swiftly upon the left of the

1803. Sept. 23. enemy's first line of infantry. These stood firm for a time and received the British cavalry with a storm of grape-shot ; but the Nineteenth, totally heedless of the fire, leaped straight into the midst of them, when the whole broke and fled across the river in their rear.

Meanwhile Wellesley had wheeled up his own left wing to the right, in order to attack the enemy's reserve by the Juah ; but thereby he necessarily exposed its left flank to the hostile cavalry and his right to the fire of the enemy's centre, which had faced about to confront him. Maxwell's charge, however, delivered him from the danger on his right ; and Wellesley's battalions, breaking into double quick time, charged the reserve and drove it across the river. The Sepoys began to disperse in pursuit, but the Seventy-eighth fortunately stood firm and daunted any attempt of the Mahratta horse upon their flank ; while Maxwell's cavalry, finding a second stream of fugitives added to that already before them, dashed over the water, hewing mercilessly among them, and for a time disappeared from the field of battle.

Wellesley then re-formed his infantry on the bank of the Juah, and found that there was a second engagement before him. The enemy's cavalry still hovered round him on the west, with Pohlmann's brigade looming in more solid menace behind them ; the unbroken infantry of their centre and a mass of rallied infantry had formed themselves into a huge half-moon with their right resting on Assaye and their left on the Juah ; and finally, scattered parties of Mahratta troops, some of which had feigned death during Wellesley's advance, had seized the deserted guns in all parts of the field and were playing upon the British rear. Wellesley detached first one native battalion and later a second against the mass of men round Assaye, but both were beaten back, having accomplished nothing. Now, however, the cavalry reappeared on the scene, for Maxwell, rallying his men from the pursuit, had led them down the bank of the Juah to a ford by the village of Borekerry, and by that passage had regained the army. The General

then ordered the Seventy-eighth and the Seventh Native 1803.
Cavalry to head a fresh attack upon Assaye, and was Sept. 23.
actually drawing up the former regiment in line when his horse was shot under him. The enemy, however, did not await the onslaught of the white infantry, but retired across the Juah and made good their retreat.

There remained Pohlmann's brigade, and the scattered gunners dispersed over the ground formerly occupied by the enemy's first line; and Wellesley, leaving Maxwell to deal with Pohlmann, led the infantry to secure the Mahratta guns. This last was not accomplished without sharp fighting, in the course of which the General had another horse badly injured under him by the pikes of Scindia's brave gunners. Meanwhile Maxwell led his brigade against Pohlmann's column, though his ranks were by this time greatly thinned, and both men and horses were exhausted by their previous efforts. Pohlmann awaited the attack in line, and Maxwell led the charge obliquely against his left. At the moment of contact Maxwell was struck dead by a grape-shot. By a convulsive movement he threw up his sword and checked his horse before he fell. The squadrons behind him swerved at the movement; and the whole body of horsemen, who had acquitted themselves so nobly an hour earlier, edged with increasing speed down the whole length of Pohlmann's bayonets, crying, "Halt, halt," and finally galloped away. The brigade was soon rallied, and retired at a walk; and Pohlmann, whose conduct throughout the day bears strong marks of treachery to his master, seized the opportunity to retreat. The Mahratta horse, which by a little energy and boldness could have ensured the victory to Scindia while Maxwell was on the other side of the Juah, lost heart and rode sullenly off. The British troops, having marched twenty-four miles before the battle began, were in no condition to pursue; and the irregular cavalry of the Peishwa and of Mysore had not mettle sufficient to attack an unbroken army. At six

1803. o'clock, therefore, the engagement closed, leaving Arthur Wellesley victorious in his first general action.[1]

Success was only gained by the most extraordinary exertions on the part of every man in the field. Had Pohlmann done his duty he might at least have embarrassed Wellesley greatly; and if the Mahratta cavalry had behaved with even a show of spirit, the issue would have been certainly doubtful, and most probably disastrous to the British arms. Colonel Orrock's unfortunate error in misleading the right of the line was responsible for the extreme hazard incurred in the fight; but Wellesley, in consideration of the terrible fire which he faced at the head of the picquets, forgave him for the blunder. For the rest, though every man, British or native, played his part with superlative gallantry, Assaye presents a roll of valiant deeds which is unsurpassed in our military history. First and foremost, Wellesley himself was throughout, in the hottest of the fray, calm, cool, and collected as if at a field-day. He escaped untouched, though, as has been told, two horses were killed under him; but of his staff eight out of ten sustained wounds to themselves or their horses. His brigadiers, Harness and Waller, together with most of the members of their staff and the mounted officers of infantry, also had their horses shot under them. Regimental and staff-officers vied with each other in heroism. Lieutenant Nathan Wilson of the Nineteenth Hussars had his arm shattered by a grape-shot early in the action, but charged on with the useless limb dangling by his side. With

[1] The best account of Assaye known to me is in *Twelve Years' Military Adventure*, i. 154 *seq.*, which should be read with *Wellington Desp.* ii. 323-329, 338, 349; *Suppl. Desp.* iv. 185-190; *Notes on the late Transactions*, etc., p. 59; Welsh's *Military Reminiscences*, i. 171 *seq.*; Grant Duff's *History of the Mahrattas*, iii. 169 *seq.*; Wilson's *History of the Madras Army*, iii. 104 *seq.*; Thorn's *Memoir of the War in India*; and Colebrooke's *Life of Mountstuart Elphinstone*, i. 63 *seq.* All of these have been admirably worked up, with some original matter, in *The Nineteenth and their Times*, by Colonel Biddulph, who has most kindly furnished me with notes taken by him in the India Office, and other valuable material collected by him from private sources.

the Nineteenth in the same charge rode a staff-officer, 1803. Captain A. B. Campbell of the Seventy-fourth. He had lost one arm in the Polygar war; he had since broken the other at the wrist by a fall when hunting; but he took his bridle in his teeth and fought fiercely with his sword in his mutilated hand. Captain George Sale of the Nineteenth galloped so impetuously at a Mahratta gunner, who was in the act of firing his gun, that his horse stuck fast between the cannon and the wheel. His covering sergeant, Strange by name, came to his rescue, and though pierced through the lungs by a pike, not only saved his officer, but rode on with his regiment to the end of the day. The Sepoys showed not less bravery; and Wellesley confessed that they astonished him. In the first battalion of the Eighth Native Infantry, which called itself "Wellesley's Own," five native officers and non-commissioned officers of a single distinguished family were killed. They were buried in one grave, and their comrades refused to mourn over men who had died in the performance of their duty.

But the loss of the British was heavy, amounting to nearly six hundred and fifty Europeans and over eight hundred natives killed, wounded, and missing; and since most of the wounded were struck by cannon-shot, their hurts were very severe.[1] The Seventy-fourth alone lost eleven officers and one hundred and thirteen men killed, six officers and two hundred and seventy-one men wounded. Wellesley never forgot their gallant service on this day, and six months later interposed to save from the gallows a murderer of infamous character, who was also a soldier of the Seventy-fourth, rather than punish a member of such a regiment with death.[2] Of the two

[1]

	Killed.	Wounded.	Missing.
European Officers . .	23	30	...
European Soldiers . .	175	412	4
Natives	230	696	14
Totals .	428	1138	18 = 1584

[2] *Wellington Suppl. Desp.* iv. 341.

1803. Sepoy battalions on the right of the first line, one had one hundred and seventy-four and the other two hundred and twenty-eight casualties. The cavalry brigade, besides nearly two hundred men killed and wounded, lost three hundred and fifteen horses killed and over four hundred wounded. Indeed there have been few actions in which horses have suffered so heavily in proportion to their numbers. The enemy left twelve hundred dead on the field; their wounded were estimated at four times as many; and they abandoned also to the British ninety-eight guns. They were hardly treated, for their infantry fought well and stubbornly, being by Arthur Wellesley's testimony the best troops in India next to our own Sepoys. But Ragogee Bhonsla fled at the beginning of the action, and Scindia followed him soon after; and with such leaders it was impossible for the men to do themselves justice.

Wellesley's army bivouacked on the field after the action, in a state of utter exhaustion after so severe a contest following upon a march of twenty-four miles. The cavalry was sent back to bring on the baggage and camp-equipage, but did not return until next morning. And meanwhile the dead were ungathered, the hurt in many cases untended, and the living lay down among them as they could. Wellesley, overcome by the reaction after intense strain of mind and body, sank down with the rest upon the ground. Close to him on one side lay an officer whose leg had been shot off; close to him on the other was a second officer, dead; but the General sat motionless with his head bent low between his knees, and spoke no word to any man.[1]

Sept. 24. When morning came it was hoped that Stevenson would arrive, bringing his medical staff to help the overworked surgeons of Wellesley; but it was evening before he appeared. Like a good soldier he had moved at once towards the sound of the cannon, but being misled by his guides had entangled his troops in a defile, so that

[1] Biddulph, p. 145, quoting from a MS. in the India Office Library.

they were wearied out with marching. All through the 1803.
25th he waited in order that his surgeons might give assistance; though even thus it was a week before the wounds of all the injured could be dressed. Then on the 26th, leaving Wellesley still encamped near the Sept. 26.
battlefield, he set out in pursuit of the enemy.

The Mahrattas had passed the night of the 23rd within twelve miles of Assaye, but, hearing of Stevenson's approach, made off on the morning of the 24th, and never stopped until on the same night they reached the foot of the Ajunta Ghaut. As they fled, they abandoned or hid several more of their guns, four of which fell into Stevenson's hands. Their force then parted into two divisions, the regular infantry retiring across the Nerbudda, towards which river Stevenson followed them; while Scindia and Ragogee, after taking some guns from the fort of Burhanpore, moved westward along the Taptee, with the intention, as was supposed, of marching ultimately southward upon Poona. Wellesley until the 8th of October was still Oct. 8.
occupied in moving his wounded to the fort of Ajunta, and in the more welcome task of attracting grain-merchants with thousands of bullocks from Scindia's army to his own. Upon hearing of the Mahrattas' movements he decided that he could not advance to northward without risk to Poona or to the Nizam's dominions. He therefore ordered Stevenson to take possession if possible of the forts of Burhanpore and Asseerghur, upon the north bank of the Taptee, and himself made a rapid movement from Ajunta southward towards Aurungabad, halting within one march of that town for the best part of a week. On the night of the 15th of October he learned that Scindia, finding Oct. 15.
his way to Poona barred, had turned again northward. Stevenson was at that moment on the point of reaching Burhanpore, which indeed he occupied without resistance on the 16th, afterwards continuing his advance north- Oct. 16.
eastward upon Asseerghur. Divining that Scindia's sudden change of direction boded no good for Stevenson,

1803. Wellesley on the 16th marched rapidly northward and foiled his enemy's plans for the second time. The fall of Burhanpore and Asseerghur, however, signified that the last of Scindia's possessions in the Deccan had been wrested from him; and the surrender of sixteen of his European officers, upon the terms offered by the Indian Government, greatly diminished his power for mischief. Wellesley therefore decided that the Rajah of Berar also must now feel the weight of his hand, and instructed Stevenson to equip himself for the siege of Gawilghur, the chief stronghold of Ragogee's government and the storehouse of his most precious possessions.

Hardly had he done so when the news was brought to him that the Rajah had separated his force from that of Scindia and moved to Chandore; whereupon, directing Stevenson to keep a sharp eye upon Scindia,
Oct. 24. he reascended the Ajunta Ghaut on the 24th, and was again ready to prevent any inroad to the south. Marching southward he reached Aurungabad on the
Oct. 29. 29th, when he turned south-eastward, making Ragogee's army shift its position five times in two days by repeated
Oct. 31. menaces, and at last on the 31st came in sight of his camp full twenty miles away. On that day one of the Rajah's detachments made an attempt upon a British convoy on the Godavery, but was beaten off; and Ragogee then hurried eastward down the river, having no mind to let Wellesley approach him too closely. Wellesley followed
Nov. 10. him as far as Patree, which lies about one hundred miles east of Ahmednuggur, when he turned northward, hoping by an invasion of Berar to recall the Rajah from his raid to the defence of his own territories.

Immediately afterwards two events of some import-
Nov. 11. ance occurred. On the 11th there arrived in Wellesley's camp a message from Scindia to sue for peace; and on
Nov. 12. the 12th Amrut Rao, Holkar's favoured candidate for the throne of Poona, joined the General as an ally of the British, with three or four thousand irregular troops. The negotiations were carried on during the movement of the army northward, which was slow owing to the

tardiness of the Nizam's government in sending 1803. garrisons to occupy the country taken by the British. On the 20th of November Wellesley reached Wakud, Nov. 20. about sixty miles north of Patree, when he turned north-westward to Rajoora; and there on the 22nd he agreed Nov. 22. to a suspension of hostilities with Scindia.

The considerations which chiefly moved him to this arrangement were that he could do no more harm to Scindia, having already captured the whole of his territory in the Deccan; whereas Scindia's horse could do a good deal of harm to him by impeding his operations against Berar in general and Gawilghur in particular. The only condition, therefore, upon which he insisted was that Scindia should retire to some position at least fifty miles east of Ellichpoor, and should preserve the same distance from any British troops. In return he engaged that the advance of the British in Guzerat should be kept within certain limits. This done, he turned eastward from Rajoora, and entering Berar on the 25th, Nov. 25. reached Akolah on the 27th, from which two days' march due north to Parterly[1] united his army on the 29th with that of Colonel Stevenson. Nov. 29.

Meanwhile, as might have been expected, Scindia had made no attempt to fulfil his part of the armistice by retiring to east of Ellichpoor, but had simply drawn his cavalry nearer to a large force of Ragogee's regular infantry, which was encamped within sight of Parterly under the Rajah's brother, Manu Bapu. Stevenson therefore had followed Scindia, but judiciously halted for a day so as to allow Wellesley to join him in the attack. On the morning of the 29th a messenger from the Rajah of Berar came to Wellesley to tell him that his master's army was only ten miles distant, and to entreat him to halt. The General's only answer was that if he overtook the army he would certainly attack it, and that the messenger had better remain with the baggage under protection of the rear-guard. Ascending a tower at Parterly immediately upon his arrival,

[1] Or, as some spell it, Pautoorla.

1803. Nov. 29. Wellesley perceived a confused moving mass some five miles distant, but, having made a long march on a hot day, was disinclined to weary his troops with a pursuit. However, bodies of Mahratta horse at once appeared in his front; and when these were chased away, in order to clear the ground on which he intended to encamp, he plainly descried the whole army of the enemy drawn up in order of battle about five miles off on the plains before the village of Argaum. This was enough. Though the troops had marched at six in the morning and it was then three o'clock in the afternoon, he resolved immediately to attack. The army accordingly marched off in three columns in a direction nearly parallel to the enemy's position, the irregular cavalry covering the left flank and rear. The country was covered with high grain, and for three miles those in the ranks could see nothing. Near the village of Sirsoni, however, the ground opened out slightly, and on the other side of it the cultivated land gave place to an open plain, perfectly flat though cut with water-courses, where the enemy's host came into full view about a thousand yards away.

The road followed by Wellesley's division of infantry entered this plain by the village of Sirsoni; and it was the General's direction that the column should leave this village on its right and, having cleared it, should wheel to the left and form line. The Mahrattas, knowing that Sirsoni marked the only access to the open ground, had trained their guns upon it, and, as Wellesley's leading battalion emerged from it, they opened a fire at long range from more than fifty cannon. The native troops of the advanced guard, who had with them a few field-pieces drawn by bullocks, were thrown into disorder; the bullock-drivers lost their heads; and the cattle, turning round, carried confusion into the ranks behind them. Next to the advanced guard were two native battalions which had behaved heroically at Assaye; but, dismayed by the backward rush and galled by the cannonade, they were now seized with panic, broke, and ran. Happily Wellesley was close by, or the day would have been lost. At the first opening of the cannonade he rode towards the enemy's line with some uneasiness, but presently observed to his secretary, "We shall have time to take those guns before night." Then, finding that the fugitive battalions would not rally to him when he stepped out in front, he rode quietly up to them and bade their officers guide them to the rear of the village, and re-form them under cover of it. When this was done, he led them as quietly once more to the front and halted them in their appointed place, while the rear battalions, which had been checked and delayed by this mishap, came up and deployed in succession. Guns were brought into action on each side of the village to cover the deployment, so far as was possible, against an overwhelming superiority of artillery; and each battalion, after taking up its position, lay down.

1803. Nov. 29.

The infantry was drawn up in a single line, standing from right to left in the following order: the advanced guard or picquets, two native battalions, the Seventy-eighth, the Seventy-fourth, four more native battalions of Wellesley's army, and then the Scots Brigade[1] and the six native battalions of Stevenson's force. The regular cavalry, consisting of the Nineteenth and five native regiments, was drawn up in second line in rear of the right, and the irregular horse occupied the same position on the left. The entire force probably numbered from ten to eleven thousand men.

The Mahrattas were formed in more primitive fashion. The centre and left were composed of Ragogee's infantry, artillery, and cavalry; the right consisted of Scindia's cavalry with a number of Pindarries or predatory horse. The regular infantry, about ten thousand strong, was drawn up, together with its guns, in one line, with a small body of foot in rear. Scindia's cavalry was massed in two huge bands, one slightly in advance, and the other in rear of the right of the first

[1] This, while it endured, was numbered 94th of the Line.

1803. Nov. 29. line; and the Rajah of Berar's cavalry likewise took post somewhat in rear of the left flank. In all, the host numbered, probably, from thirty to forty thousand men of one description or another, and covered a front of considerable extent.

After several minutes' continuance of the fire of the Mahratta artillery, the deployment of Stevenson's battalions completed Wellesley's line, and at half-past four he gave the order to advance. The whole then strode forward as if on parade, while Wellesley in person led the cavalry on to within six hundred yards of the enemy, and left it with orders to play upon them with their galloping guns and to charge as soon as the fire produced any effect. In the advance of the infantry the centre for some reason gradually outpaced the rest until, at the moment of attack, the Seventy-fourth, Seventy-eighth, and the native battalions on their left were some distance ahead of the remainder of the line. As the two European battalions arrived within sixty yards of the Mahratta array the enemy's gunners fired a final discharge of grape into them, and a large body of Arabs, with much shouting, boldly charged them with sword and buckler. A short but sharp struggle followed, in which the Arabs were beaten back with the loss of some six hundred killed and wounded; and the rest of the Mahrattas gave way almost immediately. Two feeble attacks of the cavalry upon the extremities of Wellesley's line were easily repulsed, and then the whole mass of the enemy turned and ran, leaving thirty-eight guns behind them. Wellesley instantly launched his cavalry after the fugitives; and Colonel St. Leger, who had succeeded Maxwell as Brigadier, pressed the pursuit relentlessly by moonlight, cutting down some three thousand of the enemy and capturing elephants and camels and huge quantities of baggage. It was midnight before the British troops finally lay down to rest, having been under arms for eighteen hours.

Their casualties in the action were inconsiderable,

not exceeding one hundred and sixty-two Europeans 1803.
and two hundred natives killed, wounded, and missing.[1] Nov. 29.
But the proportion of Europeans that fell was unduly large, partly, no doubt, because the enemy took care to concentrate their artillery-fire upon them. Thus the small remnant of the Seventy-fourth lost fifty-two men, the Seventy-eighth lost forty-seven, and the Scots brigade forty-one. However, even so, the cost of a great success was trifling, especially after the mishap to the leading native battalions at the opening of the action. "I am convinced," wrote Wellesley, referring to these last, "that if I had not been near them to rally them and restore the battle, we should have lost the day."[2]

On the day following the action Stevenson's division Nov. 30.
marched in pursuit of the enemy, though Stevenson himself was so ill that he was hardly fit to do duty; and, Wellesley following him a day later, the two divisions met once more at Ellichpoor, about forty
miles east and north of Argaum, on the 5th of December. Dec. 5.
Halting there for two days to establish a hospital for the wounded, Wellesley pushed on with his whole force to Gawilghur, where the defeated infantry of Argaum had taken refuge. The fort itself was situated on a lofty mountain in a range of hills between the sources of the Poorna and the Taptee; and by the natural configuration of the ground the stronghold was divided into two distinct parts, a main fort or citadel fronting to the south, and an outer or lesser[3] fort, which covered the approach to the inner, on the north. Between the

	Killed.	Wounded.	Missing.
[1] Europeans . . .	15	145	2
Natives . . .	31	163	5

One European officer was killed, and ten wounded.

[2] *Well. Desp.* ii. 565. Welsh's *Military Reminiscences* and *Twelve Years' Military Adventure* are the best authorities to read with the despatches.

[3] Perhaps this should be more correctly described as a fortified *pettah*, being in this case smaller instead of, as usual, larger than the fort proper.

1803. two forts was a deep gorge, on the inner side of which was an intermediate wall, shielding the access to the walls of the citadel from the north. One and all of these defences were well built of stone, with ramparts and towers but without a ditch. The roads which led to the fort were three. The first reached the citadel from the south, and was not only very long and steep, but so narrow as to be impracticable for cattle. The second started from the outer fort on the north-west side, circled round the western face of the main fort within range of its guns for a long distance, and finally formed the main communication with the country to southward. But it was too narrow to be used as a regular approach, besides which the rock on each side of the gate had been scarped. There remained a third road on the north side, leading to the outer fort directly from the village of Labada ; and here the ground was level with the works. But on the other hand the road to Labada from Ellichpoor wound for thirty miles through mountains and jungle, offering terrible obstacles to the transport of guns and stores, together with some uncertainty as to the supply of water on the way. In fact, as Wellesley said, the great difficulty in attacking Gawilghur was to approach it at all.

However, he decided to make his attempt from the north by Labada ; and, since Stevenson had equipped his force for a siege, the principal attack was entrusted to him, while Wellesley himself undertook to cover the operation with his own infantry and the cavalry of both armies, and to make such diversions as he could on the south and west of the fort. Accordingly on
Dec. 6. the 6th of December detachments were sent out to drive away the hostile troops which were encamped to south of the walls, and to seize the fortified village of Damergaum, which covered the access to Labada at the
Dec. 7. entrance to the mountains. On the 7th both armies marched from Ellichpoor, Stevenson's upon Damergaum, and Wellesley's on Deogaum, towards the south front of Gawilghur.

For four long days Stevenson's men struggled with extraordinary difficulties in dragging the heavy guns to their appointed place. First they had to make roads over the ruggedest of mountains and ravines, and then to haul their cannon and stores with frightful fatigue to the desired spot. The work, however, was cheerfully done; and on the night of the 12th Stevenson erected two batteries, the one of five, the other of four guns, against the northern front of the outer fort. Wellesley on his side also threw up a battery of four guns, though with little hope of success, over against the gate of the south front of the citadel. All three of these opened fire on the 13th, Stevenson's playing with great effect, while the shot from Wellesley's battery simply rebounded from the solid wall and rolled down the hill back to the very muzzles of the guns. By the night of the 14th the breaches in the wall of the outer fort upon Stevenson's side were practicable, and at ten o'clock of the following morning the assault was delivered by the flank companies of Stevenson's division, supported by the Scots Brigade. Simultaneously Wellesley launched two columns, consisting of the Seventy-fourth and Seventy-eighth regiments and one battalion of Sepoys, as a diversion, against the southern and north-western gates. Stevenson's men soon forced their way into the outer fort, and the enemy, striving to escape from their bayonets by the north-western gate, were met by one of Wellesley's columns, which forced them back, and, entering the gate with them, soon mastered the outer fort.

1803. Dec. 12. Dec. 13. Dec. 14. Dec. 15.

Then to their astonishment the British for the first time discovered that the citadel stood on a separate hill on the other side of a deep gorge, beyond which appeared the intermediate wall and its gate. However, Colonel Kenny, almost by himself, found a track which crossed the gorge towards the gate, and the Ninety-fourth, presently finding it also, crowded after him to the intermediate wall. This rose out of a steep pitch of ground, and the men could only climb it slowly and

1803. Dec. 15. with difficulty, one by one, under a heavy fire from the walls of the citadel. Meanwhile the British supports came hurrying up, and, halting on the edge of the outer fort, poured in an answering fire of musketry while the Ninety-fourth were clambering over the wall. Beyond this obstacle was a narrow rocky road leading to yet another wall and gate—those of the main fort—which seemed to be inaccessible. However, after some trouble a place was found where this last wall could be escaladed; and the light company of the Scots Brigade, fixing their ladders, forced their way into the stronghold and opened the gate to admit the storming party. These rushed in, and in a very short time the British were in possession of Gawilghur. The total loss during the siege was fourteen killed and one hundred and twelve wounded, the European share of the casualties being sixty-seven; so that the resistance was evidently ill-organised. The garrison was some four thousand strong, being composed chiefly of regular infantry which had fled from Argaum; and, the British troops being savage, the slaughter among the enemy was fearful. It should seem that the greater number of them was killed with the bayonet or driven over the walls and dashed to pieces. On a smaller scale, the assault of Gawilghur appears to have been as bloody as that of Seringapatam.[1]

Meanwhile the expedition against Cuttack had met with complete success. The total force allotted for the operations numbered close upon five thousand men, of which three thousand[2] were assembled at Ganjam

[1] *Wellington Desp.* ii. 583, 599; Wilson's *Madras Army*, iii. 118-122; Welsh, *Military Reminiscences*, i. 195-197; *Twelve Years' Military Adventure*, pp. 218-219.

[2]

Europeans.	2 companies, 22nd Foot	200
	102nd Foot	300
	Artillery, etc.	73
Natives.	20th Bengal N.I., 1/9th M.N.I., 1/19th M.N.I., Cavalry and Artillery	2468
	Total	3041

under the command, first, of Lieutenant-colonel 1803.
Campbell of the Seventy-fourth, and, upon his serious illness, of Colonel Harcourt of the Twelfth Foot. The rest of the troops were stationed in detachments at Jelasore, Balasore, and Midnapore. Harcourt marched from Ganjam on the 8th of September, and Sept. 8.
on the 18th occupied Juggernaut without opposition. Heavy rain then detained him until the 24th, when he Sept. 24.
moved upon Cuttack, and, after some skirmishing on the march, took possession of it, unresisted, on the 10th of October. The fort of Barabutty, about a mile Oct. 10.
distant from Cuttack, made some show of resistance, being surrounded by a wide ditch containing thirty feet of water, which could be crossed only by a single bridge. But after a short cannonade a storming party, on the 14th, boldly crossed the bridge and, with some difficulty Oct. 14.
and delay, succeeded in blowing open the wicket of the gate. Through this the men passed singly, and were presently masters of the place, with a loss of little more than fifty killed and wounded. After this miserably feeble struggle the greater part of the province submitted, and the operations practically came to an end, most disastrously for the Rajah of Berar.

It is not surprising, therefore, that the final stroke of Gawilghur, over and above all previous losses and disgraces, should have crushed the spirit of the unfortunate Ragogee. On the very day after Wellesley's Dec. 16.
successful assault messengers came to sue for peace; and on the 17th a treaty was signed, whereby the Dec. 17.
province of Cuttack was ceded to the East India Company, and sundry other territories to its friends and allies. Thus one member of the Mahratta Confederacy was crushed, and it was not long before another was to share his fate; but first it must be told how Scindia fared at the hands of General Lake in Hindostan.

CHAPTER II

1803. On turning from the south to the north of India, from the correspondence of Arthur Wellesley to that of his brother the Viceroy, one is struck by the advantage which Arthur Wellesley enjoyed through his greater remoteness from Government House. The order to prepare for war was issued to him at the same time as to General Lake; but Lake was required to furnish an elaborate plan of campaign, against each paragraph of which the Viceroy penned pompous comments of approval with as much solemnity as if he had been Frederick the Great. This was an entirely harmless amusement, for Lord Wellesley, despite an enormous share of vanity, was on most affectionate terms with Lake, and far too able a man to attempt to set him right upon military matters. The essence of Lake's plan was summed up in a single sentence, the defeat of Perron's army in the field. That army once destroyed, the success of any subsequent operations would be assured as a matter of course. But Perron's influence as vicegerent of the puppet-emperor, Shah Alum, was wide, and his power as leader of a large body of trained infantry was formidable; and it was therefore of the first importance to isolate him completely before giving him battle. Only thus was it possible to hold the allies of the Mahrattas in check until a successful action against Perron should induce them to change sides; and only thus could Scindia be prevented from returning suddenly from the south with his cavalry, and perhaps converting a pitched battle into a British defeat, as he might have done at Assaye. 1803.

The main army for the field was therefore fixed at the strength of one British and eleven native battalions, three British and three native regiments of cavalry, with forty-nine guns. Four native battalions and one regiment of native cavalry were stationed at Allahabad for the invasion of Bundelcund, in order to divert cavalry from joining Perron from that quarter. Three battalions and a few horse were ordered to Rohilcund to cover Rampore and overawe the Sikhs and other troublesome neighbours. A detachment of the same strength was designed to cover Benares and bar the passes to southward of it.[1] Lake had fixed his head-quarters at Cawnpore in July; but marching from that place with the garrison on the 7th of August, Aug. 7. moved up the Ganges to Kanoge, near which place his force gradually assembled. The camp was luxurious. The officers were allowed to keep their wives and families with them, and, the nights being cold, many of them fitted up their tents with glass doors and brick chimneys. There was plenty of game in the neighbourhood; and there was at least one officer who was adventurous enough to spear a tiger, and would probably have paid for his daring with his life, had not Lake himself shot the beast with a pistol in the nick of time. Lastly, there was plenty of good wine, and there was a ballroom; from all of which it may be concluded that life was merry in that camp on the Ganges.

The last of the troops having come up, the army was distributed into three brigades of cavalry and four of infantry, counting in all nine regiments of horse and fourteen battalions of foot.[2] The whole, after absorbing

[1] *Wellesley Desp.* iii. 189-193.

[2] *Cavalry.* 1st Brigade. Lt.-Col. Vandeleur; H.M. 8th L.D., 1st and 3rd Bengal N.C.
2nd " Col. St. Leger; H.M. 27th L.D., 2nd and 6th Bengal N.C.
3rd " Col. Macan; H.M. 29th L.D., 4th Bengal N.C.

1803. many of the detachments so carefully distributed under the original scheme, must have numbered about fifteen thousand men, accompanied as usual by about ten times that number of followers and about the same proportion of bullocks. The army moved in a huge square, of which the front face was formed by the picquets coming on duty, the rear face by the picquets coming off duty, one side by the cavalry and the other by the infantry. The artillery kept the high road, next to the infantry, and the rear of the interior of the square was filled
Aug. 26. with baggage and cattle. On the 26th of August
Aug. 29. the host was at Secundra, and on the 29th it entered Mahratta territory and marched straight upon the fortress of Aligarh, where Perron had concentrated his force to oppose it. The baggage was packed and left in charge of a detachment about four miles in rear, and at about seven o'clock the enemy was sighted in the act of striking camp.

Presently the Mahratta horse, about twenty thousand strong, drew itself up on the plain, taking post behind a huge morass, with their right protected by the guns of Aligarh, and their left resting on a village. Thereupon Lake, taking personal command of his mounted troops, led them away to the right in column of regiments and, turning the swamp, wheeled them to the left in two

Infantry.	1st Brigade.	Lt.-Col. Monson; H.M. 76th, 1 and 2/4th Bengal N.I., 4 cos. 17th N.I.	
	2nd "	Col. Clarke; 2/8th, 2/9th, 1/12th, 6 cos. 16th Bengal N.I.	
	3rd "	Col. Macdonald; 2/12th, 1 and 2/15th Bengal N.I.	
	4th "	Lt.-Col. Powell; 1 and 2/2nd, 1/14th Bengal N.I.	
Artillery.	2 galloper-guns to each regiment of cavalry		18
	2 battalion-guns to each battalion of infantry		28
	1 brigade of Horse Artillery		6
	6 six-pounders, 4 twelve-pounders		10
	3 five and a half inch howitzers		3
		Total of guns	65

lines for the attack, leaving the infantry to follow in 1803.
support. Some annoyance was caused during the Aug. 29.
advance by a skirmishing fire of matchlock-men, and by a fusillade from the village, until the houses were presently cleared by a native battalion ; and the enemy's horse retiring steadily, not without punishment from the guns of the British cavalry, finally abandoned the field without an attempt to come to close quarters. Perron with his bodyguard then withdrew to Agra, leaving a Colonel Pedron in the fort, with orders to defend it to the last extremity ; and Lake, disappointed at his failure to force a general action, was fain to occupy Coel and to encamp. His men had been marching from five in the morning until two in the afternoon on a day of intense heat.

Meanwhile he summoned Pedron to surrender, with the result that six of Scindia's European officers at once quitted the Mahratta service and came over to the British camp. Pedron answered with a somewhat hesitating defiance in order to gain time to improve his defences ; and Lake, hoping to obtain the fort
by bribery, took no further step until the 3rd of Sept. 3.
September. Finding then that his hopes were baseless, he resolved to assault at once rather than lose a precious month in a tedious siege. The decision was a bold one, for the fortress was deemed impregnable ; and indeed in the rainy season the swampy ground about it was so deeply inundated as to render it inaccessible. Aligarh consisted of an inner and an outer fort, with circular towers at short intervals, the configuration of the outer being exactly repeated on the inner lines ; while an immense wet ditch, "in which a seventy-four might sail,"[1] surrounded the whole, and detached works of great strength and remarkable intricacy defended the gate. The fortress mounted in all seventy-three guns of various calibres, with plenty more in the arsenal to make good casualties. Since the only possible means of passing the ditch was by the gateway, Lake decided

[1] Lake to Wellesley, *Wellesley Desp.* iii. 293.

1803. Sept. 3. that the assault should be delivered at that point. Two batteries were thrown up on the night of the 3rd, so as to bring a cross-fire to bear on the outworks of the gate; and a storming party was selected of four companies of the Seventy-sixth and as many of a native battalion, with a second Sepoy battalion in support.[1] Colonel Monson was appointed to lead the attack, his guide being Mr. Lucas, a British officer who had lately deserted Scindia's service.

Sept. 4. At three in the morning the forlorn hope moved off towards the gateway, and halted within four hundred yards of it until dawn. A small party of the enemy being visible sitting round a fire, a few men of the Seventy-sixth were sent to surprise them, in the hope that they might enter the gate on the backs of the fugitives and hold it until supported. The British soldiers, however, defeated their own object by despatching every man of the enemy; but, though the alarm was raised, it was fortunately not taken up seriously by the garrison. The men of the Seventy-sixth then retired unperceived; and the sentries on the ramparts, after firing a few shots, relapsed into calmness and security. At dawn the morning gun sounded from Lake's camp; and upon this signal the storming party, covered by a heavy fire from the two batteries, rushed at the gate. A hundred yards in advance of it was a newly erected traverse mounting three guns, but the British were in possession of this work before a shot had been fired; and Monson, pressing on with two companies of the Seventy-sixth, hoped to enter the fort with the flying garrison. He was disappointed. The traverse had been abandoned; the gate was shut; and from three different sides the guns of the batteries and outworks plied the little party with a most destructive fire.

The grenadiers of the Seventy-sixth planted two ladders by the walls and attempted an escalade, but found the attempt hopeless in the face of a forest of

[1] Four companies 17th N.I., 2/4th N.I.

pikes. A six-pounder was hurried up to force the gate, without success. A twelve-pounder was then brought forward, but owing to peculiarities in the structure of the gateway it was not easily placed in position, and four or five rounds were fired before any impression was produced. Twenty minutes were thus consumed, during which time the storming party remained helpless under a deadly converging fire of grape and musketry, while the enemy, gallantly leaving the ramparts, swarmed down the scaling ladders to close with their assailants. Monson was hurt by a thrust from a pike, several more officers were wounded with him; and the adjutant and every officer of the Grenadiers of the Seventy-sixth were killed outright. 1803. Sept. 4.

Nevertheless the first gate gave way at last, and the stormers pursued their way along a circular road, from within which a circular tower filled with matchlock-men poured a deadly fire of musketry upon them, while from without a neighbouring bastion plied them with a tempest of grape. At the further end of the circular road was a second gate, which was easily forced; and the British now hurried along the causeway which connected the outwork with the main fortress, caught the flying enemy crowded at a third gate, which lay at the end of the causeway, and seized it before it could be closed against them. Thus, always under a heavy fire from all quarters, they entered the passage between the outer and inner forts, only to be stopped by a fourth gate. The twelve-pounder was again brought up, for Captain Shipton of the Artillery, though wounded, had refused to quit his gun; but the gate was battered to no purpose, for it was too strongly secured to be broken down. At length, however, Major M'Leod of the Seventy-sixth succeeded in passing the wicket and ascending the ramparts; and then resistance gave way to despair. The garrison, seeing the inner fort entered, thought of nothing but escape, and jumped by hundreds into the ditch. Great numbers were drowned; others swam over to the plain beyond, only to find a

1803. Sept. 4. picquet of dragoons in wait for them, and, refusing to surrender, were cut down. In all over two thousand of them perished by the bayonet or the water; and after an hour's hard fighting the fort of Aligarh was won.

This was a fine feat of arms; and Lake confessed that he had never spent a more anxious time than during the long hour consumed in the attack. Nor were the losses trifling. The four companies of the Seventy-sixth lost five officers and nineteen men killed, four officers and sixty-two men wounded; the Fourth Native Infantry lost fewer officers but rather more men; and altogether the casualties amounted to fifty-five killed and two hundred and five wounded of all ranks.

The fortress had not been many hours in Lake's hands when news came that a large body of predatory horse, under the command of a Frenchman, Fleury, had attacked the cantonment of Shekoabad, some thirty-five miles east of Agra. Macan's brigade of cavalry was
Sept. 5. sent off at two o'clock on the morning of the 5th to rescue the five companies of native infantry quartered in the place, but arrived too late. The Sepoys, under command of Colonel Coningham, had faced five thousand cavalry in the open plain for two consecutive hours and had finally driven them off. But the attack had been renewed on the following day, and after a further resistance of some hours the British commander, who was himself wounded, was obliged to engage that his troops should serve against Scindia no more during the war; upon which condition he led them away with all their arms and their one battalion-gun. Five British officers and over sixty men were killed and wounded in this affair. Macan, burning to take vengeance, pursued Fleury by forced marches as far as Ferozabad, about twenty-four miles east of Agra, which he reached on the 8th. There, finding that the enemy had crossed the Jumna, he gave up the pursuit, but continued roving
Sept. 17. until the 17th, when he marched to rejoin the main army.

Lake, meanwhile, having strengthened the defences 1803.
of Aligarh and left a native battalion in it for garrison, marched on the 7th towards Delhi, having intelligence Sept. 7.
that Louis Bourquain, one of Scindia's French officers, was employing the name and prestige of the Mogul Emperor to the utmost in order to strengthen his position among the native chiefs. On the evening of the same day the General received a letter from Perron reporting that he had quitted Scindia's service, and asking for a safe-conduct to Lucknow. An escort was willingly granted, and Perron, with Fleury and another officer, after a few months' stay at Lucknow, removed to Chandernagore. Lake, not ill-pleased thus to be rid of a formidable enemy, pursued his march, and on the 8th had the satisfaction to find the strong Sept. 8.
fort of Koorjah evacuated at his approach, the garrison having no mind to repeat the experience of Aligarh. On the 10th a march of eighteen miles brought him Sept. 10.
within six miles of Delhi on the eastern side; and on the road intelligence arrived that Louis Bourquain had crossed the Jumna in the night with sixteen battalions of regular infantry, six thousand horse, and several guns, with the expressed intention of attacking him.

The troops had come into camp at eleven in the forenoon, much fatigued; but hardly had the tents been pitched, when the enemy appeared in such force as to oblige the grand guard and picquets to turn out. More and more bodies of the Mahratta army appeared, and presently Lake mounted his horse, and, taking three regiments of cavalry,[1] which were all that repeated detachments had left to him at the moment, rode off to reconnoitre them in person. He found the entire array drawn up on rising ground, with the Jumna in its rear. The infantry formed the first line, and was posted very strongly behind entrenchments; each flank covered by a swamp and the whole length of the front bristling with guns. Behind the foot stood the cavalry in second line. High grass and jungle in some

[1] H.M. 27th L.D., 2nd and 3rd Bengal N.C.

1803. Sept. 10. measure concealed the enemy's dispositions, and, as Lake prolonged his reconnaissance, the Mahratta guns opened fire upon his escort. Having satisfied himself, however, the General lost no time in sending orders to his infantry to move to the front at once. Detachments for various services had deprived him of two complete brigades of cavalry and five battalions of infantry, leaving him with three regiments of cavalry and eight and a half battalions of infantry only. Allowing half a battalion and the picquets for a baggage-guard, he could reckon on about four thousand five hundred men for the coming action; and with these he prepared to assail the nineteen thousand under Louis Bourquain.

It was a full hour before the infantry could come up; and meanwhile the cavalry suffered heavily from the fire of the enemy's artillery. Lake's horse was shot under him, and he was obliged to take that of his son, who in his turn took that of a dead trooper. At length, seeing that the battalions were approaching, Lake gave the order for the cavalry to fall back, hoping thus to lure the enemy from their position. He was not deceived. The entire Mahratta line advanced with its artillery, shouting loudly as the cavalry retired. The regiments continued the retrograde movement in line, always masking the advance of the infantry, until they reached their comrades; when upon a sudden word they wheeled right and left into column of troops and galloped away to both flanks, revealing the line of battalions perfectly formed, with the Seventy-sixth on the right and the Sepoys in succession upon its left.[1] In a few minutes the cavalry was again massed in rear of the right wing; and then, since the enemy's Sikh horsemen were advancing to threaten his right flank and rear, Lake threw out two or three squadrons with two galloping guns to check them. At the same time the left flank battalion, with

[1] The actual position of the various corps was as follows, from right to left: 76th, 2/12th N.I., 2/15th N.I., 2/2nd N.I., 1/14th N.I., 1/2nd N.I.

four guns, was thrown forward obliquely with its right 1803.
wing resting on a village, in order to cover the left. Sept. 10.
These dispositions completed, Lake placed himself at the head of the Seventy-sixth, and ordered the whole line to advance.

The Mahrattas promptly opened a tremendous fire of round, grape, and chain shot; but the battalions strode on unheeding. The Seventy-sixth kept their muskets at the shoulder, despite the concentration of the Mahratta guns upon them, until they came within range of one hundred yards, when Lake gave the order to fire a volley and charge. The effect was as crushing as at Quebec. The British dashed forward, and the Mahrattas broke and fled in all directions. The troops were no sooner halted after the charge than Lake ordered the battalions to form column of companies; and the cavalry, galloping through the intervals, fell upon the unhappy fugitives and hunted them to the Jumna, where the galloping guns made terrible havoc among the flying masses. But, while the cavalry was thus engaged on the front and right, a part of the Mahrattas had retired to the left; wherefore Lake wheeled the line of infantry also to the left, and, pursuing them among the broken ground and ravines adjoining the Jumna, completely routed them and captured all their guns and stores. The action came to an end at seven in the evening, by which time the troops had been on foot for sixteen hours, for the most part under a burning sun. The army then encamped on the bank of the river over against the city of Delhi.

It is instructive to compare this action with that of Assaye, which was fought only a fortnight later. In both cases the British commanders found their enemy very strongly posted with very powerful and efficient artillery, and in both cases they manœuvred to make him change position and then attacked. Both, also, resolved to endure the punishment of the enemy's cannon for a time, feeling sure that he could not stand

1803. Sept. 10. the ordeal of meeting their infantry. But here the resemblance ends. In Lake's action everything went right, and the cavalry was fresh for pursuit; in Wellesley's everything went wrong, and the result was a narrow escape from disaster. It may therefore be concluded that but for the unfortunate error which led Wellesley's right astray, the battle of Assaye would have been such another as Delhi. But with all his good fortune, Lake's losses were in one respect serious. The total number of killed, wounded, and missing was four hundred and seventy-eight; and of these one hundred and thirty-seven, including one officer, belonged to the Seventy-sixth. The native regiment which stood next to it lost ninety-one of all ranks killed and wounded; and the casualties among the horses of the cavalry brigade amounted to one hundred and seventy. In truth it was no child's play to face the fire of the Mahratta artillery, though, when once it had been silenced by the charge of the infantry, the action in every case came to an abrupt end. The Mahrattas on this occasion were estimated to have lost three thousand men, and they left sixty-eight pieces of cannon, all admirably made after a French design, as the trophies of the victors.

Halting for three days, Lake crossed to the western
Sept. 14. bank of the Jumna on the 14th, and on the same day received the surrender of Bourquain and of four more French officers, who were presently sent down to Calcutta. This gave a mortal stroke to the French
Sept. 16. power built up by Perron; and on the 16th Lake was welcomed by the emperor, Shah Alum, to the capital of the Mogul empire. It was the last of many vicissitudes which the unhappy potentate had been fated to experience. Old, blind, and broken down by harsh treatment, he found himself, though still a puppet, yet again by title an emperor, and entertained as such with honour. Three years later he died at the age of eighty-six, having lived to see the occupants of a few small factories become the masters of India.

After a week's halt in Delhi, Lake marched on the 24th upon Agra, his heavy guns and stores being conveyed in boats down the Jumna, while the army followed the banks. On the 25th messengers arrived from the Rajah of Bhurtpore, a powerful chief of the Jats, to beg the friendship and protection of the British Government, which proposal, being readily entertained by Lake, was on the 9th of October formulated into a treaty of offensive and defensive alliance. On the 2nd of October the army reached Muttra, Perron's principal arsenal, where Lake was rejoined by the cavalry and other troops that had been detached to Shekoabad and other quarters,[1] and was further greeted by four more of Scindia's French officers who had come in to surrender. Two days later he encamped on the south side of Agra, when he at once summoned the garrison to surrender; but the troops in the city had risen against their European officers; all was in confusion; and no answer was returned. Seven battalions of regular infantry with several guns were, however, encamped upon the glacis, occupying the town and the ravines which surrounded the south and south-west faces of the fort; and Lake realised that, until these were dislodged, it would be impossible to conduct the operations of a siege. Shifting his camp, therefore, on the 7th and 8th so as to encircle the place as far as possible, he on the 10th made two separate attacks, each with three battalions of Sepoys, upon the town and the ravines, and drove the enemy off with a loss of six hundred men and twenty-six guns. The action, however, was severe, since the troops were exposed to the guns of the fort; and the object was not attained without the loss of two hundred and twenty-eight killed and wounded, including nine British officers. Two days later, however, the remainder of the seven battalions, two thousand five hundred strong, surrendered; and on the morrow, before Lake could

1803. Sept. 24. Oct. 2. Oct. 4. Oct. 7, 8. Oct. 10. Oct. 12. Oct. 13.

[1] 8th and 29th L.D., two regiments of native cavalry, and three and a half Sepoy battalions.

1803. make any great progress with his batteries, the two
Oct. 13. English officers, Hessing and Sutherland, who commanded within the city, wrote to ask for terms, stating that they had persuaded the troops to offer no further resistance. Lake replied that he would grant protection to themselves and their private property, and continued to work at his batteries, one of which opened
Oct. 17. fire with such effect on the 17th that the conditions were promptly accepted. On the 18th the British were in possession of Agra.[1]

The capture of this great fortress, the key of Hindostan, produced a profound impression upon the native mind; and Lake, when he saw from within how formidable was its strength and calculated the loss that must have ensued upon a storm, felt devoutly thankful for his good fortune.[2] All was now going well. Enormous quantities of stores were taken in Agra, which pleased the General; a very large sum in the treasury was adjudged to be prize-money, which pleased the officers and men; and finally two thousand five hundred of Scindia's infantry had taken service with the British, while the Rajah of Bhurtpore had brought to Lake a contingent of five thousand horse. Scindia's regular infantry, however, was not yet entirely extinguished. That chieftain before the battle of Assaye had detached fifteen battalions from the Deccan to Hindostan, and these, added to two of Bourquain's which had escaped at Delhi, made up a force of about nine thousand men.[3] They were excellently equipped with artillery; they were further accompanied by four or five thousand horse, not all of inferior quality; they had a good leader in a Mahratta named Abaji; and

[1] Thorn, *Wellesley Desp.* iii. 393-396, 407.

[2] *Wellesley Desp.* iii. 415.

[3] Grant Duff, *Hist. of the Mahrattas*, iii. 179, gives the number of detached battalions as seven, and adds to them three more of Bourquain's besides the fugitives. Lake, however (*Wellesley Desp.* iii. 450), speaks of seventeen battalions. All authorities agree that the number of men, whatever the number of battalions, was nine thousand.

Lake was not disposed to allow them to wander at large about Hindostan. On the 27th of October, therefore, he marched westward, and after a day's halt at Karowly, due to a very heavy fall of rain, pushed forward on the 29th nearly to Futtehpoor, where the sound of the enemy's guns, bombarding a neighbouring town, roused him to renewed exertion. The heavy cannon and baggage were left at Futtehpoor with an escort of two battalions; and two forced marches north-westward brought him on the 31st to the ground where the enemy had encamped on the same morning.

1803. Oct. 27. Oct. 29. Oct. 31.

Intent upon overtaking them, Lake started on the same night at eleven o'clock with the whole of his cavalry,[1] hoping to keep them engaged with the mounted troops until the infantry should come up. In six hours he traversed twenty-five miles, and at dawn of the 1st of November came up with a confused mass of men, evidently in hasty retreat. Marking their disorder, Lake determined to attack at once; but the enemy contrived to gain time by cutting the embankment of a large reservoir of water, which made the road very difficult for the passage of cavalry. Turning this respite to good account, the Mahratta leaders pushed on for a short distance, and took up a strong position between the villages of Laswaree and Mohaulpore, the latter of which was fortified. Immediately in rear of Laswaree flowed a small stream, with banks so steep as to be barely accessible; and from its front a ravine ran diagonally through the right wing of the Mahratta line of battle. Along the whole length of that line extended a broad strip of high grass, which concealed their array and their seventy-two guns completely from the view of their pursuers. The dense clouds of dust raised by the enemy's movements contributed also to obscure alike their intentions and their

Nov. 1.

[1] 1st brigade, Col. T. P. Vandeleur, 8th L.D., 1st N.C., 3rd N.C.
2nd brigade . . . . 27th L.D., 6th N.C., 2nd N.C.
3rd „ Col. Macan . 29th L.D., 4th N.C.

1803. Nov. 1. dispositions, making it almost impossible for Lake to divine what they were actually doing.

None the less, having overtaken them only by uncommon exertions, he was determined not to let them escape. He therefore ordered the advanced guard and the first brigade of cavalry to move upon the point where the enemy had last been seen in motion, which, as a matter of fact, proved to be the left of their new position. The two remaining brigades were to maintain the attack, as quickly as they could be formed after passing the stream which separated them from the field of action.

The first brigade accordingly crossed the water, and, riding from end to end of the enemy's front, charged the left of their line by Mohaulpore, broke through it, drove the Mahratta gunners from their guns, and penetrated into the village. But they were unable to silence the galling fire of musketry and artillery which still played upon them. Their brigadier, Vandeleur, an excellent officer, was mortally wounded; and Lake, seeing that they could do no more, was fain to withdraw the squadrons, and to allow the guns which they had captured but had been unable to remove, to relapse into the enemy's possession. In other quarters the second and third brigades delivered their attack as gallantly and with as little permanent effect. Macan, who was directed upon the Mahratta right, crossed the ravine with his two regiments under a heavy cannonade, wheeled into line in the face of a still heavier fire, and galloped down upon the guns as if he had been at a review. Nothing could be seen through the long grass; and the Mahratta gunners, holding their fire until the horses were within twenty yards, poured upon them a storm of grape and chain shot. Yet still the squadrons galloped on, passed through the batteries, although the cannon were fastened by chains from axle-tree to axle-tree, and rallied on the other side. But already the Mahratta gunners, who had crept under their guns when the cavalry came upon them, were

serving them again ; while the infantry, entrenched 1803.
behind their waggons and carts, showered on the Nov. 1.
assembling squadrons a hail of bullets. Nothing daunted, Macan charged back through the line with the same irresistible gallantry and the same result; repeated the charge a third time, and was about to renew it for the fourth when he was recalled by Lake's order, and withdrawn with the rest of the cavalry out of range. The troopers had suffered heavily, and, though they had taken many guns, yet, for want of infantry to secure them, had been unable to retain more than two. The whole attack indeed was unnecessary, and would hardly have been delivered had not Lake been under the impression that the enemy was still retreating. When once he had found out his mistake he recalled all three brigades, resolving simply to hold the enemy with them until his infantry should come up.

At about eleven o'clock the infantry appeared, namely the Seventy-sixth and four native battalions. They had been marching since three o'clock in the morning, and, having traversed twenty-five miles under a blazing sun, were much fatigued. Lake therefore gave them an hour's halt for breakfast; and in the interval Abaji, awed by the arrival of the victorious British infantry, sent a message to the General that, if certain terms were granted to him, he was willing to surrender his guns. Lake returned an answer accepting the proposal, and granting him an hour to make up his mind; not omitting, however, to make his dispositions for a fresh attack. Abaji meanwhile shifted his ground, throwing back his right, and took up a new position. His infantry was formed in two lines, the first covering the front or east, and the second in the rear or west of Mohaulpore, while the cavalry extended beyond it almost to the stream, with its right flank in the air. Lake therefore formed his battalions in two columns along the brink of the stream ; the first, under Major-general Ware, being designed to advance

1803. Nov. 1. and turn Abaji's right flank, and the second, under Major-general St. John, to support Ware. Macan's brigade of cavalry also was to sustain the infantry, while the first and second brigades were extended widely across the plain on the British right, with the galloping guns and a few field-pieces pushed well forward in two groups, each with a squadron for escort, so as to menace and contain the Mahratta front.

Meanwhile the stipulated hour expired without a sign of the fulfilment of Lake's conditions; and accordingly his infantry advanced along the bank of the stream, under shelter of high grass and broken ground, which for some time concealed their movement. After a time, however, their march was detected, and Abaji, divining its purport, threw back his right wing, covering the manœuvre by a heavy and destructive cannonade upon the head of the British column. The result of this evolution was that the Mahratta array now assumed somewhat the form of the letter L, but with an obtuse instead of a right angle at the junction of the two lines, and that the British column, far from taking it in flank, was itself exposed to a flanking fire. The artillery which had accompanied the British infantry unlimbered and played upon the new front of the enemy's right wing, while the three batteries with the cavalry advanced and did the like upon their left wing; but the British guns were overmatched both in numbers and weight of metal by those of the Mahrattas; and matters began to look serious. The Seventy-sixth, which headed the column, had reached its appointed station, as also had a battalion and a half of Sepoys which followed immediately after it; and they had accordingly wheeled into line. But the remainder of the column had been delayed by unexpected impediments; and the three leading corps were compelled to await its coming inactive, under a furious and very well-directed fire. Lake, seeing that no troops could endure such a trial for long, ordered the Seventy-sixth and its companions to advance forthwith. They did so with alacrity; but the enemy, with great coolness allowing 1803. them to approach within range of canister shot, saluted Nov. 1. them with a murderous salvo from every gun in their front, while at the same time a body of cavalry bore down upon their left flank. Fortunately the Seventy-sixth was on the left of the line, and in spite of terrible losses, retained such steadiness and order as to repulse this dangerous attack; but the Mahratta horse soon rallied and showed unmistakable signs of delivering a second charge. Foreseeing some such trouble, Lake had ordered the Twenty-ninth Dragoons to be at hand to support the advancing infantry. These had been halted in a hollow behind the British guns by the stream, where they were partially screened from the enemy's view, but none the less exposed to rolling and ricochet shot,[1] which killed the commanding officer and wrought much mischief among both men and horses. This regiment, to its great relief, was now ordered to advance. The outlet from the depression in which they were posted was too strait to admit a broad front; and it was in narrow file that they galloped forward and formed on the left flank of the hard-pressed Seventy-sixth. The gallant infantry hailed them with loud cheers, which were echoed by the dragoons; and the Mahratta horse, which was advancing to the charge, beat a very hasty retreat.

There was now a pause. The Mahratta guns were

[1] "Nothing is so trying for troops as to stand exposed to a heavy fire from guns out of point-blank range; for it cannot be expected that ordinary flesh and blood will stand and see a shot hit it without attempting to get out of the way. I would observe for the benefit of my young military readers that they must not suppose when they see a round shot going leisurely along the ground that it is then quite innocuous, particularly if it has a spinning motion; for if when in that state it meets with a stone or any irregularity which raises it from the ground, it will fly off apparently with renewed force, but really with the force which it was before expending in its rotatory motion. I knew a person whose leg was shattered to pieces from his having thought to stop a ball in this situation by putting his foot upon it."—*Twelve Years' Military Adventure*, p. 201.

1803. Nov. 1. silent, the gunners seeming to bide their time to annihilate their assailants. On the British side there had occurred an incident which braced the troops for a supreme effort. Lake, at the head of the Seventy-sixth, had his charger shot under him. His son, who was on his staff, dismounted and offered his own horse, which the General at first refused, but after some entreaty consented to mount. The younger Lake then took a trooper's horse, and had just swung himself into the saddle when he was struck by a cannon shot, and fell very severely wounded before his father's eyes. For a fleeting moment Lake forgot everything in the agony of seeing his son, as he thought, killed; then, instantly mounting the horse, he was again directing the battle. The trumpet of the Twenty-ninth dragoons sounded the charge, and was answered forthwith by the roar of every Mahratta gun; but the troopers, galloping through a tempest of grape-shot and a general volley of musketry, rode straight into the line of guns, scattering the gunners; then crashed into the first line of infantry and broke it up; then pressed on against the second line of infantry and swept away its right; and finally, wheeling to the left, fell again upon the Mahratta horse and routed them completely. Lake meanwhile followed hard at their heels with the infantry, which by this time had been increased by a battalion and a half of Sepoys, secured the guns, and drove the enemy's right wing in confusion before him. The remainder of his infantry now came up; when, advancing with the whole of them, he attacked Abaji's second line, which fought most bravely, contesting every inch of ground. But at length it was forced back from the village into the plain, where the indefatigable Twenty-ninth, returning from the pursuit of the cavalry, swept down upon it and cut it to pieces.

Even now, however, the first line of the enemy's left wing before Mohaulpore, scorning to break and fly, strove still to retreat in good order. But by this time Lake could turn nearly the whole of his force 1803. upon them. The Twenty-seventh dragoons and Sixth Nov. 1. Native Cavalry cut off their retreat, and at length breaking into the column, after a long, stubborn, and most gallant resistance, cut them down by hundreds. A bare two thousand were left at last, and these became prisoners. The rest of the Mahratta host was slain or utterly swept away.

So ended the long agony of this most fateful and bloody fray, as fierce a fight as ever was fought by mortal men. It marked the fall of the proud Mahratta empire ; and, as on the death-day of Hyder Ali's dynasty, nothing was wanting to mark the horror of the crash. The seventeen battalions which De Boigne had trained, and which until this dawn had been known as the Deccan Invincibles, were reduced to two thousand disarmed and captured, though always valiant men. The remainder were lying on the plain in thousands, dying or dead, and with them most of their comrades of the horse. The fortified village of Mohaulpore was sinking into a smoking heap of ashes. Of the Mahratta guns, some stood in lines as during the action, with the gunners bayonetted and dead beneath them ; others, which the drivers had striven to carry away, lay scattered and overturned. The tumbrils and ammunition-waggons, in which they had kindled slow matches, exploded from time to time with a sullen roar, and veiled the sky with an ever-thickening canopy of sulphurous smoke. Beneath the canopy the British troops moved wearily or lay still, utterly exhausted by hard marching and hard fighting. Above it there advanced with startling rapidity a dense bank of clouds, which burst after sundown in a furious thunder-storm, lighting up the ghastly field with frightful vividness at every flash, and printing deep upon every mind an awful memory of the night after Laswaree.

The loss of the British was thirteen officers and one hundred and fifty-nine men killed ; twenty-nine officers and six hundred and twenty-three men

1803. Nov. 1. wounded; making a total of eight hundred and twenty-four casualties. Among the killed the British numbered eighty-two, and among the wounded two hundred and forty-eight. The chief sufferers, as usual, were the Seventy-sixth, with a loss among all ranks of forty-three killed and one hundred and forty-nine wounded. This raised their casualties in the three actions of the 4th and 11th of September and the 1st of November to eighteen officers and four hundred and twenty-eight men. Next to the Seventy-sixth came two Sepoy battalions, the one with one hundred casualties, the other with eighty-seven; but relatively the three white cavalry regiments suffered more than they. The Eighth Light Dragoons lost fifty-four of all ranks, and one hundred and sixteen horses; the Twenty-seventh, forty-eight of all ranks and eighty-six horses; the Twenty-ninth, sixty-two of all ranks, and one hundred and twelve horses. In all, the cavalry lost no fewer than four hundred and fifty-three horses killed, wounded, and missing.

But perhaps the General's staff was the most heavily punished of all. The Quartermaster's deputy and one aide-de-camp were killed; and the Adjutant-general, Secretary, Political Agent and commander of the escort were wounded. Lake himself had his coat burned by a matchlock fired at close range, though the bullet by a happy chance missed him; and two horses were killed under him, one of them a favourite charger named "Old Port," which was regretted even by the Viceroy.[1] Always in the thickest of the fire, it seemed to those with him miraculous that he escaped injury, but it is probable his presence alone saved the fight. The enemy fought, as he said, "like devils, or rather like heroes . . . and if they had been commanded by French officers the event would have been, I fear, extremely doubtful. I never was in so severe a business in my life or anything like it, and

[1] "I grieve for the loss of my poor friend 'Old Port.'" *Wellesley Desp.* iii. 458. Wellesley had given this horse to Lake.

pray to God I never may be in such a situation again." 1803. In truth in his eagerness to overtake and destroy the Nov. 1. battalions trained by De Boigne, Lake ran a more dangerous risk than he had expected. His first onslaught with his cavalry only was, as it fell out, a simple waste of men and horses; but, being unable to see anything when the attack was delivered, he was reasonable in conjecturing that an enemy which had fled from him precipitately for some days, would be more likely to continue its flight than to turn to bay. Probably, too, in both phases of the action he underrated his enemy's power of manœuvre, and, like Wellington, was somewhat taken aback to see Scindia's battalions change position with order and regularity when menaced by an attack in flank. It is impossible, indeed, not to conjecture that Abaji may have secretly nursed a vague scheme of turning upon his pursuers when they were exhausted by a long chase. His army was better appointed than Lake's, as the General confessed. He had thrice as many men to each gun as the British; he had greatly superior bullocks; and he had camels to carry the knapsacks of his infantry, which enabled them to make long marches with little fatigue. All this, however, availed him nothing. His brave army was cut to pieces; his guns, seventy-one in number, were captured, together with sixty-four tumbrils laden with ammunition, forty-four stand of colours, five thousand stand of arms, and the whole of a large train of baggage. He had the bad luck to meet very fine troops, flushed with victory and led by a General whom they trusted, and rightly trusted, to handle them to the best advantage in a battle; and he was beaten. But in spite of his failure he fought a splendid action, and his men covered themselves with glory. As to the British troops, the conduct of the Seventy-sixth ranks with the very highest that has ever been recorded of any corps in the British Army.[1]

[1] The authorities known to me respecting the battle of Laswaree are not many. There are the accounts in Thorn, p.

1803. Embarrassed by the number of his wounded, and other cares, Lake did not quit the battlefield until the
Nov. 8. 8th, when retracing his steps by leisurely marches he
Nov. 13. halted close to Agra on the 13th, sending his sick and his captured guns into the fortress. From all sides the neighbouring chieftains and Rajahs swarmed in to pay their court, and to conclude defensive alliances with the victor. Among them came Runjeet Singh, the Rajah of Bhurtpore, an elderly little man, very plain in his attire, who, having concluded his visit of ceremony, retired to his capital, doubtless thinking deeply of the future. Lake was joined by a few reinforcements; but everything pointed to the probability that they would not be required. The occupation of Bundelcund was the only one of the tasks set to him which he had not fulfilled; but the work had been progressing ever since September, and, though obstructed by a rebellious chief, was going forward rapidly under the bayonets of a small force of native infantry. With the exception, therefore, of sending a small detachment to hasten the capture of Gwalior, there was seemingly nothing more for Lake to do; and he and his army indulged in a well-earned rest.

By this time Scindia was almost at the last gasp. He had been utterly defeated in the Deccan, in Hindostan, and in Cuttack, but even so the cup of his affliction had not been filled. In spite of all the apathy and obstruction of the Government at Bombay, an expedition against Baroach had been duly organised
Aug. 21. in the months of July and August; and on the 21st of the latter month a force of about a thousand men, one half of them being of the Sixty-first and Eighty-sixth, and the remainder of Native Infantry, under Lieutenant-colonel Woodington, marched from Baroda, and sat down unresisted on the 24th before the fortress. On

210 *seq.*, in *Notes of the Principal Transactions*, p. 93, and Lake's letters in *Wellesley Desp.* iii. 439-447, 449. These are well summarised by Captain May, *From Cromwell to Wellington*.

the 26th Woodington opened fire from a single battery 1803.
of two guns; and on the 29th, the breach being practic- Aug. 29.
able, Baroach was stormed after a short resistance which cost the assailants sixty-nine of all ranks killed and wounded. Thereupon the British took possession of the entire district of the same name, a rich and populous territory which afforded a large annual revenue.

Attacked and despoiled on all sides, Scindia and Ragogee Rao were fain to sue for peace. A treaty
with the latter was concluded on the 17th of December, Dec. 17.
three days after the fall of Gawilghur; and a second
treaty on the 30th brought to an end the war with Dec. 30.
Scindia. Ragogee ceded Cuttack, and all his territories west of the Wurda. Scindia yielded all his country in the Doab between the Jumna and the Ganges, all that between the Ajunta Hills and the Godavery, and the forts and districts of Ahmednuggur and Baroach. Both engaged themselves never to employ any subject of any power that should be at war with England; and the first phase of the contest with the Mahrattas was over.

CHAPTER III

1803. WHILE Lake was lying in camp near Agra at the end of December, letters came to him from Jeswunt Rao Holkar, the only important Mahratta chief who now remained unconquered or unconciliated, in terms which the General described as arrogant and improper. After the tremendous punishment administered to his peers by the British army it was reasonable to suppose that Holkar would at least have taken up a respectful, if not a cordial attitude, and would have made his friendly overtures in a less patronising tone. The Government at Calcutta, though willing and even desirous to come to a definite understanding with him, saw no particular necessity for including him in the treaties contracted with Ragogee and Scindia, much less for entering into a separate alliance with him. If he would remain quiet and leave the British and their allies alone, Lord Wellesley was not disposed to disturb him ; and the probability was that, after all that had happened, Holkar would give no trouble, at any rate for the present. He had played false towards his brethren of Gwalior and Berar by neglecting to come to their assistance until it was too late ; and it was hardly likely that he would have now the temerity to encounter the British single-handed.

But Holkar was an ambitious man, who could think for himself; and it is possible that his reflections had led him to the same conclusion as had recently been formed by the most sagacious of his enemies. Arthur Wellesley, when summing up the position in November,

averred that the Mahrattas had made a mistake in 1803.
fighting the British with regular infantry and artillery, that their military spirit had been impaired by the importation of European officers to train them according to European ideas, and that they would have been far more formidable if they had stuck to their traditional military policy and fought a predatory war with cavalry only.[1] Be this as it may, Holkar did not give up the game for lost; and, while still expressing a friendly disposition towards the British, he proceeded to levy contributions on Rajpootana, pretending to be unaware that it had passed under British protection, and actually to threaten the territory of Jeypore. This was carrying impudence rather too far. On the
23rd of December Lake broke up his camp near Agra, Dec. 23.
and moving some fifty miles west and south, took up his station with the main army at Biana, by the pass which commands the entrance to the dominions of the Rajah of Jeypore. Thence he addressed a letter to Holkar disclaiming any hostile intentions, but bidding him desist from his depredations and, in pledge of his good faith, to withdraw to his own estates.

Holkar then took up his station about Ajmeer, and
proceeded to murder three British officers who had 1804.
taken service with him, because, in obedience to the Viceroy's proclamation, they had expressed their intention of resigning their commissions. Nevertheless Lord Wellesley was averse from taking strong measures, and instructed Lake to assure the Mahratta chief that the Government harboured the most amicable feelings towards him, though it could not permit him to injure the allies of the British. The General for his part feared that permanent peace could not be hoped for until Holkar's power should be annihilated, but promised to avoid hostilities if possible. Meanwhile he advanced westward to Dowsa, about thirty miles east of Jeypore, so as to be ready to check any hostile movement; whereupon Holkar renewed so fervently his

[1] *Wellington Desp.* ii. 518-519.

1804. professions of extreme solicitude to maintain friendship and to abstain from further aggression, that Lord Wellesley actually began to think of breaking up the army. Lake was not so sanguine. He had noticed that Holkar barely kept within the letter of the law, and, knowing that he would turn to mischief directly the British force was withdrawn, begged the Viceroy not to hasten disarmament. "I never was so plagued as I am with this devil," he wrote ; "if he does not come in to see me, which I do not suppose he will, I cannot move on towards him, as, the moment I advance and leave an opening for him, he will give me the slip, get into our territories with his horse, and burn and destroy everything he comes near." But for all his impatience Lake was loyal. "Don't, my dear Lord, from this language imagine that I shall commence hostilities with Holkar or lead you into another war, unless he comes or till I hear from you."[1]

Such a situation could not last long. The British Government could not be at the expense of keeping a large army in the field to watch a chief who refused to retire, and waited only for its withdrawal to plunder and ravage. Matters were brought nearer to a crisis by the interception of several letters which had passed between Holkar and certain chiefs of the Rohillas and Sikhs, wherein a detailed plan was set forth for the overrunning of all the British territory eastward of Benares. But Lake, while apprising Jeswunt Rao that this correspondence was in his hands, still gave him the
Feb. 20. chance to go in peace. Meanwhile, on the 20th of February 1804 he had moved eastward to Hindoun to cover the principal roads leading into British territory;
March 8. and marching thence northward on the 8th of March, halted on the 10th at Ramghar. Here again Holkar's messengers visited him and made extravagant demands; and shortly afterwards the chief threw aside all reserve, sent an emissary to Scindia to ask his assistance in an immediate attack on the British, and openly plundered

[1] *Wellesley Desp.* iv. 3-9, 19-20, 45-48.

the territories of the Rajah of Jeypore. On the 6th of April Wellesley ordered Lake to commence hostilities. 1804. April 16.

As in the case of Scindia, the Viceroy hoped to press upon his new enemy from all sides simultaneously. Arthur Wellesley, since the peace with Scindia, had retired to southward and encamped about Ahmednuggur, moving from time to time to break up bands of freebooters which hung by tens of thousands about the Nizam's frontier. These little expeditions incidentally led him to make the most remarkable march of his whole career. On one occasion he started at six o'clock on the morning of the 4th of February with Feb. 4. the Nineteenth Light Dragoons, the native cavalry that had been with him at Assaye, the Seventy-fourth, a native battalion, five hundred Sepoys from different regiments, and four guns. Having travelled by noon twenty miles, he gave his men a halt of ten hours; at ten o'clock at night he marched again, and by nine the next morning, in spite of bad roads and darkness, Feb. 5. reached his destination, only to find that the enemy had received warning of his coming and decamped. Following them up immediately, he overtook their rear, cut down many, captured all their baggage and guns, and by noon had dispersed them completely. Within thirty hours he reckoned that he had marched sixty miles, and the infantry arrived at the point of attack as soon as the cavalry. His own comment on this feat, of which he was justifiably proud, was apt and pithy. "I think we now begin to beat the Mahrattas in the celerity of our movements."[1]

With an army in such condition, it might be hoped that Holkar, even if he pursued the traditional Mahratta tactics, would quickly be brought to reason; and it is somewhat noteworthy that this chief wrote on the 1st of February to Arthur Wellesley, speaking of him personally with great civility and respect, while using very different language of Lake. But since Holkar's

[1] *Wellington Desp.* iii. 43-45, 48.

1804. possessions, with the exception of Chandore, lay outside the Deccan, it was obvious that the operations would be confined to Guzerat and the frontiers of Hindostan, unless, as Arthur Wellesley early foresaw, the Mahratta chief should establish himself among the Sikhs and Afghans in the Punjaub. Moreover, as Wellesley said, if his troops went far to the north, fifty Holkars would certainly start up in the territories of the Peishwa and the Nizam; for, in spite of the many hard lessons which he had taught to freebooters, these pests still flourished and increased in all the territories of the native princes. Also, owing to the famine that raged in the Deccan, the subsistence of any army north of Poona would be impossible. Wellesley therefore decided, upon the first alarm of a war with Holkar, to reinforce Guzerat with three of his native battalions in anticipation of any orders that he should receive from the Viceroy.

Feb. 27. On the 27th of February a subsidiary treaty of defensive alliance had been concluded with Scindia; and with Scindia's forces and the augmented force in Guzerat he reckoned that Colonel Murray should be able to penetrate from that city to Indore. Upon this plan, as he wrote to Murray, "we ought to be hanged if we do not get the better of Holkar in a short time."[1]

Great, therefore, was his surprise on learning, about the middle of April, that Lake depended upon Wellesley's own troops in the south to defeat Holkar in case of a war, while the Commander-in-chief himself should look to the safety of Hindostan. The difficulty of the situation was further complicated by the fact that for some time past not a word of instruction had been received from the Viceroy. In utter perplexity, Arthur Wellesley wrote to Lake that his plan was out of the question unless hostilities could be delayed until August, that he doubted whether the prevailing famine would permit him even to advance to Chandore, much less to traverse the six hundred miles from Poona, where his army was concentrated, to Indore. Even at Poona

[1] *Wellington Desp.* iii. 164-165, 171, 196.

the horses of his own cavalry were living on rice; 1804.
further afield his Mysore Cavalry had lost one hundred horses in a single day from starvation. He could only recommend that Murray's force should operate from Guzerat, and Scindia's army from some position north of Ujjein, so as to attack Holkar in rear, while the Commander-in-chief attacked him in front. Privately he stated his opinion that, if Lake pressed Holkar vigorously, he could end the war in a fortnight; but that if he stood upon the defensive merely with a view to foiling his enemy's raids and depredations, there was no saying when the contest would end.[1]

A fortnight later, on the 7th of May, Arthur May 7.
Wellesley received at last official intimation that hostilities had been declared on the 16th of April, whereupon he wrote careful instructions to Murray to take the field at once with his troops at Guzerat. During the war with Scindia Murray's part had, through no fault of his own, been obscure; for the insurrection of a rebel who aspired to the place of the Gaekwar had prevented him from invading Scindia's territory, and limited his exertions to the keeping of the peace in his own district. The task now assigned to him was more honourable. He had under his command at least two European and four native battalions, besides the native cavalry of the Gaekwar; and, since Arthur Wellesley could only guess at Holkar's probable movements, he left Murray a free hand, simply bidding him to march immediately, move rapidly, and attack Holkar whenever he could find an opportunity. Wellesley's information did not allow him to state positively the point upon which it would be best to march, but he divined it to be Ujjein. As for himself, in obedience to the wishes of the Viceroy, he prepared to march northward. By the 1st of June rain enough had fallen to June 1.
ensure a supply of water, and he announced his intention of sending forward at any rate his train of battering cannon for the siege of Chandore. But three days

[1] *Wellington Desp.* iii. 231 *seq.*, 235 *seq.*

1804. later he reported the dearth of food and forage to be such that it was impossible for him to move, and on the 8th he applied for leave to return home. By the
June 24. 24th he had broken up his army, having no use for it in the field; and his force therefore disappears for the present from the sphere of active operations.

Meanwhile Lake, on receiving his orders to com-
April 18. mence hostilities, had moved on the 18th of April towards Jeypore, to which town he had already pushed forward three battalions under Colonel Monson. Upon the appearance of this detachment Holkar retired precipitately to the southward; and Lake, still advancing,
April 28. encamped on the 28th at Tonga, about fifteen miles south-west of Jeypore. Holkar, meanwhile, continued his flight to the south, followed by Lake's irregular cavalry, which reported his condition to be miserable. But he completely distanced Monson's detachment, which moved in advance of the main body, and of course left Lake's principal army far in rear. After a week's halt at Tonga, Lake again moved southward and, after much delay through violent storms and rain,
May 8. on the 8th of May reached Nowai, about forty miles
May 10. south of Jeypore. From hence on the 10th he detached Lieutenant-colonel Don with two Sepoy battalions, a regiment of native cavalry and guns to attack Rampoora, a fortified town rather over thirty miles to south-eastward, which was Holkar's only stronghold to north of the Chumbul. Arrived before the town, Don, to disarm suspicion, encamped in an opposite direction to the principal gate, and at two o'clock on
May 15. the morning of the 15th sallied forth to the attack. Under his personal command he took eight companies, together with one twelve-pounder to blow up the gates. To protect his rear against a body of hostile troops which had moved up from Tonk, and to keep down any fire from the ramparts, he employed three more companies and four guns; his cavalry he reserved to pursue the garrison in the event of its flight. So incautious was the enemy that the column was within

one hundred yards of the walls before a shot was fired 1804.
from the town. The gates were then promptly blown up, and the garrison driven out into the plain, where great numbers were cut down by the cavalry. The ease with which this success was gained seems to point to extremely able management on the part of the commander.

Deprived thus of his one fortress in the district, Holkar, who had for the moment turned northward, recrossed the Chumbul; and Lake, whose troops were suffering greatly from the heat, decided to abandon the further pursuit of him. He therefore left two parties of irregulars under Captain Gardiner and Lieutenant Lucan to watch his movements, and committed the ultimate destruction of him to Murray, with his troops from Guzerat, and to Colonel Monson. Since Monson's three battalions were supplemented by auxiliaries of the Rajah of Jeypore, he reckoned that each of these officers would be strong enough to deal with Holkar independently in case of an action.

Lake therefore retired eastward, and on the 27th re- May 27.
gained his old camping-ground at Hindoun. During the last four days of his march he buried some fifty European soldiers who had succumbed to the sun, the thermometer marking one hundred and thirty degrees Fahrenheit in the shade. The mortality was greatly increased by the scarcity of water; and on resuming his march he separated his force into two columns so as to move the more quickly. Still, however, the men continued to fall down, the Sepoys and the camp-followers almost as fast as the Europeans; and a single march of eighteen miles cost the army the loss of over two hundred and fifty natives and about thirty British soldiers. Ultimately the main body, after dispersing several corps to various stations on the way, marched into Cawnpore on the
20th of June. Possibly its losses would hardly have June 20.
been greater if it had followed up Holkar and left him no rest, as had been the desire of Arthur Wellesley.

Thus the principal army was withdrawn into canton-

1804. ments, and the prosecution of the war was left to detachments, scattered in various directions for the purpose rather of preventing Holkar from doing mischief, than of ending his career for ever by hunting him until he had not a man left. And now came a series of mishaps. The operations undertaken by Colonel Powell for the reduction of Bundelcund had met with so little resistance as to be unworthy of detailed notice ; and, though the province always lay open to predatory raids from Holkar's partisans and other freebooters, of whom one, Meer Khan, was the most notable, the seven thousand troops which had been allotted to the service were amply sufficient to beat any number of banditti. It so happened, however, that Colonel Powell and the officer next senior to him died ; and that the command passed into the hands of a certain Colonel Fawcett, who, to judge by Lake's language, was an officer of unique incapacity. However that may be, Fawcett, whose headquarters were at Koonch, to west and south of Kalpee, must needs on the
May 21. 21st of May send out seven native companies, a troop of horse and five guns, under a certain Captain Smith, to reduce a small fort within a few miles of his camp. The ostensible purpose of his operation was to obtain forage, there being none left in the district except in the villages of chieftains who refused to acknowledge the British authority. At midnight came reports that five thousand predatory horse were in the vicinity ; and
May 22. two hours later native messengers hurried in with intelligence that Meer Khan himself with fifteen or twenty thousand followers was within three miles of the camp. The troops were at once turned out, and Fawcett despatched an order to Smith to return to camp immediately. To this Smith replied that he had occupied a village under the fort against which he had been sent, that he could not draw off the men quartered in it without much loss, and that he hoped to return to camp directly after dark. The truth of the matter was that he had stationed the guns with fifty European

artillery-men and two companies of infantry in the village to attack the fort, and kept the remaining five companies half a mile apart from them, being apparently possessed by the idea that, when sent with a few hundred men to reduce a petty stronghold, he must divide them into besieging army and covering army. 1804.

The predatory bands had no taste for an attack on the camp at Koonch; but they speedily discovered the two isolated companies, fell upon them in overwhelming numbers by surprise, cut them to pieces to a man, and carried off the guns. Fawcett, growing anxious as the morning wore on, marched out at two o'clock in the afternoon with his whole force to rescue Smith, and presently came upon him with his five companies, his troop of horse and one galloping gun intact, having made his way through his contemptible enemy without the slightest difficulty. Smith had retreated directly after hearing from a fugitive of the fate of his two companies, but apparently had made no effort to rescue them when firing had been first heard in the village; and to this negligence the whole of the detachment, including five European officers and five guns, had been sacrificed.[1]

But this was not the worst of the misconduct in this affair. It was presently discovered that the leader of the raid was not Meer Khan, but an ordinary robber of no great fame or station, and that his force did not exceed the strength of five thousand men. Emboldened by his success, this ruffian pursued his way to Kalpee, marking his path by cruelty, plunder, and devastation, attacked the town and attempted to cross the Jumna. But, being beaten back by two companies of Sepoys, he returned by a fresh route to Koonch, where on the 30th May 30.
of May he was met and very roughly handled by a small party of irregular levies lately taken into service by the British from a native chieftain. Yet it was from this rabble that Fawcett allowed himself to receive a very forcible and unpleasant blow, and that without

[1] *Wellesley Desp.* iv. 71 *seq.*

1804. attempting to return it; for after much aimless marching to and fro, which cost the lives of many men from heat and exhaustion, he retired to Kalpee, having done his best to spread consternation from end to end of Bundelcund.

Lake, much annoyed, superseded him instantly, and placed Captain Smith under arrest. Lord Wellesley, still more angry, ordered Fawcett to be tried at once by court-martial; but the mischief was done, and there was no saying how far it might extend. Happily one officer, Captain Baillie, though in command of no more than fifteen hundred native levies, refused to share in the panic; and, from his station at Banda, he by his firmness and courage maintained confidence and tranquillity to south of the Betwa.[1]

Meanwhile Holkar had continued his retreat southward almost to Ujjein, still followed by Gardiner, who
May 30. on the 30th of May had made a successful attack upon one of Holkar's underlings, forcing two thousand men to surrender and capturing all their baggage. Monson, also, having been reinforced by Don to a total strength of five and a half regular native battalions,
June. moved southward, and at the beginning of June reached Kotah, about sixty miles south of Rampoora. Here he was joined by a contingent of troops in the service of the Rajah of Kotah, after which he continued his movement for about thirty miles south-eastward to the Pass of Mokundra. After a short halt to collect supplies he resumed his march on the 28th of June,
July 1. and on the 1st of July arrived near the fortress of Hinglaisgurh, an ancient and much-valued possession of Holkar's family. Here he ascertained that Holkar was encamped with his whole force between forty and fifty miles to south-westward on the other bank of the Chumbul. He determined, therefore, to attack the fort at once, and accordingly carried it by assault
July 2. on the following day with little trouble but considerable loss. This done, he again moved forward, and

[1] *Wellesley Desp.* iv. 84, 127-129.

finally took up a position about fifty miles south of the 1804.
Mokundra pass, where he was informed that he would be able to secure supplies. He was expecting also to open communications with Murray, who, as he knew, had received orders to march upon Ujjein[1]; and Ujjein was, as the crow flies, not above seventy miles distant from his encampment.

Now Murray had received instructions, advice, and encouragement from Arthur Wellesley which would have stirred the spirit of almost any other man to abnormal energy and enterprise. "You have a great game in your hands," the General had written on the 22nd of May; and the unerring instinct with which, weeks before and with no information, Arthur Wellesley had selected Ujjein as Murray's destination, should have convinced that officer that by following his instructions he could not go far wrong. But instead of being full of ardour, Murray was full of complaints. He bewailed his lack of cavalry, which was indeed serious, for both Scindia and the Gaekwar had evaded the duty of providing it; he bewailed his weakness in numbers, though on the 1st of June he had five thousand eight hundred men fit for duty; finally he bewailed his want of European troops, though his army included more than had fought either with Lake or Wellesley in the previous campaign. Arthur Wellesley wrote to him in terms which showed his disapprobation of this querulous spirit; and accordingly, at the beginning of June.
June, Murray began his march from Baroda. He was much hampered by the difficulty of obtaining transport, supplies, and forage, though indeed his troubles in this way were no greater than those that had been overcome by Wellesley in the campaign of 1803. By the middle of June he arrived at Dohad, about eighty miles north-east of Baroda, where it had been arranged that he should deposit his heavy ordnance and stores; and on the 30th of June he reached Badnawar, forty miles west June 30.
of Ujjein. Here he received a letter from Monson, reporting that the main body of the army had gone into

1804. cantonments, and that he had halted his own detachment at the Mokundra Pass, pending further orders from the Commander-in-chief. At the same time intelligence reached Murray that Holkar was bringing his whole force forward to attack him; whereupon, disliking his situation at Badnawar, he turned about, and on the following day retreated towards the Myhee, intending to take up a strong position in rear of the river.

If this decision be reviewed from a strictly theoretic standpoint, it seems difficult to quarrel with it, more especially since Murray reported that the heat and fatigue of the march had already cost him three thousand men—a loss which Arthur Wellesley found it difficult, except upon very unflattering hypotheses, to account for. But it is certain that Lake blamed him very much for his retreat; and the taking up of a defensive position against a Mahratta force was the thing of all others against which Wellesley had warned him. Beyond all doubt Lake or Wellesley himself, in a like situation, would have marched straight against Holkar and attacked him; but such boldness was not to be found in Murray. He had no confidence in himself, and, as he was to prove far too often before he was finally laid aside, he was both incapable and unenterprising. He retreated accordingly for four
July 5. days until on the 5th of July he heard that Holkar had moved eastward; whereupon he faced about, and finding nothing to impede his march, arrived on the 8th at Ujjein.[1]

But meanwhile Monson also had begun to retreat.
July 7. On the 7th he received intelligence that Holkar was crossing the Chumbul with his whole army and every gun that he possessed; and his first instinct was to march at once to the spot and attack him. He remembered, however, on reflection that he had but two days' grain in his camp, that part of his force had been detached to bring up more grain, that one of his

[1] *Wellington Desp.* iii. 439; *Wellesley Desp.* iv. 374-375.

battalions was on march to join him from Hinglaisgurh, 1804.
and that he was expecting a convoy with treasure for the troops. In fact, shortly after he began his movement he heard of Murray's retreat, and could find any number of reasons for not attacking, because, though a brave man, he was afraid to attack. His force was not weak, for, over and above the five battalions already with him, he had been joined not only by Gardiner's irregulars under Lieutenant Lucan, but also by Scindia's contingent of horse which ought to have joined Murray, under the leadership of a native chief, Bappojee Scindia. This gave him in all nearly three thousand cavalry; but he had no European troops, and like Murray he had not the nerve of Wellesley and Lake. Moreover, he had been unwise in trusting to the Rajah of Kotah to furnish him with supplies, a duty which native chieftains were always ready to undertake but could never be trusted to perform; and lastly, he had certainly advanced further than was consistent with safety in order to capture a petty fort, which gave him no accession of strength or resources, but rather weakened him by the amount of a small garrison which he could ill spare. These, though serious, might be deemed venial mistakes, easily to be redeemed by a bold attack; but instead of attack Monson chose retreat.

On the morning of the 8th he began his retrograde July 8.
movement towards the Mokundra Pass, sending off his baggage and stores at four in the morning, but remaining with the main body in line of battle until half-past nine. As the enemy made no appearance, he then led the retreat with the infantry, leaving the cavalry to form the rear-guard, which was exactly the reverse of Wellesley's practice in similar circumstances. He had not traversed more than twelve miles when he received intelligence that the rear-guard was attacked by the whole of Holkar's cavalry; and soon afterwards Bappojee Scindia galloped up with the news that his men and Lucan's had been totally defeated, and

1804. that Lucan himself, an excellent and gallant officer, was
July 8. wounded and taken prisoner. There was therefore
nothing to be done but to continue the retreat to the
Mokundra Pass, which was safely reached without any
July 9. molestation at noon of the following day.

Here Monson halted with some idea of turning the
strength of the position to account, though he was still
troubled by uncertainty about his supplies. At noon of
July 10. the morrow Holkar appeared with his cavalry in great
force, and after summoning the British to surrender,
attacked them at three different points in front and
flanks, but was beaten off at all. He then fell back a
few miles to await the coming of his infantry and
artillery; and Monson, fearing to be cut off from
Kotah and starved, marched again on the following
July 11. morning. Heavy and incessant rain had set in on the
10th, and the troops suffered much from the weary
tramp through the deep black cotton soil. They did
July 12. not reach Kotah until the 12th, when the Rajah was un-
able to supply them with provisions; and Monson was
fain to drag on his men for seven weary miles further
before he could obtain food for them. Fortunately he
was able to cross the Chumbul in the Rajah's boats,
which he sank after using them, and so reached his
July 13. destination on the morning of the 13th. There he
halted for two days, first because his way was barred
by a flooded stream, and secondly because of the
imperative need for collecting a small quantity of
victuals; the natural consequences of attempting a
campaign without pontoons, transport, or supplies.
July 15. On the 15th the march was resumed, but was presently
stopped by the state of the roads; and on the following
July 16. day, the provisions being absolutely exhausted and the
guns sunk too deeply in the mud to be recoverable,
Monson abandoned his artillery and destroyed the
ammunition. He then proceeded on his way through a
country completely under water, only to be stopped again
July 17. within twenty-four hours by the Chambalee, in itself a
mere rivulet, but now swollen to an unfordable torrent.

Matters were fast becoming desperate. The 1804. European artillery-men were sent through the flood on elephants, but the rest of the army was detained, and only with great difficulty contrived to collect grain for two days from neighbouring villages. The halt enabled Holkar's cavalry to come up, though the advance of his guns also had been much delayed by the rains. Monson, however, proved that he had not served with Lake to no purpose, for he promptly attacked the nearest Mahratta camp, took several of their animals, and thus secured for himself respect. At length, on the 23rd his force was able to begin the July 23. passage of the flooded stream in rafts, while two battalions were detached under Colonel Don to find a ford. Even so two entire days were consumed in the crossing, though the enemy's cavalry made no serious attack and was easily beaten off with considerable loss. Finally, on the 27th Monson's battalions arrived at July 27. Rampoora and were able to send supplies to Don's detachment, which came in safely on the 29th. All July 29. were alike utterly exhausted, having consumed their last provisions even before the crossing of the Chambalee.

At Rampoora Monson found two battalions of Sepoys with their guns, a body of Hindostani cavalry under a British officer, Major Frith, and a certain quantity of grain ; all which had been sent from Agra by Lake immediately upon his hearing of the retreat. But here again there had been neglect. Rampoora was held as a post for the purpose of checking Holkar's movements, or, in other words, as an advanced base of operations; yet no effort had been made to convert it in reality into such a base by filling it up with abundance of supplies. Monson set himself to collect provisions, but with no great success, for up to the 20th of August Aug. 20. he had succeeded in gathering only twelve days' supply for his own force. Meanwhile Holkar, though much delayed by floods, had continued his advance; and by that same day had approached within twelve or fifteen

1804. miles of Rampoora. At this Monson became anxious. It is not easy to explain why, looking to the difficulties which he had found in obtaining victuals, he did not earlier continue his retreat; it is still less easy to explain why he did not march out boldly and attack. His mind appears to have been made up for him by Lake, from whom on this same day he received a letter, desiring him to retire to Jeypore if he thought that he might be again in distress for his supplies. Accordingly, leaving a garrison in Rampoora, he marched on the
Aug. 21. 21st with five and a half battalions and two howitzers north-eastward upon Kooshalghur.

The first march brought him to the river Banas, which, as might have been foreseen, was in flood and unfordable. Three boats, however, were found, and in these the treasure was sent forward under escort of six companies with orders to proceed at once to Kooshalghur, some twenty miles away as the crow flies. The rest of the force perforce halted; and early next morning Holkar's cavalry appeared, and encamped four miles
Aug. 24. away. On the 24th the river became fordable; and by eight o'clock in the morning Monson had thrown across it the whole of his baggage, with one battalion for escort. The enemy meanwhile had occupied a village on his right, from which he promptly dislodged them with little loss to himself; but, as the river fell lower, the Mahratta cavalry began to pass it in great numbers upon both flanks, and Monson therefore sent over three more battalions and a howitzer for the better protection of his baggage. He was now left on the south bank of the river with his picquets and a single battalion to support them, and he could see that any attempt to withdraw these before dark must lead to their inevitable destruction. Unfortunately the darkness did not come soon enough for him. At four o'clock Holkar's infantry and guns appeared, and his batteries presently opened a heavy cannonade upon Monson's little party. The Colonel at once retorted by charging the guns with his infantry and capturing one line of them; but Holkar

met this attack by a destructive fire from a second line 1804.
of cannon, while his infantry and cavalry came up on all
sides of the unhappy detachment. The Sepoys having
suffered heavy loss, gave way, and Monson ordered a
retreat to the river; but the enemy's horse pressed hard
upon him, and the retreat soon became a panic rush for
the ford. The Mahrattas plunged in after the fugitives,
and were bidding fair to annihilate the whole of them,
when one of the British battalions on the north side of
the river came down to the bank; whereupon the
pursuit instantly ceased and the enemy retired.

This respite enabled Monson and a few men to Aug. 24.
escape, but it was of short duration; for Holkar's guns
presently unlimbered before the ford, and under cover
of their fire his cavalry began to cross the river.
Monson meanwhile lost no time, but forming his
troops into a hollow square, and letting the baggage
take its chance, he pressed on to Kooshalghur, with
the enemy's cavalry clinging to his rear all the way,
and arrived there in safety on the evening of the
25th. Here he found the treasure with its escort, Aug. 25.
but not, as he had hoped, a large reinforcement of
infantry and cavalry from the Rajah of Jeypore. On
the morning of the 26th Holkar's cavalry overtook and Aug. 26.
encamped all round him; and now came the most
terrible moment of all. The native officers of two of
his battalions, Sepoys of the British service, were found
to be in correspondence with Holkar; two companies
actually deserted, and half of Frith's irregulars went off
at the same time. Happily the two remaining battalions
remained faithful, and at seven o'clock on the evening
of the 26th Monson renewed his march. Constantly Aug. 26.
harassed by the enemy's cavalry and horse-artillery, he
reached Hindoun on the evening of the 27th, with the Aug. 27.
greater part of his baggage lost and the troops in the
last stage of exhaustion.

Halting until midnight, he marched again at one
o'clock on the morning of the 28th, to be overtaken at Aug. 28.
daylight as usual by the enemy's horse. Bolder than

1804. Aug. 28. was their wont, the Mahratta cavalry made a desperate charge in three bodies up to the very bayonets of the Sepoys, but being beaten off with heavy loss, kept at a respectful distance for the rest of the day. Sunset brought Monson to the Biana Pass, at the entrance of which he halted, hoping to give a little rest to his worn and weary troops; but the Mahrattas, bringing their guns up on all sides, forced him to move on. At nine o'clock he entered the city of Biana in pitchy darkness, the baggage being mixed up with the troops in the greatest confusion; and, all attempts to restore order being fruitless, the various corps made their way to Agra

Aug. 31. as best they could. By dawn of the 31st all the survivors had arrived; and then the reckoning of the disaster was taken. Twelve British officers had been killed, two more had been drowned, two more were missing, and five others had been wounded; while of five and a half fine battalions little more than one half were left, through the sword, fatigue, and desertion. It was the heaviest blow that had fallen on the British in India since the destruction of Baillie's detachment.

There was less recrimination than usually follows upon such occurrences. Monson blamed Murray for his retreat as the cause of all the trouble; and Murray retorted that his retreat was due to Monson's own retrograde movement. Arthur Wellesley, as a friend of all parties, drew out a searching analysis of the entire expedition, which is among the most remarkable of his papers. He criticised Monson for not attacking Holkar on three different occasions, first before he began his first retreat, secondly before he retired from Rampoora, and thirdly before he crossed the Banas. He blamed him also for halting unduly long at the Mokundra Pass and, even more, at Rampoora, where his delay, as Lake said, was fatal. But Wellesley's final conclusion was that the detachment was doomed to destruction, even if Holkar had not attacked them with infantry and artillery; or, to put the truth into words which he carefully avoided setting down, the ultimate fault lay with Lake, the Commander-in-chief. 1804.

The operation assigned to Monson was in fact most hazardous. He was ordered vaguely to march far away at the beginning of the rainy season, into a country everywhere seamed with deep water-courses and rivers, without any regular system of supplies or any organised provision for crossing the waters. Nothing could better have played into the hands of the Mahrattas, whose practice in warfare had for years been the same. By means of their cavalry they ravaged the country until want of provisions compelled their enemy to retreat, followed him up with that same cavalry while in motion, and surrounded him with infantry and artillery when he halted. The way to foil these tactics was that adopted by Wellesley; namely, for a commander to amass supplies enough to make himself independent of the country, to organise the transport-service to the utmost perfection in order to carry those supplies, and finally always to possess the means of passing rivers. Attention has already been called to the fact that Wellesley made the acquisition of a pontoon-train his first object upon the menace of a Mahratta war. Failing to obtain it, he fell back on wicker-boats, made by his own troops and covered with hides; but in addition to this he had established a regular post with boats upon every unfordable river from Seringapatam to Poona. Thus it was that he was able to carry on his campaign during a famine, and chose, as a preferable time for a Mahratta war, the opening of the rainy season. In brief, by leaving nothing to chance, but thinking out every detail beforehand, he was able to organise victory.

Lake had given no such forethought to his projects when he ordered Monson's detachment to pursue Holkar to Ujjein. It seems, too, that the numbers of Holkar's infantry and artillery—for he was reported to have one hundred and seventy-five guns—came as a surprise to every one; for all previous intelligence,

1804. during his retreat before Lake, showed his force to be an undisciplined rabble upon the verge of starvation, whereas in fact he had fallen back upon his main body of infantry and guns. On the other hand, both Lord Wellesley and Lake had counted upon a respectable contingent of troops, to be furnished according to treaty by Dowlut Rao Scindia; but that chief had steadily evaded the discharge of his obligation. Nevertheless, in Monson's place Lake would by a happy instinct most probably have avoided Monson's blunders, and carried the expedition to a victorious issue. Indeed it was one of Lake's failings that he gave every commander credit for possessing that instinct, and could not understand how any man could possibly lack it. Arthur Wellesley, on the other hand, reasoned matters out, and ensured that, if the instinct were wanting, sound and logical instructions should in some measure take its place. Lake expected a man to fight his way out of any difficulty that might arise out of want of provisions, wished him good luck, and sent him on his way; and it is probable that he himself, having a real genius for a pitched battle, could have acted successfully upon his own precepts. Arthur Wellesley, on the other hand, told a commander that if he made sure of his supplies in the first instance, he could not fail of success. Lake's system might suffice for one man; Wellesley's gave a chance of success to any man.

Yet, to do the Chiefs justice, they did not turn upon Monson. Lord Wellesley had expected the ruin of his force from the first hour of its retreat, and was relieved to find that any part of it had escaped; "but," he added, "whatever the result of his misfortunes to my own fame, I will endeavour to shield his character from obloquy, nor will I attempt the mean purpose of sacrificing his reputation to save mine." Lake's answer was not less worthy and honourable. "My dear lord . . . all blame ought to fall upon me for detaching the force in the first instance . . . all censure for that measure must be attributed to me and to me alone, and

if called upon I am ready to answer for it before the 1804.
House of Commons . . . I stand perfectly at ease on that score, unless it may be said that I left too much to the discretion of Colonel Monson." Misfortunes were not likely to be irretrievable with two such men in command in India.[1]

[1] The authorities for the account of Monson's retreat are:— *Wellesley Desp.* iv. 197 *seq.*, 204, 213-217; *Wellington Desp.* iii. 438, 443, 455-463; Thorn, *Memoir of the Late War in India*, pp. 357-367.

CHAPTER IV

1804. The consequences of the disaster to Monson's detachment were not slow to show themselves. Bappoo Scindia deserted to Holkar; the Jats, lately our allies, turned against us and threatened to seize our newly-acquired territory in Hindostan; and the conduct of Dowlut Rao Scindia became more and more suspicious. Most dangerous of all was a fact revealed by a correspondence which had been intercepted by Monson during his stay at Rampoora, namely, that the Rajah of Bhurtpore, though bound to the British by recent treaty, was conspiring with Holkar to drive them from India. Indeed the political consequences of the disaster seemed likely to be far-reaching beyond all calculation; but fortunately the chiefs of every department were not men who shrank from danger or exertion. The Viceroy, even before Monson marched from Rampoora, had decided that the Commander-in-chief must take the field again in person with his army; and Lake, eager to meet his wishes and to crush the power of Holkar, gave orders for the troops at once to march from their cantonments and assemble at Agra. Arthur Wellesley, though still resolved to go home, made active preparations for the forced march to Chandore of a column under Colonel Wallace, drew up a scheme for Wallace's operations, wrote to Murray an admirable letter as to the best means of carrying out the operations entrusted to him, and, by no means the worst of his measures, recommended that Murray himself should be superseded as soon as possible.[1]

[1] *Wellesley Desp.* iv. 189, 197; *Wellington Desp.* iii. 447 *seq.*, 453 463 *seq.*, 468.

Meanwhile Holkar pursued his victorious march, and after some delay in the Biana Pass, arrived before Muttra with the whole of his cavalry; while his infantry and artillery, far in the rear, toiled forward towards Delhi. The garrison of Muttra, which counted five battalions of Sepoys, two regiments of native cavalry, and a proportion of artillery, evacuated the place on the 15th of September, apparently in some haste, for it left behind not only much baggage but a large quantity of grain, which must have been very welcome to Holkar's hungry horsemen. However, the Jumna, being in heavy flood, forbade the invasion of the Doab by any but small parties of the enemy, which were easily driven out; and thus less harm was done than might have been apprehended. Meanwhile Lake's regiments had marched from Cawnpore on the 3rd of September, at the very height of the rains, crossed to the south bank of the Jumna on the 22nd, and reached the rendezvous at Secundra, about six miles outside Agra, a few days later. The force consisted of the Eighth, Twenty-seventh, and Twenty-ninth Light Dragoons, with five regiments of native cavalry, the Seventy-sixth Foot, the flank companies of the Twenty-second, and ten battalions of native infantry. A week was lost through the necessity of awaiting supplies; and on the 1st of October Lake advanced upon Muttra.[1]

1804. Sept. 15. Sept. 3. Sept. 22. Oct. 1.

[1] *Cavalry*. Colonel Macan, H.E.I.C.S.

1st Brigade. Lt.-Col. Vandeleur, H.M. 8th L.D., 2nd, 3rd, 6th Bengal N.C.

2nd Brigade. Lt.-Col. T. Browne, H.M. 27th and 29th L.D., 1st and 4th Bengal N.C.

European Horse Artillery.

Infantry. Major-General Fraser, H.M.S.

1st Brigade. Lt.-Col. Monson, H.M. 76th, 1/2nd, 1/4th Bengal N.I.

2nd Brigade. Lt.-Col. G. S. Browne, 1 and 2/15th, 1/21st Bengal N.I.

3rd Brigade. Lt.-Col. Ball, 1/8th, 2/22nd Bengal N.I.

Reserve. Lt.-Col. Don, Flank cos. H.M. 22nd, 1 and 2/12th, 2/21st N.I.

1804. On the morning of the 2nd large bodies of hostile
Oct. 2. horse were encountered, but showed no disposition to
Oct. 3. stand and were easily dispersed. On the 3rd the enemy
succeeded in capturing some baggage as well as a small
convoy which was on its way to Lake from Agra; and on
that same evening the General reoccupied Muttra. Here
he was detained for some days by lack of vituals; but on
Oct. 7. the 7th, learning that Holkar had assembled the whole of
his cavalry about four miles away, he moved out before
dawn to attack him. But the alarm had been given
before Lake reached the camp; and the Mahrattas
instantly fled with such precipitation that only the
galloping guns of the cavalry could come into action
and knock down a few horses and men. The
General, therefore, returned to Muttra; and Holkar
promptly moved back to his former camp. On the
Oct. 10. 10th Lake made a second attempt upon him, leading
the infantry only against his front and sending the
cavalry round by a wide circuit to cut off his retreat;
but the Mahrattas were too wary to be caught, and fled
as before, though they returned, according to their
wont, directly the British faced about to retire, and
hung about their flanks and rear.

Oct. 12. At length on the 12th Lake was able to pursue his
march to the relief of Delhi, which he now knew to be
besieged. The enemy still clung round him; and two
fortified towns on the road, having been provided with
guns by Holkar, threatened resistance; but Lake
Oct. 18. passed them by, and on the 18th came up to Delhi,
from which the Mahratta infantry and artillery had
already beaten a hasty retreat. Lake started to pursue
Oct. 19. them on the 19th, hoping to capture their guns; but
once again he was detained by disappointment in the
matter of supplies, and the opportunity was lost.
Delhi, meanwhile, had made a creditable defence,
though its fortifications were in ruins. The resident,
Colonel Ochterlony, had early divined from the direction
of Holkar's march that he would attempt the capture
of the place, and had promptly called in a battalion and

a half of Sepoys which were within reach, supplementing 1804.
them further with twelve hundred local levies. On arriving before the walls on the 7th of October the Oct. 7.
enemy lost no time in erecting batteries against the south-west angle of the city, whereby in a few days the parapet was demolished and the walls greatly damaged. A sortie was therefore made upon these batteries, which were stormed with great success, the British Sepoys spiking every gun and inflicting heavy loss at small cost to themselves. The enemy then shifted their guns to the southern face, where a breach was made, but was speedily rendered useless by retrenchments; and on the 14th they attempted an assault on Oct. 14.
the Lahore gate, from which they were beaten back with considerable loss. Finally, on the 15th they raised the Oct. 15.
siege and retired, knowing that Lake was in full march upon them and having no taste for an encounter with his cavalry. It was a creditable feat that with so few men Ochterlony should for nine days have held a city ten miles in circumference.

Having failed at Delhi, Holkar sent back his infantry by a circuitous route through the hills towards Deig, a strong fortress belonging to the Rajah of Bhurtpore, about twenty-five miles west and south of Muttra; but while moving with his cavalry up the Jumna to Paniput, he himself crossed the river with the object of giving the Doab a taste of the old Mahratta tactics. As soon as Lake was apprised of these movements, he determined to divide his force, giving the bulk of the infantry, the field-artillery, and two regiments of native cavalry to Major-general Fraser to watch the force at Deig, while he himself should pursue Holkar across the Jumna with the rest of the cavalry, the horse-artillery, the two companies of the Twenty-second, and three battalions of Sepoys.

He was unable to march until the 31st of October, Oct. 31.
when he proceeded in the lightest order. The usual number of tents was reduced by one half; private wheeled carriages were absolutely forbidden; and every

1804. fighting man carried six pounds of flour, which was to last him six days. The first day's march, including the passage of the Jumna, was of ten miles; the second covered fifteen miles; and the third, in consequence of bad news, was extended to thirty miles. The single battalion which formed the garrison of Saranpoor had been withdrawn for the defence of Delhi; and the Sikhs, who were inclined to throw in their lot with Holkar, had seized the opportunity to blockade the British resident in the place. Worse than this, the battalion itself, while marching to relieve Saranpoor, had been surrounded at Shamlee, between fifty and sixty miles due north of Delhi, by Holkar's horse, and was known to be in great straits. Happily the commander, Colonel Burn, being a capable soldier, had thrown himself into a ruined fort about a hundred yards square, where, though suffering heavily from the enemy's sharp-shooters, he was able to hold his own
Nov. 3. until relieved by Lake's advance on the 3rd of November. By that time his Hindoo Sepoys had been for some days without food, their caste not permitting them to share the flesh of draught-bullocks with the Mohammedans. The inhabitants of Shamlee having joined with the Mahratta matchlock-men in shooting at Burn's men, their town was given up to be plundered as a warning to others; and after one day's halt Lake,
Nov. 5. on the 5th of November, resumed his pursuit of Holkar.

From Shamlee he turned eastward for fourteen miles, when he had the satisfaction of learning that an adjacent town, dreading the fate of its unhappy neighbour, had fired upon Jeswunt Rao's horsemen rather than admit them. Thus early was verified Arthur Wellesley's prediction, when he wrote to Lake that he had only to press Holkar hard to make every inhabitant turn
Nov. 6. against him. On the 6th of November a march of twenty-four miles brought Lake to the residence of the Begum Somroo, who, having succeeded to the command of the troops raised by her husband, Reinhardt, was

now called by his native name with the prefix of a native 1804. title. She was a very capable person, and a power in the land; for which reason Holkar was conjectured to have pressed her to join her force to his own. Lake, however, followed so closely upon the Mahratta host as to remove all weight from its chief's representations; and at noon of the 7th the British at last caught sight Nov. 7. of the enemy in full flight towards Meerut. On arriving there the next day Lake found that this town also had shut its gates upon Holkar and compelled him to double back twenty miles southward to Haper. Having left two Sepoy battalions and some irregular troops at Meerut, Lake followed him up, always from twenty to thirty miles behind, but close enough to hearten every place to resist him and to leave him little time to plunder any but unwalled towns. So the chase continued at the rate of twenty miles a day, through clusters of mischievous little forts and luckless burning villages, south and eastward from Meerut to Malagur and Shikarpoor, thence across the Kali river, some fifteen miles north-west of Aligarh, to Coriagunge, which lies twelve miles to south-east of that fortress; and thence, moving always south-eastward, by Klasgunge and Sirpoora to Aligunge, where Lake arrived on the 16th. The village was still burning as he Nov. 16. marched by it, for Holkar's banditti, having been disturbed at the work of plunder, had solaced themselves by destruction; but then came the welcome news that Holkar was certainly at Furruckabad, thirty-six miles to eastward, a distance so great that he would assuredly judge himself safe against any early attack.

At nine o'clock therefore on the same evening Lake's cavalry and horse-artillery were ready to move, without baggage or encumbrance of any kind. Just before he started there reached him the news of a great success at Deig; and, with this to excite them to rivalry, the troopers rode off under a radiant moon into the soft warm air of the night. Messenger after messenger

1804. joined the squadrons as they pursued their way, confirming former intelligence as to Holkar's position; and his encampment was not far distant, when the whole column was startled by a sudden terrific roar. By some unhappy accident a tumbril of the artillery had exploded; and there was at least one man among the sleeping Mahratta host who heard it and took fright. Holkar had received bad news from Deig on the previous evening and had retired, without repeating it to a soul, to pass a sleepless night. The dull boom of the explosion roused him to alarm; but his attendants reassured him. It was only the usual morning-gun at Futtehgarh, they said; and the chief lay down again, while his men, rolled up in their blankets, slumbered comfortably on beside their horses. But ten minutes later the true morning-gun at Futtehgarh was fired; and some at least of the Mahrattas rose uneasily, though many thousands remained buried in sleep.[1]

Nov. 17. The dawn was just breaking when the head of Lake's column, having doubtless quickened its pace after the accident, reached the skirts of the camp; and the guns actually approached within range of grape-shot without giving the alarm. Then they opened fire into the thickest of the crowded mass, and Holkar's lieutenants ran to tell him that General Lake and the British were upon him. He refused at first to believe them, knowing that his enemy had been thirty-six miles away at night-fall; but, being soon convinced, he mounted his horse and galloped off with such men as were about him south-westward towards Mainpooree; nor did he draw rein till he had passed the Kali eighteen miles away. Meanwhile his unhappy men were left surprised, panic-stricken, and leaderless. The Eighth Light Dragoons presently came spurring their jaded horses among them; the remaining regiments followed close behind; and then

[1] *Memoirs of John Shipp*: edition of 1843, p. 69. "Had it not been for the blowing up of a tumbril yesterday morning, I think we must have had Holkar." Lake to Wellesley, Nov. 18, 1804. *Wellesley Desp.* iv. 241.

followed such a slaughter as is never seen except when troops are thoroughly savage. Holkar had mutilated the prisoners taken from Monson and sent them back to Agra with right hands and noses cut off, so that there was some excuse for vengeance. Such of the Mahrattas as had horses rode for their lives, and were pursued for ten miles. Those whose steeds had foundered under the stress of the chase were cut down in all directions, or, climbing trees to conceal themselves, were discovered and shot by the pistols of the dragoons.[1] A body of infantry which formed part of Holkar's force was totally destroyed by the Eighth Light Dragoons. In all it seems that literally three thousand of the enemy were killed; and many more poor wretches were wounded, who crowded into all the villages around for shelter, or perished miserably on the plains, too much exhausted to reach any refuge. The loss of the British was twenty-eight men and seventy-five horses killed and wounded, of which the only two men killed, besides thirteen of the wounded, belonged to the Eighth Light Dragoons.

1804.
Nov. 17.

This was rather a massacre than a fight, but none the less was it a great feat of arms. The British column had traversed three hundred and fifty miles in a fortnight before it was called upon to make its crowning effort, and had actually covered twenty-two miles on the 15th when it started for its night march of thirty-six more to Furruckabad. The pursuit led the cavalry yet ten miles further afield, so that the total distance accomplished in the twenty-four hours, before the force finally encamped, exceeded seventy miles. And something more was achieved even than the total defeat and dispersion of Holkar's army. For the Mahratta chief had already burned the outer cantonment of Furruckabad; and though the Europeans, who were mostly civilians, had taken refuge in the fort and defended themselves bravely, they would probably have

[1] This is the only instance which I have ever encountered of pistols being of the slightest use to dragoons.

1804. succumbed to an assault on the 17th but for Lake's swift march and most opportune arrival.

Here therefore was Holkar's cavalry shattered to pieces; and meanwhile his infantry had already undergone the like fate. A few days after the departure of Lake, General Fraser, who had been detained at Delhi by want of supplies, was able to march due south

Nov. 11. towards Deig. On the 11th of November he reached Goverdun, a short distance from that fortress, and discovering the enemy to be close at hand, encamped there for the night. The Mahrattas had taken post in a narrow space running to southward from the south-east angle of the walls, and confined between a large deep tank[1] on one side and a still more extensive morass on the other. They had secured their flanks by resting their right on an eminence crowned by a fortified village, and their left on the fortress itself which, though it belonged to the Rajah of Bhurtpore, was in perfect understanding with the commanders of Holkar. Their strength, so far as could be ascertained, was twenty-four battalions, or at a moderate estimate fourteen thousand infantry with one hundred and sixty guns, besides a considerable body of horse. Fraser had two British regiments, the Seventy-sixth and the Hundred-and-first,[2] the latter of which had recently joined the army, besides a detachment of recovered European invalids, six battalions of Sepoys, two regiments of native cavalry[3] and artillery. These may be taken at about one thousand British infantry, four thousand native infantry and seven hundred sabres, or about six thousand bayonets and sabres altogether.[4]

[1] A tank is of course simply a pond; the earlier form of the word, *stank*, being indeed identical with the French *estang*, *étang*. Why this archaism should have been preserved in India is a curious question.

[2] Then the First Bengal European Regiment.

[3] 2nd and 3rd Bengal N.C. 1/2nd, 1/4th, 6 cos. 8th, 1 & 2/15th, 2/22nd N.I.

[4] The official returns on the 23rd of November were (including all sick, etc.) :—

Leaving a battalion and eight companies, together with his irregular horse, to guard the baggage, Fraser marched to the attack at three o'clock on the morning of the 13th. He had to fetch a wide compass southward to turn the morass, but, on arriving at the fortified hill which covered the enemy's right, he wheeled his column to northward in two lines; the first consisting of the Seventy-sixth, and the second of the Hundred-and-first, each forming a centre between two battalions of native infantry.[1] In this order he advanced upon the village, where the enemy's sharpshooters, firing from loopholes, caused his troops much annoyance. This petty stronghold was, however, speedily carried, when the Mahratta dispositions became clearer, and as usual were found to be skilful enough. Their first line with several guns barred the front of the inlet between the pond and the morass; a large body of infantry and artillery being drawn up with particular cunning on their left, and another on the right, so as to enfilade the British advance on both flanks. In rear of this was a second line, equally powerful in artillery; and beyond this again was a succession of batteries stationed at such an angle to each other as to ensure a cross-fire. On their right, in 1804. Nov. 13.

Cavalry	677
76th	626
101st	281
6 batts. Sepoys	4176
Total	5760

[1] First Line. Monson's Brigade. 1/2 N.I. (on left); 1/4th N.I. 76th (on right).
Second Line. Browne's Brigade. 101st (on left), 2/15th N.I. 1/15th N.I. (on right).

Such is the order shewn in the large plan attached to vol. iv. of *Wellesley Despatches*; but for reasons which will presently appear, I believe the order to have been, from left to right:—

Monson's Brigade. 1/4th N.I., 76th, 1/2nd N.I.
Browne's Brigade. 1/15th N.I., 101st, 2/15th N.I.

It was the old rule that the white regiment should be in the centre between the two Sepoy battalions.

1804. Nov. 13. the open ground outside the tank, their cavalry hovered about in large masses, ready to pursue if not ready to fight. Their position, in fact, resembled that of the French at Malplaquet, with this further access of strength, that at the apex of the re-entrant angle between pond and morass stood the fortress and guns of Deig.

Fraser, however, never hesitated for a moment. Ordering his two regiments of native cavalry to check the Mahratta horse, he placed himself at the head of the Seventy-sixth, and with that regiment alone charged down the hill to his left upon the nearest line of guns, under a tremendous cross-fire of grape, chain, and round shot. The enemy gave way as soon as the British came near them, and falling back to their second line, continued to ply them with a murderous cannonade. Fraser quietly re-formed his troops, and was advancing against the second line when a cannon-shot carried away one of his legs, and compelled him to relinquish the command to Monson, the officer next senior to him. Monson, however, knew Fraser's plans, and, being a man of extraordinary bravery, was well fitted to execute them. The British second line having reached the village, two native battalions,[1] taken from both lines, faced half right and moved forward with their battalion-guns under command of Major Hammond, to check the outflanking corps of the enemy at the southern end of the morass; while the Hundred-and-first, seeing the Seventy-sixth engaged far ahead of them, ran forward to support their comrades, followed by the two remaining battalions of Sepoys. Monson meanwhile had without hesitation led the Seventy-sixth forward against the second line of the enemy; and from thence this intrepid band pressed on for two full miles, capturing battery after battery, till they fairly drove the mass of fugitives against the walls of the fortress, where hundreds perished in the swamp which adjoined the south-east angle and many were even drowned in

[1] These were the 1/2nd and the 2/15th N.I.; the right-hand battalions, if my order of battle be accepted.

the ditch. Had not our nominal allies in the fort 1804.
opened fire upon the British, the pursuit would Nov. 13.
probably have been still more destructive.

Thus the front was swept clear, but there still remained the powerful body at the southern end of the morass which Major Hammond with his Sepoys was gallantly holding back, though his three little six-pounders were utterly overmatched by the far heavier and more numerous artillery of the Mahrattas. Moreover, a party of horse belonging either to the enemy or to the Rajah of Bhurtpore's troops which were serving with our own army, had stolen round the cavalry that opposed them, and, recapturing the first line of guns, had turned them against the British. Captain Norford of the Seventy-sixth with twenty-eight men (who presumably had been left to guard them) at once charged this hostile body and drove it off; but he fell himself in the attack, and his little party remained in great peril. Monson, therefore, re-formed his troops, and, marching back to Hammond, first reinforced him with some of his battalion-guns, and then led his infantry round to the left flank of the party of Mahrattas that opposed him. These did not await the attack, but at once gave way and fled. Many ran back into the morass and were lost; the rest were scattered in all directions. The cavalry then moved down to assist in protecting the wounded and the captured guns, and the escort of the baggage arriving at the same time, soon put an end to further resistance. The British encamped upon the field of battle.

This was a fine and gallant action, which Lake declared to have surpassed anything hitherto done in India. He added, however, the significant remark: "I have reason to believe that the action of the 13th inst. was a very near business. The personal courage of Monson alone saved it." In any case the native infantry appears to have done its duty gallantly, though the casualty list shows that, as usual, the British bore the brunt of a very severe fight. Six European

1804. Nov. 13. officers, including General Fraser, were killed or died of their hurts, and seventeen were wounded. Sixty-three European soldiers were killed, and one hundred and eighty-one wounded; and among them forty-two of the killed and one hundred and twenty of the wounded belonged to the Seventy-sixth. Of the natives of all ranks ninety-nine were killed, and two hundred and seventy-four wounded; and it is significant that not one of these belonged to the two regiments of Native Cavalry. The fact that the Mahratta horse was able to pass them by and recapture the guns, added to the further fact that the infantry of the baggage-guard was brought up to support them, tends to show that they needed a squadron or two of British dragoons to hearten them; and it was, presumably, owing to their failure that the action at one moment evidently bore an extremely ugly aspect. However, the bravery of Monson and his officers saved the day, and all was well. The loss of the Mahrattas was reckoned at two thousand killed, including those who perished in the swamp. The trophies of the day were eighty-seven guns, thirteen of them being those which Monson had lost on his retreat from Malwa, and which he now most honourably recovered.[1]

It is an extraordinary fact that, though he had thus brilliantly redeemed his fame, Monson decided immediately after the action to fall back to Agra. Lake was in despair. Most of Holkar's defeated infantry had taken refuge in the fortress of Deig; and there was every chance that Monson's retirement would allow them to escape and that, his movement being construed as a retreat, the whole country would rally to support the Rajah of Bhurtpore. Monson's ostensible motive was that he must go back to Muttra for provisions. "There are sufficient supplies there for

[1] The authorities for the battle of Deig are meagre. I know of none but the account in Thorn's *Memoir of the War in India*, eked out by Monson's report and Lake's comments in *Wellesley Desp.* iv. 233, 245, 251.

the whole army for two months," wrote Lake, "and 1804. from thence he ought to have drawn them. He might have spared a battalion or two to have fetched them. . . It is somewhat extraordinary that a man brave as a lion should have no judgement or reflection. . . . It really grieves me to see a man I esteem, after gaining credit in this way, throw it away in such a manner immediately." However, the only remedy for the mischief was that the Commander-in-chief should hasten to Deig himself, which he resolved forthwith to do; and meanwhile he comforted himself with the news that Colonel Wallace of the Nineteenth Light Dragoons had, towards the end of September, captured the fortress of Chandore with little trouble or loss.

On the 20th of November Lake's cavalry marched Nov. 20. from Furruckabad, leaving the infantry to follow, and pursued its way on the track of Holkar, first south-westward upon Mainpooree, thence north-westward Nov. 22. upon Etah, and thence westward by Assan to Muttra. Nov. 26. There on the 28th Lake crossed the Jumna and rejoined Monson, who had fortunately halted at Muttra when apprised of the Commander-in-chief's approach. After a stay of two days, Lake advanced towards Deig on the 1st of December. The treachery of the Rajah Dec. 1. of Bhurtpore had, since the battle of Deig, been so obvious, that hostilities against him were inevitable; and these were to be opened by the siege of the fortress. On the 2nd Lake encamped within sight of the strong- Dec. 2. hold; and, since the heavy artillery had not yet arrived from Agra, the next nine days were spent in reconnaissance and in skirmishes with the Mahratta horse under Holkar's personal command. At length, on the 10th, the siege-cannon came up under the escort of Dec. 10. Colonel Don; and on the 11th the entire force moved forward, formed in a huge hollow square, with the transport and followers, amounting to some sixty thousand human beings and over a hundred thousand animals, in the centre. Finally, on the 13th the army Dec. 13. encamped on the western side of the fortress.

1804. Being almost surrounded by marshes and lakes, Deig was during the greater part of the year nearly inaccessible to an enemy. The town, of considerable size, was defended by a strong mud wall with the usual round bastions, and by a deep ditch which surrounded it on every side except at the south-west angle, where the works were prolonged to a high rocky eminence called the Shah Bourj. Before this eminence stood what was practically a distinct fortress, consisting of a square enclosure with four commanding circular bastions at the four cardinal points, and a smaller bastion midway between the northern and western of them; while the northern bastion and north side of the western were further covered by external entrenchments of the pointed form used by European engineers. A few hundred yards to south of these was an old detached mud fort, named Gopalghur, which was filled with matchlock-men and sharp-shooters. Within the town and about a mile to north-east of the Shah Bourj stood the citadel, of quadrate form, with circular bastions, and surrounded by a deep ditch faced with masonry. The ramparts were high and thick; the approaches were guarded by massive gateways and towers; and the whole was in excellent preservation and repair.

On the very night of his arrival Lake broke ground in a grove over against the western front of Gopalghur;
Dec. 14. and by the next dawn a mortar-battery, besides another for two field-guns, was completed. On the evening of the 14th, volunteers from the British regiments of dragoons began the construction of a breaching battery seven hundred and fifty yards to south-west of the Shah Bourj. The workmen, despite much annoyance from the sharp-shooters in Gopalghur, completed their
Dec. 17. task by the night of the 16th; and on the morrow fire was opened from ten heavy guns and four mortars. The result was disappointing; and the enemy meanwhile brought guns out into the plain, where, utilising the inequalities of the ground with great skill, they sheltered their artillery from all possibility of damage

by the British batteries, while pouring upon them in 1804. their turn a destructive enfilading fire. Fresh cannon were therefore disposed by Lake to keep these in check, and on the 20th a new battery of heavy guns was Dec. 20. erected farther to the north and closer to the Shah Bourj. These measures proved effective. Many of the enemy's guns were silenced; a practicable breach was made in the Shah Bourj; and the assault was fixed for the night of the 23rd December.

The attacking parties were divided into three Dec. 23. columns. The right column, consisting of four battalion-companies of the Hundred-and-first and five of Sepoys, was led by Captain Kelly, and was ordered to carry the enemy's batteries and trenches on the high ground to south of the Shah Bourj. The left column was in charge of Major Radcliffe, who, with four more companies of the Hundred-and-first and five companies of Sepoys, was appointed to capture the hostile works to north of the Shah Bourj. The central column was commanded by Colonel Macrae. This last, being the storming party proper and entrusted with the assault of the breach, was composed of the flank companies of the Twenty-second, Seventy-sixth, and Hundred-and-first, supported by a battalion of Native Infantry.

The whole, under the supreme direction of Macrae, moved off at about half-past eleven, the enemy firing an occasional gun and burning blue lights to show that they were on the alert. The two flanking parties came first into action, drove the enemy from the outworks and spiked the guns. The storming companies, however, were much hampered by broken and difficult ground, and were met by a cross-fire from a strong entrenchment which lay between them and the breach. Fortunately the cannon were mostly trained too high, for the artillery-men stuck most gallantly to their guns and were actually bayonetted where they stood. Thus this outer defence was carried, and the British rushing at the breach, after a desperate fight made

1804. Dec. 23. good their footing in spite of every kind of missile, and ran down into the fort. Here again they were met by guns at the corner of every street and by a galling fire of musketry from the buildings; while some of the enemy rallied under cover of the darkness and tried to recover their captured ordnance. But at half-past twelve the moon rose, and, with its light to help them, Macrae's men were able to work more freely without fear of firing on one another. The columns to right and left had been equally successful in carrying the detached batteries and entrenchments; and by two o'clock the Shah Bourj, with the whole of its outworks, was in Lake's possession. The flanking columns then rejoined Macrae and attacked the main walls of the town, which were speedily carried. Preparations were made for the battering and assault of the citadel, but
Dec. 24. the enemy evacuated it during the ensuing night; and
Dec. 25. on Christmas morning of 1804 the town and fort of Deig, with most of the artillery that still remained to Holkar, besides a large quantity of grain and two lacs of rupees in specie, were surrendered into the hands of the British.

The losses of the assailants were slight considering the difficulties of the assault. Forty-three, including two British officers, were killed, and one hundred and eighty-four, of whom thirteen were British officers, were wounded. Of the two companies of the Twenty-second no fewer than four officers were wounded, among them being Captain Lindsay, who, though twice severely hurt by a pike-thrust and a sabre-cut before he reached the breach, yet led his men on into the Shah Bourj. Lieutenant Forrest of the Pioneers received over twenty wounds and was left for dead, but recovered with the loss of one arm. Considering that the issue of all these desperate actions hung upon a handful of British officers, it is marvellous than any of them should have survived.

Having repaired the defences of Deig so as to make
Dec. 28. it again secure, Lake, on the 28th of December,

marched south-eastward, picked up a convoy of stores, 1805. together with the Seventy-fifth regiment, which had formed its escort, and on the 2nd of January 1805 Jan. 2. encamped before the maiden fortress of Bhurtpore.

There appears to be no detailed description of this stronghold before its capture by Lord Combermere in 1826, when it had been much enlarged since 1804. But, even when Lake came before it, it was a place of great extent, the circumference of the fort and town being upwards of eight miles. The whole of this vast perimeter was surrounded by a mud wall of great height and enormous thickness, with round bastions, mounting innumerable guns, at short intervals, and by a very wide and deep ditch. The fort, of quadrate figure, was situated at the eastern extremity of the town, upon elevated ground, with three sides within the town and the fourth overlooking the country. Its walls were higher than those of the town, and its ditch wider and deeper. The whole lay within a belt of jungle and swamp, the water of which could be drained off to fill the ditch. Indeed upon the arrival of Lake's army a large expanse of water on the north-west side suddenly disappeared; and not for some time was it discovered that the whole of it had passed into the ditch, insomuch that in this case also it was said that "a seventy-four could have floated there."

The complete investment of so great an enclosure was beyond the strength of Lake's army, but this consideration had never weighed with British generals in the siege of an Indian fortress; and accordingly he concentrated the whole of his force opposite the selected point of attack at the south-west angle of the city. On the 4th of January a grove in advance of Jan. 4. his camp was first cleared of the enemy to facilitate the opening of the trenches; and on the night of the 5th a breaching battery of six eighteen-pounders was Jan. 5. erected, which opened fire on the 7th. By noon of Jan. 7. the same day a second battery of eight mortars was

1805. completed; and both plied the town with a heavy cannonade, which was answered as vigorously from the
Jan. 9. walls. On the afternoon of the 9th a breach was reported to be practicable; and it was resolved that the storm should take place on the same evening, before the enemy should have time to pursue their usual practice of covering the breach with a stockade.

The assault was to be delivered in three columns. Of these the left was composed of one hundred and fifty men of the Hundred-and-first and a battalion of Sepoys under Lieutenant-colonel Ryan, his orders being to attempt to enter a gateway on the left of our batteries. The right column, led by Major Hawkes, was made up of two companies of the Seventy-fifth and a battalion of Sepoys, and was designed to capture the advanced guns of the enemy outside the walls and to the right of our batteries. It was hoped that one or both of these parties might make their way into the town upon the backs of the fugitives; but, if they failed in this, they had orders to turn and support the central column. This last counted a strength of five hundred Europeans, consisting of the flank companies of the Twenty-second, Seventy-fifth, Seventy-sixth, and Hundred-and-first, besides a battalion of Sepoys, the whole being under command of Lieutenant-colonel Maitland of the Seventy-fifth.

At seven o'clock these three bodies moved off to the trenches; and upon the firing of the evening gun at eight o'clock they advanced to the assault. Ryan and Hawkes to right and left succeeded in their task of carrying the outer entrenchments and spiking the guns, but failed to enter the town with the fugitives. The central column advanced unperceived to within fifty yards of the breach, when a tremendous fire of musketry and cannon was opened upon them. Hurrying forward, the leaders of the column found themselves arrested by a deep trench about twenty yards wide and full of water, which branched off from the main ditch and enclosed a small island, on which stood a strong

force of the enemy with two guns. These at once 1805.
opened a destructive fire; and the storming party, Jan. 9.
finding that the obstacle was too deep to be filled by the fascines and gabions which they carried, plunged waist-deep into the water and dashed straight at the enemy. The companies of the Twenty-second and part of the Seventy-fifth, who were at the head of the column, followed hard after the forlorn hope and quickly cleared the island; but the companies in the rear broke off to the left in the darkness, leaving the leaders in isolation. The little band in front, however, pressed on over the ditch, but on reaching the breach found nothing but a perpendicular curtain descending sheer down to the water, with no footing but stones and logs that had fallen down from above under the fire of the guns. No more than three men abreast could ascend it; but none the less, Sergeant John Shipp of the Twenty-second, Colonel Maitland, and Major Archibald Campbell of the Seventy-fifth made their way to the top, supported by such few of their men as had not fallen. Here they found their way barred by a stockade of stakes, stones, bushes, and pointed bamboo, through the crevices of which a forest of moving spears made continual thrusts at them; while a shower of stones, stink-pots, and bundles of lighted straw fell on them from above. Staggering on the loose and treacherous rubbish up which he had climbed, Shipp drove one of his feet through it, and through the hole thus made caught sight of the interior of the fort swarming with men. His foot was instantly seized, nor could he withdraw it except at the sacrifice of his boot. Meanwhile the enemy in the bastion to the right of the stormers set fire to some dead underwood which they had hung from the wall for the purpose, and, being thus lighted to their work, trained a gun upon the little party in the breach. At the first discharge Maitland, Campbell, Shipp, and most of the few with them fell dead or wounded, and the remainder were ordered by

1805. Jan. 9. Lieutenant Mauser to sit down at the foot of the breach while he went in search of the rest of the column. But the whole of the supports had gone astray, being stopped by the ditch. Some of them had halted by it, while others had turned either to right or left until they joined the columns of Hawkes and Ryan, the former of which, pursuant to its orders, was returning towards the breach after doing its work on the right. But meanwhile the little party at the breach's foot, finding itself unsupported and success hopeless, had retired; and the order was given to retreat. The enemy jubilantly redoubled their fire; and the troops suffered far more during this retrograde movement than during the advance. In all, five officers and sixty-four men were killed, twenty-three officers and three hundred and sixty-four men wounded. The flank companies of the Twenty-second, in particular, were terribly cut up; while those of the Seventy-fifth lost not only their colonel, Maitland, killed, but seven other officers severely hurt. Worst of all, some of the killed were men who had been left badly wounded near the breach, and had been murdered in cold blood by the enemy.

The failure of the assault was doubtless due to insufficient means, and consequently to insufficient preparation and excessive haste. No adequate facilities had been devised for crossing the ditch; and, if the ditch had been easier, the so-called breach was really no breach at all. The troops were not discouraged; but it was ominous that on the following day the enemy's working parties repaired the breach in broad daylight, Lake's four battering-guns being unable to fire until repaired. Other materials too were so scanty that during the three days following the attack there were not sufficient for more than the repair of the batteries already erected. However, the engineers now decided to batter the wall a little further to the right, or south; and accordingly an additional breaching battery mounting four eighteen-pounders and two twenty-four pounders was erected immediately to the right of the old one, while other batteries of twelve-pounders were thrown up wide on 1805. both flanks so as to divert the fire of the fortress. On the 16th the newly mounted cannon opened upon the Jan. 16. wall in the appointed place, but with disappointing results. The mud wall crumbled down before the shot and disappeared into the ditch, which had been deepened by the enemy, leaving no foundation for the slope of a practicable breach, but merely a pile of light dust in which a man would sink waist-deep.[1] Moreover, as fast as a breach was made, it was forthwith stockaded by the Rajah's working parties, so that each morning saw the previous day's work undone.

No effort, however, was made to bring the batteries within nearer range of the wall so as to ensure greater and more thorough destruction. The truth was that the number of the troops was insufficient for the work. On the 18th there arrived from Agra a reinforce- Jan. 18. ment under Major-general Smith, but this was not enough to supplement the losses arising from the unsuccessful assault, and from the daily and insidious attacks of sickness and fatigue. At this time also the freebooter, Meer Khan, threatened to appear upon the scene with a huge body of horse, having been hired by the Rajah with six lacs of rupees. Lake's cavalry had already been fully employed in keeping Holkar's plundering horsemen at a distance, and the arrival of fresh predatory bands promised to tax their vigilance to the utmost. This necessarily threw the task of protecting the camp more heavily upon the infantry, which, besides severe duty in the trenches, was required to take a share in all foraging parties and escorts for convoys. Hence the horse was harassed by constant troublesome service, the foot was overtasked, and the artillery and pioneers, being very few in number, were simply worked to death. Scarcity of forage was already

[1] *Memoirs of John Shipp*, chap. vii. I should attach little importance to this observation of a private soldier were it not confirmed in its main features by the journal of the siege in Creighton's *Siege of Bhurtpore*, p. 154.

1805. serious; and the deficiency of stores was such that the two twenty-four pounders were withdrawn from their
Jan. 20. battery on the night of the 20th, the supply of their shot being exhausted.

However, on that same day the breach which had been made was declared to be practicable. During the afternoon three brave troopers of the Native Cavalry contrived by an ingenious stratagem to ascertain the width and depth of the ditch over against it; and on
Jan. 21. the following morning the troops were marched down to the trenches on the right, in order to assault shortly after noon. A bridge lightly constructed of bamboos, and made buoyant by inflated skins, had been devised to facilitate the passing of the ditch; and picked men had been trained to bring it forward and handle it. It remained therefore only to choose the storming party, which was made up of the surviving men of the Twenty-second's flank-companies, one hundred and twenty of the Seventy-fifth, one hundred and sixty of the Seventy-sixth, and one hundred of the Hundred-and-first. As soon as these should have forced an entrance, the remaining men of the same four regiments, together with three battalions of Sepoys, were to support them. The Twenty-second was to lead the way, and the foremost among them, with eleven volunteers, was Sergeant John Shipp, who had held the same place in the assault of the 9th and, over and above many smaller wounds, had been struck in the shoulder by a grape-shot. Immediately behind him was Captain Lindsay of the same regiment, who, owing to previous hurts, had only on that very day thrown aside his crutches, and still carried his left arm in a sling. A second column under Colonel Simpson was also appointed to make an attempt to force the Anah gate, to the right or east of the storming party.

The British batteries played upon the breach throughout the morning, and at three o'clock in the afternoon opened fire again to cover the advance of the stormers. A shell from a howitzer was the signal to move, and this bursting in the muzzle of the gun killed two British grenadiers. However, Shipp's little party led 1805. the way, followed by the bridge, which was carried on Jan. 21. men's shoulders ; and the enemy at once poured on them a tremendous fire of musketry and artillery. At the edge of the ditch Shipp and Lindsay fell, severely wounded, the former in the head, the latter in the knee ; and the bridge on being launched was found to be too short by one-third, the enemy having dammed up the water and thereby immensely increased its width and depth. A hurried effort to lengthen the bridge by means of scaling ladders had no further effect than to overset it; when it floated away uselessly down the ditch. Thereupon Lieutenant Morris of the Hundred-and-first, with Lieutenant Brown and twelve men of the same regiment, swam the ditch and mounted the breach ; but they were too few to effect an entrance by themselves, and the rest of the column remained halted under a terrible fire. At length Colonel Macrae, who commanded the storming party, seeing no hope of success, gave the word to retreat ; and then it seems that there was a general rush back to the shelter of the trenches. Simpson's column, however, now came up in Macrae's rear, on the way to the Anah gate ; whereupon the storming party rallied and again advanced, though to no purpose. After a time Simpson returned, finding the entrance by the Anah gate impracticable ; and the whole presently retired in good order, though leaving many of the wounded behind. Morris, finding himself unsupported in the breach, where he had already been wounded, swam back over the ditch and, though struck by a bullet in the neck, was brought safely into camp. The enemy then swarmed out in triumph to murder the wounded and mutilate the dead ; and thus disastrously ended the second assault of Bhurtpore.

The loss of the British amounted to twenty-eight officers and five hundred and seventy-three men, European and native, killed and wounded. The flank companies of the Twenty-second lost sixty-five of all ranks killed and wounded, and the small party of the

1805. Jan. 21. Seventy-fifth, one hundred ; so that there was no lack of daring and devotion. Yet no advantage whatever was gained, and the troops were much shaken and disheartened. Lake issued a consolatory general order, and distributed a reward of money to every corps, with assurances that success was ultimately certain. It was all that he could do, and his outward firmness no doubt made some impression upon the enemy ; but in truth he had throughout the day been overmatched. During the assault the cavalry had been engaged with the confederate force of Holkar and Meer Khan which, though successfully prevented from doing any mischief, refused to be brought to close action, and at sunset followed the retiring squadrons of the British almost up to the camp, being kept at bay only by a battery of horse-artillery in the rear-guard.

Jan. 22. On the following day the enemy worked busily to repair the breach, unmolested by any fire from the British cannon ; and the engineers sought for a more promising site for their batteries to the eastward of the existing trenches. But meanwhile a new difficulty, which might have been foreseen, arose to distract the British commander. A large convoy of twelve thousand bullock-loads of grain was on its way to the camp at Muttra by way of Deig, and on the 22nd a regiment of native cavalry and a battalion of Sepoys under Captain Welsh were sent to bring it in. The escort duly joined the convoy, and encamping with it at a distance of twelve miles from Bhurtpore, marched again
Jan. 23. with it early on the morning of the 23rd. All went well until they reached Combir, half-way between Deig and Bhurtpore, where the convoy was attacked by the entire force of Meer Khan, numbering some eight thousand horse and foot with four guns. The four hundred troopers being too few to protect such a multitude of bullocks, Welsh took post in the village with his escort and such of the animals as he could gather round him. Here, though beset on all sides, he held his own gallantly, beating off attack after attack until, two of

his guns being disabled, the enemy by a desperate effort 1805. succeeded in capturing a part of his position. The firing, Jan. 23. however, had been heard at Bhurtpore, and at half-past eight the Twenty-seventh Light Dragoons and a regiment of native cavalry under Colonel Need rode hastily out of camp to the rescue. The dust raised by the column was soon perceived by Welsh's Sepoys, who, making sure that Lake himself was on his way to them, raised loud cheers, and dashing at the enemy's guns, captured the whole of them at the bayonet's point. Need came up in time to scatter the enemy's cavalry in all directions, and catching the fugitives of the infantry as they fled from their cannon, cut them down without mercy. Six hundred of Meer Khan's men were killed on the spot, and the chief himself only escaped by throwing off his clothes and arms, and running away with the press of his followers. Altogether the affair was highly creditable to the troops engaged, whose loss in killed and wounded did not amount to fifty of all ranks; and inasmuch as the enemy left forty standards and four guns in the hands of the British, the story was capable of being expanded into a lively despatch. But the fact remains that of twelve thousand bullocks only eighteen hundred came into the British camp, the remainder with their loads going to feed Holkar's army. How it came about that only fourteen hundred men were sent to escort twelve thousand bullocks, when Meer Khan was known to be in the neighbourhood with a large force, is a matter that was left unexplained.

However, this unpleasant lesson was not neglected. A second and much larger convoy of fifty thousand bullocks laden with grain, and about eight hundred cart-loads of stores, ammunition, and treasure was on its way from Agra; and it was of vital importance to bring it in safely, for there was not seven days' grain left in the camp. Accordingly on the 24th Lake sent Jan. 24. Colonel Don to that place with the Twenty-ninth Light Dragoons, two corps of native cavalry, and three battalions of Sepoys. Arriving there on the 26th, Don

1805. Jan. 29. marched with the convoy on the 28th, and on the 29th, at a distance of about sixteen miles from Bhurtpore, fell in with the united forces of the Rajah of Bhurtpore, Holkar, Meer Khan, and Bappoo Scindia, all of them intent on securing so rich a prize. Lake instantly marched with the rest of the cavalry and two battalions of Sepoys to reinforce him; and such was the terror of his name, that no attack was attempted in his presence. His whole camp was surrounded by the enemy that
Jan. 30. night; but on the morrow he marched in a huge hollow square, and brought in the convoy safely without the loss of a man or bullock; while his cavalry and horse-artillery succeeded in inflicting some damage upon the hordes of the enemy. "Nothing," said a critical observer, who was not always friendly to Lake, "could have been better planned or more steadily and coolly executed than the protection of the convoy upon this occasion."[1]

A little respite was thus gained; and the preparations for the renewal of the siege, which had gone forward somewhat languidly owing to lack of supplies and stores,
Feb. 5. received new life. On the 5th of February a new parallel was opened towards the Neemdar gate, on the southern front of the fortress; and on the following day the whole camp was shifted to a new position in rear of it. Now, however, Meer Khan essayed a fresh kind of diversion. His recent failure to capture the great convoy had caused complaint among the chiefs subordinate to him; and the quarrels between them became so hot that he determined to separate from his friends, and try his fortune in his native country of
Feb. 7. Rohilcund. Accordingly on the 7th of February he crossed the Jumna with the whole of his own body of horse and as many banditti as would join him, concluding that Lake could detach no force in pursuit of him without raising the siege of Bhurtpore.

No sooner, however, was Lake informed of his departure than he despatched Major-general Smith with

[1] *Journal of Lord Lake's Siege of Bhurtpore* (apparently by an officer of Engineers), appended to Creighton's *Siege of Bhurtpore*.

the Eighth, Twenty-seventh, and Twenty-ninth Light 1805. Dragoons, and three regiments of native cavalry, to hunt him down. This detachment marched on the 8th, Feb. 8. crossed the Jumna by the bridge of boats at Muttra on the 9th, and at once took up the chase. Reaching Aligarh on the 11th, Smith was there reinforced by two Feb. 11. regular battalions of Sepoys, some irregular infantry, and Skinner's Horse. Proceeding north-westward, the column, after meting out some punishment to predatory chieftains on its way, dropped the infantry and part of Skinner's Horse at Arropshehar, and on the 14th en- Feb. 14. camped on the bank of the Ganges. There intelligence was received that Meer Khan had failed in an attempt to traverse the river and had followed it upwards in the hope of finding a suitable crossing-place. Smith at once pursued him to a point due east of Meerut, where, finding that his quarry had succeeded in passing the stream, he at once led his troops into the water, a mile broad at that place, and reached the eastern bank in safety with the loss of a few followers and baggage-animals.

Thence the chase lay due east by Moradabad to Rampoor, which was reached on the 20th, and from Feb. 20. thence south-eastward to Sheergur, where Smith halted, having driven Meer Khan to the foot of the bleak hills to northward where he could work little mischief, while he himself held a good central position for the defence of Pillibeer, Rampoor, and Bareilly. Moving between these places for some days, Smith on the 27th turned Feb. 27. northward from Moradabad, and on the 2nd of March Mar. 2. received the welcome intelligence that Meer Khan with the whole of his force was but nine miles distant at Afzulghur. Marching at once to that spot, he found the chief's forces drawn up in order of battle behind a ravine; and at once attacking, cut the whole of his infantry to pieces, killed three of Meer Khan's principal officers, and dispersed his cavalry with heavy loss in all directions. Smith's casualties in the action did not exceed forty killed and wounded.

1805. Deserted by many of his followers, Meer Khan fled by a circuitous route to Moradabad; and after another week of defeat in sundry attacks, being hustled in every direction by columns detached from the British garrisons in the country, he recrossed the Ganges on
Mar. 11. the 11th, having lost alike his baggage, his following, and his reputation. Smith also crossed the Ganges,
Mar. 23. and on the 23rd, after a month of excessive exertion and fatigue during a chase of seven hundred miles, rejoined the army before Bhurtpore.

There, unfortunately, matters had not prospered since the departure of the cavalry. In itself the detachment of so many troops was an embarrassment to Lake, which was not lessened by his losses in the two unsuccessful assaults. It was imperative that he should obtain reinforcements from some quarter; and finally it had been decided to call up from Malwa a part of the Bombay contingent commanded by Murray. That officer, indeed, had played a singularly inconspicuous part in the operations. As far back as September 1804, Arthur Wellesley had recommended that he should be superseded by Major-general Jones. This was not immediately done; and Murray accordingly remained inactive at Ujjein, until in November Wellesley advised that he should be recalled towards Guzerat, where his force might be re-equipped with facility and would ensure the safety of that district. Lake, however, at this same time bade him move northward from Ujjein, apparently with the view of using his column to head back Holkar if he should again turn towards the south. The defeat of Holkar at Deig and Furruckabad made these orders useless; but Murray, to Arthur Wellesley's consternation, marched northward to Kota, leaving Holkar's forts of Partabghur and Hinglaisghur untaken in his rear, and sacrificing his communications with Guzerat. In December 1804, explicit directions came from Lake that he should join him on the Jumna, which seemed to justify his movements; though Wellesley did not conceal his apprehensions lest Murray should share the fate of Monson in Malwa. However, in due time 1805. General Jones reached the army and took command; when it was discovered that Lake's orders for the force to move northward, far from being due to carelessness and imprudence on the part of the Commander-in-chief, had actually been suggested by Murray himself. Yet this was the same officer who in the previous year had been so nervous about his supplies and communications that he would hardly move. The truth seems to be that when Murray learned that he was to be superseded he was prepared to march anywhere at any risk, so long as he could prevent his successor from joining the army.[1]

However, on the 11th of February Jones arrived Feb. 11. before Bhurtpore with eight companies of the Sixty-fifth, the Eighty-sixth, five battalions of Bombay Sepoys, a troop of Bombay cavalry, and a few irregular horse, in all about seven hundred Europeans and twenty-four hundred natives. By that time a new breaching battery of four eighteen-pounders had just been completed, and a second battery to left of it had been begun, both of them within four hundred yards of the wall. A new breach was made by these guns; but the enemy built a mud wall in rear of it and kept stockading it and restockading it as fast as the palisades were shot away. However, something more of science was shown in the general prosecution of the siege. Trenches of approach were carried forward so as to shelter a storming party almost to the edge of the ditch; a mine was begun at the end of them with the idea of blowing up the counterscarp; powerful mortar-batteries were erected on each flank of the breaching battery; and outlying works of sandbags were thrown up for lighter ordnance to keep down the fire of the defence. On the other hand, the enemy erected batteries and threw up trenches outside the walls of the fortress so as to enfilade the British guns. Nor did the besieged lack enterprise in

[1] *Wellington Desp.* iii. 468, 547, 556, 570, 592, 599, 597, 631, 642.

1805. Feb. 19. other respects, for on the morning of the 19th they attacked an unfinished work which was erecting within seventy yards of one of their towers, drove out the Sepoys within it, emptied the sandbags and carried them off. Lake, however, was satisfied with what had been done by his engineers, and determined to storm the breach as soon as the batteries should have swept away the stockade.

Three columns in all were formed. The left was made up of most of the European soldiers of Lake's own army, supported by three battalions of Sepoys, and was placed under command of Colonel Don for the assault of the breach. The centre column was committed to Captain Grant of the Bombay forces, who, with two hundred of the Eighty-sixth and a battalion of Bengal Sepoys, was to carry the enemy's guns and trenches outside the town. The right column, composed of three hundred of the Sixty-fifth and two battalions of Bombay Sepoys under Colonel Taylor, was to attack the Beem Narain gate at the south-eastern angle of the fort, which was reported to be accessible to guns, and therefore capable of being broken in.

During the night of the 19th some parties of the enemy made a sally and crept into the nearest approach unperceived, the British troops being for some reason always withdrawn before the relief arrived to take their place. Here they remained for some time unmolested, demolishing the preparations that had been made for a
Feb. 20. mining chamber, and carrying off the tools. At daybreak the British storming party arrived, whereupon the enemy at once rushed out with pikes and swords along the top of the trench, thrusting and slashing at the men below, and occasionally jumping down and closing with them. Every man of these aggressors was intoxicated, and their onslaught was most furious. The trench being very deep and narrow, without banquette-steps to enable the men to ascend it or to fire over it, the British were caught at a disadvantage and were thrice driven back, until the remnant of the

flank companies of the Twenty-second came up and swept the savage assailants out. The British guns were then turned upon them, as well as the guns of the fortress, which throughout had played indiscriminately upon all parties; and few of this desperate band escaped alive. But the loss of the British also had been severe; the wounded and dying were left where they lay, exposed to the enemy's fire; and their miserable groans and writhings threw gloom and discouragement over the storming party. 1805. Feb. 20.

At three o'clock the three native battalions of Don's column marched into the trenches; and a little later Grant's detachment sprang forward and dashed at the entrenchments and batteries without the walls on the right of the British guns. The enemy was at once driven out; eleven guns mounted in the batteries were captured; and Grant's men following close upon the fugitives, pursued them to the walls and on to the Anah gate, which was barely closed in time to shut out the foremost of the British. Having no guns, Grant was powerless to blow in the gate; and he therefore established himself under the bank of a dry pond immediately outside it, having only narrowly missed forcing his way into the fortress.

Grant's attack was the signal for the storming party to move forward, and accordingly Don gave the word to assault. The orders were that the Europeans at the head of the column should advance from the left of the breaching battery, and that the Sepoys should follow them to the breach. Fifty men with fascines were to take the lead, throw their fascines into the ditch, and then wheeling outwards spread themselves along the glacis to keep up a fire upon the breach while the forlorn hope rushed on. But the men, though they were the remnant of the Seventy-fifth, Seventy-sixth, and Hundred-and-first regiments, which had covered themselves with glory during the past weeks, refused to move out. They were depressed by past failures before Bhurtpore; they were dismayed by the ghastly agony

1805. Feb. 20. of the wounded men all round them; they were discouraged by the success of the hostile sally in the morning. They had only too readily caught up an idea that the enemy had established a mine in the unfinished gallery of their own engineers; they found their task made doubly difficult and perilous by the faulty construction of the parallels and the enfilading fire which consequently swept the approaches; and in fact they had come to the conclusion that the operations before the fortress had been and still were mismanaged, and had lost confidence in their leaders. In vain their officers exhorted them by words, gestures, and example: they would not advance; and, until they moved, the native troops in their rear could not pass to the front. Some of the flankers of the Twenty-second alone responded to the appeals of their officers, but, finding themselves unsupported by their comrades, presently retired.

In desperation Don at last led two battalions of native infantry to the right of the breaching battery, and from thence to the ditch. The Sepoys followed him most gallantly; but the ditch opposite to the breach was found impassable, and the column swerved to its right to the nearest point which had suffered damage from the besieging cannon, namely a bastion known to the British as the Tower bastion. Here the ditch was found to have little water in it; and the men began to climb up the bastion by clinging to the shrubs that grew on its face. On reaching the slope of the tower most of the party stopped, though a few of the bravest clambered on and even planted their colours close to the summit; but there was no chance for the ascent of a number sufficient to maintain a footing united at the top. Those that would not face the peril of the final climb, hung in crowds round the foot of the tower; but no order nor entreaty could induce them to move round it or to push on to the breach in the curtain. There they remained huddled together, while the enemy from above showered on them logs

of wood, fire-pots, and missiles of every description. 1805.
Meanwhile the European regiments, observing the Feb. 20.
attack on the tower, imagined that the place was taken; and a small party of them left the trenches and pushed on after the Sepoys. Two of these soldiers actually reached the summit of the tower, where one was blown to pieces by a gun, but the rest joined the Sepoys at its foot, where they endured the enemy's fire for an hour and a half. At length they were ordered to retire, when the whole suddenly took to their heels and rushed back in panic to their trenches. Taylor's column, meanwhile, having lost its scaling-ladders and had one of its guns dismounted, had found the forcing of the Beem Narain gate absolutely impracticable, and had already retired. Thus the third assault, like its fellows, issued in a disastrous repulse.

Twenty-eight British officers were killed or wounded in this affair; and the total loss amounted to forty-nine Europeans and one hundred and thirteen natives killed, seventy-six Europeans and five hundred and fifty-six natives wounded, making in all little short of nine hundred casualties. Nevertheless on the same night it was reported to Lake that if the tower which had been assaulted by the storming party were battered for half a day, it might easily be stormed; and accordingly the whole of the guns in the new breaching
battery were turned upon it. In the morning Lake Feb. 21.
came on parade and, addressing the European regiments rather in sorrow than in anger, expressed his regret that they had not followed their officers and so had failed of success, but added that he would give them an opportunity of retrieving their reputation. He then called for volunteers; and the whole stepped forward as one man. Two hundred were selected, to each of whom a reward of one hundred rupees was promised if the fortress were taken. Lieutenant Templeton offered to lead the storming party, and Sergeant John Shipp, though still disabled by wounds, insisted for the third time on leading the forlorn hope. Lake therefore

1805. Feb. 21. decided to assault once more in the afternoon, his supplies and stores having fallen so low that unless he captured the city he had no alternative but to raise the siege.

The guns therefore played upon the tower with such ammunition as was left, and beat so large a gap about its base as to raise hopes that the upper portion would fall by its own weight. This expectation was, however, disappointed; and Lake was duly informed that the higher part of the tower was still steep. It was thought, even so, that it might by some means be surmounted; and, since it was reported that the breach was still unrepaired, Lake decided to make the attempt. The shattered remains of the Seventy-sixth and of the flank companies of the Twenty-second, the Sixty-fifth, Eighty-sixth, the flank companies of the Hundred-and-first, two battalions of Bengal Sepoys, and one of Bombay Native Infantry formed the storming party, the whole being under the command of Monson. Before four o'clock the signal was given, and the detachment, cheering loudly as they passed the General, marched forward to the assault.

The advance was made with the greatest boldness and regularity, and the men showed all their old bravery in attempting to scale the tower. The gap in its base gave shelter to a few, but the breach was still too steep to be climbed. Determined to carry the fortress if it were humanly possible, some of the stormers drove their bayonets into the rampart, one above another, to make a ladder; while others tried to scale the ascent by the holes made by the British guns; but only two men abreast could advance in that way, and numbers so small were easily overpowered. The enemy heaped missiles upon them, logs of wood, pots of gunpowder, flaming packs of cotton dipped in oil, heavy shot, all that came to hand; while the guns of the adjoining bastion poured in a sweeping and most destructive fire. For two hours the men wrestled with the impossible, striving to ascend the curtain at any point which promised the least semblance of success. Templeton 1805. was killed just as he had planted the colours near the Feb. 21. summit. Major Menzies, Lake's aide-de-camp, begged leave to join in the assault, and was slain at the head of the old breach. All was in vain. Monson at length gave the order to retire, and the survivors rushed back under a furious fire to their batteries. Four hundred and seventy-nine Europeans, thirty-four of them officers, and five hundred and eight natives had fallen ; making in all nine hundred and eighty-seven killed and wounded. The various attacks had cost over three thousand men, and the fortress was as defiant as ever.

There was no doubt now as to what must be done. On the night between the 22nd and 23rd the troops Feb. 23. were withdrawn from the trenches, and the ordnance from the batteries. The guns were unfit for service, the vents being so much worn that most of them would hold four fingers, and had only been stopped, in the later days of the siege, by bags of sand. This, in fact, was one cause of Lake's failure ; six iron guns of no great calibre and eight brass mortars comprehended the whole of his siege-train, which was far too small and too weak for his purpose. His force of men also was inadequate, for he began the siege with little more than six thousand effective infantry and two thousand cavalry, the latter of which was constantly absent in chase of predatory horse of one description or another. Lord Combermere, when he sat down before Bhurtpore in 1826, had with him eighteen battalions, eight regiments of cavalry, six troops of horse artillery, one hundred and twelve siege-pieces, and fifty light field-guns. The historian of Combermere's siege, with these figures before him, most generously strives to vindicate Lake against all hostile criticism ; but it cannot be gainsaid that the main cause of his failure was his own impatience. "They must have blundered that siege terribly," wrote Arthur Wellesley from St. Helena, when he heard the news ; "for it is certain that with adequate means every place can be taken ; and,

1805. Lord Lake having been so long before the place, adequate means must have been provided or in his power. The fault lies therefore in the inapplication of them or, most probably, in the omission to employ all those which were necessary to accomplish the object in view, either through the ignorance of the engineers, or the impetuosity of Lord Lake's temper, which would brook no delay." Even the Viceroy, greatly as he esteemed and admired Lake, begged him, upon the report of the last assault, not to accelerate operations at Bhurtpore, if he resumed the siege, but to await the arrival of a sufficient battering-train rather than risk another failure. Lord Wellesley's confidence must have been greatly impaired before he would write in such terms to his beloved General.[1]

Lake, however, was still resolute and unshaken.
Feb. 24. On the 24th he drew off his army six miles to north-eastward of the fortress and encamped so as to cover the roads to his magazines at Agra, Muttra, and Deig; the enemy's horse making the movement both difficult and hazardous owing to the absence of the cavalry under General Smith, which had not yet returned from the chase of Meer Khan. The troops were then employed in making fascines and in bringing in large convoys of supplies and stores, including the battering-train which ought to have been summoned earlier. The
Mar. 10. Rajah began to lose heart, and on the 10th of March, two days after Lake had received the news that he had been raised to the peerage, his emissaries were admitted to headquarters to negotiate for peace. Holkar, meanwhile, with what remained of his force, lay about eight miles westward from Bhurtpore in ease and comfort, since Lake had no cavalry with him. On the
Mar. 23. 23rd, however, Smith returned with his regiments to
Mar. 29. camp; and at one o'clock on the morning of the 29th Lake led them out to surprise Holkar's camp, he himself intending to attack its right, while another

[1] *Wellington Suppl. Desp.* v. 511; *Wellesley Desp.* iv. 301; Creighton's *Siege of Bhurtpore*, xx. *seq.*

column moved round its left. But the enemy were 1805. warned of the movement and were so far prepared for flight when he came upon them that, after a long pursuit, he succeeded only in making an end of about two hundred men and capturing a few animals. Holkar, therefore, took up a fresh camp some way to the south-west of Bhurtpore, where he thought himself more secure; but at daybreak of the 2nd of April Lake April 2. came upon him with his cavalry and horse-artillery, and pursuing him for eight miles, made large captures, besides working great havoc among the men. Numbers of Holkar's followers deserted him; and he was forced to cross the Chumbul with a mere remnant of eight thousand horse, half as many foot, and twenty or thirty guns. A week earlier a detachment of his infantry with three guns had been routed and dispersed Mar. 26. near Ahmednuggur by a small column of Sepoys and irregulars, which weakened him still further. The Mahratta chief was now little more than a wanderer and an outcast, having lost all his strong places, nearly all his artillery, and the great bulk of his once-powerful army.

These successes were not without effect on the Rajah of Bhurtpore; and Lake presently accelerated the nego- April 8. tiations with him by marching back to his old encampment at the south-east angle of the city. On the 10th of April accordingly the Rajah signed the preliminaries April 10. of peace; and a few days later he bound himself by treaty to hold no correspondence with the enemies of Great Britain, to leave Deig in the hands of the British Government until it should be assured of his fidelity, and to pay an indemnity of two hundred thousand pounds. Thereupon, on the 21st, the army broke up April 21. from before Bhurtpore and moved south-eastward upon the Chumbul.

There was indeed more than enough to require its presence there. Ever since the first reverses of the British Scindia had waxed warlike or pacific according to the prospect of their failure or success in

1805. the field ; and as disaster followed disaster at Bhurtpore, he became more and more forgetful of former lessons. His ostensible ground of complaint against the Viceroy was that the fort of Gwalior and the territory of Gohud had, under the recent treaty, been wrongfully withheld from him. Moreover, it seems that Lake, Arthur Wellesley, and in fact every one except the Viceroy, thought that he had a just claim to Gwalior.[1] But other of his grievances were simply impudent ; and in the autumn of 1804 he had gone so far as to march towards Bundelcund, attacking the allies of the British in violation of the treaty, and openly communicating with Meer Khan and with other followers of Holkar. After repeated protests, the British resident at his
Jan. 23. court quitted his camp on the 23rd of January 1805, but was at once brought back by force and virtually detained as a prisoner, with every circumstance of humiliation. Lord Wellesley, seeing that Lake's strength was already overtaxed, contented himself with
April 23. mild remonstrances ; and Scindia, on the 23rd of April, intimated to the resident his intention of marching to Bhurtpore to mediate between the Rajah and the British. The consequences of this movement would undoubtedly have been serious ; but they were averted by Lake's treaty with the Rajah, which came both to Scindia and to Holkar as a staggering surprise. None the less, the two last remained in open communication, and at last both Holkar and Meer Khan joined their forces to Scindia's, the whole virtually forming one united camp.

April 30. Lake crossed the Chumbul near Dholpore on the 30th of April ; and Scindia, thinking better of his big words, withdrew up the river to Kotak, though he still refused to liberate the British resident, even when Lake threatened a renewal of hostilities. The Viceroy, however, was determined not to precipitate matters; and the desertion of a part of Scindia's army to the British gave that chief warning that he must be careful. Lake

[1] Wellington, *Suppl. Desp.* iv. 386.

detached a force to watch him, and meanwhile employed 1805.
himself in negotiating a treaty with the ruler of Gohud, whereby the latter pledged himself, by what was called a subsidiary treaty, to take three battalions of the East India Company's Sepoys into his pay. This done, the army broke up in the third week of May; the May.
Bundelcund detachment marching to Gwalior and the Bombay force to Tonk. Lake with his head-quarters at Muttra threw his army into cantonments there, at Agra, at Secundra, and at Futtehpore; the whole being kept ready to march and to concentrate at a moment's warning.

On the 25th of July Lord Wellesley, weary with July 25.
waiting, sent Scindia an ultimatum, bidding him deliver up the British resident or take the consequences; but his term of office had come to an end before any answer could be received. He had sent home his resignation at the end of 1803, and had waited only until the negotiations with the Mahratta chiefs, which subsequently gave place to war, should have been terminated. Meanwhile his ambitious and costly policy had commended itself neither to the East India Company nor to the British Cabinet; and war and conquest in India, ever since the trial of Warren Hastings, could be always held up as wicked and unnecessary. Hence when his successor, Lord Cornwallis, arrived at Calcutta on the 30th of July 30.
July, he brought with him both the hopes and the instructions of the Government for a new era of economy and peace.

The faith reposed by British ministers in Cornwallis is somewhat remarkable, for he was not a man of great ability, and his career had by no means been of the most successful. In America he had proved himself decidedly a failure. In India he had been within a hair's-breadth of actual disaster before Seringapatam; and, though he had redeemed his first mishaps in the field by subsequent victory, his neglect or misgovernment had left to his successor very formidable difficulties. As chief military adviser to Pitt's Cabinet and as Master-

1805. general of the Ordnance, his career, whether by his fault or not, was the reverse of creditable to him; and though he had done well in Ireland in 1798, he had cut a deplorable figure as a diplomatist at Amiens. He was beyond doubt a man of sterling integrity, with a high sense of duty as a public servant; and these are gifts which are not so common as to be valued lightly. But his chief merit in the eyes of the Government seems to have been what was termed his moderation, of which it can only be said that it bore a dangerous resemblance to mediocrity. But in any case his health was so much broken that, though he most nobly and unselfishly undertook the heavy charge, it was simple folly to despatch him to India.

Arriving by no means the better for his long and tedious voyage, Cornwallis was dismayed to hear that hostilities with Holkar were not yet ended, and that even with Scindia they were likely to be renewed. Within twenty-four hours he decided that no further military success could be of any profit, but that the contest must be terminated forthwith by negotiation; and he at once set out on a journey to the Upper Provinces. Examination of the Company's finances, which were certainly in a deplorable condition, confirmed him in his opinion; and he made up his mind at once to restore to Scindia both Gwalior and Gohud, to withdraw Wellesley's demand for the liberation of the resident, to reinstate Holkar in the whole of his dominions, and to renounce the connexions made by Lake with the native princes on the Jumna. By happy chance Lake was able, before Cornwallis's instructions reached him, to insist that Scindia should set free the resident; and indeed, when apprised of their purport, he took upon himself to keep back the Viceroy's letter to Scindia and wrote a strong remonstrance against such proceedings. But Cornwallis was past all work before Lake's letter reached him. For a month he lingered in a state of weakness which allowed him to transact little
Oct. 5. business, and on the 5th of October he died at Ghazipore.

Meanwhile Holkar who, with such troops as remained 1805.
to him, had again betaken himself to Ajmeer, marched northward at the beginning of September, announcing Sept.
that he expected assistance from the Sikhs and even from the Ameer of Cabul. Lake, being determined to allow no mischief of this kind, thereupon ordered the troops at Agra and Secundra to move to Muttra on the 10th of October, sent a detachment to Saharanpoor for the protection of the Doab, and himself marched on the 28th of October with two brigades of cavalry, one Oct. 28.
of infantry and sufficient artillery,[1] to pursue Holkar in person. On the 7th of November he arrived at Delhi, Nov. 7.
whence moving northward by easy marches he reached Paniput on the 17th, and entered Sikh territory by way of Kurnah. On the 24th he was at Pattiala, where Nov. 24.
the Rajah reported that Holkar had endeavoured to attract the Sikhs in those parts to his standard, but without effect. On the 29th Lake was reinforced by Nov. 29.
three battalions of Sepoys and two bodies of irregular horse; and still moving north-westward, he reached Ludhiana on the 2nd of December. Here he crossed Dec. 2.
the Sutlej, being received everywhere in friendly fashion, and marched on in the hope of coming up with Holkar, who had failed to cross the Beyah still further to north-west. He was disappointed, however, for his advanced guard arrived at the Beyah just in time to see Holkar's rear-guard cross it before their eyes; and by the time Lake's main body reached the river, Holkar was at Amritsar. Lake continued to advance to Jallundar; Dec. 9.
where, under the terror of his name, the chiefs of the Sikhs declined to give aid to Holkar, sending an emissary to welcome the British and to offer their mediation. On the 20th of December Holkar's messengers arrived; and on the 24th a treaty dictated Dec. 24.
by Lake brought the long contest to a close.

[1] 1st Brigade—H.M. 24th (late 27th), 25th (late 29th) L.D., two regiments of native cavalry.
2nd Brigade—H.M. 8th L.D., one regiment native cavalry.
Infantry—H.M. 22nd, 101st (E.I.C. Regt.), two native battalions.

1805. But the treaty was such that the General would never have agreed to it except under instructions. After Cornwallis's death Sir George Barlow succeeded to the Government as Senior Member of Council; and he pushed his predecessor's views to extremes. A treaty was negotiated with Scindia by which Gwalior and Gohud were ceded to him as a matter of grace, though not of right; and to Holkar there was restored the whole of his dominions intact. This would have been comparatively a small matter, had not Barlow renounced also all treaties whereby British protection was granted to native princes. This abandonment of men, who had given the British invaluable aid at critical times, to the mercy of a ruffianly robber like Holkar, was a bitter grief to Lake, who pleaded earnestly on behalf, at least, of the Rajahs of Jeypore and Boondy. But Barlow was inflexible, and even went so far as to order that the treaty of protection with the Rajah of Bhurtpore should also be abrogated. But here Lake refused to give way, and drew such a picture of the confusion which must inevitably follow, as to frighten the acting Viceroy into compliance, at any rate for the present, with his will.

The war therefore ended, as have so many British wars, with the concession of all that had been gained by great expenditure of blood and treasure, in order that more blood and treasure might be expended in fighting another war for the same object in the near future. British Governments—perhaps it would hardly be fair to say the British nation—are seized from time to time with these revulsions of feeling, which they call remorse and ascribe to conscience, but which should be called weariness and ascribed to timidity. The sufferers on such occasions are not the British themselves, but the unhappy allies whom they have drawn to their side in the course of the contest, and whom they desert at the hour of trial; and it is from them, and not from formidable rivals, that Britain has truly earned the title of perfidious Albion. The work, which had been left unfinished, needed of course to be done anew. The

power of the Mahrattas was in great measure broken; 1805.
but two more wars, and the victories of Maheidpore and of Maharajpore and Punniar, were necessary in 1817 and 1839, before the descendants of Sevajee would accept the fact that the British and not they were to be final masters of India.

Long before that time most of the chief actors in the drama of the great Mahratta war had passed away. Jeswunt Rao Holkar, after a few years of excessive indulgence in brandy, died in 1811. Lake embarked for England in February 1807, but died soon after his return on the 28th of February 1808, in time to be spared the pain of mourning for the gallant son who had been wounded by his side at Laswaree, and who fell at Roliça in the same year 1808. Though he can hardly be reckoned a great general, Lake left behind him such fame as had been gained by few British officers among the native troops of India; and worthily he had earned it, for on the field of battle he was not only a grand leader but a great commander. Had he been born a Frenchman and served under Napoleon, he would assuredly have won a marshal's baton by sheer hard fighting; and the Great Captain, who loathed the very name of supplies,[1] and declared that twenty thousand men could live in a desert, would have pardoned him many shortcomings for the sake of his surpassing prowess in action. Lake's military experience had been remarkable, for he had been matched first against the crafty and tenacious Americans in the most difficult and dangerous of all the wars fought in the eighteenth century, then against the tumultuary armies of France in 1793, and lastly against the Mahrattas in the plains of India; and he had seized victory by the hair at Linselles as at Laswaree. As a disciplinarian he was strict; but, like Abercromby, he took thought for the comfort of his men, and while making great demands upon their courage and endurance, never subjected them to fatigue for no object. He spared himself as little as

[1] "Les vivres! Ne m'en parlez pas."

1805. he spared his men, and whether it was the cavalry or the infantry that was bearing the brunt of action, Lake, for all his sixty years, was always to be found at their head in the thickest of the press and the hottest of the fire. With such qualities and with natural affability of manner and kindness of heart, he was adored by all ranks of his army; and under his leadership they wrought marvels. Few, unfortunately, now know anything of the battles which he won; and his most famous battalion, the Seventy-sixth, which should at least bear Lake's crest upon its colours, has, under a new organisation, become associated with the still greater name of Wellington.[1] None the less should it always be remembered as the fighting battalion of one of Britain's greatest fighting generals.

But here the praise of Lake must end. The siege of Bhurtpore stands out as a sad example of his impatience and his love of rough-and-ready methods; but the despatch of Monson's detachment on its isolated march to the south remains a still greater blot upon his fame. For this measure showed that he had not studied his enemy, nor thought out the means of making every movement of the campaign contribute to his ruin. His fault, it is true, was not greater than Napoleon's when he sent Dupont's corps in similar circumstances to Andalusia; and it was, perhaps, a misfortune for Lake that such a man as Arthur Wellesley should have been his rival in the field; but against the background of Wellesley's achievements the defects of Lake became very conspicuous. If it were only Assaye that were to be compared with Laswaree, the elder General would have nothing to fear; but beneath Assaye is the solid structure of communications thoroughly guarded, magazines and advanced bases carefully stored, transport laboriously organised; everything provided that prudence and sagacity could foresee, nothing left to

[1] It is now the second battalion of the Duke of Wellington's (West Riding) Regiment.

chance which could be assured by industry and care. 1805.
It must at the same time be admitted that Lake, unlike Wellesley, fought his campaigns in a country of which very much was absolutely new and strange to the British; and that he had not Wellesley's good fortune in possessing Mysore bullocks for the transport of his army. Moreover, though Wellesleys are rare, Gerard Lakes are rare also; and an honourable place in the Army's history must always be reserved for this indomitable Guardsman, whose magic of leadership could make men march and fight beyond their ordinary powers. Loyal to his men, loyal to his officers, loyal to his superiors, brave as his sword, a cool strong master in the direction of a battle, a fiery youth in the leading of a charge, he was a type of English gentleman which is of untold worth to the Army.

CHAPTER V

The reader has been detained for long in the East, but there remains still to be narrated the story of a forgotten little war in that quarter which, from its extreme inopportuneness, threatened at one moment to carry with it very serious consequences.

The British, it will be remembered, had in 1796 captured from the Dutch their settlements in the island of Ceylon. We of this generation have generally assumed that those settlements embraced the entire country; but they did not. The Dutch possessed indeed the whole coast-line of the island, measuring in circumference some seven hundred miles; but the mountainous country of the centre was still unconquered, and owed no allegiance except to the King of Kandy. The Kandians were not comfortable neighbours. They were not formidable and they were not aggressive, but they were amazingly conceited, jealous, and suspicious; unwilling to enter into any negotiation with the Dutch, except as superiors treating with inferiors, and therefore requiring extravagant concessions alike of solid gain and of outward respect. Such an attitude never commends itself to a commercial nation; and it was galling to the Dutch to find themselves unable to push their trade, as well as inconvenient to possess no road from Colombo to Trincomalee except that which followed the coast. At last in 1766 the Dutch declared war, and after many skirmishes and considerable loss in the field, took possession of Kandy, only to find themselves very little the better for their exertions. Their object was either to conquer the country outright, or to dethrone the reigning king; but they had not troops enough to accomplish the former, and there was no means of dethroning the king except by capturing him, which in spite of desperate efforts they completely failed to do. The operations were prolonged for some time with no very decisive result, and in the end a treaty of peace was concluded, of which it need only be said that it left the position of Kandy wholly unweakened.

When the British captured the island in 1796, they too sent an embassy to Kandy, offering concessions in the matter of navigation which were thought too liberal; but the treaty was none the less rejected by the King. It unfortunately happened also that the expedition which took Ceylon was sent from India, and was therefore at first administered by Indian civil servants. These gentlemen brought with them not only their detestable system of inflated correspondence, but also Malabar agents as their underlings, who superseded the native headmen. By oppressive abuse of their masters' authority, these subordinates soon drove the unfortunate Cingalese into spasmodic rebellion; and, although the Malabar agents were presently removed and the native officers restored, the incident was not likely to give the Kandians, who hated all white intruders impartially, a favourable impression of British rule.

In 1798 the King of Kandy died; whereupon 1798.
Pelime Talauve, the chief minister or (to give him his local title) First Adigar, contrived to oust all members of the royal family in favour of a young Malabar of obscure extraction, whom he seated on the throne as his puppet, becoming himself the true governor of the country. The relations of the deceased sovereign he placed in confinement, from which they presently escaped; and one of them, named Moottoo Sawmy, who had the strongest pretension to the Crown, solicited for himself and his fellow refugees the protection of the

1798. British Government. The legitimate claimant of an usurped throne is always a tempting instrument to a diplomatist who has an object to gain; but the Governor, Mr. Frederick North, declined to take advantage of it in this case. The Kandians seemed to be content with their new King; and North therefore put Moottoo under surveillance, so that he should be unable to give any trouble to the government in Kandy.

1799. Not long afterwards, in February 1799, the First Adigar approached North with mysterious proposals, which in December he made clearer by inviting the Governor directly to assist him in making away with the new King, and in placing himself, Pelime Talauve, upon the throne; which done, he promised to make the British masters of the country. North naturally rejected this overture with indignation; and the Adigar then addressed himself to the Secretary of Ceylon, declaring that he hated the royal race of Malabars, the oppressors of his fatherland, and that he had raised his puppet to the sovereignty with the object of bringing the whole clan into contempt and rousing the people to drive them out for ever. The Secretary answered that the British would never conspire to depose a foreign prince who had been guilty of no aggression against them; whereupon the Adigar innocently inquired whether an invasion of British territory would be a sufficiently aggressive act to answer the purpose, a question which not unnaturally stimulated North to excessive anxiety and suspicion.

What real purpose, if any, may have underlain these dark overtures of the Adigar, it is difficult to say; but in any case North thenceforth was filled with apprehensions concerning the murder of the King of Kandy and the invasion of British territory. He now tried to approach that potentate more directly, and proposed that General Macdowall, who commanded the troops in Ceylon, should go ambassador to Kandy with a sufficient escort, in order to remove the person of the

King to British ground if he was in danger, or if not, 1799. to negotiate what was called in India a subsidiary treaty. Macdowall accordingly started on his mission in March 1800; but most of his escort was stopped at the 1800 frontier, and though he himself proceeded to the capital, the embassy came to naught. A new negotiation, opened soon afterwards by one of the nobles of the Kandian court, was equally a failure, as were also sundry efforts made by North to approach the King through other channels than the First Adigar. Throughout this time Pelime Talauve was reported to be active in inciting his countrymen to war, and the natives in British territory to revolt.

Early in 1802 the First Adigar or his instruments 1802. twice approached Governor North with the old invitation to join in dethroning the King of Kandy, with the usual result, of course, of indignant refusal. In April matters took a more serious turn. Certain April. native merchants, British subjects, were arrested in Kandian territory while carrying on a commerce which was sanctioned by long usage; and their goods were taken from them. Rightly or wrongly, North interpreted this as deliberate provocation to war; but it was not until September, after minute investigation of Sept. the case, that he forwarded a remonstrance to Kandy. He fully expected at this time that he would be compelled to resort to force to bring the King to reason; but to his astonishment he was answered not only by a promise of speedy redress but by an expression of the First Adigar's wish to conclude a friendly treaty. North replied that he was equally anxious for an amicable arrangement, but that, before any further negotiation, he must insist upon knowing the King of Kandy's sentiments with regard to the treaty already submitted to him by Macdowall. This answer was decisive. The Kandians were an ignorant and unwarlike people; but they, and particularly those about the court, were filled with extravagant conceit of their greatness and superiority; and, however unreasonable it may have seemed to North,

1802. they were not disposed to place their foreign policy under British direction, to exclude all Europeans except those who bore a British passport, to see their native troops disarmed and a British force quartered in the capital, to yield up a part of their territory in payment for this privilege, and to see the frontier between their own land and the British thrown open for purposes of trade. They wished to keep their country for themselves in all its primitive sanctity and isolation. It was bad enough that foreigners should rule the seven hundred miles of coast that ringed the mountains about, but it was intolerable that they should be masters of Kandy. The First Adigar therefore evaded the grant of the promised redress to the merchants who had been despoiled, and in spite of all protests, massed such rude warriors as he possessed upon the frontier. His action was easily to be explained by a natural desire, by no means alien to British sentiment, to preserve the independence of his country. North, however, could see in it nothing but the nefarious perversity
1803. of an incorrigible evil-doer. On the 31st of January 1803 he ordered his troops to march upon Kandy.

The garrison of Ceylon at this time consisted of the Nineteenth, Fifty-first, and a small detachment of the Eightieth Foot,[1] a battalion of native infantry, two companies of artillery lent temporarily by the Indian Government, and a battalion of Malays, the last-named extremely untrustworthy and dangerous troops. The Europeans numbered about fourteen hundred men altogether ;[2] and these, as well as the native troops, were distributed in small detachments over a dozen different stations, with no advantage, as may be supposed, to their discipline. The force was amply sufficient to overcome such resistance as could be offered by the Kandians ; but this was the least of the difficulties of the coming campaign. In the first place, there was from climatic causes but one month in the year when

[1] The rest of the Eightieth was in Egypt.

[2] There are no returns of their strength in 1803.

the force could take the field; in the second place, the Kandian territory was unexplored, the passes in the mountains were extremely dangerous, and the tracks and paths were so bad as to forbid not only wheeled traffic but even pack-animals; and in the third place, it was more than doubtful whether the mere capture of the capital would in itself produce the slightest effect in reducing the King of Kandy or his advisers to submission. These obstacles, however, North appears either to have appreciated insufficiently or to have ignored. He had little doubt but that in a month he would bring his recalcitrant neighbour to reason. 1803.

The advance upon Kandy was to be made by two distinct columns operating from two distinct bases, the one from Colombo on the west coast, the other from Trincomalee on the east. The first column, under the command of General Macdowall, was made up of the Fifty-first, two companies of the Nineteenth, a thousand native infantry, two weak companies of Bengal Artillery, and a small force of pioneers; in all from eighteen to nineteen hundred men. The second column, under Colonel Barbutt, was of slightly inferior strength, comprising five companies of the Nineteenth, the greater part of a battalion of Malays, and one company of Madras Artillery.

On the evening of the 31st of January Macdowall marched out of Colombo, and after an inspection of his troops by the Governor on the next day, crossed the Kalany Gunga at daybreak of the 2nd of February. Thence his march lay northward upon Ja Ela to Halpè, from which point he turned a little north of east to Feb. 4. Allugalla on the Maha Oya river, and on the 6th of February reached Kotadeniyawa. This place, having good communication by water with Negombo and the coast, had been selected as the site for a magazine; and Macdowall halted for four days to throw up a small redoubt for its protection, the work receiving the name of Fort Frederick in honour of the Governor. Then leaving a garrison of a hundred Sepoys and a few

1803. Europeans to hold it, he resumed his advance on the
Feb. 10. 10th, and fording the Maha Oya on that day at Giriulla, entered Kandian territory.

From this point forward, owing to the difficulty of the roads in the interior, men's shoulders formed the only possible means of transport, and all baggage was therefore reduced as low as might be. The country, however, was still fertile and well cultivated, and the troops had to wade for a part of the first two marches through paddy-fields, knee-deep in mud and water; but the men were healthy and the inhabitants friendly, being ordered, as they said, by the King to supply the
Feb. 11. English with all that they wanted. The second day's march brought the column to Dambadeniyawa, little more than five miles in a straight line from Giriulla; and here supplies failed owing to the death of a commissary. The force therefore again halted for four days, formed a magazine, and threw up a redoubt to protect
Feb. 16. it. On the 16th Macdowall resumed his march in an easterly direction, and for the first time traversed a distance of rather over ten miles. But the roads were so bad that it was necessary to dismount the three-pounder guns which he had with him, and to employ men to carry them. The baggage-coolies fell far behind, and
Feb. 17. the column was consequently unable on the morrow to advance more than six miles to the Magroo Oya river. A picquet of the enemy was surprised fast asleep on this day, and fled with such precipitation on being awakened, as to diminish any anxiety that the British might have felt about an active resistance.

Still moving eastward, Macdowall, after a very fatiguing march of fifteen miles, reached the Deek
Feb. 18. Oya on the 18th, and on the following day encountered
Feb. 19. the two most formidable posts upon the road. The first, a square and open redoubt,[1] built of hewn stone and seated at the top of a rocky mountain, completely commanded the narrow pass which led to it; but the

[1] Macdowall calls it Galle Gidehu; Cordiner calls it Galle Gedera.

Kandians, making no effort at defence, fled instantly, 1803.
abandoning three guns and a quantity of ammunition. Feb. 19
The next stronghold, Geriagame, lay beyond it, very similar in construction, and so situated that a few resolute men might, as was said, have defended it with a shower of stones. The approach to it was by a kind of natural stairway, winding up the side of the mountain between impervious thickets, and intersected by a series of perpendicular rocks, all of which were within range of the cannon above. The Grenadiers of the Nineteenth, being in advance, were the first to draw near the fort, and were at once saluted by a very noisy and ineffective fire, under which they toiled up to the enemy's guns and walked into the battery. The enemy promptly fled as they entered, carrying their wounded with them; but Macdowall in the rear, judging from the prolonged cannonade that there was serious resistance, hurried the entire column with all haste over the pass. The casualties amounted to no more than two men wounded; but the rapid ascent of the rugged path seems to have strained the men beyond belief; and it appears that many soon afterwards succumbed to the effects of the exertion, or at least were so much weakened by it as to be unable to stand against the fever which presently beset them.

A garrison was left in this important post, the capture of which threw open the road to Kandy. Macdowall now turned south, and halting in the afternoon at Kattugastotte, on the Maha-villa-ganga, fired three guns as a signal to Barbutt, whose artillery he had heard after the storm of Geriagame. The signal was promptly answered, for Barbutt was in fact within two miles of him. He had met with a trifling resistance at a pass close to Kandy, and again at the Maha-villa-ganga, but had overcome both by a few cannon-shots; and thus the two columns starting from opposite coasts of the island effected their junction almost to an hour within three miles of their destination. On the 21st Feb. 21.
therefore the two commanders entered the city, each

1803. with a strong detachment of his force, in great content.
Feb. 21. Barbutt had not a single casualty nor even a sick man in his camp. Macdowall could hardly say as much, for some of his Sepoys had fallen down with fever, but the Europeans were in remarkably good health. Both of them, and still more Governor North, looked upon their work as well done.[1]

The aspect of Kandy, however, was not reassuring. The main street with its two miles of mean houses, its innumerable branching lanes, its palace and its temples, stood untouched in the plain within its ring of wooded mountains; but not a living creature, with the exception of a few dogs, was to be seen in it. The city in fact was deserted; the treasure and everything of value had been carried off; the magazine had been blown up, and several of the buildings were in flames. After 1812 such a scene would inevitably have reminded a general of a like desolation at Moscow; but this was in February 1803, when Napoleon was still First Consul. Macdowall, Barbutt, and North were perfectly easy and satisfied, and knew exactly, as they thought, what was best to be done. On his march from Trincomalee Barbutt had reported that if Moottoo Sawmy, the rightful claimant to the throne of Kandy, would but join him, every Kandian on that side of the country would flock to his standard. This done, provisions for the army could be obtained without difficulty. North grasped eagerly at the idea. He at once gave directions that Moottoo Sawmy should be escorted to the capital, intending that in return the new King should cede to the British two large and rich districts, known as the Seven Korales and the Saffragam Korale, lying on the west and north of the Kandian territories. Barbutt accordingly marched with the Malay regiment to meet
Mar. 4. Moottoo; and on the evening of the 4th of March the poor puppet was duly brought by the British troops into Kandy.

[1] Macdowall to North, 5th, 19th, 20th, 21st, 24th Feb.; Barbutt to North, 19th, 20th Feb. 1803.

In due course North's proposals were submitted to him, and not a little to Macdowall's surprise, were resisted with considerable spirit. North, to do him justice, willingly abated his claims; and finally a convention was signed whereby the British Government agreed to deliver to Moottoo the town of Kandy and the whole of the Kandian territory at that time occupied by British troops, receiving in return the district of Seven Korales, the two hill-forts of Geriagame and Galle Gedera, a strip of ground sufficient to make a road from Colombo to Trincomalee, and certain facilities for commerce. All this would have been highly satisfactory had the Kandians but shown the slightest disposition to receive Moottoo as their ruler; but on the contrary not a soul would go near him, so that he found himself in the palace at Kandy with no further adherents than his own servants and the British guard. On the other hand, the deposed King and the First Adigar, who had fled to a royal palace two days' march from the capital, enjoyed full control of their bands of followers and were not slow to prove it. Parties of armed men skulked continually round the British outposts, hiding themselves by day but firing at the sentries by night, and slaughtering every straggler, coolie, or armed follower, with barbarous mutilation. 1803.

But this was not the worst. A few days after the occupation of Kandy the effects of fatiguing marches began to tell upon the troops; and presently jungle fever attacked them, especially the Sepoys, with terrible virulence. On the 9th of March Macdowall reported that he had little more than eighteen hundred bayonets fit for duty, that, unless the people should speedily declare for Moottoo Sawmy, all hope of reducing the interior must be abandoned, and that the army, with the exception of a thousand men to hold Kandy itself, must be withdrawn without delay to Trincomalee and Colombo. Then a sudden gleam of hope appeared in the shape of a message from the First Adigar, giving full information as to the position of the King's refuge Mar. 9.

1803. at Hangaramkatty, as to the easiest roads by which to approach it, and the nature of the resistance to be expected. He also requested that two strong columns might be sent out to converge upon it simultaneously by different routes, promising that he personally would be present to assist in delivering the monarch into the hands of the British. Nothing doubting, Macdowall,
Mar. 13. on the morning of the 13th of March, sent out two detachments, the one of five hundred, the other of three hundred men. The country through which they had to pass was by nature difficult, and they had not marched many miles before they realised that the enemy had turned its strength to account. Guns were posted upon every height that commanded the path of the columns, and sharp-shooters lurked in ambush in the thickest of the jungle. Heavy firing soon began, and a single volley struck down two officers and several men, both British and native. With incredible labour and harassed at every step, the troops forced their way forward through a perpetual fire; and after traversing nearly thirty miles, the two columns
Mar. 14. found themselves on the evening of the 14th before Hangaramkatty. The palace was instantly taken without much resistance; but the King had fled; and pursuit, owing to want of transport and supplies, was impossible. The building was therefore burnt, and the two detachments reached Kandy safely on the evening
Mar. 16. of the 16th. The loss of the troops was slight, not much exceeding twenty wounded, thanks to the bad marksmanship of the Kandians, but nineteen unfortunate transport-coolies were killed, and that at a time when their numbers were already seriously diminished. In fact, the entire movement was a complete and rather humiliating failure.[1]

The monsoon was now near at hand; it was evident that the object of the expedition could not be secured without another campaign; and North began to grow

[1] Macdowall to North, 5th, 9th, 14th, 18th March; Colonel Baillie to Macdowall, 16th March 1803.

anxious. The refusal of the Kandians to accept Moottoo Sawmy as their King had upset all his calculations; and that unhappy man's failure to perform the part which the British Government had put him forward to enact, was quite sufficient, in the Governor's view, to absolve it from all engagements. On the 23rd of March, therefore, North instructed Macdowall to dissuade Moottoo from being proclaimed King, since the British could not undertake to support him. He spoke too late. On that very day Macdowall, though acknowledging that the authority of the fugitive sovereign was now greater than it had ever been, with singular want of judgment installed Moottoo Sawmy as King of Kandy amid all the ceremony of a royal salute. Twenty-four hours later came news from Madras that General Arthur Wellesley was on his march from Hurryhur to Poona, and that at such a conjuncture not a man could be spared from the Presidency for Ceylon. North instantly wrote to Macdowall that the quarrel with Kandy must be made up at once, and that overtures must be reopened with the First Adigar; but he was fain to add that the city of Kandy must be held until some convention had been agreed to. He was soon to learn that the contest with Kandy was not so easily to be concluded.[1]

1803. Mar. 23. Mar. 25.

While North was thus hurriedly multiplying orders to Macdowall, that officer became unpleasantly aware, during the last fortnight of March, that his communications with Colombo were interrupted. Several small parties of coolies with provisions had been murdered; one mail had been captured from its escort of Sepoys at Dambadeniyawa; the rest had been stopped through want of sufficient protection; and it was only by sending down a powerful detachment that Macdowall, on the 30th, contrived at last to bring in despatches and supplies. Moreover, tumultuous bodies of Kandians had broken at more than one point into British territory, and

Mar. 30.

[1] North to Col. Sec. of Ceylon, 19th March; to Colonel Barbutt 23rd March; to Macdowall, 25th March 1803.

1803. March. though easily dispersed by a few dozen British soldiers, kept the country in constant agitation and alarm. Even this was not the worst. Many of the posts on the line of communication proved to be extremely unhealthy, Fort Frederick in particular being the most deadly of all. On the 13th of March, when its first commandant had already been carried from it to die, it was reinforced by seventy-five men of the Sixty-fifth and fifty Cingalese infantry. Every individual of this detachment was struck down by fever; and orders were despatched for the redoubt to be destroyed and the post to be evacuated; but none the less within a month of the 13th of March one officer and two men were all that survived of the whole party.

However, North's negotiations seemed at first to
Mar. 30. bear fruit, for on the 30th of March the Second Adigar came to Kandy bearing the emblems of peace; and with him Macdowall arranged what he thought to be a satisfactory truce. Thereby the First Adigar was to be invested with supreme authority in Kandy, paying an annual allowance to Moottoo Sawmy, who was to retire to Jaffnapatam; and the British were to receive the province of the Seven Korales, the road to Trincomalee and Fort Macdowall, and a fort which commanded that road at a distance of about eleven miles due north of Kandy, together with the district around
April 1. it. This done, on the 1st of April the General marched back to Colombo with the Fifty-first, and sent a part of the Nineteenth to Trincomalee; leaving in Kandy the rest of the Nineteenth, detachments of the East India Company's artillery, and some companies of Malays. In all three hundred Europeans and seven hundred natives remained as a garrison for the city under the command of Colonel Barbutt.

April 2. On the next day after Macdowall's departure the First Adigar advanced with a large force to within three miles of Kandy; but the movement excited no alarm, for it was generally supposed that the truce would shortly be converted into a durable peace. Nor did these favourable appearances seem likely to be belied, for not many days later the Adigar sent a message to North requesting an interview for the final settlement of the treaty. A meeting was accordingly held on the 3rd of May at Dambadeniyawa, the capital of the province so greatly coveted by North—the Seven Korales. The terms agreed upon by Macdowall and the Second Adigar were discussed and ratified, with the stipulation, which to North seemed a mere matter of form, that the execution of the treaty should be delayed until the King of Kandy should be delivered into the hands of the British. Until that time hostilities were to cease.[1] 1803.

All now seemed to be in train for a happy ending to the quarrel. Some slight embarrassment was caused by the sudden illness of Barbutt, to whom, as commandant of Kandy, the execution of the treaty was to have been committed; but at the request of the First Adigar, Macdowall went up temporarily to take his place. The General duly arrived at the capital on the 23rd of May, and found a miserable state of things. May 23.
The garrison, both black and white, was reduced to a shadow by fever; many had perished, and nearly all of the European soldiers were in hospital. Macdowall's brigade-major had been stricken on the journey upward and sent back to Colombo, and both he himself and his one remaining staff-officer were attacked by the same malady a few days after their arrival in Kandy. In weakness and misery they awaited in vain the coming of the First Adigar; until at last, on the 2nd of June, June 2.
arrived an ominous message that he could not attend the General without the permission of the King. Therewith all hopes of a treaty vanished, and North found himself for the twentieth time the dupe of his crafty antagonist. Macdowall and his aide-de-camp, still prostrate with sickness, left Kandy on the 11th of June 11.
June, and by good fortune reached Colombo alive on the 19th. They were the last white men to set eyes upon the isolated garrison in the hills.

[1] North to Hobart, 4th May 1803.

1803. The epidemic fever had by this time spread over the greater part of Ceylon, attacking blacks and whites alike with savage virulence. In Colombo itself it reduced the Fifty-first from four hundred to one hundred men in less than three months; and within the Kandian territory its ravages were even more frightful. The Kandians, though themselves not spared by it, welcomed it as an ally and seconded it with vigour. The newly appointed commissioner to the Seven Korales was driven from his post within a month, leaving his secretary dead of fever behind him. The unhappy transport-coolies, who were still employed to carry supplies up to Kandy, covered the road with their corpses, falling victims some to the sword, some to fever, some to small-pox, some even to famine. In Kandy itself by the third week in June the British soldiers were dying at the rate of six a day; and the Malay troops, their only comrades, were beginning to desert. The Kandian warriors meanwhile crept nearer and nearer to the city, entrenching themselves in strong positions until their time should come. The First Adigar, wishing to cut matters short, proposed to Major Davie, upon whom the chief command had devolved, to make a second expedition to Hangaram-katty in pursuit of the fugitive king. To give colour to his suggestion, he alleged that he himself was out of favour, and that this was the only method whereby peace could be obtained; but Davie was not to be deceived by this trick, even if he could have collected men enough for the enterprise. For his British soldiers did not cease to die, nor his Malays to desert.

North now realised that it was high time to evacuate Kandian territory; and accordingly a small detachment
June 17. of Ceylon native infantry was ordered, on the 17th of June, to proceed at once to Kandy in order to help to escort the sick. But from the extreme difficulty of procuring coolies the party was unable to set out until the 26th; and meanwhile the Kandians struck their
June 23. decisive blow. On the 23rd the posts of Geriagame

and Galle Gedera were surprised and taken, a mishap 1803. June 23. which seems less extraordinary when the amazing truth is told that in each of them there were stationed but one sergeant and twelve privates of the Malay regiment, of whom one-third had deserted already to the enemy. By the fall of these two strong places communications between Colombo and Kandy were finally severed; and on that same day the First Adigar warned Major Davie that, in spite of all his efforts to prevent it, the British garrison in Kandy would shortly be attacked.

Davie made his dispositions for defence; and at four June 24. o'clock next morning the Kandians assailed a post on the hill in rear of the palace where the British troops were quartered. This small guard, which consisted of but ten native soldiers with a light field-gun, was easily overpowered; and an hour later a strong body of Kandian Malays attempted to storm the palace by the eastern barrier, where Davie had stationed a second gun. They were met by a Lieutenant and a few men of the Nineteenth; and the leaders of the two bands closed in a hand-to-hand struggle, wherein the Malay mortally stabbed the British officer, but was himself immediately slain by the Adjutant of the Nineteenth. The alarm was at once sounded; and a single discharge of grape swept away twenty-four of the Kandians, who thereupon withdrew to a distance and kept up a galling fire from their light native field-pieces. The British guns replied; and the duel was maintained continually until two o'clock in the afternoon, when many European officers entreated Davie to enter into a capitulation, since the enemy was advancing in such numbers that the palace could not be held for much longer. Nor was this merely pusillanimous counsel, for the British soldiers were reduced to a handful of twenty men, nominally fit for duty but in reality convalescents who were not yet recovered. Of their comrades one hundred and twenty were helpless in hospital, and the remainder were dead. There were left the Malay regiment,

1803. June 24. which recent events had proved to be not over faithful, and the lascars of the East India Company's artillery. Moreover, the officers themselves were so weak and exhausted that they were hardly equal to further resistance. After some hesitation, Davie hoisted a white flag, and was presently escorted, together with a loyal native officer of the Malays, to the quarters of the First Adigar. It was then agreed that the British garrison should march out with its arms on the road to Trincomalee, and that Moottoo Sawmy should be allowed to accompany them; in return for which the Adigar undertook to feed and tend the British sick until they could be removed. The conditions were reduced to writing and signed; and the Adigar further gave Davie a passport in the King's name to enable him to proceed towards Trincomalee unmolested.

At five o'clock on the same evening the garrison marched out, fourteen British officers, twenty British soldiers, about one hundred lascars, two hundred and fifty Malays, and in the midst of them the unfortunate Moottoo Sawmy.[1] After proceeding for a mile and a half they were stopped by the river Maha-villa-ganga, when, finding neither rafts nor boats to enable them to cross, they bivouacked for the night in pouring rain.

June 25. Next morning the troops were engaged in making rafts when a number of armed Kandians appeared; and some chiefs, approaching Davie, said that the King was much enraged that the garrison had been allowed to leave Kandy, but that he would give the troops boats and forward them on their way, if they would yield up Moottoo Sawmy to him. Davie reminded the messengers of the terms of the capitulation, and refused. Two hours later another party of chiefs came up with an intimation to Moottoo Sawmy from the King that

[1] These are Cordiner's figures, which seem to me to be probably correct. The last return of the garrison shows sixteen British officers and thirty men, eleven native officers, and four hundred and sixty-five native troops fit for duty.

he desired to embrace and protect him. Once again 1803.
Davie refused to let him go; and the messengers June 25.
presently returning threatened that, if Moottoo Sawmy were not given up, the King would send his whole force to seize him and prevent the British troops from crossing the river. Finally Davie, after consultation with his officers, told Moottoo that he had no longer power to detain him, and that the King had promised to treat him kindly. Moottoo answered with a bitter reproach, which was only too well merited. Davie was in a difficult position; but it is plain that he and his garrison hoped to buy their own salvation by throwing this unfortunate puppet, whom their own arms had set up, as a sop to the Kandians. Though, as it turned out, Moottoo Sawmy's fate could hardly have been different whatever the decision of the British commander, yet it was none the less base and mean to abandon him. The victim was led away to Kandy and to instant death; and Davie was destined to pay dearly for the sacrifice.

In the afternoon a few Kandians joined the British, and made ostensible preparations to help them to cross
the river, both then and on the following morning. June 26.
Still no boats appeared; and when, after many difficulties, a British officer succeeded in passing a warp to the opposite bank, the rope was presently cut by the Kandians. Upon this the Malays and lascars began to desert in small parties to the enemy; and at eleven o'clock a mob of Kandians ranged themselves close to the forlorn British, while a chief advanced to bid them in the King's name lay down their arms and march back to Kandy, on pain of being immediately surrounded and put to death. With extraordinary infatuation, Davie and his officers decided to obey; and the whole party was then marched off. Presently the British were halted between two ranks of Kandians; and the Malays were bidden to advance, which, with a few exceptions, they did. The Europeans were then led out two by two, and their brains were dashed out with the butts of muskets. Two officers, Davie and another,

1803. alone were preserved and taken back to Kandy; a third
June 26. made his escape, but was captured and soon afterwards died; one corporal of the Nineteenth, named Barnsley, though desperately wounded and left for dead, recovered his senses and contrived to crawl back to Fort Macdowall. Meanwhile the whole of the Europeans in hospital at Kandy had likewise been murdered in cold blood, to the number, according to one account, of one hundred and twenty; but it appears more likely that the full tale of the victims amounted to nearly one hundred and ninety. In a word, between desertion and massacre, the entire garrison of Kandy was annihilated.

This attack was the signal for several others in various quarters, one and all of them so feeble, spiritless, and contemptible, as to make Davie's weakness more than difficult of explanation. Captain Madge of the Nineteenth, who was in command at Fort Macdowall,
June 25. was assailed on the 25th and on the two following days, but held his own stoutly, though he had but thirteen men, fortunately all Europeans, fit for duty. Then Corporal Barnsley brought the news of the massacre at Kandy; and Madge thought it prudent to evacuate the post by night, unfortunately leaving nineteen sick men of his regiment behind him for want of transport, but bringing off three officers. For four days he marched towards Trincomalee under an incessant fire, until he met a small column of a hundred men from that garrison, on the sight of which the enemy instantly fled. At Dambadeniyawa also the fort, a feeble structure of fascines and earth, was from the 23rd onwards completely blockaded by the Second Adigar, who sent in a daily summons to surrender, with promises of peaceful evacuation, transport of the sick, and similar temptations. Ensign Grant of the Malay regiment, who held the post, had no more than fourteen convalescent men of the Nineteenth and twenty-two invalid Malays; but though himself so enfeebled by ill-health that he could hardly walk, he refused to hear of terms of surrender. He
June 30. was reinforced on the 30th by a detachment of sixty

men which had been designed to escort coolies to Kandy; 1803.
but their ammunition was soon exhausted, and the little garrison defied its enemy with the bayonet only, until brought off by a party of one hundred men on the 2nd of July. The relieving force had to storm July 2.
more than one battery during its advance; but this was not a dangerous service, for the Kandians were too cowardly to stand for a moment after they had once fired their guns. Never was there a more miserable enemy than that to which Davie had surrendered.

However, the fact remained that the Kandians had now taken the offensive, and that through pestilence, massacre, desertion, and general mismanagement, there were very few troops with which to repel them. In fact the European infantry in Ceylon was reduced to little more than six hundred, and the native infantry to fewer than three hundred bayonets. North therefore sent urgent messages to Madras, Bombay, and Calcutta for reinforcements, which request was not the more welcome for arriving just when Arthur Wellesley was opening his campaign. That General bluntly characterised the whole of the proceedings at Kandy as disgraceful folly;[1] and Lord Wellesley seems to have sent no answer. Governor Duncan, on the other hand, appears to have been really anxious to oblige North, probably with the object of disobliging Arthur Wellesley. But the danger of Ceylon upon a renewal of the war with France, which though not known was expected in India, made it impossible to refuse all help. Lord Clive therefore prepared to send at once from Madras two hundred of the Thirty-fourth Foot, and five hundred native infantry known as the Bengal Volunteers. North, meanwhile, in despair over the mortality in the native regiments from jungle fever, began to buy African slaves, in order to form a corps on the model of those which had been so successful in the West Indies. Thus in Ceylon there was witnessed

[1] North to Sec. of State, 31st August 1803; *Wellington Desp.* (ii. 143, 165).

1803. the extraordinary spectacle of a military establishment numbering less than two thousand men, but including British, Bengalis, Madrasis, Cingalese, Malays, and Africans; and all to repel an enemy of which two thousand would hardly have faced one hundred British soldiers in the open field.

However, the King of Kandy, elated by his success, now sent emissaries to all quarters to detach the native subjects of the British from their allegiance; and by the end of July he had massed large forces at various points on the frontier to second any rebellious rising. The sphere entrusted to the First Adigar was the district of Matura, at the extreme south of the island; while the King formed the ambitious design of marching on
Aug. 13. Colombo itself. On the 13th of August intelligence of the renewal of war with France reached Ceylon; and a few days later the Adigar advanced within twenty miles of Matura, the rebellious inhabitants meanwhile severing communication between that place and Galle. The commandant at Matura was seized with panic, and was about to withdraw to Galle, when North sent round a small reinforcement by sea, and an officer to supersede the nervous leader. The threatened mishap was thus averted. A little activity soon sufficed to drive the Kandians back and to restore order among the inhabitants in this quarter. Nor was the King's invasion
Aug. 21. much more successful. On the 21st of August his bands occupied the little fort of Hangwell, about twenty miles east of Colombo, and even advanced five miles nearer to the town; but the place was easily retaken and
Aug. 27. the invaders driven back with some loss. Another raid upon the ruined fort of Chilaw, on the west coast to the north of Colombo, was as futile, for two young civil servants and twenty-five Sepoys contrived to hold the miserable post against an immense number of Kandians for twenty-four hours until relieved. Finally a second grand attack upon Hangwell delivered by the flower of the Kandian army under the King in person was beaten off with very heavy loss by a garrison of fifty Europeans

and about thrice as many native troops. The casualties 1803.
of the British on this occasion were two men wounded ; Aug.
those of the enemy were known to have exceeded two hundred and seventy killed ; but the most welcome result of the victory was the recapture of the lascars of the East India Company's artillery, who had been made prisoners after Davie's surrender. Another week saw the whole of the district cleared of the enemy ; and
though in September the Kandians made a raid upon Sept.
Batticaloa, the invasion for the moment came to an end.

In October the First Adigar reappeared in the fron- Oct.
tier as if to make an inroad upon the district of Saffragam ; but North, having received his reinforcements from India, to which Clive had added three hundred men of the Tenth Foot[1] over and above the forces already promised, now initiated a new system of counter-raids by small detachments upon Kandian territory. These little columns, which rarely numbered one hundred men, simply hunted the unfortunate inhabitants away from their homes, burned their houses, destroyed their crops, and cut down their most valuable trees. The service meant much fatigue though little danger to the troops, but since it left them free to plunder and destroy, was by no means unpopular. North was much elated by the successes of these columns, and wrote home that he hoped to open a decisive campaign in July 1804, capture the First Adigar, depose the King, and annex Kandy. General Macdowall went home at the end of
1803 ; and was replaced in March 1804 by Major- 1804.
general Wemyss, who entered warmly into North's projects, and cheered on the troops against their unfortunate victims with a zeal worthy of a better cause. North then conceived the extraordinary idea of combining with his incursions a general blockade of the Kandian territories, so as to cut off their supplies of salt, and put an end to all commerce ; hoping that the people would thereby be incensed against the King and depose him. He accordingly divided his three thousand troops

[1] These were drafted into the Nineteenth and Fifty-first.

1804. into minute fractions, with the fond expectation that by so doing he could close a frontier of some seven hundred miles. Wemyss made no attempt to undeceive him; indeed it seems rather that he fully shared the imbecility of North; and thus the British troops were urged on still further in their career of demoralisation.[1]

Upon the news of the first disasters at Kandy Lord Hobart wrote drily in March 1804 that he refrained from all comment, but would send reinforcements. These, however, did not arrive until September; and meanwhile a sickly season wrought havoc among the
July. British soldiers. Thus when July came and the question of transport-coolies with other kindred difficulties required to be faced, North decided to abandon the decisive campaign, and to maintain what he was pleased to call his blockade. So fully did he believe in its efficacy and in the reports of the sufferings of the Kandians under it, that he made condescending offers to grant them peace if the King were deposed and the authors of the massacre punished. The whole of these overtures were rejected with scorn, for as a matter of fact the Kandians were none the worse for the blockade, though the villagers were incensed to madness by the devastation of their fields and the shooting down of their fathers and brothers. North, however, so reported these predatory chases as to make them appear great operations. This, unfortunately, as a rule, they were not; but one exception must be mentioned. The officer in command at Batticaloa misunderstood the order countermanding the general attack upon Kandy, and boldly led his column, consisting of sixty men of the Nineteenth and two hundred native troops, straight upon the capital by a new and untried route. He reached it after a march of nearly two hundred miles, without the loss of a man; but waiting for some days for the remaining columns to come up, he found his retreat cut off by large bodies of Kandians. Without hesitation, he attacked and forced his way through, nor

[1] North to Hobart, 3rd March 1804.

would he have suffered much loss had not his ammunition become exhausted, which caused a panic among his native troops and transport-coolies. Finally he returned safely to British territory with the loss of nine Europeans, sixty native soldiers, and seventy-six coolies killed and wounded. Contemptible though the enemy was, this was a creditable feat of courage and endurance.[1] 1804. Oct. 16.

At length at the end of 1804 a letter written by the commanding officer of one of North's predatory columns found its way to the hands of the Duke of York, who sent it to the Colonial Office, asking if these stories of destroying paddy-fields and shooting villagers were true, since in his opinion they were very disgraceful to the British arms. Several months necessarily elapsed before the question could be passed on to Governor North; and meanwhile in February 1805 an exceedingly trivial matter encouraged the Kandians to renewed aggression. General Wemyss and the Puisne Judges of Ceylon fell at variance about a minute point in which each party conceived that its dignity was concerned. The General behaved with extreme foolishness, the Judges with ridiculous conceit; and the Judges eventually haled the General before them while he was immersed in the business of directing the blockading columns, and bound him over to keep the peace. The Kandians, hearing of the quarrel, seized the moment to make simultaneous attacks in every direction. They were of course repelled; and their rashness brought upon them the usual reprisals of death and devastation until July. Nor would their punishment have ceased even then, had not North resigned the government from ill-health; when the British Ministers, suspecting that all might not be right about this war, sent out General Thomas Maitland to succeed him.[2] 1805.

[1] North to the Sec. of State, 25th May, 25th, 30th Sept. 1804, 11th Jan. 1805.

[2] Colonel Gordon to the Colonial Office, 15th Nov. 1804; North to the Sec. of State, 8th, 21st Feb., 11th March, 13th April, 10th July; Sec. of State to North, 21st Feb. 1805; Colonel Wemyss to Colonial Office, 14th Feb., 10th March 1805.

1805. Maitland arrived on the 17th of July, and quickly realised the situation. Overtures for peace had been made by the Second Adigar in June in consequence of the King of Kandy being stricken with small-pox, which was interpreted as a mark of the divine displeasure; but these were as little genuine as any of the previous proposals. Maitland resolved to wait for a few weeks in case the King should feel disposed to open negotiations with a new Governor, being determined, in the contrary event, to take the initiative himself. He did not ostensibly discontinue preparations to meet further aggression, but he was resolved to make no further offensive movement from his side; and he issued a stern order to forbid the cruel and useless burning and plundering with which North had indulged his columns. It was none too soon, for the troops were already thoroughly demoralised. Owing to the laxity and incompetence of Wemyss, and indeed not of Wemyss only but of the entire administration both civil and military, public money had been issued lavishly to every subaltern in command of twenty men who chose to ask for it; and the result was an enormous military establishment, scandalous waste, and great financial distress in the Colony. All this Maitland brought summarily to an end with a strong hand. The Sepoy regiments he condemned as useless, the Malays as both useless and dangerous; and he marked out both for speedy disbandment. But above all he deplored the condition of the British regiments. They were lamentably weak in numbers; for the service in tiny detachments had killed many by useless fatigue, and enervated the rest by giving them unlimited opportunities to drink. Their discipline also was very seriously impaired. The Nineteenth, which had been, by Maitland's own testimony, one of the finest regiments in the Service, had lost all sense of subordination; and the General only checked the evil by trying the Major and a Captain by court-martial and cashiering the Major. By this timely severity and by massing the troops in two divisions only, at Trincomalee and Colombo, order was presently restored, and the men regained the good tone and the discipline that they had lost. 1805.

Meanwhile, owing to the withdrawal of the British raiding columns, the war died a natural death. "I want peace," wrote Maitland, "first in order to regain our prisoners, and secondly to enable Ministers to tell Parliament that there is peace. In point of security we are just as well off as though peace were signed." Here Maitland's experience as a member of the House of Commons stood him in good stead; but, notwithstanding all possible moderation in his proposals, he was unable to persuade the powers at Kandy to enter upon any formal discussion of a treaty. He therefore set secret agencies to work in the hope of aiding the prisoners to escape, and contrived not only that letters should be conveyed to Major Davie, but that his answer should be safely brought to hand. That answer told a miserable story. "I, Davie, am the only prisoner left," so it ran, "the rest are all dead, murdered, or starved. I am without meat or clothes. I expect not to survive many days. Do not tell my friends that I am alive." Then followed advice as to the conduct of an expedition to Kandy, with a plan for his escape, and near the end the ominous sentence, "I am told that I am to be murdered when my countrymen come to Kandy."

Maitland's schemes for the captive's escape, though he spared neither pains nor money to make them successful, proved abortive; and for months and years no more was heard of the unfortunate Davie. At home a piteous petition came from his mother, praying for payment of his allowances to herself; for she had six daughters, three of them still unmarried, and no means of support but her son's little estate near Edinburgh, which hungry creditors were threatening to seize. In Ceylon, in the year 1812, when Maitland had left the island and a new General had

1805. come to take his place, there arrived at Colombo two ragged scraps of native paper, bearing a few faint and scarcely legible lines scrawled in pencil by a feeble and exhausted hand.[1] These pitiful fragments, which may still be seen deeply buried among the pompous folios of official despatches, were the last sign that any white man saw of Davie. Maitland's agents soon afterwards reported that he had died at length of dysentery and had been buried secretly in the jungle. If his weakness on his march out of Kandy was culpable, assuredly he atoned for his fault by such a penance as is laid upon few men; for he languished a prisoner for years within one hundred miles of British regiments, which practically on any day could have marched up to deliver him. Yet Thomas Maitland did his duty when he refused to move a man to save him; for it was more important that there should be peace in Ceylon even than that murdered Englishmen should be avenged. While Davie was yet living, Maitland, as shall in place be told, was summoned

[1] Here is the full text.

"*August* 1811.

"Gen. Wilson—Oh be expeditious in saving me. Is there any question that my wishes are to be released hence without delay? I have no means to propose than those formerly mentioned. I have wrote several times within these 10 months and have got three small slips of paper without signature. Messenger is of no use being in (*sic*) daily sick unto death without money, clothes, or food; please send me a little opium or laudanum to alleviate my pains; expect to die daily; could be carried by dooly by way of Gambo and Ganda. [Here follow illegible scraps about mohurs and rupees.] If you no intentions (*sic*) of speedily doing something send me a pair of pistols to terminate my painful existence, twelve months unable to rise from mat [illegible] a pen-knife, a little rum, gin, or brandy and laudanum, stopping at Kalug [illegible] and when night falls sending a party with a dooly might get out of the country [illegible] distance without a shot being fired at as my anguish [illegible]. (signed)

"Ad. Davie."

Second scrap about $4\frac{1}{2} \times 2$ inches.

"My anguish of body is insupportable, and I see but imperfectly my dear friend. No paper. My complaints are [illegible]."

to reinforce the Indian Army at a moment of supreme 1805.
danger, and was able to answer to the call.[1]

So ended this forgotten episode of the Great War, an episode which perhaps may be thought undeserving of the space that has been allotted to it. Yet it came at a most critical time alike for England and for India, when both were required to send to Ceylon regiments which could ill be spared, and both made shift to despatch them; and to India this might well have been of most serious consequence. The losses in action were trifling; yet this futile enterprise, thoughtlessly undertaken and thoughtlessly carried out, must have cost the lives, directly or indirectly, of little fewer than a thousand British soldiers and of fully as many natives, and that at a moment when every soldier's life was precious. The arrival of a French armament before Ceylon in 1805—and North was warned that one was likely to appear in August—would have found the British troops thinned, worn out, and demoralised; while the capture of Trincomalee would have so heartened the Mahrattas and their allies that they might have gone near to sweep the British out of India. None of these things occurred, and the Kandian war of 1803 to 1805 has been utterly forgotten; but it may serve at least as a warning of the mischief that may be done by a foolish Governor seconded by a foolish General.

It is idle to rail at the treachery of the Kandians, and to exalt the good faith and virtuous intentions of the British. Independence is as dear to primitive races as to the most highly civilised nation. Deceit is the natural resource of the weak against the strong, and duplicity has nowhere been carried to such perfection of art as in the East. The story of Kandy is one that will be frequently repeated in this history, the story of a column which marches to an oriental capital with easy triumph, and returns not again. Usually the destruc-

[1] Maitland to the Sec. of State, 19th, 28th July; 4th, 18th, 19th Aug.; 19th, 28th Oct.; 22nd Nov. 1805; 28th Feb.; 20th Sept. 1806.

1805. tion of the first column is followed immediately by the advance of a second ; but it was not so in Ceylon in 1803. The tattered scraps which record Davie's agony are the crown of the whole enterprise ; and it is a crown of thorns. No long time was, however, to elapse before the Kings of Kandy should cease to be, and their historic throne should find a new home in Windsor Castle.

The authorities for this account of the Kandian war are: *Colonial Correspondence*, Ceylon, vols. vii.-xxiv.; and Cordiner's *Description of Ceylon*, vol. ii. The latter is based principally upon official papers, supplemented by private inquiries by the author, and bears strong marks of having been inspired by Governor North.

CHAPTER VI

FROM the troubles in the East, which it has been necessary to follow by anticipation until far into the renewed contest against Napoleon, I return now to England, which we left enjoying the hope rather than the fruition of peace in March 1802. It was somewhat significant that within three weeks of the signature of the Treaty of Amiens the Government thought it necessary to introduce a bill to consolidate the militia-laws and augment the Militia. "The benefits of peace," said Mr. Secretary Yorke, when proposing the measure, "can only be derived from placing the country in a proper position of defence," an eternal truth which for once was accepted by the House of Commons, thanks to the national dread of Bonaparte and the military organisation of France. The establishment of Militia was fixed by this Act at seventy-two thousand men for Great Britain; forty-nine thousand of whom were to be at once enrolled for twenty-one days' training, and the remainder to be called up in case of emergency by proclamation. The bill, of which more shall presently be said, was passed without opposition, rather indeed with the approval of all parties; and the fact was extremely significant. It is true that many prominent members, and notably Fox, were absent from Parliament, being attracted by very pardonable curiosity to the court of the First Consul at Paris. But no one felt any confidence that peace could endure for long; and hence this unique acceptance of the proposition that, in the event of war, England ought to be able to

1802.

1802. lay her hands at once on one hundred thousand men for purposes of defence.[1]

May 4. Not many days later a bill was brought in to enable the country to accept an offer from certain corps of Yeomanry and Volunteers to continue their service; and on this occasion a gentleman was found to protest against the maintenance of such an establishment, "when the country was in a state of profound tranquillity," as "adverse to the ancient constitutional practice of the realm." The unfortunate British Constitution has been invoked as the protectress of many foolish sentiments, but rarely of an opinion quite so foolish as this. However, the voice of this objector passed unheeded, for the times were too serious for the pastime of pedantry; and without further examination at present into its provisions, it must suffice to say that the bill was passed. New estimates were shortly afterwards introduced for the Army; and for the first time in history the regiments were designated to the House of Commons by their numbers as well as by the names of their Colonels; a welcome change, which, slight though it was, signified that the proprietary rights of Colonels were beginning to lose their primeval sacredness. The establishment was fixed at rather over seventy thousand men for the United Kingdom, over twenty-five thousand, including six West India Regiments, for the Colonies, and over twenty-six thousand for India; which, added to ten thousand artillerymen, made a total of over one hundred and thirty-two thousand men. The regiments of cavalry included, besides the Household regiments and those of Dragoon Guards, twenty-three regiments of Dragoons, the three last being those which we have seen fighting with such distinction in India. Among the infantry neither the Ninetieth, the Ninety-second, nor the Ninety-third found a place, the order for their disbandment having gone forth on the 6th of May; but the Scots Brigade still bore prophetically the number Ninety-four, and Manningham's Rifles, at a

[1] *Parl. Hist.* xxxvi. 535 *sq.*

ridiculously low strength, were still at hand to claim 1802. that of Ninety-five. Fencible corps had received their death-warrant at the same time as the Ninetieth; and second battalions were passed or passing into the first battalions of their own or of other regiments. But these estimates were calculated to be valid only from June to December; and many things were to happen before December.

As has already been told, the first alarm to the Ministry was given by Bonaparte's expedition to St. Domingo. But Bonaparte, unfortunately for himself, had always a new project upon the stocks before the first was fairly launched. Now, in the negotiations at Amiens the King of Sardinia had been one of the potentates for whom the British envoy had made special efforts, in the hope of gaining for him some indemnity for the territory which the French had taken from him in Italy and merged in the Italian Republic. On the 21st Sept. 21. of September 1802 Bonaparte by formal decree annexed Piedmont to France, thus reducing the dominions of the King to the island from which he took his title. Valid excuse for this proceeding there was none; but there was a sufficiently valid reason in that the possession of Piedmont assured that of the pass of Mont Cenis. A month later, upon the death of the Duke of Parma, his duchy was likewise annexed to France, though Bonaparte had raised the legitimate heir to the rank of King of Etruria, and had thereby gained from Spain the vast province of Louisiana. Finally the First Consul laid violent hands on a country which appealed far more than Piedmont or Parma to the sympathy of the British of all parties. Ever since the first interference of the Directory with Switzerland in 1798, that unhappy land had been impoverished and oppressed by the presence of large bodies of French troops. Its independence, and its right as the Helvetian republic to decide upon its own form of government, had been guaranteed by the Treaty of Lunéville; but still the French battalions remained in their old quarters and

1802. showed particular reluctance to loosen their hold upon Swiss ground. The result was that the unfortunate people were unable to arrive by any peaceful process at a decision regarding the government which they really required. There were two parties in the country, of which the one favoured a strong centralised administration, and the other the retention of large independent powers by each canton. This latter had, for very good reasons, been the system of the old Swiss Confederacy. But, as fast as one party came into power, the French authorities after a few months arranged or connived at a revolution to displace it, so as to keep the country in continual commotion and afford constant pretexts for the intervention of Bonaparte. The truth was that his heart was set upon gaining possession of Valais in order to construct a military road over the Simplon pass; and until he could obtain this he was not disposed to relax his grip upon Switzerland. At length in July he was prevailed upon to withdraw his troops, and to leave the country to determine for itself the form of its government. The issue was submitted to the vote of the whole body of the people; and the majority against centralisation was so great as to leave no room for further doubt. None the less the minority refused to accept their defeat, whereupon their opponents rushed to arms, and were in mid career of a victorious enforcement of their vote at the polls, when Bonaparte
Sept. 30. suddenly interfered. His troops once again crossed the frontier; and he declared that the new Constitution of Switzerland must be arranged at Paris under his mediation.

So shameless a violation of the Treaty of Lunéville naturally caused agitation at every court in Europe; but the excitement was short-lived. Prussia, in the hope of gaining further territory in Germany, was too abjectly subservient to the First Consul to protest. Austria was too jealous of Prussia to think of Switzerland; Russia showed indifference; and England alone stood out heartily for the cause of Swiss independence. So seriously did Addington's Ministry treat the question that vessels were at once despatched to the West Indies, the East Indies, and the Cape to cancel, until further directions, the orders for the restitution of the Dutch and French colonies ; and, as has been seen, Pondicherry and Chandernagore were still in the hands of the British when the war was renewed. But, finding themselves unsupported by other powers, the British Ministers gave way about Switzerland ; and fresh commands were issued for the redelivery of the French and Dutch colonies to their former masters. Bonaparte then regulated the new Constitution of Switzerland according to his own ideas, which were calculated, as a Swiss patriot complained, to assure to the country all domestic happiness, but to annihilate it as a political factor in Europe. 1802.

The Swiss difficulty was only one of a series which were beginning to arise between England and France. French troops still continued to occupy Holland, though nominally the Batavian Republic was independent ; and this was a matter upon which the British were peculiarly sensitive. Moreover, commercial relations between the two countries were strained ; for Bonaparte, less perhaps from unfriendliness than from extreme ignorance of everything pertaining to trade, had determined to shut out British goods from all markets controlled by France. Remonstrance from England upon any one of these matters was met at once on the part of the First Consul by the demand that the British should evacuate Malta. But on this point the Ministry stood firm. It had been weak enough to restore its conquests in the New World even in the face of Bonaparte's high-handed proceedings in Europe ; but the experience of the last war had shown that, under existing conditions, the Mediterranean was the true field of operations for England against France ; and Addington was not disposed lightly to yield up Malta. In fact Lord Whitworth, our ambassador in Paris, held instructions

1802. which empowered him practically to claim Malta as indemnity for the various annexations of France.

All this, however, was hidden from the country at large, or at any rate Ministers seemed to think so. A new Parliament met in November, and was opened by a speech from the Throne so colourless that no one, on reading it, could have guessed that England had not for years been living in a state of profound peace. Grenville in the Lords and Windham in the Commons, as became men who had disapproved the Peace of Amiens, did indeed call attention to Bonaparte's proceedings in the bitterest terms; but Pitt was silent; Fox, of course, took the opposite view; and, after the effusion of a suitable volume of prose by Addington, the address of thanks was passed with little ceremony. When, however, the estimates came up for discussion in the first week of December, the case was different. For the Navy, Ministers had begun by proposing thirty thousand seamen. This number they suddenly increased to fifty thousand, alleging first that the additional twenty thousand would be wanted for a few months only, but finally asking for them as part of the establishment for the year.[1] The estimates for the Army likewise testified to a certain uneasiness. The Secretary at War began by reciting at length the various forces of France, setting down their total at over nine hundred thousand men, after which he asked money for an establishment of over one hundred and forty-three thousand men; sixty-six thousand of them for the United Kingdom, twenty-three thousand for India, forty-two thousand for the Colonies, and twelve thousand artillery. Of those detailed for service at home five thousand represented the men who had formerly been called Invalids, and had been organised into independent companies. They were now distributed into seven Garrison Battalions. Among the troops abroad were over three thousand foreigners, comprehending the regiments, nominally Swiss, of

[1] *Parl. Hist.* xxxvi. 1054.

Meuron, Rohan and Watteville, together with Stuart's battalion, at first Minorquin but now composed chiefly of Germans, which had distinguished itself so greatly in Egypt. Lastly eight thousand volunteers, principally cavalry, had enrolled themselves for continued service in England, and nearly thrice that number in Ireland ; and altogether it was reckoned that the country could count upon two hundred thousand men, exclusive of the troops in India. 1802.

It is satisfactory to be able to add that the Commons showed no backwardness to vote the money required of them. Bonaparte's treatment of Switzerland had so incensed all parties that even Sheridan gave his voice heartily for a large military force. Fox almost alone advocated a reduction, making light of any idea of invasion, and apparently contemplating with perfect serenity a disembarkation of Bonaparte in England with fifty thousand men, which he declared to be the largest possible army that could be conveyed across the Channel in the relative state of the forces of England and France. He even committed himself to the characteristic proposition that by maintaining twenty-five thousand men less, the country would shortly gain twenty-five million pounds more to apply to her defence against aggression. It is precisely from acting upon this fallacious opinion that England has built up her national debt. Fox must have known perfectly well that time as well as money is needed to produce trained and disciplined soldiers, and that no number of millions can abridge that time. Pitt took no part in the debate ; and, seeing that he had actually reduced the Army in 1792, he was probably prudent to hold his peace when ten years later his great rival proposed to outdo that egregious blunder.

Meanwhile at Paris matters were coming rapidly to a crisis. Since the publication of Sebastiani's menacing report as to Egypt, Lord Whitworth had been instructed to declare that England would not evacuate Malta until reassured as to Bonaparte's designs upon the

1803. valley of the Nile and the Ottoman Empire at large.
Feb. 18. The First Consul thereupon took the occasion of a reception at the Tuileries to treat Whitworth to a torrent of menace and invective which lasted for nearly two hours. Such an outburst was ill-calculated to produce any great impression upon an English gentleman, who was not to be intimidated, and was, perhaps, not ill-pleased to see how low so great and formidable
Feb. 20. a man could abase himself. But two days later Bonaparte addressed an inflated message to his own Legislative Assemblies upon the state of the Republic, in which his threats were renewed. "In England," he said, "there are two parties that struggle for power; one of them has made peace, the other has sworn implacable hatred to France. While this strife of parties continues, the Republic must take its measures of precaution. Half a million men must be and shall be ready to defend and avenge her. . . . England will never be able to draw other nations into new coalitions. . . . Alone England cannot stand up against France." This, together with Whitworth's report of the scene at the Tuileries, roused the spirit of the British Ministers and still more that of the King. On the
Mar. 8. 8th of March a Royal message was brought down to both Houses setting forth the need for measures to countervail the preparations which were said to be going forward in the ports of France and Holland. As a matter of fact those preparations were as yet trifling;[1] and Bonaparte's activity was more easily to be traced at home, where French spies and agents of disaffection had been freely dispersed both in England
Mar. 9. and in Ireland. However, the message was met by an unanimous address of thanks from both Houses; Fox carping but not opposing in the Commons, and Moira warmly supporting in the Lords. Bonaparte used this proceeding as a pretext for another violent
Mar. 13. address to Whitworth, which was only cut short by the freezing silence of the Ambassador; but the First

[1] Desbrière, *Projets et tentatives de débarquement*, iii. 6-8.

Consul did not deceive himself as to the true meaning 1803.
of the situation, and sent a despatch-vessel in all haste Mar. 16.
to divert Decaen's expedition from Pondicherry to Mauritius. He had made the enormous blunder of treating the Court of St. James's as if it had been the Court of Naples; and the result was that the renewal of hostilities was not to await his good pleasure until October 1804, but was to be forced upon him at once, while his preparations were still incomplete, and his great West Indian expedition hopelessly compromised. The British Ministry made a last effort to come to an understanding; but Bonaparte was so furious at the British retention of Malta, as a pledge for proper concessions from France, that no one durst broach the matter to him. He made a final attempt by a shallow device to gain time; but Whitworth was not to be hoodwinked;
and on the 16th of May 1803 England declared war. May 16.

The First Consul instantly retorted by an order that all Englishmen in France between the ages of eighteen and sixty should be detained as prisoners of war. The pretext for this decree, which condemned some ten thousand innocent men to indefinite detention and in many cases to ruin, was that two French merchantmen had been captured by British frigates before the declaration of hostilities. This, as was so frequent with Bonaparte's statements, was entirely and demonstrably false. There was no excuse for this outrageous action; there was no reason for it except the spiteful rage of an ungovernable man who had been unable to have his own way. It is too often forgotten that Bonaparte the First Consul could be quite as mean and petty, when thwarted, as Bonaparte the captive of St. Helena. The result of the decree was that England entered upon the war not only with indignation but with intense and implacable hatred.

Since the crisis in Switzerland, Ministers had suspended many of the reductions ordered in the Army. The disbandment of the Ninetieth, Ninety-second, and Ninety-third, as well as of the second

1803. battalion of the Fifty-second, had been revoked between October and December 1802; and the last named was in January erected into a separate regiment and numbered the Ninety-sixth. The Cavalry and Guards had also been slightly augmented in March, so that preparations were far less backward than usual at the beginning of a war, and the Ministry could take the offensive at once. There was no doubt as to the quarter in which the first blow should be struck. In St. Domingo the French were barely holding their own against the negroes, and their chief support was the fleet under Admiral Latouche Tréville which lay at Cap François. Before the French ships could escape, Admiral Duckworth had brought his squadron to blockade them, thus not only hemming in the ships but cutting off all supplies from the troops ashore. This was a serious matter, for, unless they have been grievously maligned, many of the French generals used the campaign simply as a means of enriching themselves by plunder and embezzlement.[1] The negroes welcomed the unexpected aid of the British exultingly; and Duckworth's cruisers played havoc among the French transports and smaller men-of-war which were on the coast. A frigate with a General Morgan and five hundred French troops on board was the first capture; and Morgan reported that the army and the fleet together had already lost sixty thousand men since the first invasion of the island. Within a week or two the Commandant of the French garrison at Léogane entreated the Captain of H.M.S. *Racoon* to take himself and his men on board as captives; and he was refused only because the frigate, already encumbered by prisoners from a captured transport, could hold no more. Then the *Duquesne*, a French seventy-four, tried to escape from Cap François, but was taken; though a more fortunate consort, the *Duguay Trouin*, together with a frigate, contrived to sail safely away. The

[1] Intercepted letter from Commissaire Ordonnateur Colbert to Rochambeau, enclosed in Nugent to Sec. of State, 20th May 1804.

garrison of Jérémie, driven from its post by the negroes, and not by negroes only but by some hundreds of Poles and Germans, deserters from the French army, surrendered to a British man-of-war, and was brought to Jamaica. Other detachments submitted to the like fate, and on the 30th of November the garrison of Cap François yielded themselves to the British fleet as prisoners. By the end of the year nothing was left of the French army but a garrison, strictly blockaded by the English, in the town of St. Domingo itself. Of the soldiers and seamen by far the greater number were dead. Of the survivors seven thousand, including one thousand officers, were prisoners in Jamaica, where over five hundred Germans and Poles entered the ranks of the Sixtieth. Three hundred invalids, left behind in hospital at Cap François, were placed on board a ship and sent to the bottom by the negroes. A few soldiers escaped to America, and about eleven hundred to Havanna, where they were hospitably received by the Spaniards. But still misfortune dogged the poor wretches to the end. Eight hundred of these last sailed in four transports from Havanna to Carolina. One of these ships with four hundred men on board was captured by the escort of a British convoy; two more were lost with every soul on board in the Bahama Keys, and one only was left to pursue her solitary course. As to the men-of-war, the greater number found their way as prizes to Port Royal, which was full of captured vessels of all kinds; and thus ignominiously ended Bonaparte's expedition to St. Domingo.

1803.

Nov. 30.

History has been strangely silent as to this enterprise, and yet surely it must be reckoned as one of the most disastrous ever recorded. It is probably within the truth to say that it cost France forty thousand good soldiers and sailors not disabled but dead; but even so this is not the most terrible part of the story. There are signs enough in the English archives alone to show that the conduct of the senior officers was infamous. "Your predecessors," wrote Commissaire Colbert to

1803. Rochambeau on his arrival, "have committed atrocities which I cannot trust myself to speak of. Our magazines are empty. I show you[1] what we have legitimately consumed and what our generals have embezzled. Sarrazin and La Valette are governed only by the most cruel egoism and the most sordid avarice. . . . The Generals have done their best to oppress the people and make the soldier discontented. The officers and men are groaning under terrible misery and want. La Valette and the head of the Administration think only of enriching themselves and giving favours to their Creole girls." Add to this that not only two educated mulattoes, one of whom had come out with Leclerc as a general of division, but several hundred white men, were driven by maltreatment to take sides with the brigands, and also that Rochambeau by his cruelties gained for himself the name of Robespierre, and we can form some idea of the degradation to which a French army could sink even under one of the greatest military administrators that ever lived. It may be pleaded that Napoleon, being in Paris, was not responsible. No doubt much of the rascality and embezzlement was kept hidden from him; yet it was he who gave the tone for the deliberate and perfidious maltreatment of the blacks which was at the root of all the mischief; and he cannot have been ignorant of the outrageous oppression practised by his generals. The like evils had flourished among British officers for a time during their occupation of St. Domingo, but never among the Generals; and, upon the first suspicion at home of such mischief, Simcoe and Maitland were sent out to restore order with a stern hand. Beyond doubt a little severity would speedily have recalled the French also to a sense of their duty; for it would be absurd to suppose that originally they were in any way inferior to the British. Yet it is certain that they sank far below the British in demoral-

[1] Evidently the letter was accompanied by returns, which are not now to be found.

isation; and that the British officers in Jamaica, who 1802. usually were glad to meet their gallant brethren of France, could not bring themselves to consort with the prisoners of St. Domingo. "Their generals as a rule," wrote General Nugent from Jamaica, "are a low ignorant set of people who talk of nothing but their own prowess and the supremacy of the Great Nation. . . . The incapacity and atrocious conduct of their chiefs in St. Domingo are proverbial." Yet these were the men sent out, with excellent soldiers under them, by Bonaparte; and the fact is a very grave reflection upon either his honesty or his judgment.[1]

But it was not only to leeward that the British Ministers turned their eyes. Pitt's example was still before them, and the conquest of the French Windward islands promised to be easy, for on that side also Bonaparte's treacherous policy towards the negroes had borne fruit. Martinique, it is true, had been taken over from the British practically unchanged; but when Richepanse came before Guadeloupe in April 1802 he found the two divisions of the island, Grande Terre and Basse Terre, each under the rule of a mulatto. In Grande Terre the French troops were received without opposition, but in Basse Terre they were defied, and for a time successfully. In truth the French force was so abominably ill-provided and equipped that Richepanse was forced to buy clothing and shoes wherever he could find them, and even to borrow ammunition from the British. However, by the end of May he had virtually crushed all resistance, though with the loss of about two thousand out of three thousand French troops, dead or disabled in action or by sickness. In fact it was mainly by the exertions of a corps of black troops under a chief named Pelage that Richepanse finally prevailed; yet no sooner had this force done its work than the French General ordered every man of it to be embarked and

[1] *Col. Corres.* Jamaica. Nugent to Sec. of State, 21st July, 9th Sept., 8th Oct., 19th Nov., 19th, 21st, 25th Dec. 1803; 14th Jan., 10th, 11th March, 20th May, 10th June 1804.

1802. deported to Rattan, from whence there was every prospect that they would ultimately be shipped off to the mines on the Spanish Main. Before the hurricane season was ended Richepanse was dead of yellow fever; but his successor, as was natural, steadily carried forward the disarmament of the negroes, regarding all black regiments as an accursed thing. He was really only trying to execute Bonaparte's avowed policy of re-establishing slavery.[1]

It was therefore tolerably certain that the French negroes would not take up arms with any great enthusiasm for their new commanders; and, apart from this, the extreme aversion of the French authorities from black troops worked by a curious chain of circumstances greatly to their damage and to the profit of the British. In April 1802 the British islands were startled by the news that on the night of
April 9. the 9th the Eighth West India Regiment at Dominica had risen in mutiny, and had murdered three of their officers and the whole of their white non-commissioned officers with shocking and hideous mutilation. The mutineers were quelled after a short pitched battle which cost them over one hundred casualties and their assailants nearly thirty killed and wounded. A court of inquiry was held, and it was discovered that the mutiny was due to an idea that the regiment was to be disbanded and the negroes sold as slaves; the Governor, a certain Mr. Cochrane Johnston—who gained later an unpleasant notoriety—having employed the men in clearing the jungle off his estate, nominally for purposes of fortification, without giving them working pay. Such a practice was strictly contrary to the orders of the General in command, who knew the value of the West India Regiments and desired nothing more strongly than to raise the self-respect of the black soldiers who composed them. Before the news of this mutiny could reach England, orders came from

[1] C.O. *Windward and Leeward Islands*, General Trigge to Sec. of State, 17th, 24th, 30th May, 11th June, 1st, 10th July 1802.

the Colonial Office for the West India Regiments 1802. to be reduced from twelve to six, upon the conclusion of peace, by the simple process of disbandment. The execution of these directions would, in the circumstances, have been dangerous, for it would have confirmed the general suspicions which had caused the outbreak in Dominica, and would probably have brought about a mutiny of the remaining regiments. With great good sense General Trigge had issued an order to reassure the negroes, directing that his own guard should always be formed from the two West India Regiments at headquarters; and he resolved at any rate not to precipitate the disbandment. Still the position was difficult, for England was nominally at peace and the British public would certainly be clamouring for the reduction of establishments; and it therefore occurred to Trigge, since one of the regiments had been raised in Martinique, to offer it to the French authorities, provided that the men were willing to take service with them. The answer, as might be expected, was an uncompromising rejection by the French of any such proposal; and it was finally decided not to risk the danger of disbandment, but to draft the men of the last six West India Regiments into the first six, and to allow time to reduce their numbers.[1]

Hence it was that at the outbreak of the war the 1803. West India Regiments were still in fair strength; while, owing to the delay in restoring the captured islands to the French, there was an unusually large force of white troops at disposal for work in the field. In April there were, in the Windward and Leeward Islands, not far from ten thousand men of all ranks and colours fit for duty, of whom between three and four thousand could be spared for active operations. Nor was the British Government negligent in giving early warning that war was approaching, for General Grinfield, who

[1] Trigge to Sec. of State, 16th, 23rd, 30th April, 4th, 29th May, 13th June, 1st, 10th July; Grinfield to Sec. of State, 17th Sept.; Sec. of State to Trigge, 6th May 1802.

1803. had succeeded Trigge in the chief command, began to prepare for all emergencies before the end of April 1803. By the beginning of June a rupture seemed so certain to the British in the West Indies that one of the British cruisers detained a French transport, which was carrying troops to Martinique, and sent her to Barbados. Grinfield also embarked six weeks' supplies for four thousand men, and Commodore Hood made every arrangement for the embarkation of the men themselves at twenty-four hours' notice. About the middle of the month arrived the news of the declaration of war, with orders for attack upon Martinique, St. Lucia, and Tobago, each or all of them. Grinfield at once summoned the
June 20. Commodore, who arrived on the 17th of June; and on the 20th the fleet and transports got under way and made all sail to leeward.

The British Ministry had been over-sanguine in expecting the conquest of Martinique, which, well-garrisoned as it was, required ten thousand men to master it; but St. Lucia and Tobago were within the powers of Grinfield's force, and the former being the more important as a check on Fort Royal, was clearly marked out as his first object. He had three thousand excellent troops,[1] with at least two senior officers who were of more than ordinary ability. These were Thomas Picton, who was on his way home from Trinidad after enduring shameful persecution by certain malignant commissioners sent out from England, and Edward Pakenham, who was destined after a brilliant career to fall before New Orleans. By day-

[1] Staff	17
2/1st	487
64th	744
68th	765
3rd W.I.R.	714
Royal Artillery, with 14 field-guns and 16 siege-guns	271
Royal Military Artificers	80
Black Pioneers	71
Total of all ranks	3149

break of the 21st the armament was off St. Lucia, and 1803.
during the course of the day the greater part of the June 21.
force was disembarked in Anse du Choc, the bay which lies immediately to the north of Castries. In the evening the enemy's outposts were driven in, and a summons was sent to the French commander on Morne Fortuné. This officer, General Nogués, was very much inclined to surrender; for the inhabitants of St. Lucia had welcomed the British with open arms. Indeed the Prefect and several officers actually entertained Grinfield and his staff at supper, not without friendly messages from the General himself. Duty, however, prevailed with Nogués, who finally returned an answer of defiance; and at four o'clock on the morning of the
22nd the British attacked the fortress in two columns June 22.
under Brigadiers Prevost and Brereton, and carried it, despite a spirited resistance, in half an hour. The Royal Scots and Sixty-fourth bore the brunt of the work, Pakenham being wounded at the head of the latter; but the fortifications were in too ruinous a condition to be very formidable, and the casualties did not exceed one hundred and thirty-eight.[1] The troops on both sides became very friendly directly after the surrender; and, when the six hundred prisoners had been embarked for France, Nogués and a few of his officers gratefully accepted permission to retire to Martinique. Altogether the first contest in the new war was marked by the best of good feelings.[2]

Leaving General Brereton with the Sixty-eighth and three companies of negroes to hold St. Lucia, Grinfield
sailed again on the 25th, and at daybreak on the 30th June 30.
made Tobago. By five in the evening the troops were landed, when they at once marched straight upon the town. A dangerous defile on the way being found

[1] 20 men killed, 9 officers and 109 men wounded.
2/1st, 9 men killed, 2 officers and 45 men wounded.
64th, 6 " " 4 " " 34 " "
3rd W.I.R., 2 " " 23 " "

[2] Sec. of State to Grinfield, 7th, 16th May; Grinfield to Sec. of State, 28th April, 9th, 10th, 20th, 22nd, 24th June 1803.

1803. June 30. unguarded, Grinfield took the hint and at once sent a summons to General César Berthier, who capitulated forthwith with the honours of war. Berthier had indeed no choice in the matter, for his garrison numbered but two hundred men, half of them sailors, while the whole of the population was hostile to him. He revealed, however, to Grinfield that his orders had been to fortify Man-of-War Bay thoroughly and to make the island a French naval depot, with a garrison of twelve hundred men. This plan, if fulfilled, would have placed Trinidad and the whole of the southern islands at his mercy.

Eight companies of the Royal Scots and a company of negroes were left at Tobago; and therewith Grinfield prudently returned to Barbados. The conquest of islands might be easy, but the supplying of garrisons in such a climate was a costly process, and might become still more costly if the French, with a powerful force at Martinique, should attempt reprisals. There was, of course, a British squadron to windward, and Commodore Hood was an active and zealous officer; but his ships were not too many, and Antigua and Dominica lay invitingly close to Guadeloupe and Martinique. Moreover, the Assembly of Antigua, with characteristic perversity, was declining to vote any money for its defence or to call out its militia; and Grinfield, like other commanders in the West Indies before him, was beginning to discover the difficulties of guarding the precious sugar-islands. Ships passed in and out of their harbours, he knew not on what errand, and he had not the slightest power to stop them. The forts, though garrisoned by the King, were mostly Colonial property, and as such owned no master but the civil government. Signals were likewise under the domain of the Colonial authorities, and all flags of truce were claimed by the civil Governor as concerning him only. In fact all control was in civil hands, but all responsibility for protection against the enemy was thrown on military shoulders. Yet this was the sphere and these were the conditions in which Pitt delighted to make war.[1] 1803.

Nor did Addington lag behind his great master. Before Grinfield had been at Barbados a week there arrived fresh orders from England. Victor Hugues had recently visited the Dutch settlements on the main- July 20.
land; and the Dutch planters, dreading a repetition of the scenes which had troubled Guadeloupe in 1794, had appealed to England for protection. Ministers promised to afford it; and accordingly on the 10th of June Lord Hobart instructed Grinfield to make immediate arrangements for taking over Demerara, Berbice, and Surinam, summoning the Governors to surrender and attacking them if they refused. Since the Batavian Republic was dragged into war against England a week later, the General was of course at liberty to attempt the capture of Curaçoa also, if he thought fit. Grinfield, like all officers, was eager for active service; but on receiving the first conditional orders for the expedition to the Dutch colonies, he very rightly pointed out to Ministers that they might not be aware what they were doing. St. Lucia and Tobago had already swallowed up nearly two thousand of his men; and the occupation of Demerara in addition would not only deprive him of the whole of his expeditionary force but would leave all his garrisons dangerously weak. The Government had promised to send him one battalion from Gibraltar, and he had been able to save three hundred negroes from a regiment that had been doomed to disbandment; but to make good the daily losses from sickness in the islands, quite apart from those sustained on active service, he would need reinforcements of at least five thousand men.[2]

All this the Government knew or should have known without Grinfield's information; but it either ignored

[1] Grinfield to Sec. of State, 1st, 5th, 15th July, 11th Aug. 1803.

[2] Sec. of State to Grinfield, 30th May, 10th, 16th June 1803; Grinfield to Sec. of State (private), 24th June 1803.

1803. or defied these plain facts, and committed itself, without hesitation, to a large permanent increase of the West Indian garrisons. The General waited over a month for his promised battalion from Gibraltar, but in vain; the fact being that it had never received its orders to go to the West Indies. At last, at the end of August, he decided to eke out his force with Marines and to delay the attack on Demerara no longer, having ascertained with tolerable certainty that the Colony would make
Sept. 1. no resistance. He sailed accordingly on the 1st of September with some thirteen hundred men,[1] and anchoring off Georgetown on the 16th, sent an offer of good terms which brought about the surrender of
Sept. 20. Demerara and Essequibo. A detachment of five hundred and fifty men received the capitulation of Berbice a few
Sept. 25. days later; and thus three rich but pestilent possessions were gained not only with no loss, but with actual increase of the British force. For the Dutch garrisons numbered fifteen hundred men, half of whom, rather than starve, were well content to enter the British service, which they did under the name of the York Light Infantry Volunteers.[2]

With this the operations of 1803 in the West Indies came to an end. The deaths from sickness in the Windward and Leeward Islands during the last six months of 1803 numbered close upon seven hundred, or more than nine per cent of the force, though the season was by no means remarkably unhealthy. One of the Brigadiers, Clephane, died before he had been in the Antilles three months, and Grinfield had hardly reported this death before he too, with his work still in-
Nov. 19. complete, succumbed to yellow fever. But the Government had not yet done with conquests. Early in November the Sixteenth and Forty-sixth regiments, both of them strong battalions, were ordered to the

[1] Artillery, 90; R. Military Artificers, 30; 64th, 983; detachments of the 3rd, 7th, and 11th W.I.R., 208. Total 1311 of all ranks.

[2] Grinfield to Sec. of State, 17th, 29th Aug., 22nd, 27th, 28th Sept., 16th Oct., 4th Nov. 1803.

West Indies; and though in January 1804 a sudden order was despatched from London that no further operations were to be undertaken, yet on the arrival of these two regiments and of a new Commander-in-chief, Sir Charles Green, towards the end of March, an expedition was at once arranged for the capture of Surinam. The people of that settlement were believed to be friendly, but the secret of the project had been allowed to leak out, so that it was necessary to employ a large and imposing force. During the last weeks of March both Green and Commodore Hood worked strenuously at their preparations; and on the 7th of April the armament, numbering over two thousand troops,[1] sailed before the trade wind from Barbados, and anchored on the 25th off the Surinam River.[2]

1804. March. April 7. April 25.

Paramaribo, the capital of Dutch Guiana and in those days a thriving town of twenty thousand inhabitants, lies about twenty miles up the Surinam. This great river, though swelled to a breadth of two or three miles at its mouth by the influx of a large tributary, the Commewyne, is full of banks and shoals, which render its navigation difficult. It was therefore by no means a formidable task to defend the passage, and, if the waterway were closed, effective entrance into the

[1] Advanced Corps. Flank companies of the 16th and 64th.
Rifle companies 2/60th and York L.I. Volrs.
Light company 6th W.I.R.

1st Brigade.	Advanced corps, 493 16th Foot, 573	Brig.-Gen. Fred Maitland.
2nd Brigade.	64th Foot, 604 6th W.I.R., 305	Brig.-Gen. Hughes.
Royal Artillery	. . . 106.	
Ordnance.	6 light six-pounders 2 ,, three ,,	4 howitzers, $5\frac{1}{2}$ in. 4 ,, ,, light.
	2 medium twelve-pounders 2 light twelve-pounders	1 mortar, 8 inch. 2 mortars, 10 inch.

Royal Artificers, 26; Black Pioneers, 20; Staff, 21.
Total. 2148 of all ranks.

[2] Grinfield to Sec. of State, 4th, 9th Nov.; Brig.-Gen. Fred Maitland to Sec. of State, 19th Nov. 1803; Green to Sec. of State, 22nd March, 2nd April 1804; Sec. of State to Gen. Moncrieff, 2nd Jan. 1804.

1804. Colony was practically impossible; for the country, though a level plain, was marshy and overgrown with thick jungle for some distance inland from the sea. For defence of the river, therefore, the Dutch engineers had constructed a series of powerful works. The first of these was a battery of seven eighteen-pounders situated at Bram's Point, at the eastern side of the entrance to the river. Further up the stream stood Fort Amsterdam, mounting altogether eighty guns, which was placed on the southern bank of the Commewyne at the point of its confluence with the Surinam. Over against it to northward, and at about two thousand yards' distance on the opposite bank of the Commewyne, stood Fort Leyden, armed with twelve heavy guns; and another work called Frederick's Battery, also of twelve heavy guns, lay about a mile below Fort Leyden. Nearly opposite to Fort Amsterdam, on the western bank of the Surinam, stood Fort Purmerend, containing ten heavy guns, and having its flanks and rear protected by a marsh. Further up, and on the same bank, stood Fort Zeelandia, a battery of ten guns, for the immediate defence of Paramaribo. The whole of these works could bring a cross-fire to bear upon the one channel by which ships could ascend the river; and the problem set to Green was to open a passage for the fleet in despite of them.

April 26. On the 26th the Advanced Corps, augmented to six hundred rank and file by men of the Sixteenth, Sixty-fourth, and Sixth West India Regiment, and by one brigade (or, as we should now say, one battery) of light artillery, was detached on different ships under General Maitland's command to Warappa Creek, about thirty miles to east of the Surinam. Maitland's orders were to land, find communication by water with Commewyne Creek, collect boats enough from the various plantations to carry his troops down the Commewyne to its junction with the Surinam, take up a position in rear of Fort Amsterdam, and cut off a strong detachment of the enemy which was stationed in a less important work hard by. On the same day 1804. the men-of-war *Pandora* and *Emerald* engaged and silenced the fort at Bram's Point, whereupon a small party of the Sixty-fourth landed and took possession, capturing over forty of the garrison. The ships then entered the river, and Green sent a summons to the Governor to surrender. He was answered on the 28th with defiance, and proceeded at once with the April 28. task before him.

His chief difficulty was that, owing to the shallowness of the river, landing was everywhere difficult except at the top of the tide, and below Fort Frederick was almost impossible on account of the marshes and jungle on the banks. On the 28th he tried to disembark a force for the capture of Fort Purmerend, but was completely foiled by the unfavourable state of the tide; and it was not until the following day that he obtained April 29. information of a path which led through the woods upon the rear of Fort Leyden and Frederick's Battery. On that night between ten and eleven o'clock Brigadier-general Hughes with one hundred and eighty men, chiefly of the Sixty-fourth, besides a party of black pioneers carrying axes, landed quietly and entered the bush under the guidance of some native negroes. Heavy rain had rendered the path nearly impassable, and it was only after five hours of an intensely fatiguing march that the column at last approached the rear of Frederick's Battery. The alarm was given in the fort, and a heavy fire of grape was poured upon the men as they deployed, which was seconded by musketry as they advanced; but they speedily entered the work and swept the enemy out with the bayonet. The fugitives fled to Fort Leyden, though not before they had kindled the powder-magazines, which presently exploded, killing and wounding many of the British. Hughes, however, quickly rallying his little force, pushed on to Fort Leyden along a narrow road which was enfiladed by the enemy's guns, and charging up to the Battery in face of a

1804. April 29. furious fire, captured over one hundred and twenty prisoners. Thus the defences of the eastern bank north of the Commewyne were secured, and with them a position from which Fort Amsterdam could be cannonaded and communication assured with Maitland's detachment.

April 30. The following day was employed in throwing up shelters in the captured works against the fire of Fort Amsterdam, which, however, was soon silenced when two British mortars were brought into play; and on the same evening Green received intelligence that Maitland had accomplished his disembarkation successfully, having defeated a small party of the enemy which guarded the landing-place at Warappa Creek, and captured two guns. Accordingly in the course of the
May 1, 2. next two days the bulk of the force that still remained upon the ships landed at Fort Leyden, and marched for some distance up the north bank of the Commewyne
May 3. to await the arrival of Maitland. On the 3rd Maitland appeared, with his entire column afloat, passing comfortably down the Commewyne, as had been prearranged. He presently landed on the south bank; and, his boats being thus released, Green's troops were likewise transferred from the north to the south bank. The operation was not completed till the afternoon of
May 4. the 4th, when Maitland advanced by a road through the jungle to within a mile of Fort Amsterdam, and drove in the enemy's advanced parties. Shortly afterwards a flag of truce reached Green, and on the
May 5. following day Surinam was delivered over to him by capitulation. His casualties were trifling, as were also those of Commodore Hood, the total number of killed and wounded in Army and Navy not exceeding thirty, though of these no fewer than ten were officers. The enemy's force numbered about thirteen hundred white troops and four hundred negroes, besides the crews of two small men-of-war, which brought the full roll of the defenders up to two thousand men. With such strength, and with over two hundred and eighty guns of

one kind and another, the Dutch should have made a 1804. better resistance, but for the fact that their officers were divided among themselves. Ministers in England had supposed that the province would be delivered up at once by a people eager for protection; but, as usual, not a man of the inhabitants would move to help the British until he saw that they were likely to be successful. Addington's Cabinet had made the old mistake, so often made by Pitt and Dundas between 1793 and 1801; and only by good fortune did it fail to be again disastrous.

With Victor Hugues at Cayenne, Green judged it imprudent to leave fewer than fifteen hundred men to guard the new conquest; though he was fortunate enough to enlist some hundreds of the Dutch soldiers into the British service. But none the less here was another hostage given to fortune, and another British battalion relegated to a distant station where the annual casualties by sickness and death could not be reckoned at less than one-third of the whole. Nor was this all; for still earlier in 1804 England had only narrowly escaped being saddled with Curaçoa as well as Surinam. Admiral Duckworth, without saying a word to General Nugent at Jamaica, had sailed in January to Curaçoa with two line-of-battle ships, as many frigates, and a schooner, intent upon playing the general. Landing eight hundred men without artillery, he found himself powerless against a garrison of six hundred men within fortifications, failed to make the slightest impression upon the defences, and was fain to re-embark his men ignobly and sail away. Had he but communicated his ideas to the General, he would have received a few gunners and mortars, with which, as he himself acknowledged, he would have forced the Dutch to surrender in two or three days. Having, however, like most naval officers in those days, a keen and pardonable taste for prize-money, he tried to be soldier as well as sailor and, very fortunately for all parties, over-reached himself. But for Pitt's mistaken

1804. policy during the last war, the gallant officer would have been less eager to capture sugar-islands without orders from the Cabinet.

In truth Surinam, superadded to previous conquests, was already far too much. The Commander-in-chief to Windward naturally begged for reinforcements as soon as the Colony had fallen, sending a return which showed his entire force to be eleven thousand men, scattered over thirteen different islands and settlements, with a sick list, which he truly pronounced to be normal, of two thousand. In September the Secretary of State promised him two battalions; "but," he added, "every soldier is imperatively needed to repel a possible invasion of England by France." Nevertheless General Myers at Barbados and Commodore Hood still hankered after Curaçoa, ostensibly as a station for the distribution of British manufactures in the Spanish Main. This was a plea likely to commend itself to British manufacturers and therefore to the Chancellor of the Exchequer; but for once the British Government returned a decided and unmistakable negative. "Multiplication of garrisons," wrote the Minister for War, "weakens the whole of our islands." The comment was just, though it came a little late, after the West Indian garrisons had been multiplied by two through the orders of Ministers themselves. It is now time to return to England, and to examine the causes which had converted Addington's Ministry to principles so sound, so sober, and so novel.[1]

[1] Green to Sec. of State, 13th May (2 letters); to Sullivan, 14th May; Myers to Sec. of State, 7th, 31st Aug.; Sec. of State to Myers, Nov. 1804.

CHAPTER VII

It has already been told that England's declaration of war came to Bonaparte as a surprise, his preparations being still altogether incomplete; and in truth the weakness of France at sea in May 1803 was such as would have daunted many men. Forty-eight vessels, carrying each from eighty to ten guns, were at St. Domingo, of which number seven ships only were destined to escape capture or destruction by taking refuge in different ports of Spain. The whole, therefore, might be practically looked upon as lost. In March the French Admiralty reported that all the ports of France could in a month's time produce but five ships of the line and ten frigates ready for sea, and in six months' time no more than twenty-one ships of the line and nineteen frigates. In June matters had not improved. There were but three line-of-battle ships at Brest, all of them short of their complement of men, and as many more at Toulon. In such circumstances it is not astonishing that Bonaparte's first care was for the protection of his own coasts, and that he should have shown particular anxiety for the safety of the island of Walcheren as the gate of the Scheldt. But even for defence his maritime resources were dangerously small, for, though nearly two hundred gunboats remained on the list of the French Navy, only twenty-seven of them were even tolerably sound. The naval impotence of France, as their own writers confess, was as great in 1803 after three years of the Consulate, as in 1793 after four years of revolution.

1803. May. June.

1803. Powerless to strike at sea, Bonaparte lost no time in doing England such mischief as he could on land. A few days before the declaration of war he began to concentrate his garrisons in Holland; and on the 31st
May 31. of May Mortier invaded Hanover at the head of twenty-five thousand men, brushed away such feeble opposition as was made to him, and on the 3rd of
June 3. June took over the entire province under a convention. The Hanoverian troops retired for the moment to the east of the Elbe, but were destined to avenge themselves, as shall in due time be seen, in another land and under another name. The chief mischief wrought to England by this stroke was the shutting of the Elbe and the Weser to her trade; but to Bonaparte the gain of the province was indirectly most valuable, for he could use it, as he said, as a bone for Prussia to gnaw; and, with such a prize to dangle before her, he could be sure of attracting her to his side. Simultaneously he called upon Spain for the help that she was bound to afford him under the Treaty of San Ildefonso, ordered Gouvion St. Cyr to invade Neapolitan territory and occupy Tarento, Otranto, and Brindisi, and directed Leghorn to be placed under martial law. He also forbade the entry into the ports of France or her allies of all colonial produce coming directly from England or from any of her possessions. If he could not meet the British fleet at sea, he would at least exclude British merchantmen from as many harbours as possible, especially in the Mediterranean; while the occupation of the peninsula of Otranto served the additional purpose of threatening the Levant, the Morea, and Egypt. If he could not prevent England from foiling his colonial projects and sweeping the whole of the Antilles into her net, he would at any rate close against her every market that he could control, and so lay the foundation of the Continental System.[1]

But these measures, however formidable, were

[1] Sorel, vi. 309.

secondary to a still vaster project which was ripening 1803. in his brain for more signal humiliation of the inveterate enemy. In March he had given orders for the creation of a flotilla of five hundred craft at Dunkirk and Cherbourg, the whole of which were to be ready by September; and in June he compelled the Batavian Republic to provide ten ships of war, transports for twenty-five thousand men, one hundred gunboats, and two hundred and fifty flat-boats for a descent upon England. From Spain he claimed fifteen ships of the line besides smaller vessels, though finally after months of haggling he accepted a subsidy of £240,000 a month in their stead. From Hanover he required the construction of flat-bottomed boats in the Weser and the Elbe. From France herself he demanded that twenty ships should be fit for sea at Brest by the third week in November; and, after many changes Aug. 22. of plan, he decreed that two thousand small craft should likewise be constructed by the same date. On the 14th of June he had ordered the concentration of the Grand Army in six camps, one in Holland, and the rest at Ghent, St. Omer, Compiègne, St. Malo, and Bayonne; and therewith his original design was, on paper, complete. The small craft for the conveyance of troops were one and all to be armed, with the object apparently of fighting their way through the British fleet, if necessary. One hundred and ten or twenty thousand men would be embarked on them; they would slip across the Channel on some favourable night of fog and darkness during the winter; a revolution would break out in London at the sight of the French Army, and England would become a vassal of France.[1]

Such was the project which from the end of May onwards possessed the brain of Bonaparte. For the present it was, as we shall see, both wild and vague; but possibly for that very reason it struck the greater alarm into the British Ministry. The First Lord of

[1] Sorel, vi. 310; Desbrière.

1803. the Admiralty at this time was Lord St. Vincent, who, in the enthusiasm of an economic crusade against the corruption in the dockyards, had not only allowed artificers to be discharged and valuable material to be sold, but had omitted to replenish the stock of necessary stores. His instinct for strategic dispositions was as sound as ever; and squadrons under renowned commanders were soon watching every one of the French naval arsenals. Nelson lay before Toulon; Pellew shut in the fugitive vessels from St. Domingo at Ferrol; Collingwood cruised off Rochefort; Cornwallis, a seaman unsurpassed in vigilance, nerve, and resolution, blockaded Brest. But the numbers of their ships were insufficient; and Nelson complained bitterly, though to no purpose, that the majority of those under his command were unfit for sea. Looking to the contemptible strength of the French Navy at the outbreak of the war, an invasion of England may seem to us now a plan so hazardous as to be absurd; but our ancestors may be forgiven if, with a Bonaparte on the other side of the Channel, they wished to be ready for any contingency.

In virtue of the large establishment voted in 1802, and by the timely suspension of the disbandment of many condemned corps, the British Government had ready to its hand a regular army incomparably stronger and more efficient than had ever before been seen at the beginning of any war. Moreover, despite of St. Vincent's failure at the Admiralty, England's superiority at sea was overwhelming. Here, therefore, was an opportunity, such as is not often afforded, for augmenting the Regular Army to formidable strength by means of the tens of thousands of men trained during the last war, and disconcerting the whole of Bonaparte's plans by a vigorous offensive movement. The obvious sphere for such a movement was the Mediterranean. The French invasion of Calabria was of course a glaring violation of the neutrality of the Kingdom of the Two Sicilies. The Court of Naples, though utterly corrupt

and inefficient, at least preferred British protection to 1803.
the encroachments and menaces of Bonaparte. The Apulians hated the French invaders, and might easily be brought to turn against them savagely, both as individuals and in masses. Gouvion St. Cyr lay weak and isolated at the very heel of Italy, almost the remotest point to southward that could be reached by French troops. Thirty thousand British soldiers, or forty thousand if transport could be found for them, concentrated in Sicily, with their ships ready, would have stirred up dangerous unrest in the whole of the Peninsula. They would have compelled Bonaparte to drain men from France for reinforcement of the Italian garrisons, and would have constrained him either to double the strength of St. Cyr's corps, or to recall it altogether and to relieve Nelson from all anxiety as to the safety of the Levant, of Egypt, and of India. If Austria, later on, were drawn into hostilities, forty thousand British troops could give her most effective help on either flank of Italy; while, on the other hand, such a force might well harden Spain in her reluctance to yield to Bonaparte's claims upon her under the Treaty of San Ildefonso. Italy, in fact, the scene of Bonaparte's triumphs, the acquisition that was dearest to his heart, was the sphere where a British fleet and a British army, under command of such a man as Moore, might have made a diversion that Bonaparte himself could not have ignored.

But no such ideas occurred to Addington or to his colleagues. Dumouriez, whom they consulted late in the year, advocated an attack upon Walcheren and an expedition to Portugal as the best means of checking a descent upon Ireland, which he justly held to be the most vulnerable point in the Empire. Ministers may well have been justified in rejecting both projects; but they were equally deaf to all the protests of Dumouriez against an inert defensive.[1] Their only notion was to

[1] Rose and Broadley's *Dumouriez and the Defence of England*, pp. 332-337.

1803. leave to Bonaparte all initiative, and suffer the strength of England to be paralysed by a menace from Boulogne. The only augmentation ordered for the army was an addition of eleven men to every troop of dragoons and of ten to every company of Guards; and Mr. Yorke,
June 6. the Secretary at War, when introducing the estimates took credit for the moderation of the increase. Ministers, in fact, were resolved to stand wholly on the defensive, except in the West Indies, and, moreover, considered the resolution to be exceedingly clever.

The Militia Act of 1802[1] had been framed wholly with this view. It provided for raising by ballot, and by no other means, fifty-one thousand five hundred men between the ages of eighteen and forty-five, and at least five feet four inches in height, from all the parishes of Great Britain; giving the King power, moreover, on menace of invasion or rebellion to augment that number by one-half on calling Parliament together within fourteen days. Any parish which failed to produce its quota of men was fined annually £10 for every man deficient. The men were to be trained for twenty-one days annually; and enlistment from the Militia into the Regular Army was positively forbidden. They were to be chosen by ballot, and, if they accepted the lot that fell upon them, were to serve for five years; receiving from the parochial rates, if they were worth less than £500, a sum equal to half the cost of a substitute. Such men were at liberty to prolong their service on giving notice four months before the expiration of their term, and stating the sum which they demanded for such prolongation. But there were several ways whereby service in the Militia could be evaded. In the first place, parishes could produce parochial substitutes and levy a rate to purchase them, up to the price of £6 a head. In the second place, a ballotted man, or to use the contemporary name, a lotman, could provide a personal substitute, towards the cost of which the parish gave him, if he were worth

[1] 42 Geo. III. caps. 90, 91.

less than £500, half the current price of a substitute, 1802.
such substitutes being required to be drawn from the "same or some adjoining county or place." And thirdly, he could purchase exemption for five years by the payment of £10. But whereas ballotted men, who accepted service, were enrolled for five years only and then released until their turn to be ballotted should come again in rotation, substitutes were retained until the disembodiment of the Militia, or, in other words, until the end of the war. All sergeants and drummers, again, were enlisted for life. Hence, unless the majority of the lotmen were ready to serve in person, which was contrary to all experience, Addington's Militia Act promised to lock up a vast number of men in the Militia, who would otherwise have enlisted in the Army.

To this enactment the Ministry added another in the same session of 1802 for dealing with the Volunteers. The Volunteer Acts passed by Pitt during the late war had expired with the war; and, in the uncertainty of the continuance of peace, the Government thought it expedient to enable such of the corps as were willing, to prolong their service. Now the Volunteers called into existence by Pitt had been established upon a totally false principle. They had been dependent mainly upon private subscriptions, and governed by committees of the subscribers, who were not necessarily officers; and it was therefore extremely doubtful whether they were commanded by their titular commanding officers or by their committees. Jealousy and self-importance had prompted a vast majority of the corps to organise themselves into small and insignificant units, so that they might reserve to themselves the greater independence, and indulge to the utmost their peculiar ideas and idiosyncrasies. They were subject to no discipline excepting their own rules, which could only be enforced by public opinion. They were, therefore, practically under no control; and, as an inevitable consequence, they were for the most part utterly useless. Here,

1802. therefore, was an opportunity for reconstituting them upon some sounder basis, if they were to be revived at all; but Lord Hobart, who, though Secretary of State for War, had for some reason taken over the charge of the Volunteers from the Home Secretary, was far too incapable to think of any such thing. Hence the Volunteer Act of 1802, without attempting to remedy a single defect, simply empowered the King to accept any offers from Yeomanry and Volunteer corps to prolong their service, and, in return, guaranteed such corps exemption from the Militia ballot in consideration of their undergoing five days' exercise annually

A fair number of corps accepted these terms in 1802, but a great number refused them, seeing no occasion for any such patriotic display in time of peace. As the prospects of war became more certain, however,
1803. the Government issued on the 31st of March 1803 a Circular calling for more Volunteers, at the same time submitting a scale of allowances which they proposed to grant for their maintenance and encouragement. The response to this was ready and even eager. But presently Ministers bethought themselves that if they created too many Volunteers they would leave no men to be ballotted for the Militia; wherefore, after effusive acceptance of a great many offers of Volunteer corps, they suddenly and abruptly declined to answer further applications. Many thousands of men who had tendered their services were thus kept in suspense, and, as was natural, murmured loudly at such treatment; and, since they had really been inspired in the vast majority of cases by truly patriotic motives, they complained that the Government was deliberately damping the ardour of the people. This was unjust. Addington and his colleagues were only hesitating until they should have ascertained their own minds. But this was a lengthy process, for it was extremely doubtful whether they possessed any minds beyond such fragments as their lofty patron, Pitt, might choose to dole out to them.

Meanwhile, on the 11th of March a proclamation 1803.
was published for the embodiment of the Militia; when that force in Great Britain was found to be in an extremely unsatisfactory state. Notwithstanding that the ballots had been going on ever since the previous December, the levy was still incomplete, and very seriously incomplete. Even in Ireland, where Militiamen were raised almost entirely by voluntary enlistment for a bounty of two guineas, there was a considerable deficiency. In Great Britain there had been a rush for substitutes, the price of which had already run up to an extravagant figure. There had been some recalcitrance in Scotland, and persistent evasion everywhere; and crimps and insurance-societies[1] had been driving a roaring trade. This was a serious matter, for war was drawing nearer every day. An Act was passed on the 24th of March to prolong the annual training of the Militia from twenty-one days to twenty-eight; and another Act of the 7th of April made an attempt to ensure that there should be some men to be trained, by doubling the bounty for the Irish Militia from two guineas to four. Then on the 16th of May, as has been told, war was declared; and on the 28th the Government called out the additional contingent of Militia, known as the Supplementary Militia, which was authorised by the Act of 1802. This signified that Great Britain, which so far had failed to produce fifty-one thousand men in four or five months, must now produce another twenty-five thousand;[2] and, in order to quicken the process, an Act of the 11th of June levied a cumulative penalty of £10 every quarter upon the counties for every man deficient of their quota, raised the fine for exemption from £10 to £15, and made substitutes who had deserted liable, upon conviction, to serve in the Regular Army abroad. This, however, did not prevent but rather stimulated a

[1] Societies which, for a certain premium, undertook to provide men with a substitute or with the amount of the exemption-fine.

[2] Ireland had no Supplementary Militia.

1803. second rush for substitutes, with the natural result that their cost again increased rapidly. With high prices, which were commonly called, and to all intents actually were, high bounties, crimps grew rich, and desertion and fraudulent enlistment flourished more abundantly.

These hasty measures did not escape sharp criticism, for, when men could gain from £20 to £30 as substitutes, they were not likely to accept a bounty of £7 : 12 : 6 to enter the Regular Army. Windham attacked the whole system fiercely, pointing out that if men could earn large sums by serving for a few years at home, they could not be expected to enlist for life to serve in the Regular Army in any part of the globe. Pitt echoed Windham's strictures, and both agreed in condemning a purely defensive policy as alike ruinous and dishonourable.[1] But Addington was popular with the country members; and the House accepted his assurance that he was only dealing with defensive measures first, in view of the vast preparations of the enemy. When the opportunity for offensive operations should arrive, he added, no doubt the country would afford means for supporting them with honour.

The dull, pompous man was therefore permitted to proceed with his defensive measures. He had long paltered with the Volunteers, sometimes urging them to tender their services, sometimes refusing to accept their offers; and he now passed what was called a Defence Act, the object of which seems to have been to stimulate them to come forward. It directed the Lords-Lieutenant to furnish lists of all able-bodied men, between the ages of fifteen and sixty, who were willing to serve in defence of their country; distinguishing among these such as were Yeomen or Volunteers, and such as were ready to serve as waggoners, pioneers, or the like. It also required returns as to the vehicles, horses, cattle, forage, and so forth in the country, giving powers for the destruction or removal of them in case of invasion, and for the acquisition of land for military purposes.

[1] *Parl. Hist.* xxxvi. p. 1574, 6th June 1803.

Lastly it ordained that persons enrolled in Volunteer corps after the passing of the Act should not be called out except according to their own conditions of service, nor except in case of invasion or imminent danger thereof. A more foolish enactment, except as regards the registration of horses and kindred matters, was never proposed; for it was and is the undoubted right of the Sovereign to call up all able-bodied men to serve in defence of their country, willing or unwilling; and there was little object, therefore, in ascertaining whether they were willing or not. 1803.

Moreover, the enactment as to the Volunteers was nugatory, for, a few days after the Act had been passed, Ministers finally made up their minds what they would do about them, and issued a code of regulations which became known as the June Allowances. Hereby June 20. they offered to the Volunteer Corps pay for eighty-five days' exercise in the year, as well as salaries for a limited number of officers and for a permanent staff; requiring from them in return an agreement to serve in any part of their military district. On the other hand, the Government announced that no Volunteer enrolled after the 16th of June would be exempted from the ballot for a new force, shortly about to be called into being. Nevertheless the terms were so liberal that they were readily embraced on all sides, and produced many additional tenders of service from new Volunteer corps. But now the Cabinet took alarm at the expense; and once again, amid deep groans from disappointed patriots, their offers were left unanswered.

On the 20th of June the bill for creating the new force above-named—the most important of the Government's measures—was duly brought forward in the House of Commons, and on the 6th of July became July 6. law under the name of the Additional Force Act. It ordained that within the year there should be raised by ballot in the United Kingdom an Army of Reserve of fifty thousand men, namely thirty-four thousand from England, six thousand from Scotland, and ten thousand

1803. from Ireland, the whole to be duly apportioned among the counties and parishes as in the case of the Militia. In Ireland the Lord-Lieutenant was empowered to enlist the men by beat of drum instead of by the ballot, at his discretion. The standard of height was to be five feet two inches; and service could be commuted by any ballotted man either by the production of a substitute, which assured permanent exemption, or by the payment of £20, which sum purchased immunity from the ballot for one year only. All men were to be enrolled for service in the United Kingdom and Channel Islands alone, principals for five years, substitutes for the same term or until six months after the signature of a definitive peace. Parishes failing to produce their appointed quota of men were subjected to a cumulative fine of £20, to be repeated every quarter, for every man deficient. Exemption was granted to all Volunteers and Yeomanry enrolled before the 22nd of June, provided that their offers of service extended, in the event of invasion, to every part of their military district, or in other words, provided that they had accepted the June Allowances. Finally the members of the Army of Reserve were permitted to enlist into the Regular Army.

The augmentation of the Regular Army was the principal purpose of the Act, though the fact does not appear upon its surface. Nor, in theory, was the plan upon which it was based by any means essentially bad. The fifty thousand men were to be formed into fifty second battalions to as many regiments of the line, and were to be tempted by bounties to fill up the gaps in the first battalions as occasion might require. The Duke of York, ever since he had been Commander-in-chief, had been striving hard to give a second battalion to every regiment of regular British infantry; and he it was, no doubt, who had suggested this organisation. But Pitt, who had originally urged the measure upon Addington, had, under the inspiration of the Horse Guards, very wisely designed to enlarge its scope, and to add to it further machinery for filling up the gaps in the Army of Reserve itself every year, so that it should be maintained at a constant strength. This most important detail was wholly omitted by Addington and Hobart. Entirely ignorant of all military matters, they provided simply for sudden increase of the Army by a spasmodic and costly effort, not for its permanent support, nor for making good the waste of war. What they actually did was to augment the number of men to be raised by ballot in a single year to one hundred and ten or twenty thousand men, admitting throughout the principle of substitution, which as a natural consequence swept into the Militia and Army of Reserve every man who might with better management have been recruited into the Army. The policy was furiously attacked by Windham, who looked upon it as fatal to all chance of ever creating an offensive force. He maintained that no enlistment ought to be permitted for any troops except the Regulars, and that for the Militia there should be no alternative between personal service or heavy fines for exemption, the proceeds of which fines should be gathered into a general recruiting-fund. "I would sooner leave the Militia incomplete," he said, "than introduce that fatal principle of substitution."[1] He spoke to deaf ears. Pitt, for reasons best known to himself, defended the measure as it stood; and his voice prevailed. The race for substitutes naturally became a headlong scramble after the passing of the Act; but still Addington and Hobart had not exhausted their powers of ineptitude. 1803.

Their next action, however, showed some return of sense, for it consisted in a bill to amend the absurd Defence Act of the 11th of June, which became law on the 27th of July as the Levy en Masse Act. It was based upon the undoubted right of the Sovereign to demand military service of all his subjects to repel invasion, and provided the following machinery for that purpose. July 27.

[1] *Parl. Hist.* xxxvi. p. 1622, 23rd June 1803.

1803. The Lords-Lieutenant, to whom the entire execution of the Act was entrusted, were required to obtain lists of all men between the ages of seventeen and fifty-five, and to sort them into four classes, namely: first, unmarried men under thirty years of age, with no child living under ten years old; secondly, unmarried men between thirty and fifty years of age, with no child as aforesaid; thirdly, married men from seventeen to thirty years of age, with not more than two children living under ten years old; fourthly, all other men whatsoever. Exemption was granted to the infirm, to the judges, to clergymen, schoolmasters, persons actually serving in the Army, Navy, and Reserve Forces, Lords-Lieutenant, their Deputies, and peace-officers. The King was empowered to direct any parish to be provided with arms; and to order the three first classes to be trained, under the superintendence of the Deputy-Lieutenants, for two hours on every Sunday or other convenient day in the week from Lady Day to Christmas, and moreover, until Christmas 1803, on at least fourteen and at most twenty successive days. Deputy-Lieutenants were authorised to hire instructors and to appoint four officers to every six-score men; and provision was made for enforcing attendance by means of fines, and for punishing misconduct on parade by fine, and by imprisonment for seven days in default of payment. In case of invasion or imminent danger thereof, the whole or any part of the men enrolled under the Act were liable to be embodied in new battalions, or in existing corps of Regulars or Militia, and marched to any part of Great Britain. If only a part of the classes was to be embodied, the required number was to be selected by ballot; but in places where Volunteer corps had been formed, or where a number of men of any age between seventeen and fifty, equal to three-fourths of the first class, engaged themselves to serve as Volunteers and to march to any part of Great Britain in case of invasion, the King was empowered to suspend the compulsory training prescribed by the Act. An amending Act, passed a fortnight later, provided further that if the 1803. number of Volunteers in any county were satisfactory to the King, he could suspend the operation of the Levy en Masse Act, even though such number did not amount to the prescribed tale of three-fourths of the first class.

This measure amounted practically to an Act to compel men to become Volunteers, and was meant to be interpreted as such. The Government on the 30th July 30. of July had sent a Circular to the Lords-Lieutenant limiting the numbers of men to be immediately trained to six times the quota of the Ordinary Militia, or in round figures to three hundred and nine thousand privates, and directing that the enrolment of Volunteers up to that number should be encouraged. This instruction was supplemented on the 3rd of August by pro- Aug. 3. mulgation of a new set of allowances, known as the August Allowances, for all Volunteer corps accepted after the 22nd of June. The Circular set forth the impossibility, on financial grounds, of extending the June Allowances to a greater number of men than already received them; and offered in their stead to such infantry corps as might in future be formed a grant of £1 a man for clothing every three years, and one shilling a day for twenty days' exercise in the year. No allowance for clothing and appointments was to be made in future to men entering corps of Yeomanry; but, under the Levy en Masse Act, men who appeared on horseback, properly armed and accoutred at their own expense, were excused from service in the infantry, and might either be attached to existing corps of Yeomanry, or formed into new troops or regiments.

Having done this, the Government proceeded, on the 11th of August, to pass an Act known as the Aug. 11. Billetting Act, to enable Volunteers and Yeomen to be billetted upon occasion. Incidentally this enactment subjected both Yeomanry and Volunteers to military law, if called out to repel invasion, and transferred them in the same emergency from the control of the

1803. Lords-Lieutenant to that of the General commanding their districts. It made likewise some kind of provision for discipline at other times by vesting the funds of all Volunteer corps in their commanding officers, and making the collection of fines, which had been imposed upon the Volunteers under the rules of their corps, recoverable by distress. Lastly it ordained the qualification of an effective Yeoman to be attendance at twelve days' exercise, and of an effective infantry Volunteer to be attendance at twenty-four days' exercise in the year; and exempted all such effective men from the ballot, not only for the Army of Reserve, but for any other Additional Force that might be raised in future. How this last clause ever passed through both Houses of Parliament is and remains a mystery. Sir William Yonge averred that it had been surreptitiously introduced into the House at a time when most of the members had left London for the country in order to drill with their various regiments;[1] and this is possible, for the provision was certainly contrary not only to the Army of Reserve Act itself but, by their own admission, to the actual intention of Ministers. Indeed, in spite of the plain words of the Act, they could not believe that the section really exempted Volunteers from the ballot for the Army of Reserve, until their own Law-Officers pronounced that undoubtedly it had such force; when with infinite mortification they communicated the unwelcome news to the Lords-Lieutenant. Thus, with a masterpiece of careless imbecility, ended the summer session of 1803.

The effect of all these measures concerning the Volunteers was, of course, immediate. There was a general rush for enrolment; and the offers of service poured in with such abundance that the War Office
Aug. 18. was fairly swamped with them. On the 18th of August the Lords-Lieutenant were informed by Circular that the classes need not be called out under the Levy en Masse Act, and that the operation of the

[1] *H.D.* Commons, 14th Dec. 1803.

measure in regard to training was suspended. It was further intimated to them that the voluntary system could not be carried to an unlimited extent, and that no additional corps would be accepted in counties where the number of effective Volunteers, including Yeomanry, exceeded the appointed number of six times the quota of the Ordinary Militia. In truth Ministers were already appalled at the monster that they had called into being without any adequate means of controlling it; and, moreover, they had quite overlooked the difficulty of arming this host of men. Another Circular, therefore, was issued to the Lieutenants on the 22nd of August, asking what number of arms could be procured from public or private sources in each county, and intimating that for the present the Government did not propose to issue firelocks for more than one man in four of the appointed quota, which number would, in its opinion, suffice for purposes of training. The remainder would be provided with pikes, of which there was an amply sufficient supply. 1803.

The answers to these Circulars was a howl of discontent. The nation was ablaze with the first furious flame of patriotic ardour, and felt such announcements to be drenches of cold water. Ministers had asked for Volunteers to defend the country, and every able-bodied man was eager to respond to the summons. What manner of Government was this which presumed to say that thousands should be excluded from the performance of an honourable duty, and to trifle with the supply of arms? The clamour was loudest in the maritime counties, which, being the most exposed to danger, were naturally and reasonably the most eager to equip themselves for defence; and the Government had put itself in the wrong by the egregious blunder of making the quota the same for all counties, whether inland or upon the coast. In the height of the crisis the direction of the Volunteers was re-transferred from the War Office to the Home Office; and the unhappy Mr. Yorke found himself confronted with a vast mass Aug. 22.

1803. of unanswered letters containing offers of Volunteers from all quarters. For a week he wrestled with them, and then giving up the attempt in despair, he issued on
Aug. 31. the 31st two Circulars to announce that all the offers were accepted, provided that they did not exceed the quota laid down in Lord Hobart's Circular of the 18th of August; also that a certain number of supernumerary volunteers might be attached to accepted corps, which supernumeraries, however, should be entitled to no allowance whatever from Government and should enjoy no exemption from the ballot. For the rest, all troops and companies must be of a certain strength, and muskets would be issued for one-fourth of the appointed quota, unless the arms already provided by corps for themselves rendered so large a proportion unnecessary. For the remainder of the infantry and for the artillery there was abundance of pikes, which could be furnished to any number that was required.

These concessions, though more apparent than real, stilled the clamour for a time; and at this point it will be well to show exactly what the Government had accomplished. First, it had ordered some hundred and twenty thousand men to be raised by ballot within a few months for the Ordinary Militia, Supplementary Militia, and Army of Reserve. The general terms of service for the three were the same, but the standard for the Militia, until the 27th of July, was five feet four inches, and for the Army of Reserve five feet two inches. An Act of the 27th of July,[1] however, had lowered the standard for substitutes in the Militia to five feet two inches; so that according to the letter of the law there was one standard for principals and another for substitutes. Substitutes for the Militia might not have more than one child born in lawful wedlock, while substitutes for the Army of Reserve might have an unlimited number. In the Ordinary Militia a fine of £10, and in the Supplementary Militia a fine of £15 purchased exemption from the ballot for five years; in the Army of

[1] 43 Geo. III. cap. 100.

Reserve a fine of £20 purchased exemption for one 1803. year only. Lastly, men who served in person or by substitute in the Militia were exempt from the ballot for the Army of Reserve, and *vice versa*; but men who had only paid the exemption-fine for one of these two forces were not immune from the ballot for the other. Again, five days' exercise sufficed to deliver any Yeoman or Volunteer from the ballot for the Militia, but a Yeoman must undergo twelve days' drill, and an infantry Volunteer twenty-four days' annually to obtain deliverance from the Army of Reserve. These distinctions were not all of them made quite clear in the Acts, with the consequence that they were imperfectly grasped by the county authorities and hardly apprehended at all by the body of the people. The natural result was enormous correspondence between the Home Office and the Lords-Lieutenant, endless confusion in making the levies, and deep resentment among all classes that were liable to the ballot. The task of the Lieutenancies in raising so great a body of men would under the most favourable conditions have been very arduous; but the action of the Government made it practically impossible of performance. The wholesale exemption from all ballots of over three hundred thousand Volunteers, chiefly unmarried men, threw the obligation upon married men, to whom personal service was often ruinous. Once again, therefore, the price of substitutes rose with a bound to £30, £40, and even £60. The proceeds of the exemption-fines which, in theory, were supposed to enable the parishes to purchase substitutes for the men who had paid them, were of course inadequate. The parish officers resorted in despair to the crimps. The crimps—and there was probably at least one crimp, professional or amateur, in every parish—observant of the daily increasing value of their goods, were in no haste to place them on the market. Menaced, therefore, by exorbitant prices on the one hand, and the spectre of cumulative quarterly fines on the other, the parochial authorities finally sat

1803. down in despair, hoarding the exemption-fines against the day when the price of recruits should fall, or a lucky chance should throw them some poacher or beggar who would be glad to enlist in order to escape from the law.

Much of the trouble had been brought about by the anxiety of the Government to create a force of Volunteers; yet the Volunteers themselves were in the same confusion as the ballotted levies. In the first place, they were divided into two totally distinct sections, supported by two different scales of allowances, enrolled under two different conditions of service, and governed by two distinct Acts of Parliament. Those under the June Allowances, who may be called the Old Volunteers, were liberally supported, liable by the Government's own deed of service within their military district only, and were administered under the Volunteer Act of 1802 and the supplementary provisions of the Billetting Act of 1803. Those under the August Allowances—the New Volunteers, as they may be termed—were stinted in the matter of grants from the Treasury, liable for service in any part of Great Britain, and administered under the Levy en Masse Act. The more favourable position of the Old Volunteers naturally gave rise to much jealousy and incidentally led to much friction. The Government very rightly encouraged the amalgamation of isolated troops and companies into regiments and battalions; and hence it frequently happened that corps were composed in various proportions of units engaged on varying terms of service, half of the companies perhaps under the June Allowances, and half under the August Allowances. Thus a man in one company who absented himself from drill was liable only to the penalty imposed by the rules of the corps, while a similar offender in another company of the same battalion could be fined under the Levy en Masse Act. Again, a man of one company who misconducted himself on parade was subject to the fine prescribed by the rules of the corps; but a man guilty of the like offence in another company could not only be mulcted, probably, in a different sum of money, but could be imprisoned in default of payment. Yet again, the Old Volunteers, being but men, were not immortal, and therefore were constantly diminished by casualties. Though in theory no more Volunteers were to have been accepted after a certain date, except on the August Allowances, it was impossible to break faith with officers who had raised corps on the understanding that they should receive the June Allowances; and it was therefore laid down that these should be permitted to fill any vacancies which left their corps short of establishment. The commanders of the Old Volunteers, therefore, enjoyed a peculiar kind of patronage. Being able to offer the best terms, they could, of course, be sure of obtaining the best men; and it was no uncommon thing for commanders of New Volunteers to find that some of their most promising recruits had left them without a word and gone to some troop or regiment of Old Volunteers. 1803.

Incidentally this brought up the whole question whether Volunteers at large had or had not the right to resign when they pleased. The Law-Officers of the Crown decided against any such right; and the Government circulated their opinion to the Lieutenancies for their guidance. On the other hand, Erskine, the famous advocate and future Chancellor, who commanded with extreme inefficiency the Inns of Court Volunteers, upheld the opposite contention in letters to the public prints, with all the pomp of florid and redundant verbiage which was to be expected from a man whose rhetorical powers were only exceeded by his consuming vanity. The letters spread like wildfire all over England, and were not only eagerly devoured but were quoted as of paramount authority by Volunteers in all quarters. Commandants were in despair, for their powers of discipline were already insufficient. The great mass of the Volunteers were ordinary labouring men, who had already discovered that the only penalty for not attending drill was a fine, which had little terror for

1803. those who possessed no property. The remainder were men of superior education, though by no means always of superior character, who had given to their corps the form of a club, and in many cases claimed the right to elect their own officers. If every sulky or discontented man could resign whenever he pleased, then, in the opinion of many commandants, there was an end of all discipline. The question agitated the force all through the winter of 1803; the Government striving to comfort themselves with the reflection that men who declined to serve as Volunteers could be trained compulsorily under the Levy en Masse Act, but forgetting that it would be almost impossible to find officers and instructors for such levies, and that the establishment of yet another description of force for home defence would only further confound the existing confusion. At length the controversy came before the Courts of Law, when the Judges of the King's Bench decided, on the 6th of February 1804, in favour of Erskine's contention that every Volunteer had the right to resign at his own will.

Much trouble was engendered also by the dearth of arms; the muskets in the arsenals being utterly insufficient to meet the enormous demand. Great numbers of Volunteer corps, with excellent spirit, came out and drilled for week after week without weapon of any kind, until at last they very pardonably lost patience and declared that they would proceed no longer with such a travesty of training. Ministers in vain offered to supply pikes to any number: the men would not receive them. The Volunteer infantry, by the Government's own direction, had been clothed in scarlet like the Regulars; and it had no intention of being armed except as the Regular Infantry, with firelock and bayonet. Was not the pike the weapon of regicide French and rebel Irish? and of what service would it be against a French musket? The discontent was so acute in many quarters that the Lords-Lieutenant apprehended the dissolution of very many corps; and incidentally this same dearth 1803. of arms gave birth to a legitimate grievance. The law laid down that Volunteers, to gain their exemption from the ballot, must appear at exercise properly armed and accoutred for a certain number of days before the 21st of September. Many commanders, naturally unwilling to waste all the days of drill without training in arms, reserved a certain number of them against the time when the long-expected muskets should arrive; and waiting too long, sacrificed the exemption for their corps. These naturally protested against the strict enforcement of the law in their case; and many others indignantly asked how it was possible for them to appear properly armed and accoutred when Government failed to supply arms and accoutrements. The situation was most awkward, for the Secretary of State could not override the law; and he could only promise to pass a short Act of Parliament at the earliest possible moment, which he duly did on the 13th of December 1803, to remove the grievance and to grant exemption for drills thus attended without arms.

However, in spite of all obstacles, the Volunteers continued to increase steadily during the autumn and winter of 1803. There was much sound patriotic feeling as yet at the heart of the movement. Private subscriptions for the foundation and maintenance of corps had been abundant and generous, so that officers of regiments on the August Allowances were practically able for the present to give their men the June Allowances; this being the one means whereby harmony could be kept up between the New Volunteers and the Old. Enormous sums were foolishly squandered upon dress and frippery at large; but for the moment enthusiasm averted any serious financial pressure. The men were delighted with their smart new uniforms, and the officers supremely well satisfied not only with their gold and silver lace, but with their new titles. In the session of 1803 there were already so many Colonels in the Commons that Robert Craufurd, the future leader of

1803. the Light Division, was nicknamed the "Regular Colonel," to distinguish him as the one man who had any right to the appellation. It may be reckoned also that at least as many women as men were well pleased by all this cheapening of rank and uniform. And yet, if Napoleon had landed at the end of September or beginning of October, he would have found little to oppose him but a half-armed, undisciplined rabble, composed in many instances of fragments of corps, whereof part had marched out to meet him, while the remainder, agreeable to their terms of service, had refused to move out of their military districts.

But Napoleon had been guilty of blunders as serious in their own kind as those of Addington and Hobart, and his preparations were as backward as theirs. On the 21st of July he had mapped out his scheme of invasion as follows:—There were to be ready three hundred vessels at Flushing to bring over the Dutch contingent of his army; three hundred more at Nieuport and Ostend to embark thirty thousand men; three hundred more at Dunkirk, Gravelines, and Calais for conveyance of six thousand horses and baggage; two thousand three hundred and eighty at Wissant, Ambleteuse, and Boulogne; and a few hundred more at Étaples for transport of three thousand horses and one hundred and twenty-five guns. All this was clear enough on paper; but in practice things were different. Nearly all of the ports above enumerated were small and bad, with bars, shoals, or other impediments, so that it was admittedly impossible for more than a limited number of vessels to leave them by one tide. This made it necessary that the craft which left the ports by one tide should lie in the roadstead till another tide should release their fellows, during which interval they would need protection both from British attack and from the weather. Fortifications were therefore erected in some quarters to cover the anchorage; and very extensive works were also undertaken for the improvement of the harbours. But excavation and dredging are lengthy operations; and, even supposing them to be completed, many of the flotilla, having been constructed in distant ports, would have to run the gauntlet of the British frigates, which cruised off every promontory, before they could be concentrated in the Channel. Moreover, all was by no means well with the flotilla. Too many of the craft had been put into building at once, which caused delay. Many others, particularly the vessels designed to carry horses, were found to be clumsy sailers and so faulty in many ways that their construction was suspended. In fact, by the spring of 1804 little more than three-fifths of the two thousand vessels were ready. Furthermore, fishing-vessels of light draught were found to be unobtainable in the number required, and it was necessary to replace them by large merchantmen of too great draught for any anchorage but the Scheldt. Even of the smaller craft many of the heavier boats had, by Napoleon's perverse rejection of his Admirals' advice, been apportioned to harbours which had not water to float them. In a word, the great plan of the 21st of July had broken down completely; the building of the flotilla was in arrear; the construction of the vessels themselves was defective; their efficiency for attack was extremely doubtful; they could only with great difficulty be brought into the ports of the Channel, and, if brought in, they could only with equal difficulty be brought out again in any large numbers. By the end of January 1804 Napoleon therefore renounced the project of invasion by surprise during the darkness of winter, and determined not to cross the Channel until his ships of war had cleared the way for him. The whole of his armed boats, of which some four hundred and sixty were concentrated by the end of March 1804 at Boulogne, Wimereux, Étaples, and Ambleteuse, thereupon became useless. Had they been designed merely as transports they would still have been valuable, but, having been intended also for fighting purposes, they had been spoiled for any useful object. The whole of the money spent upon them had thus

1803. been wasted; and meanwhile the preparations for strengthening the French Navy proper had been very seriously retarded. In brief, Napoleon had lost a year's work by devoting himself, contrary to all naval advice, to the wrong object.

It was well for England that this was so; for when Nov. 22. the Government met Parliament in November it had only a miserable story to tell. The casualties in the Regular Army during 1803 numbered rather over thirteen thousand; the recruits gained in the same period were rather over eleven thousand; so that upon the whole the Army had been diminished by over two thousand men. It must not be supposed that Ministers were so methodical as to have produced any such figures, but such was the actual state of the case. The much vaunted Army of Reserve was in an equally lamentable condition. Of the fifty thousand men to be raised within the year, there had been obtained by the 31st of December just under forty-one thousand, of whom rather more than one-tenth had deserted. This loss, together with other casualties, reduced the effective total to thirty-four thousand five hundred, of which number rather more than seven thousand, tempted by an additional bounty of ten guineas, had enlisted into the Regular Army and had thus brought the number of recruits during the year to the figure above quoted. In fact, the Army of Reserve Act was a failure. Addington himself confessed in April 1804 that, since November 1803, its inconveniences had exceeded its advantages; and by the end of 1803 it was in practice already dead. The Militia also, in spite of endless ballots, was still short of its establishment by seven thousand men. In short, there was little to show for the past year's work but about three hundred and eighty thousand Volunteers and Yeomanry of all ranks, of whom three hundred and forty thousand claimed to be effective rank and file, in Great Britain, and eighty-two thousand in Ireland; making a total of some four hundred and sixty thousand men, unorganised, undisciplined, expensive, and for the most part useless. 1804.

The Government's first measure was a Consolidated Volunteers' Act, whereby it was hoped to amend some of the appalling blunders committed during the last session. As a vast number of the members of both Houses were Volunteer officers, the measure was sure of a stormy reception. Bitter and scathing comment was passed upon the confusion over the matters of arms, exemptions, and various allowances; and, since the question of exemptions touched not only the Volunteers but the Militia and the Army of Reserve, the bill brought the entire military policy of the Government under legitimate review. Yorke declared that the points which chiefly needed attention for the improvement of the Volunteers were the election of officers, the control of corps by committees, and the general question of discipline. As to the evils that followed upon the two first, there should have been no question; but the election of officers was defended not only by Sheridan but by so shrewd and sensible a man as Whitbread; while it was declared by Yorke himself, in absolute defiance of the truth, that the committees devoted themselves exclusively to financial business. As to discipline, one member, Mr. Giles, maintained that the Volunteers might secure it for themselves by their own rules, but that Parliament had no right to impose it. The more the whole matter was thrashed out, the more clearly it appeared that this huge mass of men was absolutely uncontrollable; and even Pitt, after many protestations that he approved of Volunteers in principle, was fain to admit that "it was impossible to trust continually to the operation of the Volunteer spirit."

Colonel Robert Craufurd, more ingenuous and with greater insight, declared that the entire Volunteer system was faulty from beginning to end: faulty in its constitution, its finance, its committees, its exemptions, its training, even its clothing. It was

1804. wrong to allow the Volunteers to be of all descriptions, old and young, sound and infirm, married and single; for, if they were called out for service, half of them would go home unless a decisive action were fought at once. It was wrong to allow Volunteers to be self-controlled by elected committees, and in some cases by general assemblies; for that meant almost as many parliaments as corps. It was wrong to let them be supported by private subscription, for this signified the taxation of the generous and patriotic for a burden that should fall upon all: if the expense of Volunteers were defrayed from Imperial funds there would be no occasion for committees and assemblies. The exemptions were wrong, for they crippled every branch of the forces, even the Volunteers themselves, since they limited the number of men who could be trained to arms lest none should be left for the ballot. Moreover, the Volunteers were a privileged body, the envy and dislike of the poorer classes, upon whom, by the exemptions, the whole weight of the ballot was thrown. The training was wrong, for the Prussian system of drill was utterly useless for fighting in England, and was only taught to the Regulars because they were intended to fight abroad. The clothing was wrong, because it confused Volunteers with Regulars. The sight of Volunteers retreating would dishearten the Regular troops by making them believe that regiments of the Line had been beaten, and would for the same reason encourage the French. He himself would much have preferred to call out the whole of the first class under the Levy en Masse Act, put them under half-pay officers, clothe them and train them, with the help of poachers and gamekeepers instead of drill-sergeants, to load, fire, and hit their mark, and to advance or retire rapidly from shelter to shelter. As things were, if Parliament tried to enact regulations for them, it was told, not that the rules were just or unjust, but that they were not agreeable to the Volunteers. "So delicate a machine," he declared very truly, "is unfit for war."

Craufurd spoke at enormous length and probably to an empty House; and though Windham echoed every word, his protests fell upon deaf ears. Nevertheless the bill made little progress. The Government, represented by feeble men who did not know their own minds, was constantly overborne and brought into contempt. By the end of March the bill had been committed and recommitted four times; twenty-four new clauses had been added, nearly all the original clauses had been altered or abandoned, and yet the measure was as far from passing as ever.[1] 1804.

At the same time Ministers had been fighting a losing battle with the New Volunteers over another point. These last needed adjutants, instructors, and so forth, as much as their brothers on the June Allowances; but Ministers began by refusing to allow any pay whatever to provide them with a permanent staff.[2] This of course provoked much outcry, and the Government then offered to concede pay for adjutants and sergeant-majors in all corps of a certain strength, provided that the New Volunteers, like the Old, would agree to be exercised for eighty-five days in the year. It was hardly a fair arrangement, for the Old Volunteers under the June Allowances received pay for the whole of their eighty-five days, whereas the New Volunteers, under the August Allowances, received pay for but twenty days; the theory being that drill on every Sunday made up fifty-two days in the year, which, added to the twenty above mentioned, left only thirteen days of exercise to be performed gratuitously. But it was out of the question that labouring men should give up a day's work for nothing; and this regulation therefore signified simply that the officer must pay the men for thirteen days out of his own pocket. The inevitable result was fresh discontent. Practically the

[1] *H.D.* Commons' Debates, 8th, 27th, 29th Feb.; 6th, 9th, 19th, 22nd March 1804.

[2] Circular to the Lords-Lieutenant, 28th Sept. 1803.

1804. entire burden of providing parochial substitutes and of paying parochial fines for the Militia and Army of Reserve fell upon the landed interest ; and there was great resentment at the imposition of this new tax, for such in effect it was, upon shoulders that were already aching. The Government, therefore, was compelled in February[1] to grant a day's pay to all officers and privates who should attend inspection of their corps by a General Officer or Field Officer, provided that such inspection did not recur oftener than once in two months. The pretext for this allowance was a desire to ensure regular attendance at inspections ; but it was in reality only a cloak to disguise a surrender to the clamour of the Volunteers.

Meanwhile, however, Ministers had for once taken a wise and sensible step, which helped to extricate them from their difficulties. In October 1803[2] Mr. Yorke had invited the Volunteers of many of the maritime counties to go out upon permanent duty in successive reliefs for ten days or a fortnight, receiving daily pay and voluntarily subjecting themselves to military law during their period of service. The men responded heartily ; and the improvement to their discipline was so great that in March 1804[3] Yorke renewed the invitation not only to the maritime but to the inland counties also. At the same time he intimated that he would grant permanent pay, as before, for any period not exceeding a month and not shorter than ten days, which should count as part of the exercise required to obtain exemption and the pay for a permanent staff, and would add to this an allowance of a guinea a man for necessaries, any surplus from which would be paid into the men's hands. The concession having been yielded late in the day of course provoked less gratitude than contempt.

Fighting thus an unsuccessful battle against the

[1] Circular to Lords-Lieutenant, 10th Feb. 1804.

[2] Circular to Lords-Lieutenant of 12th Oct. 1803.

[3] Circulars to Lords-Lieutenant, 5th and 6th March 1804.

Volunteers both in and out of Parliament, Addington's Ministry showed increasing signs of weakness. Awed by the incessant attacks of Windham, Craufurd, and finally of Pitt upon their neglect of their Regular Army, the Government, at the end of March, brought forward a plan for augmenting it. Mr. Yorke, in introducing the measure, confessed that the Army of Reserve Act had broken down completely, the recruits gained during the past three months having hardly outbalanced the desertions. He proposed, therefore, to suspend the Act for one year, and, in view of this removal of competition in the recruiting market, to raise eight new regiments and ten new battalions, each one thousand strong, at a bounty not exceeding ten guineas. He also brought in a bill to increase the Irish Militia to twenty-eight thousand men, so as to enable ten thousand of them to serve in England, which they had offered to do, and to liberate that number of Regular troops for service abroad. An augmentation of two thousand men to the Guards and of three thousand five hundred to the cavalry, for both of which recruits were always easily gained, had already been ordered; so that upon the whole, the Army would, by one way and another, be increased by twenty-five thousand men. It does not appear, however, that Yorke at once announced the means by which he intended to raise his new battalions. This was no other than the old resource of raising men for rank; and he had already, in fact, set this objectionable machinery in motion for the augmentation of the cavalry.[1] The Commander-in-chief, however, had no intention of allowing the abuses of 1794 to be repeated; and he laid it down as a rigid rule that no officer should gain more than one step, no matter how many recruits he might produce, and, that unless the men were forthcoming within six months, no step should be granted at all. Permission was accordingly given for the officers of the Fourth, Eighth, Twenty-third, Fifty-sixth, Seventy-eighth, and Seventy-ninth to enlist men for

1804.

Mar. 29.

[1] *S.C.L.B.* 3rd Oct. 1803.

1804. their own promotion in second battalions.[1] Letters of service were also granted on the 14th of May to Lord Matthew and Colonel Brown, and on the 24th to Colonels Falkiner and Burke to raise four new regiments in Ireland, of which three formed part of the Line until 1818, and Brown's was swept into the Eighty-seventh Foot.[2] But besides this a contract was concluded with a certain Colonel French and Captain Sandon for raising five thousand men, of which four thousand were to be produced within nine months, and the entire number within thirteen months. The levy-money granted for each man was thirteen guineas, raised subsequently to nineteen guineas, with an additional ten guineas upon the delivery of each batch of five hundred recruits; and it was conceded that ten boys should be allowed among every hundred men. This levy was a complete failure, the Deputy-inspector-general of Recruiting in Ireland having set his face

[1] The terms were as follows:—

Major for Lieut.-Colonelcy	to raise	82	men	82
2 Capts. for Majorities each	„	90	„	180
10 Lieuts. for companies each	„	45	„	450
12 Ensigns for Lieutenancies	„	12	„	144
8 gentlemen for ensigncies	„	21	„	168
				1024

	£	s.	d.
Bounty to Recruit	£10	10	0
„ to recruiting officer, per man	2	2	0
„ „ party „ „	1	1	0
	£13	13	0

Besides the regiments named in the text, the 2nd, 5th, 6th, 7th, and 18th, were also selected to raise second battalions.

S.C.L.B. 19th and 24th April 1804.

C.C.L.B. 15th May 1804.

[2] *C.J.* vol. 60, p. 620.

Burke's was numbered 98th, became the 97th in 1815, and was disbanded in 1818.

Matthew's was numbered 99th, became the 98th in 1815, and was disbanded in 1818.

Falkiner's was numbered the 100th, became the 99th in 1815, and was disbanded in 1818.

against it from the first, not without insinuations 1804. that French was a crimp, and not without some justification for using that term. At the end of twelve months the Duke of York cancelled the letter of service, French having produced only two hundred men instead of five thousand; and therewith this extremely objectionable mode of recruiting came to an end, as it seems for ever. It was none too soon, for the notorious Mary Anne Clarke, the mistress of the Duke of York, was mixed up in the affair. Indeed she contrived, with her customary dexterity, to extract £1700 from the pockets of French and Sandon in return for her good offices (which were very ineffectual) with the Duke of York to promote the success of the levy.[1] This scandal was not exposed until 1809; but meanwhile it seems astonishing that, after the experience of the past war, either Ministers or Commander-in-chief should have countenanced any such agreement as was made with French; though it must be admitted that the supervision of the recruiting service had been greatly improved, that the Inspector in Ireland had at once put his foot firmly upon all malpractices, and that he had been most loyally supported by the Horse Guards.

These measures, however, were practically the last of Addington's Ministry. Pitt had long been growing weary of the attitude of patron and protector which he had assumed towards it in the first place, and which his supporters had from the beginning condemned. At last on the 23rd of April, upon the motion for going into committee on the Army of Reserve Suspension Bill, he rose to oppose it and turned violently on the Government. "No one measure for public defence can they be said to have originated," he declared, "and several they have enfeebled and retarded," and therewith he proceeded to sketch his own plan for setting

[1] The whole of the papers disinterred upon this unsavoury affair are printed in Stratford's authentic edition of the Investigation of the charges against the Duke of York, vol. ii. 355 sqq.

1804. matters right. His motion was lost by a majority of thirty-seven; but the fate of the Government was hardly doubtful from that moment. The bills for the augmentation of the Irish Militia and for enabling it to volunteer for service in England were passed on the 3rd of May, and on the 7th the House was informed that Pitt had been called upon to form a Ministry in the room of Addington resigned.

[For the authorities upon which the foregoing narrative is based I must refer the reader to my work, *The County Lieutenancies and the Army*, 1803-1814.]

CHAPTER VIII

THE formation of Pitt's new administration took some time, and when completed was anything but satisfactory. The Prime Minister had desired to include in it the ablest men of all parties without any exception; but George the Third would not hear of admitting Fox to his councils; and, having regard to the instability of the King's mental powers at the moment, Pitt forbore to press his wishes upon the Sovereign. Fox very generously accepted the situation without a murmur, and promised to advise his followers to accept places in Pitt's Government; but they with one voice refused to take office without their chief, and, worse still, Lord Grenville and his political adherents declared likewise that they would enter no Cabinet from which Fox was excluded. Pitt's position was one of extreme difficulty; but he decided that at any cost he would supplant Addington's inefficient administration. This is no place to discuss the question as to whether he was right or wrong, but it is certain, at least, that he was actuated by none but patriotic motives. The result, however, was that the list of the new Ministers showed a deplorable number of nonentities; and their weakness was not least conspicuous in the departments with which this history is chiefly concerned. Lord Chatham, capable though indolent, became Master-general of the Ordnance. Lord Camden, a nobleman of tried mediocrity, took charge of the War Office and Colonies. Henry Dundas, Lord Melville, succeeded

1804. May.

1804. May. St. Vincent at the Admiralty. The Home Office, more happily, was committed to Lord Hawkesbury, a man whose reputation is far below his deserts; and, best of all, India was entrusted to one still greater and abler, Robert Stewart, Lord Castlereagh. On the other hand, the Opposition, headed by Fox, was rendered doubly formidable now that it had gained the uncompromising resolution of Grenville and the insight, eloquence, and wit of Windham. The parting of these men from Pitt, in a political sense, had not been friendly; and the great Minister now found himself confronted no longer by a powerless though venomous minority, but by lost friends whose criticism was sharpened by the feeling that their late honoured leader had, ever since the Peace of Amiens, fallen below his reputation and forfeited their confidence.

When at length Pitt was able to meet Parliament, June. his first business was to pass the Volunteer Consolidation Act,[1] the stormy career of which came to an end on the 5th of June. Of this it must suffice to say that by it the Volunteer Act of 1802 and the Billetting Act of 1803 were repealed; that Yeomanry were required to attend four days' drill and Volunteer Infantry eight days' drill every quarter to gain them exemption from the ballot for the Militia or any Additional Force; that Volunteer Infantry, assembled of their own will for permanent duty, were subjected to military law, but not so Volunteer Cavalry or Yeomanry; that no rules of any future corps were to be binding unless approved by the King; that rules made in the past could be annulled by the same authority; and that greater powers of discipline at large were granted to the Commanding Officers. Several troublesome questions were thus finally set at rest, and means were assured for turning the chaos brought about by Addington's folly into some kind of order. But the original blunder in respect of the Volunteers, due as much to Pitt as to Addington, was for

[1] 44 Geo. III. cap. 54.

the present beyond correction; and it was with the whole weight of this blunder round his neck that Pitt grappled with the more serious problem of maintaining the Regular Army. 1804. June.

The Army of Reserve Act had by this time died a natural death; and it behoved Pitt to devise some new scheme which should replace it. The objects which he set before himself were sound and statesmanlike. First, the existing competition for recruits between the Regular Army and the multifarious forces designed for home service only must be ended, and the enormous height of bounties must, by this and other means, be brought low. Secondly, all obstacles in the way of establishing a Permanent Additional Force as a standing foundation for the maintenance of the Army must be done away. He had already sketched his device for attaining these ends in a speech on the 25th of April; and on the 5th of June he introduced a Permanent Additional Force Bill which embodied his scheme in its maturity. In substance the bill was as follows:—First, the Militia of Great Britain would be reduced to its original quota of 1802, namely fifty-one thousand men. Next, the quotas of the Supplementary Militia and the Army of Reserve would be merged into one, making a total of seventy-nine thousand men.[1] This would provide a permanent reserve for the Army; and machinery would be devised for making good any drains upon it to the extent of one-sixth, or thirteen thousand men, annually. The intention of his proposals was therefore excellent; it remained to seek out the means for their fulfilment.

In the first place, both the Army of Reserve and the Supplementary Militia were seriously short of their establishment, to the extent altogether of nearly twenty

[1]
Army of Reserve for United Kingdom . .	49,880
Supplementary Militia for Great Britain . .	29,071
Total .	78,951

Ireland had no Supplementary Militia.

1804. June. thousand men;[1] and it was necessary to raise that number before the Permanent Reserve could be said to exist. In addition to these there must be levied also by the 1st of October 1805, the first annual instalment of one-sixth, which was modestly set down at eleven thousand men, to replace those who should have enlisted from the Reserve into the Army. On the whole, therefore, the scheme required thirty-one thousand men to be supplied within the ensuing fifteen months. How was this number to be obtained? The ballot of 1803, owing to the false principle of substitution, had produced only inferior men and a gigantic rise in bounties. Pitt resolved, therefore, to dispense with it altogether, and to call upon every parish of Great Britain for its quota of the number of men required. In brief, he threw the work of raising the levy upon the parochial officers. To preserve its local character, he limited their range of recruiting to a distance of twenty miles around their parishes within the same county, or of ten miles in an adjacent county. To ensure that they should not compete with the recruiting parties of the Regular Army, he restricted their bounty to twelve guineas, being three-fourths of that allowed to the Regulars, which was sixteen guineas. The parochial recruits were to be enlisted for home service only, and for five years or until six months after the cessation of war, but were to be encouraged by a further bounty of ten guineas to take service with the Regulars. To stimulate the zeal of the parochial officers, they were to receive one guinea for every man that they produced, whereas, if they failed in their new duty, their parishes were to be mulcted in £20 for every man deficient of the quota. The fines thus collected were in the last resort to be paid to the general recruiting fund of the country; and the commander of the battalion concerned was then to

[1]

Deficiencies in Army of Reserve . . .	12,477
In Supplementary Militia	7,305
Total .	19,782

fill the vacancy or vacancies in his regiment by ordinary 1804.
recruiting, paying the same bounty as that offered by June.
the parish and no more. Finally the whole of the men, when raised, were to be formed into second battalions to the Regular regiments of the Army.

The plan was bold and, if the expression may be used, conciliatory. The ballot had become very oppressive during 1803: Pitt proposed to leave it unused. There had been loud complaints of the burden laid on the agricultural interest by parochial rates and fines under the Militia and Army of Reserve Acts: Pitt transferred the entire weight of the bounties under his new measure to the Imperial Treasury. Nevertheless, critics were not wanting to call into question every advantage expected from the measure. Windham prophesied that, if any men at all were brought forward by the parochial officers, they would be purchased from the crimps. Another member predicted that the bill might produce money but would never produce men, and that, far from giving any relief to landed proprietors, it would inflict on them the equivalent of a doubled land-tax. Yet another pointed out that to offer a man £16 : 16s. to enter the Line directly, and £23 : 2s. to enter it through the new force was on the face of it absurd. Lastly, Colonel Robert Craufurd condemned the whole plan as worthless, advocating in its stead compulsory training for all men of a certain age, with short service and liberal pensions to tempt them to enlist voluntarily into the Line. Pitt, however, turning a deaf ear to any croakings of failure, stood up firmly for his bill, which on the 29th of June was duly passed into law.

Meanwhile the general preparations for defence against invasion progressed steadily towards perfection. Orders had already been issued on the 31st of October 1803 for the removal of all live-stock and provisions—"driving the country" as it was called—but this procedure, which had been first suggested in 1779, was so strongly opposed by such capable authorities as Sir

1804. John Moore and the Duke of Richmond that it was abandoned. Far more valuable was the Duke of York's recommendation, that, among the vehicles registered under the First Defence Act, one light cart should be set apart and marked as regimental transport for each company of Volunteer infantry, and that waggons should likewise be marked, set apart, and provided with seats to convey the men from the remoter districts to any threatened point. Indeed, the organisation for speedy moving of troops was so far perfected that they could be readily concentrated in any quarter. The Volunteers and Yeomanry in each military district were also organised into brigades, and their brigadiers duly appointed. The quality of the levies steadily improved as more and more of them took their turn of permanent duty; though their unwillingness to submit to any officers but their own made their discipline, already a doubtful quantity, more uncertain than ever.

Nor was fortification, permanent and temporary, forgotten. Addington's Ministry had already made a beginning in this matter by forming entrenched camps in chosen positions, as rallying points for the forces of each district; but these, though, of course, designed by military men, did not always escape criticism from officers of the Army. Thus at Chelmsford there had been constructed at great expense, not a chain of detached works, but a single line of entrenchment. What, asked Robert Craufurd in the House of Commons, was the use of this? No enemy would pause to attack it, but would push straight on to London; and, if the force in the camp closed in upon his rear, the enemy would be none the worse, for having no communications he could not be cut off from them. This challenge was answered, not very effectually, by General Thomas Maitland; and the subject was allowed to drop. Pitt, however, infused far greater vigour into the work of fortifying the country, even riding about to inspect the works in person with an energy which Lord Grenville, no longer his supporter but now his critic, condemned as ridiculous. It is 1804. difficult to say who was Pitt's principal adviser in such matters, for he seems to have been eclectic in his tastes. Some would have us believe that it was Dumouriez who was chiefly consulted by him; and it is at least certain that Dumouriez, after many wanderings, settled in England in 1803, received a pension from Government, and produced a general scheme for the defence of the country. This, as he had planned a scheme of invasion in 1779, he claimed to be well qualified to do. But the military authorities, not unreasonably feeling some distrust of the man, declined to permit him to make a close military survey of any ground; and, since he was therefore compelled to rely wholly upon inaccurate maps for his premises, his conclusions must necessarily have been of doubtful value. Furthermore, amid much that is probably sound in Dumouriez's plans, there is such a wealth of what can only be described as nonsense, that it is impossible to suppose that they can have received much attention.[1] One costly work may, however, perhaps, be ascribed to the French General, namely the military canal from Hythe to Sandgate.[2]

[1] Dumouriez's plans of defence have been recently published in *Dumouriez and the Defence of England against Napoleon*, by Dr. J. H. Rose and A. M. Broadley, together with a certain number of the projects which Dumouriez was eternally sending to the Government unasked, and which are to be found by the dozen scattered among the papers in the Record Office. Except in a few instances, which I shall duly point out, I cannot find that his advice carried much weight, nor can I think, after examination of a good many *projets*, that it deserved to do so. Dumouriez was no doubt a man of exceptional talent and in some respects an exceedingly able soldier; but his vanity was portentous, his hold upon facts was never strong, and he was an inveterate schemer. I am unable, therefore, to accept the authors' valuation of Dumouriez, or their assurance that he rendered great service to this country. For the rest, this book, together with the two bulky volumes entitled *The Great Terror* by A. M. Broadley and H. Wheeler, appear to have been published chiefly to call attention to a private collection of documents and caricatures; for with space to contain much that would be of priceless value to a serious historian, they provide disappointingly little.

[2] But it appears from a letter from the Commander-in-chief to the Duke of Richmond that the canal, with its ultimate extension

1804. This was made in order to isolate the Romney marshes, where, according to Dumouriez, an invading force could otherwise have secured all the cattle and horses which fed on the marshes. But Pitt is more generally remembered by the martello towers, which were advocated by Craufurd among many other officers, and are still to be seen on the coast. Indeed it seems probable that Pitt leaned greatly upon Sir John Moore, whose good work at the camp of Shorncliffe came under his immediate notice while he was organising the forces of the Cinque Ports, and was thoroughly appreciated by him.

Meanwhile Napoleon, since the 18th of May 1804 Emperor of the French, remained throughout the year with his plans in a state of flux. He had realised that he could not throw his army across the Channel until his line-of-battle ships had cleared the way for him; and, having abandoned the idea of an invasion during the foggy nights of winter, he was inclined to take advantage of the calmer days of summer for the operation. It was, however, essential first that the boats which were building in every port of France should be concentrated in the harbours of the Channel; and this, in the face of the British cruisers, was no easy matter. The flotilla in the Scheldt was strictly blockaded; and, though the Dutch Admiral Verhuell with considerable skill contrived more than once to baffle the vigilance of Sir Sidney Smith, and to bring vessels down by Ostend and Dunkirk to Boulogne, yet little was really accomplished by him owing to his want of seamen. At Havre the blockade was equally strict, and was varied by occasional bombardments which caused much alarm even if they did little damage. The passage to the Channel from the ports in the Atlantic was even more difficult, so closely did the British frigates watch every promontory and headland. It was necessary for French cavalry and

to Cliff End in Sussex, was suggested by Sir David Dundas. *H.O. Internal Defence*, Duke of Richmond to C.-in-C., 13th Nov.; C.-in-C. to Duke of Richmond, 19th Nov. 1806.

artillery on land to follow the course of the boats at sea 1804.
in order to ensure their safety; and, in spite of aid from the troops and from countless batteries on the coast, only thirty five vessels out of two hundred and thirty-one succeeded in reaching the Channel from the Ocean at all. Moreover, even when they did reach it, they were glad to put into the first port that they could find; and from this cause there were in Boulogne nearly three times as many boats as had been allotted to that place. Nor were they safe even then, for the difficulties of leaving and entering the port had been little diminished by Napoleon's extensive improvements; and a light gale was quite sufficient to throw the whole of the craft in the roadstead into confusion.

On the other hand, the British attempts against Boulogne were one and all unsuccessful. Early in 1804 Addington countenanced a plan from which great results were expected by the thoughtless. Three ships were to be filled with masonry, carefully built and clamped together, and, having been run aground upon the shoal at the entrance to Boulogne, were then to be burned, with the intention that the masonry should remain, block the mouth of the harbour permanently, and shut in the whole of the flotilla for ever. This brilliant idea emanated from a smuggler, by name Etches, who was supposed to know the navigation about Boulogne better than other men. Extensive preparations were carried out, and an effort was actually made to put the plan into execution, with the help of a few light vessels of the Royal Navy. It need hardly be said that the entire project came to a ridiculous end, with the usual recriminations between the parties concerned therein; the smugglers laying the whole of the blame upon the naval officers, who had viewed the proceedings with a surly contempt which was fully justified by results.[1]
Later in the year, on the 2nd of October, a more Oct. 2
sensible attack was made upon Boulogne by vessels

[1] The whole story is in W.O. *Orig. Corres.* 184, *The Stone Expedition*.

1804. which were practically torpedoes; but, though five of them were exploded, the damage done was trifling. In fact, the most serious loss inflicted upon the flotilla at Boulogne was caused by Napoleon himself. In July he
July. paid a visit of inspection to the port and ordered out the craft for a review. Admiral Bruix, seeing certain signs of the approach of bad weather, declined to obey; and after a stormy scene, in which the two men nearly came to blows, Bruix was dismissed and the Emperor had his way. The result was that twenty or thirty craft were lost, and from fifty to two hundred men drowned. The whole affair was, of course, smothered under a mass of lies, as was Napoleon's manner; but the experience can hardly have weakened his dislike for the naval profession at large.

Meanwhile his sea-going fleets had made little progress during the summer of 1804. At Brest there were twenty-six ships paralysed by want of seamen; at Isle d'Aix and Orient nothing had been accomplished; and only at Toulon, under the impulse of Latouche Tréville, eleven line-of-battle ships were slowly made fit for service. In May, and again in July, Napoleon had sketched speculative instructions for the Toulon fleet, to which were appended the pompous words, "Let us be masters of the Channel for six hours, and we shall be masters of the world." But in August Latouche Tréville died, and the Toulon fleet had achieved nothing. However, at the end of
Sept. September Napoleon at last produced a more definite plan. According to this, the Brest squadron was to carry eighteen thousand men to Ireland, first going far to westward so as to approach it as if from Newfoundland; it was then to enter the Channel so as to favour the passage to England of the flotilla from Boulogne, or failing this, to go to the Texel and escort twenty-five thousand men more to Ireland. At the same time the squadrons from Toulon and Rochefort were to sail to the West Indies with reinforcements, raid all the British islands, return to Ferrol to release the five

ships blockaded there, and then, united, to put in to Rochefort. 1804.

Napoleon's orders concerning the attack on Ireland went astray, and their purport reached the British Government, curiously enough, through the smuggler Etches.[1] Whether this happened by design of the Emperor or not is doubtful. All that is certain is that in October he renewed his orders to the squadrons at Rochefort and at Toulon to embark their troops at once, while nothing more was said as to the action of the Brest fleet. It seems, however, that the British Government now became more nervous about Ireland, which only in the previous year had been disturbed by the abortive insurrection of Robert Emmett. Dumouriez had dwelt with great emphasis upon the fact that it was the most vulnerable spot in the Empire; wherefore, urging that there could be no safety in an attitude of passive defence, he had advocated attack upon the points from which an expedition might be expected to sail for Ireland, namely the ports of the Peninsula and the Scheldt. Whether moved by this counsel or not, Ministers in November consulted Sir John Moore as to the possibility of an attack upon Ferrol with twenty thousand men, alleging that in the opinion of the naval officers the destruction of the place by a *coup de main* would be an easy matter. Unable to find any warrant for this view in the papers laid before him, Moore undertook to reconnoitre the place secretly in person; and, though prevented by the suspicions of the Spaniards from making any close survey of the defences, he was able at least to satisfy himself that Ferrol was fully prepared against attack. Upon his report, therefore, the enterprise was abandoned.

But in the interim the situation had again changed. Spain, equally afraid of France and of England, and longing only to remain perfectly neutral, had so far yielded to the stronger pressure of Napoleon that the

[1] Desbrière, iv. 199, calls him the Reverend Cadman Etches; having apparently construed Rd. (Richard) to mean Reverend.

1804. British Government lost patience with her undisguised, though unwilling, inclination towards the French cause. On the 30th of September the capture of three Spanish plate-ships by Sir Graham Moore, the brother of Sir John, brought matters to a crisis. Napoleon seized the moment to stimulate Spain to open hostilities; and after two months of hesitation the Court of
Dec. 14. Madrid, on the 14th of December, declared war upon England. The Spanish fleet was therefore now at the disposal of Napoleon, though it was in no very efficient state. There were a few fine ships and a great many indifferent. Some were overburdened with an excessive spread of canvas, others with an excessive weight of guns; and seamen, owing to an epidemic in the Mediterranean ports, were extremely difficult to obtain. However, the ships were at any rate to hand;
1805. and on the 4th of January 1805 Admiral Gravina on
Jan. 4. behalf of Spain and Decrès on behalf of France signed a convention, under which at least twenty-five Spanish sail of the line and some seven thousand Spanish troops were to be ready by the 30th of March for a secret expedition. Meanwhile the squadrons at Toulon and Rochefort had embarked the troops assigned to them, and on the 12th, 14th, and 23rd they received their first instructions. Both were to break the blockade at the first opportunity, and sail for the West Indies. Villeneuve, with the Toulon fleet, after picking up three French ships from Cadiz, was first to reinforce the garrison of Cayenne, and then, dividing his squadron, to attack Surinam with one division and Demerara, Berbice and Essequibo with the other; but in any case he was, within sixty days after his arrival at Surinam, to return to Ferrol, liberate the blockaded squadron there, and proceed with it to Rochefort. Missiessy with the Rochefort squadron was to sail straight to Martinique, capture Dominica and St. Lucia, and levy contributions upon the remaining British islands. Napoleon reckoned that Missiessy would be master of the Caribbean Sea for at least thirty days, which period he was to turn to the

best possible account. Missiessy likewise was to make Ferrol his first port on his return. The Emperor also sketched a suggestion for the use of the Brest, Cadiz, and Ferrol squadrons, which were to descend upon Ireland on Villeneuve's reappearance; but so far he had no thought of using his fleets in the Channel upon their return from the Antilles. Indeed, he seems to have had no design in the expedition to the West Indies beyond a plundering raid, which could have little or no influence upon the course of the war. 1805.

Thus, to the disgrace of England, the French were actually the first to send an offensive expedition across the sea; nor was the reason far to seek. The British after eighteen months of war, following upon a brief truce which had been preceded by ten years of another war, did not yet possess an Army. Addington was chiefly responsible for this, but Pitt also must bear some part of the blame, for his favourite scheme, the Permanent Additional Force Act, had proved a dismal failure. The parochial authorities, conceiving that funds and not men were expected from them, christened the measure the "Twenty Pound Act" and resigned themselves to pay their fines. According to the strict letter of the law, the twenty thousand men deficient in the Army of Reserve and Supplementary Militia were to have been raised by the 9th of August; but there were symptoms in the country which led Ministers to inquire as to the progress of the levy. The answer from every county was uniformly the same. Not a man had been raised; the areas of recruiting were too much restricted, the bounties to recruits too low, the rewards offered to parish officers too paltry. The Government extended the time for raising the men until the 15th of November and issued circular after circular, half coaxing, half menacing, to stimulate the parochial authorities to their new duties; but in vain. By the 1st of November fewer than eight hundred men had been enlisted, and of these a full eighth had deserted. Parliament met in January 1805, 1804.

1805. and a motion was at once brought forward in the Lords for the repeal of the Act. The measure was defended by Lord Hawkesbury, who alleged that, under the spur of many circulars, the parishes had begun to move, and that the Act was now producing men at the rate of three hundred a week, or eleven thousand men a year. Upon this very inconclusive assurance the Lords rejected the motion for repeal; but the attack was
Feb. 21. renewed in the Commons a week later by far more formidable critics; and on the 6th of March Sheridan definitely moved the repeal of the Act. The motion was lost by a very large majority; but the situation was ser ous; and Pitt knew it. The casualties in the Regular Army for the first nine months of 1804 exceeded the recruits gained during the whole year by over three thousand; and Lord Grenville openly asserted in the House of Lords that the numbers of the Regular Infantry were actually smaller on the 1st of January 1805 than on the 1st of January 1804. If the war were to be conducted on such lines, the ruin of the nation could only be a matter of time.

Pitt was the last man to trifle with such a situation. With his usual courage he looked facts in the face,
Mar. 31. and on the 31st of March brought in a bill to enable a number of men, equal to the actual strength of the Supplementary Militia in each county, to be enlisted in the Army. To attract recruits it was enacted that they should receive a bounty of ten guineas, should be allowed to choose their own regiments, and should not be drafted from them without their own consent; and special provisions were inserted to reconcile the Colonels of Militia, so far as possible, to this weakening of their battalions. Under this Act about eleven thousand men passed into the Regular Forces between the 10th of April and the 26th of June, four-fifths of them into the infantry, and the remainder into the Marines. Pitt had named seventeen thousand men as the figure for which he had hoped; but nine thousand were by no means to be despised, the less

so as they were not raw but trained and disciplined troops. 1805.

Nor had Pitt's diplomacy been idle since his accession to office. At the outset of the war England had at once sought the friendship of Russia, which the Tsar Alexander was very ready to grant; for he had dreams of constituting himself the protagonist of Europe against the Revolution and its representative, Bonaparte. Where Russia led there was good hope that Prussia would follow, her despicable King being very willing to attach himself to Alexander's skirts, though his greed for Hanover was such that he would have broken any faith to obtain it. Austria was also approached by Addington but would commit herself to nothing, which was not unnatural considering all that she had suffered during the last war. Napoleon, however, who was also on the search for allies, unwittingly forwarded England's interests. In the west he could gain what he wanted in many cases by threats. Holland and the Italian Republic were virtually French provinces and were treated as such. Spain he had intimidated, as has been told, into furnishing a large monthly subsidy until she should openly break with England; and from Portugal also he had extorted a convention, under which that helpless kingdom gave him money and commercial advantages as well as a promise of strict neutrality. Naples, likewise, he overawed, as we have seen, by an armed occupation. The lesser German states, Bavaria, Würtemberg, Baden, and Hesse, he had gained early in 1803 by allotting to them the confiscated property of the ecclesiastical states; thereby so whetting the appetites of the princes who controlled them, that Bavaria proceeded to seize all the lands lying within her borders that were held directly of the Emperor Francis. The aggrieved owners appealed to Austria for protection, and the Emperor occupied all the immediate lordships (as they were called) both in Bavaria and Würtemberg with troops. He withdrew them, however, upon a threat of invasion

1804. from Napoleon; but from the end of 1803 he prepared quietly for war, and began to hope for alliance with England and Russia. After this affair Napoleon could hardly hope to gain Austria, and his main object, therefore, was to neutralise her by winning Prussia to his side. He had also made overtures to Russia, but without success, and by the execution of the Duke of Enghien on the 20th of March 1804, he alienated the Tsar beyond any hope of speedy reconciliation.

Such was the state of affairs when Pitt returned to power. His great objects were three: to secure the neutrality of Holland; to paralyse Spain by capturing her treasure-ships and stirring up revolt in her colonies, unless she either joined England or remained strictly neutral; and to treat with Russia so as to draw Austria, Prussia, and Naples into a general war. The Tsar, who was already busily preparing to fight France, welcomed Pitt's proposals, and on the 24th of May invited Austria to concert operations with him; but the Emperor Francis, wishing first to be sure of a subsidy from England before the war, and of an accession of territory after it, would not sign a formal alliance. Simultaneously Alexander turned to Prussia; but King Frederick William was also averse from a treaty, hoping to gain Hanover by adroit mediation between Napoleon and the Tsar, which was as though a jay should mediate between an eagle and a condor. However, he was so far alarmed by Napoleon's seizure of
May 24. Cuxhaven and Hamburg that he came to a secret agreement with Alexander to resist any further encroachment of the French upon the North German states. There remained Sweden; and here England was sure of King Gustavus the Fourth, who loathed the very name of Bonaparte, and used the proclamation of the French Empire as an occasion to exchange insults with him. A half-witted king, as England was later to discover, is not a very profitable ally; but at the time it sufficed that he should keep open to her the port of Stralsund.

At the end of May 1804, therefore, matters had

advanced thus far towards a Coalition, not without 1804.
vigorous efforts on the part of Napoleon to check them. At Naples his threats extorted the dismissal of the English Minister, Acton, and the appointment of his own emissary, Alquier, in his stead. Prussia he surprised in the midst of her negotiations with Russia by a question whether King Frederick William would refuse a passage to Russian troops through Prussian territory, if it were demanded; and he actually drew from the miserable king a declaration that, unless the French encroached further on the neutral states of Germany, he would close his frontier to any troops directed against them. To Austria Napoleon addressed a mixed language of hectoring and cajolery, first hinting at the coalition and threatening to crush it at once, then offering her Wallachia, Bosnia, and Servia in exchange for Venetia. For the moment Austria deferred to him, and sent assurances of peaceful intentions; but at the beginning of October there was an open rupture of relations between France and Russia, and the Tsar, putting further pressure upon Austria, persuaded her to consent to an alliance. The agreement was put into the form of a declaration, so that the existence of a treaty could
be denied. Hereby Austria engaged to enter upon Nov. 6.
military operations conjointly with Russia, in the case of any further augmentation of the French forces in Naples; but Russia was to warn Naples not to provoke France thereto either by manifesto or insurrection.

Finally, in November a special emissary from St. Nov. 16.
Petersburg reached London, and on the 11th of April 1805 a Treaty between England and Russia was signed at the Russian capital. Its objects were defined to be the evacuation of Italy, Hanover, and North Germany by the French, the security of the Kingdom of Naples, the re-establishment of the King of Sardinia, and the independence of Holland and Switzerland. The means were to be half a million men, for which England was to pay at the rate of a million and a quarter sterling for every hundred thousand. Russia was to place

1805. eighty thousand men on the Austrian, and sixty thousand on the Prussian frontier. Austria and Prussia were to be invited to join the alliance, and on agreeing to do so were to receive a million sterling apiece for the initial expenses of the campaign. Spain and Portugal were to be invited likewise to include themselves in the alliance within three months of the opening of active operations. The condition for payment of the subsidies was that, within five months of the signature of the treaty, Russia and Austria, or one of them, should set her forces in action against France. Sweden was comprised in the agreement; and meanwhile she had already come to a separate arrangement with England, whereby, in return for an annual subsidy of £60,000,[1] the port of Stralsund and the Isle of Rügen were placed at the disposal of the British as military and commercial stations.

Such was the storm that was gathering round Napoleon's head at the opening of 1805. He was not unaware of it, and was ready with counterblasts in every direction. He prepared to crush Austria if she did not disarm. He sent Marshal Junot to Portugal to demand the closing of her ports against the British and the expulsion of all British agents before the 22nd of March, on pain of immediate war; and he hung out the crown of Portugal as a bait to attract Godoy, the actual ruler of Spain. He wrote letters to the Shah and to the Sultan of Turkey to stir them up against Russia. When Holland complained of the burden that was laid upon her, he transformed her into a
March. French province. The Italian Republic he converted into a kingdom, first for his brother Joseph and, when
Mar. 17. Joseph upon second thoughts refused it, for himself. If he could not persuade the really independent states to throw in their lot with him, he would at least make sure of his own vassals.

Meanwhile his two fleets put to sea, Villeneuve from
Jan. Toulon on the 18th of January, Missiessy on the 11th

[1] Pierrepont to Sec. of State, 3rd Jan. 1805.

from Rochefort. Villeneuve, meeting at once with heavy weather which seriously damaged three of his ships, put back to Toulon, with loud protests against sending ships to sea ill-fitted, undermanned, and encumbered with troops.[1] Missiessy, on the other hand, made a fairly good passage, and on the 20th of February arrived safely at Fort de France, Martinique, with his entire force of five ships of the line, five smaller vessels of war, and thirty-three hundred troops. In the British West Indies, General Myers, the commander-in-chief, had been sadly harassed by privateers, by the weakness of the British squadron both in quality and quantity, and above all by a sickly season, which had wrought special havoc in Dominica, Antigua, and St. Lucia. In the last-named island in particular the Sixty-eighth Regiment had lost over five hundred men dead and over one hundred and seventy invalided to Europe during the last six months of 1804,[2] while in Myers's own staff, civil and military, twelve out of sixteen persons had perished. He had asked for reinforcements but none had yet arrived; and Missiessy may therefore be said to have come at a good moment for himself.

1805.

Feb. 20.

Obedient to his instructions, the French Admiral wasted no time, but on the 21st sailed for Dominica, and arriving off Roseau early on the 22nd under British colours, was received by the harbour-master, who came aboard the flag-ship not doubting but that he was welcoming the British Commodore. General Prevost, who was in command ashore, speedily perceived the mistake and opened fire from the batteries upon the French squadron. The bulk of the ships then remained in position before Roseau, while two small divisions parted from them north and south to cover the disembarkation of the troops.

Feb. 21.

Feb. 22.

The landing-place selected by General Lagrange, who was in command of the French, was between two

[1] Desbrière, iv. 299-300

[2] Gen. Myers to Sec. of State, 30th Sept., 14th Oct. 1804; 5th Jan., 10th Feb. 1805.

1805. Feb. 22. and three miles south of Roseau and a little to the north of Point Michel; and at about seven in the morning nineteen barges full of troops made for the shore at this point, under protection of a schooner and of several boats armed with carronades. Prevost's entire force for the defence of the island consisted of about three hundred men of the Forty-sixth, a score of Royal Artillery, about four hundred of the First West India Regiment, and a few companies of Militia; but even this handful of men he was compelled to divide between Roseau and Prince Rupert's Bay, the maintenance of the harbour at the latter point being vital to the safety of the island. However, he was resolved to contest every foot of the ground; and with three selected companies, one from each of his three corps, he drove back the first of the French boats. Two French ships then stood in shore to cover the disembarkation with their guns, whereupon Prevost withdrew the three companies further inland to a defile which defended the approach to Roseau. Then, reinforcing them with two additional companies of Militia, more men of the Forty-sixth and two light guns, he handed the command of the whole to Major Nunn of the First West India Regiment, with orders not to yield an inch of ground. The French thereupon landed over two thousand men and advanced with great impetuosity to the attack. But the position was strong; Prevost's dispositions were good; the detachment of the Forty-sixth, which did not exceed two hundred men, set a fine example; and Nunn's tenacity was beyond all praise. The French column suffered much during its advance from the British artillery, especially from a single gun so cunningly placed behind a wall that it could only be approached in single file; and a whole company of French grenadiers sacrificed itself, man after man, in a vain endeavour to capture it. At ten o'clock Nunn was mortally wounded, and the command passed to Captain O'Connell of the same regiment. He also was wounded almost immediately, but remained in

the field until two o'clock, when the French, repulsed 1805.
in repeated attacks with heavy loss, fell back out of Feb. 22.
range.

Further north the French ships were retarded by contrary winds, but at nine o'clock they landed another strong detachment a mile and a half to north of Roseau at the foot of Morne Daniel. Prevost had but one hundred Militia at this point to oppose to over a thousand of the enemy; but his handful of men attacked the boats gallantly as they came up through the surf, killing eight French soldiers and wounding several more, till they were driven from the beach by the guns of the men-of-war. There remained now only a small redoubt on Morne Daniel, which was defended by a sergeant of the Forty-sixth with four men of his own regiment, five of the West India, and a few Militia with a single three-pounder. This gallant little party fought desperately, inflicting much loss on the enemy until the ten men of the Regular troops had fallen, when the redoubt was carried by sheer weight of numbers. The French then landed two hundred men midway between their two points of attack; and Prevost, observing them on the march to get into the rear of O'Connell, at about two o'clock hoisted the white flag. The French fire thereupon ceased, and Prevost, ordering the Militia to remain at their posts, directed the civil Governor to negotiate the capitulation of Roseau. He himself then drew off the whole of his Regular troops, white and black, and made a forced march with them along the whole length of the island to Rupert's Bay. So steep was the country and so rough were the tracks that the troops, carrying their wounded, took four days to accomplish the journey; but Prevost himself with two companies, by great exertion, reached Fort Cabril at Rupert's Bay in tweny-four hours, and at once made every preparation for a stubborn defence. With an adequate garrison, as he knew, the French were powerless to hurt him except by a regular siege. Thus though

1805. Roseau was lost, Dominica and its precious anchorage were saved.[1]

This little affair was extremely creditable to all concerned on the British side. Prevost had evidently thought out his plan of operations in every detail, and, though in a measure surprised by the French attack, was never for a moment at a loss. His officers also knew their duty and did it; and of the many tiny detachments scattered along the batteries on the coast, every one with a single exception was safely brought in, without direct orders, to Rupert's Bay. One officer and seven gunners only were captured, and the losses of the Regular troops did not exceed thirty-seven in killed and wounded. Those of the Militia are unfortunately unknown, but they were considerable, for this force behaved with admirable gallantry and spirit. The casualties of the French were reckoned by Prevost at about three hundred; but the General's spirited defence produced more important consequences than the death or mutilation of French soldiers. General Lagrange had begged Missiessy to divide his squadron so as to attack Roseau and Rupert's Bay simultaneously, and Missiessy had refused; so that when it was realised that Prevost had secured Fort Cabril, Lagrange felt anything but kindly disposed towards his naval colleague. The French squadron reconnoitred Rupert's Bay, but seeing that an attack upon it was hopeless, sailed first to Guadeloupe, and then to St. Kitt's, Nevis, and Montserrat, where Missiessy levied contributions and ransoms on a few captured ships. Returning thence to Martinique
Mar. 12. on the 12th of March, he found new orders from Napoleon awaiting him. Their purport was that Villeneuve had been driven back by weather to Toulon, that his squadron had since been detailed for another service in a different quarter, that Missiessy was now to act independently, according to the spirit of his first instructions, and that Rochefort

[1] Prevost to Myers, 1st March 1805; Desbrière, iv. 311-313.

would probably be the safest port for him to make for 1805.
on his return.[1]

Missiessy interpreted this as an order to visit St. Domingo and then return home. Admiral Villaret Joyeuse, Governor of Martinique, on the contrary, was urgent that he should first attack the Diamond Rock, which had been fortified and garrisoned by the British Navy as a thorn in the French side; but Missiessy refused to listen to him, alleging that any such operation was contrary to the tenor of his instructions.
On the 22nd of March, therefore, he sailed for the port Mar. 22.
of St. Domingo, which was then besieged by the rebel negroes, threw a reinforcement with supplies and stores
into it, and on the evening of the 28th sailed for Mar. 28.
Rochefort. Myers, however, knew nothing certain of these movements and remained in the greatest anxiety. He had received a welcome reinforcement of three battalions[2] at Barbados on the 11th of March, but in the presence of a superior French squadron he was at a loss to know how to distribute them. Commodore Hood was indeed collecting his ships at Deseada; but with only one vessel of the line and a few frigates he could not hope to engage Missiessy. Moreover, a convoy from England carrying troops for Jamaica was known to be on the way; and one straggling ship from it actually arrived at Barbados on the 27th of March, so that Myers could not tell what disaster might be impending. A little more enterprise on the part of Missiessy might have made things very uncomfortable for us at this time in the West Indies.

It is now, however, necessary to forsake the Antilles for a moment in order to follow the fortunes of Villeneuve. On the 16th of January, two days before that Admiral left Toulon, Napoleon had produced another plan, namely, that the squadrons from Brest, Rochefort, and Ferrol should embark twenty-two thousand men and sail to the East Indies. Since Missiessy had

[1] Decrès to Missiessy, 27th Jan. 1805; Desbrière, iv. 313.
[2] The 15th, 90th, and 96th.

1805. started on the 11th with the Rochefort squadron, his participation in this wild expedition was impossible; but when Villeneuve returned on the 22nd, he was ordered to refit his ships and re-embark his troops as speedily as possible for a new enterprise which, though the fact was not actually revealed to him, could only have been in the East. Evidently, therefore, with Missiessy detached on an independent service, and the remaining squadrons appointed for East Indian waters, the idea of invasion of England had been for the moment dropped. The attitude of Austria was, indeed, too threatening to permit of it.

Towards the end of February, however, French relations with Austria had so far improved that Napoleon returned to his darling project; and, heartened by the assurance of full co-operation of the Spanish fleet, he

Feb. 27. framed, on the 27th of February, his final plan. First, directions were sent to Missiessy to stay in the West Indies and await further order; though these, not arriving until after the Admiral had sailed for Europe, were given to no purpose. Next, Admiral Ganteaume was ordered to weigh anchor at once with the Brest fleet—twenty-one ships of the line—release Vice-admiral Gourdon's squadron at Ferrol, and sail with it to Martinique, where he would take the squadrons of Missiessy and Villeneuve under his command, and with the combined fleets make for Ushant, attack the British vessels there, and proceed to Boulogne. If the combined fleets at Martinique were fewer than twenty-five ships of the line, Ganteaume was to return straight to Ferrol; but he was authorised to wait thirty days at Martinique for the Toulon fleet.

Supplementary to these orders, instructions were given to Villeneuve to sail to Martinique, unblockading Cadiz if necessary on the way, to take Missiessy under his command there, and to wait forty days for Ganteaume. If the last-named did not appear within forty days, Villeneuve was to return to Europe by way of St. Domingo, wait once again twenty days for

Ganteaume at the Cape de Verde Islands, and put back from thence to Cadiz. 1805.

This done, the Emperor drew up on the 23rd of March and the following days the detailed orders for the embarkation of the invading force. But these were at once found to be impossible of execution. In Ney's corps two divisions had too many boats for their men and one division too many men for its boats, with the result that, upon the whole, over fifteen hundred men were left without any boats at all. In Soult's corps five thousand men were left without means of embarkation; and altogether it was found that transport for twenty thousand men and for over five thousand horses was still wanting. Yet, when the matter was examined, it appeared that after all there were numbers of vessels to which no men had been assigned. But this was all part of the general confusion; for though the total number, both of troops and boats, might correspond exactly, yet the distribution was so faulty that in some places there were too many craft for the men, and in others too many men for the craft. In truth, the boasted organisation of the army flotilla of invasion existed only on paper, being, when reduced to practice, a very chaos. Napoleon had in fact wasted time and money irrecoverably by adherence to his own ignorant methods in maritime matters, while neglecting the advice of his skilled and experienced naval officers. Mar. 23.

However, he had now set on foot a naval campaign upon a grand scale; and it is necessary to see what operations the British Government was contemplating at this same time. It must be premised that the Admiralty's great difficulty was to divine the service upon which the Toulon fleet was to be employed. By the occupation of the peninsula of Otranto and the ports at the heel of Italy Napoleon threw out a standing menace to the Mediterranean at large; and the British Ministers were in constant apprehension as to the point where the blow would fall. Napoleon by admirable management contrived that the suspicions of Downing Street should

1805. be turned entirely towards Egypt. He had spread constant reports of an Egyptian expedition during 1802, which were greedily swallowed by General Sir John Stuart, at that time the Commander of our troops at Alexandria.[1] After the evacuation of the country by the British, again, the French agent at Cairo, M. de Lesseps, declared continually and with firm conviction that a French fleet was on its way to Alexandria to seek for a passage thence to the East Indies; and Major Missett, the British agent left behind by Stuart, never ceased to urge the importance of sending a British force to avert such a catastrophe.[2] Lastly, Nelson, to whose vigilance the watch upon Toulon was entrusted, was firmly imbued with the idea that Egypt was Villeneuve's ultimate destination.

But there were other objects besides Egypt within reach, most notably Sicily, the possession of which in French hands would have shaken, if not destroyed, British ascendancy in the Mediterranean. There was no counting upon the Court of Naples. The King, a degenerate Bourbon like his brother of Spain, was incapable of any fixed resolution; and the Queen was a false, dangerous, and scheming woman, who was more likely than not to favour Napoleon, if by so doing she could advance any small interest of her own. From the very outbreak of war Nelson had urged the occupation of Messina; and Addington had given the Governor of Malta discretionary orders to employ two thousand men for the purpose, if Nelson and Mr. Hugh Elliot, the resident at Naples, should ask for them.[3] The Court of Naples, however, would not hear of permitting the British to protect Messina for them, dreading, according to Nelson, the jealousy of the Russians at Corfu rather than that of the French. Yet at any moment the King

[1] *W.O. Egypt*, 346; Stuart to Sec. of State, 20th Jan., 26th Oct. 1803.

[2] *W.O. Egypt*, 346; Missett to Sec. of State, 25th Aug. 1803; 25th, 26th Jan., 27th Feb., 2nd, 16th March, 28th May 1804.

[3] Nelson to Addington, private, 28th June 1803; Nelson to Hobart, 22nd Dec. 1803.

might be compelled to fly from Naples to Palermo; and 1805.
the internal state of Sicily was as bad as it could be, with an oppressive nobility, an enraged middle-class, and not so much as a company of troops. When, therefore, Villeneuve broke the blockade in January 1805, Ministers took the peril to heart and resolved to strengthen the British garrisons in the Mediterranean before it was too late.

Accordingly towards the end of March Lieutenant-general Sir James Craig received orders to take four battalions together with a small detachment of cavalry and artillery to Malta, and to assume command in the whole of the Mediterranean excepting Gibraltar. The principal object of his force was to be the protection of Sicily, and this object he was to fulfil with or without the consent of the King of Naples, but always in his name. If that potentate had gone so far as to exclude British ships from his ports, then Craig was to take possession of Sicily for King George; but if the French had invaded it, or threatened invasion, he was to dislodge them or repel them, according to circumstances, in the name of King Ferdinand. As regarded the further destination of the force, it was necessary to keep several contingencies in view. The Russians were preparing to attack the French in the Mediterranean, and might drive them from the Neapolitan dominions; or again the French might attack Naples before Sicily, and the Russians might call upon the British for assistance. In either case Craig might co-operate with the Russians, if summoned either by Elliot or by the Russian commander, putting himself under the orders of the latter if the foreigner were his superior in rank. Yet again the French might attack Turkey, in which case the occupation of Alexandria might be necessary; or, as Nelson dreaded, they might turn their arms against Sardinia and block the way to the Levant. For these cases no special instructions were given; but they were indicated to show the possible scope of Craig's duties.[1]

[1] *W.O. Entry Book*, 52, Sec. of State to Craig, most secret, 28th, 29th March 1805.

1805. April 17. Craig, accordingly, sailed on the 17th of April, carrying with him two battalions for Gibraltar besides the troops assigned to his own command. The whole of them filled thirty-seven transports, which were escorted by a small squadron of three ships under Rear-admiral Knight. But meanwhile Villeneuve had slipped out of
Mar. 30. Toulon on the 30th of March with eleven sail of the line and eight smaller ships of war, carrying in all over three thousand troops besides the crews. He was seen by two British frigates; but obtaining by good luck intelligence that Nelson was at Palma, on the south-west coast of Sardinia, he shaped his course to evade him by hugging the coast of Spain. At Carthagena Villeneuve found six Spanish ships of the line, which were placed at his disposal by their commanders; but he decided to leave them behind and, profiting by a favourable wind, passed the Straits of Gibraltar on
April 9. the 9th of April. Arrived before Cadiz, he dispersed the blockading force under Sir John Orde, and liberating Admiral Gravina's squadron, hurried on without waiting to incorporate it with his own. Orde fell
April 30. back to the Channel fleet; and on the 30th of April Admiral Knight, being at the moment off Finisterre with Craig's army under convoy, learned to his great dismay that the Toulon fleet was at large. The Admiralty had written to Nelson on the 15th of April to provide for the safety of Knight and his charge on their passage from Gibraltar eastward; but the Board had never dreamed, apparently, that the convoy might be cut off before it reached the Rock. Unaware that Villeneuve was hastening westward
May 7. with all speed, Craig was much alarmed; and on the 7th of May the convoy, with the exception of two transports which had parted company, took refuge in Lisbon. Not knowing whether the French and Spanish squadrons might not attack him even there, Craig made every preparation to land, seize the Portuguese forts and turn the guns upon the enemy's ships. It was a desperate expedient and by no means in

accordance with the so-called law of nations; but men 1805.
must not be too hardly judged when they find themselves, by no fault of their own, thrust unexpectedly into a false position.

Meanwhile Nelson, on receiving news of Villeneuve's departure, had made at first for Sicily; and it was not
until the 19th of April that he ascertained that the April 19.
French Admiral had passed the Straits of Gibraltar. Nelson then followed him, much delayed by foul winds and greatly apprehensive lest Craig's force might have come to disaster. On this point, however, he was presently satisfied. Owing to the protests of Junot, the French Ambassador at Lisbon, Knight was com-
pelled on the 10th to remove his convoy from that May 10.
port, and on the following day he fell in with Nelson May 11.
off Cape St. Vincent. Nelson thereupon made his decision, reinforced the convoy by one line-of-battle ship, and sailed straight for Barbados; while Craig pursued his way safely to Gibraltar.

Upon the first news of Missiessy's appearance in the West Indies the Admiralty had ordered Admiral
Cochrane thither. On the 3rd of April that officer April 3.
reached Barbados with five ships of the line and three frigates. Thence, after adding to this squadron Hood's flag-ship the *Centaur*, he sailed away to leeward on the
5th in pursuit of the French Admiral. For more than April 5.
a month General Myers at Barbados waited anxiously for news of his success; and then there came on the
13th of May a warning from England that a large May 13.
French fleet had been seen off Cadiz. This was
followed on the 18th by a report from Martinique itself May 18.
that a fleet of twenty-nine sail in all, with the flags of one Spanish and two French admirals among them, were coming into Fort de France. "Of course none of the islands are safe for long with the enemy so strong here," wrote Myers. "A more deplorable force than our Militia in Barbados was never seen." He prepared, therefore, for the worst, never doubting that Napoleon's object was to harry the whole of

1805. the British West Indies. The British Government also interpreted the mission of Villeneuve's fleet in
May 18. the same sense; and on the 18th of May ordered Sir Eyre Coote to take command of some seven thousand troops,[1] and to sail with them at once to the rescue of the British islands. Nevertheless, if the French movements should prove to be a feint only, Myers was ordered to send these troops back again; and even if Villeneuve should have captured an island or two, it was left to the General's discretion to decide whether he should recapture them at once or send Coote's force to Halifax to await the healthy season. The appalling experience of 1793 to 1795 had not been wholly thrown away upon Pitt; and he was not prepared again to squander soldiers by the ten thousand in fighting over sugar-plantations. Still it was a time of anxious suspense for the authorities at Whitehall as well as in the Antilles, for the West Indian merchants were powerful, and a destructive raid upon their cherished property would have damaged the Government greatly.[2]

Napoleon's plans, however, had been but imperfectly realised. Villeneuve's squadron with five thousand
May 14. troops on board had indeed arrived on the 14th at Martinique, where three of his missing Spanish ships had anchored before him; but Ganteaume had failed to make his escape from Brest. On the 24th of March, when only fifteen British vessels were blockading him, he had asked permission to go out and fight them with his own fleet of twenty-one, but Napoleon forbade him. Within the next few days the British fleet was reinforced, and Ganteaume, after a vain attempt to put to sea on the 27th, retired once more on the 29th within the inner harbour. Villeneuve, of course knowing nothing of this, set himself to wait

[1] The 8th, 24th, 32nd, 38th, 62nd, 71st, 72nd, 83rd, 89th, and 93rd Infantry of the Line; in all 6493 rank and file; besides artillery.

[2] Myers to Sec. of State, 14th, 18th, 24th May; Sec. of State to Myers, 18th, 25th May 1805.

patiently for Ganteaume's arrival, according to his 1805.
orders. He projected vaguely an attack upon Dominica, as the nearest island to Martinique, but finally reduced his offensive operations to the recapture of the Diamond Rock, a tiny islet which had been occupied by the British in order to harass the French merchantmen. On the 30th there reached him a frigate, and on the 4th of June two line-of-battle ships and eight June 4.
hundred additional troops under Admiral Magon, bringing final orders from Napoleon dated the 14th and 17th of April. These were to the effect that Villeneuve was to wait thirty-five days after Magon's arrival for news of Ganteaume, and, if he received none, that he should return at once to Ferrol, release and take under his command the fifteen French and Spanish vessels blockaded there, proceed with them to Brest, and, having set Ganteaume also free, sail with the united force to the Channel. Meanwhile he was to capture St. Lucia, Dominica, and as many other islands as possible; but due arrival before Boulogne at the appointed time was the duty above all imposed upon him. There he would find the Emperor in person; and the fate of the world would depend upon the punctuality of his coming.[1]

At last, therefore, it had occurred to the Emperor to turn his raid upon the West Indies into a feint which should give him the mastery of the Channel; but on the 2nd of June Admiral Cochrane, having ascertained June.
that Missiessy had sailed for Europe, returned with his ships to Barbados; and on the very day that Villeneuve received his new orders, Nelson likewise put into Carlisle Bay with his fleet. By the addition June 4.
of Cochrane's vessels Nelson saw his force raised to twelve ships of the line; and, though the French fleet counted half as many again, neither he nor Myers had an idea of remaining idle with such strength at their disposal. Myers's latest intelligence reported, falsely, that Villeneuve's fleet had been seen heading for

[1] Desbrière, iv. 513-515.

1805. Trinidad; and he at once proposed to Nelson to embark two thousand troops and sail to the relief of the threatened island.[1] The Admiral eagerly complied;
June 5. and early on the morning of the 5th the armament departed. On the 6th it passed Tobago, on the 7th Trinidad, and on the 9th Grenada, and found all safe; but off the island last named a British man-of-war brought the news that the French had passed Rupert's Bay on the morning of the 6th. Nelson at once stood
June 12. over to Antigua and ascertained on the 12th that the French had passed Antigua on the 8th, steering north; whereupon he promptly dropped Myers and his troops, and sailed in pursuit. With bitter disappointment Myers saw him go, for he had looked to a campaign with Nelson as the happiest chance of his life; and the great Admiral had been so much struck with the spirit of the General and of his troops that he had written with his own hand a letter in warm commendation of both.[2]

Thus within, not thirty-five, but fourteen days of Magon's arrival, Villeneuve had taken hasty flight. He had already written to Paris on the 1st of June that the state of his supplies did not permit him to carry out the new instructions received through Magon; but nevertheless he had made some show of activity, so that the information of Myers was not altogether at fault. On the 5th of June Villeneuve had stood over to Guadeloupe to embark additional troops for an attack upon Barbados; on the 6th he had sailed for Barbados with close on nine thousand soldiers; and on the 8th he had captured fourteen merchantmen to leeward of that island. But from them he learned of Nelson's arrival and of his junction with Cochrane; and this was enough for him. After consultation with Gravina,

[1] The force consisted of the 15th, the 96th, and detachments of the 4th and 6th W.I.R. with artillery, altogether 2024 of all ranks, nearly 600 of which were black troops.

[2] Myers to S.S. 3rd, 4th, 12th June; Nelson to S.S. 11th June 1805.

he decided to send his troops back to Martinique in 1805. frigates, and to take his own fleet straight to Ferrol; and on the 10th he finally turned his back upon the June 10. West Indies. Nelson, as we have seen, followed hard after him, sending warning both to England and to the British squadron before Ferrol.

In England, of course, nothing was known of all this. The War Office, upon the news of Missiessy's return to Europe, had counter-ordered the despatch of Coote; but, on hearing of Villeneuve's arrival in the West Indies, it decided again on the 5th of July to send him July 5. with four battalions only to Barbados, so as to provide for the safety both of that island and of Jamaica; the latter being suspected to be the object of the French attack. It was a small force for the purpose, but the season was a very deadly one, and the Government would not risk the loss of more. On the 8th of July, July 8. however, intelligence of Villeneuve's departure for Europe reached London; and Coote's sailing was again delayed until further orders, though the troops were still kept on board their ships at Cork to prevent desertion. Such, indeed, was the loathing and dread of West Indian service that several men jumped overboard and swam ashore to escape it. Finally, on the 26th of July Coote received an intimation that the July 26 troops were required for a different object; and the idea of extraordinary military reinforcement for the West Indies was abandoned.

As to naval reinforcement, it has already been told how the Government sent Cochrane westward immediately upon hearing of Missiessy's destination, and how Nelson followed Villeneuve to the Antilles upon his own initiative, though with the full approval of the Admiralty. On the first intelligence of Villeneuve's departure from Toulon there had been great alarm lest he should release the blockaded squadrons at Cadiz, Ferrol, and Brest, and enter the Channel to cover an invasion from Boulogne. "During the week just past," said the *Morning Chronicle*, "no one has slept in

1805. peace." The Government, however, had early intelligence of Villeneuve's true destination; and on the 27th
April 27. of April the squadrons of Collingwood and Orde were ordered to meet at Madeira and pursue the French fleet. Lord Gardner took upon himself to delay this movement, which was cancelled when it was certainly known that Nelson had sailed to Barbados; and on the 16th of May the *Sun* newspaper commented with satisfaction upon this, remarking that the departure of Villeneuve westward might well be a feint to draw the English fleet after him to the West Indies, while he doubled back to appear in force in the Channel. Admiral Decrès called Napoleon's attention to this in a letter
June 1. of the 1st of June;[1] but the Emperor none the less kept multiplying impossible instructions to Villeneuve as to junction with the fleets at Cadiz, Ferrol, and Brest, all with a view to securing a few days' control of the Channel. "If," he wrote on the 8th of May, "your presence makes us masters of the sea for three days before Boulogne, we shall have every chance of forwarding our expedition of one hundred and fifty thousand men embarked in two thousand vessels." In vain Decrès urged that these junctions of fleets were not so easily effected, that winds and tides might well prevent them, and that Nelson would infallibly hang on to Villeneuve's skirts wherever he might go. The Emperor answered only that the mind of Decrès was too small for great operations, and continued to frame vague and speculative plans. However, as none of the Emperor's letters of this period ever reached Villeneuve, no great result could follow from them.[2] On both sides
June. of the Channel throughout the month of June the directors of the naval operations were at fault for lack of information. In England, indeed, there seems to have reigned a curious sense of security, which on the 28th of June called forth a remarkable warning from

[1] Desbrière, iv. 596.

[2] Decrès to Napoleon, 1st June; Napoleon to Decrès, 6th June 1805; Desbrière, iv. 596, 602.

Colonel Robert Craufurd in the House of Commons. 1805.
The danger of invasion, he said in effect, was not yet over. The French fleet after a raid in the West Indies might return unexpectedly, gain temporary superiority in the narrow seas, take possession of the Downs, and bring over Napoleon's immense army of invasion. The Secretary at War, William Dundas, greeted the suggestion with a smile, to which Craufurd replied by asserting that such a plan had certainly been suggested by de Bouillé to Count de Grasse before the latter encountered Rodney in 1782.[1] There can therefore be no doubt that Napoleon's much vaunted scheme of naval operations was not so subtle but that it could be penetrated both by journalists and military officers.

In July the situation began to clear itself up. On
the 9th the British Admiralty received intelligence of July 9.
Villeneuve's departure from the West Indies; on the
19th Nelson, having outstripped his quarry, arrived July 19.
at Gibraltar, and, finding no news of Villeneuve,
anchored on the 21st at Tetuan for rest. A day later, July 21.
Villeneuve with twenty ships encountered the fifteen July 22.
vessels of Sir Robert Calder's fleet about fifty leagues west of Ferrol, and after an indecisive action, which cost him the loss of two Spanish ships, entered Vigo on the
27th. Finding no instructions or information there, July 27.
he left three crippled ships in the port and sailed for Ferrol, but, in obedience to orders received from
France, anchored on the 2nd of August at Coruña, Aug. 2.
with his crews very sickly and his fleet generally in a miserable plight.

Now for the first time he could form some idea of the course of events and of his master's matured plans, for so far he had received no intelligence of later date than the 3rd of May. First he was informed that Admiral Gourdon at Ferrol had been instructed to move to Coruña. He was therefore ordered to add this force to his own, which having done, he was to pick up either

[1] *H.D.* v. pp. 668-669.

1805. the Rochefort squadron or the Brest squadron, and manœuvre to gain the mastery of the Channel for four or five days. If through any cause unforeseen circumstances had altered the situation, he was to release the squadrons at Rochefort and Ferrol only, and anchor with them by preference at Cadiz. In comment upon these orders it must be mentioned that Gourdon had found it impossible to move from Ferrol to Coruña, that a wind which was fair for ships leaving Coruña was foul for ships leaving Ferrol, and that the Rochefort squadron, under Admiral Allemand, who had superseded Missiessy, had put to sea on the 16th of July. Allemand had vague instructions to make a raid upon Ireland so as to draw off some of the British ships from before Brest, and then to slip away, join Gourdon not earlier than the 3rd of August or, failing that, wait at an appointed rendezvous at sea until the 13th of August.
Aug. 3. However, poor Villeneuve wrote dutifully on the 3rd of August that he would try to enter Brest or evade the British and enter the Channel, if he saw any chance of success, but in the contrary event would put into Cadiz. He then sent out a frigate to find Allemand and, waiting till the 8th for its return, received the news that Nelson had arrived at Gibraltar on the 20th and sailed out into the Atlantic again on the 26th of July. The frigate never returned, having been cap-
Aug. 13. tured by a British ship, and on the 13th Villeneuve picked up the squadron at Ferrol, which increased his fleet to twenty-nine ships in all, and again put to sea.

Meanwhile Napoleon had continually reiterated his orders to him, to release the various French fleets from Cadiz to Brest and proceed to Boulogne. "Make me master of the Channel for the space of but three days," he wrote on the 26th of July, "and with God's help I will put an end to the career and existence of England. . . . One hundred and fifty thousand men are embarked in two thousand vessels." On the 3rd of August the Emperor betook himself to Boulogne in person, and then for the first time he learned not only of Villeneuve's return to Vigo, but of Nelson's arrival in European 1805. waters also. On the 13th of August he ordered Decrès to censure Villeneuve's inaction; at the same time directing the force in Holland to make a feint of sortie in its transports, in order to keep twelve British ships employed. He was now very anxious for an action to be fought off Ferrol, and gave Villeneuve positive orders to attack the British fleet if it did not exceed twenty-four ships. All this was useless. After two days' battling against northerly winds, Villeneuve on the 15th turned southward and put into Cadiz. Aug. 15. On the same day Nelson joined the Channel fleet before Brest, bringing it up to a total of thirty-nine sail, so that, had Villeneuve persisted in making his way northward, he would have been beaten. And even if the French admiral had reached Boulogne triumphantly, Napoleon would not have had one hundred and fifty thousand men ready to cross the Channel; for at no time had he more than ninety thousand men assembled at the ports of embarkation. The truth is that the great plan had failed at all points, and that the Emperor knew it.

Since the middle of July, too, the attitude of Austria had become more and more menacing. On the 9th of Aug. 9. August that power formally joined the alliance with Russia and England; and on the 13th, the very day on Aug. 13. which Napoleon ordered Villeneuve to be rebuked for inaction, he informed Talleyrand that he had suspended the invasion of England in order to defend his southern frontiers. He still continued to write stimulating letters to Villeneuve. "Lose not a moment, but enter the Channel with my united fleets," so ran one of the 22nd Aug. 22. of August, "England is ours; we are quite ready, and everything is embarked. Come only for twenty-four hours and all is over." Yet on this very same day he gave his first orders for the army to break up and march upon Ulm; and by the 1st of September not a man Sept. 1. was left at Boulogne. Other letters followed, containing unfair censure of Villeneuve; and yet others implying

1805. that the flotilla had been from beginning to end no more than a feint. All of this was nothing but clumsy lying, designed to cover the Emperor's own blunders. Historians will debate for ever the question whether Napoleon really intended to invade England or not. Personally I have no doubt that he did so intend, provided that he could see any reasonable chance of transporting a sufficient force across the Channel. It was one of the dreams of his life, to which he constantly reverted, even as was the wild project of an invasion of India. The man was continually conjuring up attractive visions of conquests over the sea, and amusing himself and distracting his officials by executing them upon paper. Twice he endeavoured to realise them, in Egypt and in St. Domingo, and on each occasion the attempt ended in disastrous failure. In the case of England, he might have gone nearer to success had he not wasted untold sums in building boats of the wrong kind, according to his own untutored ideas, and had he acknowledged more fully his complete ignorance of all naval matters. The true secret of the flotilla is probably to be found in his passionate impatience of making war without the possibility of taking the offensive; and it must be freely confessed that he successfully reduced the feeble Addington to a passively defensive attitude. At least, therefore, he should receive credit for having scared a British Government into the most foolish and futile preparations conceivable for an effective war.

The further problem of the failure or success of an invasion, had Napoleon succeeded in passing a large force across the Channel, must remain insoluble. Without details as to the number of men disembarked, the place of landing, the time of disembarkation, and, above all, of the warning received of his coming, all speculation is useless. In the early winter of 1803 his chances would not have been bad; but in 1804, and still more in 1805, they would have been less promising. By that time the people knew what they must do, and

were prepared to do it. The positions for rendezvous 1805.
and for defence had been chosen, and effective measures had been taken for concentrating large bodies of troops at the point of attack. The general tactics of defence had also been thought out. The invaders were to be confined as far as possible to a narrow front and perpetually harassed in flank and rear, a task which the British superiority in cavalry would have made easy. The best Generals in the Southern District, Sir David Dundas and Sir John Moore, had fully made up their minds to retreat to a flank if defeated, so as to make pursuit the more difficult and hazardous. If Napoleon had succeeded in reaching London, his task would not have been done, for every provision had been made for transporting the seat of Government to Worcester; and, with the stout old King to show an example, there would have been no talk of surrender. Once in London, the French Army would probably have taken leave of all discipline for a time; the sick list would have been enormous; and the force must have been much scattered to secure the entrance to the Thames and the capital at large. Moreover, after a few months, supplies would have failed; and it would then have been necessary to procure grain and forage, by sending out armed parties which would certainly have been attacked and probably defeated in detail. Upon the whole, if the French Army had managed to get into England, it could never have got out again. The capture of London would not have been such a death-blow as it would now be; and, though the loss and suffering to England would have been enormous, it is probable that an army of Russians and Austrians would have made France suffer even more.[1] Thus a successful disembarkation of a French army in England might well have abridged the troubles of Europe by ten years, for it is hardly possible that the rule of Napoleon could have survived it.

[1] But Napoleon himself thought that if he captured London no one in Europe would dare to move. Marmont, *Mémoires*, ii. 216.

CHAPTER IX

1805. THE dread of invasion was past. The Third Coalition was come into full play; Napoleon's columns were streaming away towards the Danube, and the time was fully ripe for England to take the offensive. Pitt, before he came into office, had sketched the spheres of employment for the troops of the various nations. The Neapolitans, ten or fifteen thousand British, and as many Russians were to be employed in South Italy, the Austrians and sixty thousand more Russians in Northern Italy. Forty thousand Russians, with a body of Hanoverians and the Swedish Army in Northern Germany, were to advance towards Holland, where a second British force would make a diversion.[1]

Here, as usual, may be observed Pitt's incurable failing—the passion for frittering England's little force away in minute divisions, instead of keeping it united at a single point. As has been seen, he had already sent a force to the Mediterranean with Craig, a detachment so puny as to call forth strong censure from the House of Commons. "The force is unnecessarily strong for the defensive," was Robert Craufurd's criticism, "and too weak to take the offensive." Napoleon was openly and justly contemptuous. "The celebrated secret expedition," he wrote, "entered Lisbon on the 7th of May and left it on the 10th. Whither is it bound? . . . If it is destined for Malta, all the better. Nothing can better prove the folly of the English Cabinet; for these combined Continental move-

[1] Stanhope, *Life of Pitt*, iv. 223-225.

ments founded on a few thousand men are pygmy 1805.
combinations. If, therefore, you find the expedition is gone to Malta, you may rub your hands, for the English will have deprived themselves of six thousand men and of a certain number of ships."[1]

During June and July, while the British and French fleets had been restlessly moving from side to side of the Atlantic, Craig's position had been an anxious one. The naval operations had reduced the escort of his forty transports to a single frigate and a sloop; and when
the armament reached Gibraltar, it was met by a May 13.
command to halt there until further order. Rear-admiral Knight dared not keep the ships at anchor for fear of the Spanish gunboats at Algeciras. For six weeks, therefore, the convoy cruised on and off
Gibraltar in anxious suspense, until at last on the 22nd June 22.
of June Rear-admiral Bickerton received directions to furnish ships sufficient to bring it safely to Malta. Even then the passage was delayed by a gale; and it
was not until the 18th of July that Craig finally carried July 18.
his detachment into Valetta.

In the meanwhile the British Government had ordered him to consider the feasibility of an attack upon Minorca; and the General was able to report that, though the garrison of the island had been raised to five thousand men, these could only defend themselves by meeting his own six thousand in the field, and that therefore the enterprise offered no great difficulty. On arriving at Malta, however, he found that Ministers had after all pushed forward their original project for British co-operation with Russia on the mainland of Italy. A letter from General Lascy, the Russian Commander-in-Chief in the Mediterranean, was awaiting him, asking what force he could spare for active service; and, as this had been written from Naples on the 9th of July, it was clear that the court of King Ferdinand had for the present decided to throw in its lot with the Coalition. Moreover, before long there

[1] *Corres. de Napoléon*, 8787.

1805. reached Craig a further letter from London, to say that fifteen thousand tons of shipping would be placed at his disposal to convey Russian troops from the Black Sea or elsewhere, and that he must do his best to give them transport for twenty-five thousand men, while reserving enough to carry eight thousand of his own force.[1]

The outlook, therefore, seemed promising. An army of thirty thousand men, though none too strong, might at least make some diversion in the Mediterranean. But further inquiry into the Russian resources revealed some doubts as to the strength of their expeditionary force. General Lascy gave it as fifteen thousand; General Anrep, commanding the Russian troops at Corfu, reckoned on twelve thousand from Odessa and nearly ten thousand more from the garrison of that island; though both agreed that nothing could be done until the arrival of the detachment from the Black Sea. Nor was Lascy's plan of operations calculated to inspire confidence. The bulk of the French forces, about fourteen thousand men, were, according to his information, in the districts of Bari and Otranto, whereby they secured a country rich in corn and cattle, to the privation of the Allies. It was most important alike to dislodge them from this and at the same time to exclude them from other fertile provinces, notably from La Terra di Lavoro, wherein Naples itself is situated. Lascy therefore purposed to land fifteen thousand Russians in the Bay of Naples, and to advance rapidly to the first good position to be found within twenty miles of the city, so as to cover both the district and the city itself and to enable the Neapolitan levies to be organised. Meanwhile the British, counting about seven thousand men of all ranks, would create a diversion by landing in the Gulf of Tarento, a little to the north of the river Crati, occupying the Castle of Roseto so as to close the road to Tarento, and advancing

[1] W.O. Mediterranean, 142, Craig to Sec. of State, 15th, 16th May, 17th, 22nd, 24th June, 21st July; W.O.E.B. 85, Sec. of State to Craig, 1st May, 8th June, 27th July 1805.

to a strong position in the mountains, which could 1805.
certainly be found within a few miles. The French corps nearest to this point (so urged Lascy) would be at least seventy miles distant, and, if extended towards that side, would be exposed to the risk of being cut off by the advance of the Russians from Naples eastward upon the province of Puglia. Hence the British disembarkation would probably be unmolested and their march practically unopposed until they reached Matera or Tarento. At that point the Russians would come into line with them, forming up on their left; and further operations in Puglia and Abruzzi could be subsequently concerted.

With admirable moderation Craig put forward his criticisms upon this absurd plan. The final embarkation for active service could not take place until the third week in September. By that time strong winds would have begun to blow, and the slightest surf would make disembarkation impossible. The selected landing-place for the British was not sheltered; the transports would not dare to remain close to the coast; and the troops would have to be landed in the ships' boats, for there were no others. The disembarkation of the men would therefore take, in the most favourable circumstances, one whole day, and that of the supplies and stores another. If in the middle of the operation a strong breeze sprang up, the ships would have to stand off, when perhaps half of the force or half of its stores was afloat, and the other half ashore. In such circumstances there was imminent risk of the destruction of the British in detail. Nor would any movement of the Russians serve to protect them. In the first place, the disembarkations of the British and of the Russians could hardly be simultaneous, for they were to be carried out on opposite sides of the same peninsula, so that the wind which was fair for the one would be foul for the other. The Russians being based upon Naples and all its resources, and being also superior in number, might have little to fear if the British disembarkation failed or was delayed.

1805. But the British force, weak, isolated, and without horses, would be liable to be overwhelmed. Supposing both disembarkations to be simultaneously accomplished, the French, being warned of the coming storm, would concentrate their troops and either occupy Naples or take up some such central position as Matera, from which they could fall upon either division at their choice. The British, even if safely landed, could not draw supplies from the country, owing to the enemy's cavalry, but would be obliged to stick to the coast; and the landing of the Russians would not prevent the French from overpowering them. For the Russians would need some days to collect transport before they could advance; they would be obliged to weaken themselves by guards for depots and magazines; and they would find it hard at once to cover Naples and to cut off the French. The whole force, Russians and British, ought therefore to land together in the Bay of Naples; but even so it could hardly be expected that the French would not evacuate Bari and Otranto, if they saw the slightest risk of being intercepted.[1]

Lascy, an easy-going gentleman of Irish descent and near eighty years of age, was convinced by this reasoning, though his Quarter-master-general, Oppermann, drew up a long memoir in support of the original plan, which was of his own designing and was dictated not merely by ignorance but by treachery. Naturally the concerting of a campaign between two commanders at points so far distant as Malta and Naples took much time; but Craig was able to turn the delay to account in equipping his army for the field, though he was driven to his wits' end to obtain horses and mules, which were equally few and equally bad both in Neapolitan territory and in Sicily. Meanwhile the Austrians had set their troops, under General Mack, in motion for the Black Forest, while ninety thousand men under the Archduke Charles were concentrating on the Adige; and Craig now learned for the first time

[1] Craig to Sec. of State, with enclosures, 16th Aug. 1805.

that Lascy's operations were to depend on those of the 1805. Archduke, of which he knew nothing. At length at the end of September the Russian troops at Corfu sent for their transports, which were duly despatched to them on the 1st of October. But at about the same time the British Minister at Naples reported that Napoleon had reinforced his troops in that Kingdom to twenty thousand men, notwithstanding that Massena had but fifty thousand with which to oppose the ninety thousand under the Archduke Charles on the Adige. St. Cyr, therefore, was in a condition to seize Naples in a few days, whereas the Allies could not reach it in less than a month, and would even then be unable to move from want of transport. King Ferdinand at once took the alarm. On the 11th of September he had Sept. 11. ratified a secret convention with Russia; but on the 21st he sent a mission to Paris with an abject offer to Sept. 21. observe perfect neutrality if Napoleon would be pleased to withdraw the French troops from his kingdom. The Emperor, however, had not reinforced St. Cyr without a purpose. He had already exacted a treaty of neutrality from the Neapolitan Minister at Paris, and he now presented this to Ferdinand through his representative at Naples, with a demand that it should be ratified at once. Quaking with fright, the miserable old King complied; but at the same time he delivered to the Russian Minister a declaration repudiating this convention with France, as having been extorted by threats, and calling upon the Russian and British troops to repair to Naples as though no such instrument had ever been signed.

Meanwhile the campaign on the Danube was approaching its crisis. General Mack had concentrated the Austrian army at Ulm to block the usual line of the French advance from the Black Forest. But by the 7th Oct. 7. of October one hundred thousand men had reached the Danube in his rear, and a few days more saw two complete French corps astride the line of his communications with Vienna. Then followed a succession

1805. of bloody combats, one and all adverse to the Austrians; and urgent orders were despatched to the Archduke Charles to stand on the defensive in Italy and to send every man that he could spare to the rescue of
Oct. 20. Mack. Finally on the 20th of October came the crowning disaster, when Mack surrendered with thirty thousand men, and the Austrian Army of the Danube virtually ceased to exist. Thenceforward there could be no hope of an Austrian offensive campaign in Upper Italy.

Lascy, however, knowing nothing of all this, on the
Oct. 30. 30th of October gave orders for his projected expedition to go forward; and on the following day Craig embarked his troops, numbering just over seven thousand of all ranks.[1] The British commander did so with no very good grace, for the treacherous behaviour of the Court of Naples towards Napoleon had been brought to his notice; and he vowed in disgust that, but for his pledge to support Lascy, he would not have countenanced such double dealing. Putting to sea,
Nov. 3. however, on the 3rd of November, he joined the Russian fleet near Cape Passaro; and after a very long passage
Nov. 20. the united corps landed at Naples on the 20th. There they were met by the news of Mack's capitulation at Ulm, and of the consequent withdrawal of the Austrians from Upper Italy. The Archduke Charles, as a matter
Oct. 29-31. of fact, after repelling a desperate attack of the French at Caldiero, was in full retreat, with Massena pressing closely upon his rear-guard. The French in the Neapolitan dominions who, after the signature of King Ferdinand's convention with Napoleon, had been

[1] 2 squadrons 20th L.D., 335 of all ranks; R.A., 273; R.E., 19; 20th Foot, 801; 27th, 1063; 35th, 1003; 58th, 973; 61st, 834; Watteville's, 725; Chasseurs Britanniques, 645; Corsican Rangers, 740; Staff Corps, 20. The force was organised as follows:—*Advanced Corps:* Brig.-gen. Broderick, 1 batt. Corsicans, L.I. battalion, Grenadier battalion, Chasseurs Britanniques. *First Brigade:* Brig.-gen. Acland, 20th, 35th, 61st. *Second Brigade:* Brig.-gen. Cole, 27th, 58th, Watteville's. *R.A.:* 2 light brigades and one heavy brigade, 4/12-prs., 4 howitzers, 8/6-prs.

hastening northward to join the Marshal, were halted; 1805.
and Eugene Beauharnais was collecting thirty thousand men to re-occupy Naples. But so far Craig had no knowledge of anything except of the disaster at Ulm and the Archduke's retirement; and, though instructed to second the Austrian operations on the Adige, he had never been placed in communication with their commander nor with the Court of Vienna. He could, indeed, obtain no information whatever except through Russian channels, which he believed, not wholly without reason, to be untrustworthy. Not until long after his arrival at Naples did he hear that on the 21st of October Nelson had broken the naval power of France and Spain at Trafalgar.[1]

However, after disembarking his troops, he collected draught-animals as fast as the miserable Neapolitan Government could supply them, and, by cutting down the baggage of the army to the smallest possible bulk, gradually brought his brigades forward from the coast. Lascy had so arranged his line of cantonments on the northern frontier that seven thousand Neapolitan troops occupied the mountains of the Abruzzi on the right, with the fortress of Pescara in their rear; the strong fortress of Gaeta, on the extreme left, being guarded by a Neapolitan garrison under a hard-drinking, most gallant old soldier, the Prince of Hesse-Philipstadt. The Russians held the centre, with headquarters at Sulmona, being fourteen thousand strong and professing daily expectation of six more battalions; and the British formed the left, in Sessa and other villages about the Lower Garigliano. And there the twenty thousand men lay, holding a defensive position, with no enemy, except the garrison of Ancona, nearer to them than the Po. Had Lascy on hearing the news of Ulm —or even earlier, seeing that on the 16th of October he knew the neutrality of Naples to be secured—directed his troops to Trieste or Venice, Massena could never have pressed the Archduke as he did, and

[1] Bunbury, pp. 206, 207.

1805. Napoleon's campaign might have ended differently. But Lascy had been chosen not for his ability but for his age, so that at all costs he might be senior to Craig; and it was vain to expect great energy from the veteran.

So the little army lay still; and from time to time came French reports of Napoleon's steady advance into Upper Austria, of the reverse suffered by Marshal Mortier's corps at Krems on the 11th of November, of the retirement of the Emperor Francis to Pressburg in order to organise continued resistance in Hungary, and finally of the presentation of an ultimatum, in circumstances which shall presently be described, by Prussia to Napoleon. Amid these hopeful signs arrived a letter from the Archduke Charles himself, written from Laybach on the 22nd of November during his retreat through Carinthia. Until that day, through extraordinary negligence in some quarters,[1] he had remained uninformed of the withdrawal of the French troops from Neapolitan territory; but now, realising that Lascy's force was lying idle, he urged the Russian commander to embark it at once for Venice, which was held by a strong Austrian garrison, and from thence to fall upon Massena's rear. But as Craig pointed out, the Archduke had no intention of standing at Laybach; wherefore Massena would either continue to follow him beyond hope of being overtaken, or would mask Venice with part of his force and beat Lascy with the remainder. Moreover, the British and Russian divisions possessed no cavalry whatever except two squadrons of the Twentieth Light Dragoons; that of the Neapolitans was thoroughly contemptible; and to attempt to harass superior numbers of the French, under such a leader as Massena, with twenty thousand infantry and only three hundred horse was utterly absurd.[2]

Meanwhile the campaign on the Danube had pur-
Nov. 13. sued its course. On the 13th of November the French

[1] Bunbury hints strongly at treachery on the part of the Russian Minister at Naples. P. 20.

[2] Craig to Sec. of State, 2nd Nov., 9th Dec. 1805.

entered Vienna; and Napoleon bent all his energies to 1805.
the task of preventing the junction of the retreating Austrians with the Russians. He failed: the allied commanders united their forces successfully at Wischau on the 19th, and the game was in their hands. They Nov. 19.
needed only to wait under the guns of Olmütz for the arrival of the Archduke Charles who was hastening, though necessarily by a wide detour, to join them with the Army of Italy, in order to place Napoleon in a most dangerous position. The Russians, however, were presumptuous and headstrong. They preferred to advance and fight at once; with the result that on the 2nd of December they were utterly overthrown at Dec. 2.
Austerlitz.

This news, together with that of the armistice concluded with France by Austria on the 6th of December, Dec. 6.
was speedily passed on to Naples by French agents, and reduced Lascy to great embarrassment. He had no instructions to guide his action, nor had the Russian agent at Naples; and he did not even know whether there was or was not a suspension of arms between Russia and France. As a matter of fact there was not. Napoleon, having granted to the Tsar a safe retreat and restored to him the prisoners which he had taken among the Russian Imperial Guard, never doubted but that the war was over; but Alexander was too young in misfortune to yield after a single defeat, and waved aside all proposals of peace. Napoleon, therefore, had a campaign in Poland still before him; but nevertheless Austria had been separated from Russia by the armistice, and this was sufficient to make Lascy's position most critical. His information was still imperfect; but he knew at any rate that French forces were moving southward, and that Napoleon had publicly declared his resolution to drive the Bourbons from Naples and to take possession of their kingdom. Nor were these his only causes for disquietude. His own troops were extremely unhealthy; he had more sick in each of his battalions than the British in their whole division; his

1805. fourteen thousand bayonets had shrunk to a bare eight thousand, and the six additional battalions expected in November had never appeared. A few days more passed away; and at the end of the year came definite information that from thirty to thirty-five thousand French soldiers were in full march southward and would reach the Neapolitan frontier in ten days. It behoved Lascy therefore to come without delay to a decision.

It was not difficult to determine that defence of the Neapolitan frontier was hopeless. In spite of all efforts Craig had been unable to find horses even for the whole of his artillery, to say nothing of his baggage-waggons. It would have been possible to take up a strong position to cover the plains of Naples, and even to repulse for a time a force of superior numbers. But the Allies, having no transport, could not move, and the French could always have covered their retreat with cavalry and renewed their attacks until they succeeded, in which case the re-embarkation of the British and Russians would have been difficult if not impossible. Lascy, in council of war, broached the proposal to retire into Calabria and there hold out, depending upon a small port in the Gulf of Policastro for supplies; and this found favour with every officer present, British and Russian, excepting Craig and Major-general Campbell, his second in command. The harbour was reported by a British naval officer to be unsafe for shipping, too small for its purpose, and unapproachable on the side of the land except by the roughest mule-tracks. This was one drawback; and there was another which Craig did not venture to mention, namely, that the Russians, having neither money nor credit, must live upon the country and would thus infallibly bring upon the entire force a savage and dangerous struggle with the Calabrese. Lastly Craig retained a lively recollection of his instructions to secure Sicily, and on that account was anxious to re-embark at once. Lascy, however, dared not re-embark without orders; and the Court of Naples

in an agony of rage and fear would hear of nothing but 1805.
a desperate resistance which would cover the capital till the last moment. In this mood King Ferdinand absolutely prohibited any withdrawal to Calabria; and the situation was becoming extremely dangerous to the Allies, for Craig, though utterly disapproving as a soldier any futile attempt to resist the French, thought himself bound in honour not to forsake the Russians.

Fortunately, however, on the 7th of January 1806 1806.
Lascy received orders, dated a full month back, from Jan. 7.
the Tsar that he should return at once to Corfu; and the two armies parted not unwillingly, for the Russians had not yet forgotten their supposed grievances in North Holland in 1799. The Russians marched to Naples, and the British to Castellamare, where on the
14th they began their embarkation. Craig's health, Jan. 14.
always uncertain, had broken down under the anxieties of the past weeks; but now came the most trying time of all for him. Mr. Hugh Elliot, our Minister at Naples, always a witty and usually a sensible man, for some reason set his face against a retreat of the British troops to Sicily, and would have had them return to Malta. The jealous imbecility of the Court of Naples was of course offended by the thought of the British repairing to Messina; and King Ferdinand went the length of announcing that, if they occupied Sicily without his consent, he would join forces with the French to drive them out. Elliot so far humoured this folly that he offered to open a negotiation on the Queen's behalf with the advancing enemy. In vain Craig protested that such a course would assuredly sacrifice Sicily. The faithlessness of the Neapolitan Government was proverbial; Napoleon would accept nothing but a French occupation of Sicily in redemption of King Ferdinand's misdeeds; Collingwood's squadron had left the Mediterranean for Cadiz, leaving the sea open to the French; and, if the British troops retired to Malta, they would probably be unable to return before Syracuse and Messina had received French

1806. garrisons. All arguments were thrown away. Elliot persisted in his mad scheme of negotiation; and Craig finally taking matters into his own hands sailed away
Jan. 19. on the 19th, and on the 22nd anchored at Messina. The French marched on, playing meanwhile with King Ferdinand's emissaries as a cat with a mouse, and within three weeks the King himself came flying over to Sicily, where Craig's foresight and firmness had provided for him a safe refuge.[1]

Before quitting Mediterranean affairs for the present, it is worth while to emphasise the extreme futility of this expedition under Craig. The criticisms of Craufurd and Napoleon were amply justified. The combination which Pitt had projected was a pygmy combination, and deserved no success; yet, paltry though the British force was, no true effort was made that it should be fit for the field. At Malta, instead of a reserve, there was a positive dearth of ammunition; and Craig, who had only brought with him four hundred rounds for each of his six thousand men, was obliged to give one hundred and sixty of this proportion to the garrison. Again, though he was supposed to co-operate with the Austrians and might therefore find himself in the plains of Northern Italy, only two squadrons of cavalry were granted to him, and no notice was taken of his urgent requests for more. Yet again, though Abercromby had done his best to impress upon the Cabinet in 1799 that an Army cannot move without horses and waggons, yet Craig's handful of dragoons and the whole of his artillery were shipped abroad without their horses. It would have been easy to ascertain from the officers who had served with Charles Stuart in the Mediterranean in 1798 whether horses and mules were procurable in Naples and Sicily; yet Craig was sent upon his mission with easy assurance, as though the animals could be obtained for the asking. As to his instructions, they show plainly that the Government

[1] Craig to Sec. of State, 11th Feb. 1806, enclosing correspondence with Elliot.

had no definite military policy and no distinct object 1805. in dispatching a division of infantry to Malta at all. Craig was to go to the Mediterranean and do something somewhere within its limits between Alexandria and Cagliari. In brief, the whole enterprise bears upon it the unmistakable mark of Pitt's military administration.

But Pitt's efforts to take the offensive were not limited to this paltry expedition of Craig. Holland had for some time been virtually a province of France;[1] and it therefore behoved England to look well to the Cape of Good Hope. It has already been told how, upon the first alarm of Villeneuve's departure to the West Indies, large reinforcements had been prepared for the British islands under the command of Sir Eyre Coote. Nelson's pursuit and Villeneuve's return rendered the departure of these reinforcements unnecessary, and, as the troops were on their transports at Cork, it was resolved to send a portion of them under Sir David Baird to capture the Cape. Baird received his instructions to this effect on the 26th of July, and sailed a few weeks later for his destination, whither in due time we shall follow him. It will be remarked that the decision to send his force out of the country was taken a full month before the break-up of the camp at Boulogne; and it was therefore reasonable to suppose that, when Napoleon was in full march for the Danube, some far more formidable operation would be undertaken. Troops might now be easily spared from England, and moreover Pitt had had the good fortune to meet with a windfall. Officers and men of the Hanoverian Army, which had been broken up by the capitulation of 1803, soon afterwards drifted over to England, where in rage and shame they entreated George the Third to re-form them and take them into his service; and in December 1803 was begun the levy of a King's German Regiment which was very soon expanded into that of a King's German Legion. The force grew apace. In January 1805 it already included

[1] Sorel, vi. 423.

1805. one regiment of dragoons, another of hussars, two battalions of light and four of heavy infantry, with two batteries of horse-artillery and three of field-artillery. Negotiations were opened with Sweden to procure recruiting depots at Stralsund and Rügen, which were duly accorded by a convention of the 3rd of December 1804;[1] and before the end of 1805 the Legion counted in all five regiments of cavalry, ten battalions of infantry, and six batteries of artillery, in all some fourteen thousand men. And these were no mere mercenaries like the Hessians of former days. They were not only excellent soldiers under excellent officers, but loyal and patriotic subjects, devoted to the King, and burning to avenge themselves for their humiliation in 1803. They had their will; and these Hanoverians enjoy the proud distinction of being the only Germans who from 1803 to 1814 bore arms unceasingly against Napoleon.

With so valuable an addition to his offensive force, Pitt was really in a situation to make the arm of England felt on shore as well as at sea. His first thought, not unnaturally, was to end the fear of invasion at once by destroying the flotilla in Boulogne and the adjacent ports. The project was entrusted to Sir John Moore, who, after careful investigation, reported that, unless undertaken by a really formidable force and with a sure port for re-embarkation, the enterprise was unduly hazardous. Ministers very reasonably decided to abandon the idea. But, with Napoleon's army plunged into the heart of South Germany to meet the Austrians and Russians on his front, there could hardly fail to be good opportunity for dealing a stroke upon his flank or rear. Such a blow might fall either upon Holland or upon Hanover, both of which were reputed to be weakly held by French troops; or it might be dealt by a force landing at Stralsund, where the King of Sweden could without difficulty be persuaded to permit a disembarkation. But in this last case the

[1] F.O. Sweden, 33; Pierrepont to Sec. of State, 3rd Jan. 1805.

co-operation of Prussia was essential; and indeed without at least the countenance of Prussia, it would be difficult if not impossible to effect anything decisive in North Germany. All therefore turned upon the attitude of the Court of Berlin. 1805.

Some account has already been given of the artful fashion in which Napoleon kept Hanover dangling before the greedy eyes of Frederick William, and of the King's infatuation in believing that he, weakest and stupidest as well as falsest of men, could contrive to obtain the coveted province from the Emperor and yet remain friendly with the Tsar. As the outbreak of hostilities between France and Austria became more and more certain, Napoleon strove more and more to bind Prussia to himself. In July he invited her to occupy Hanover and to keep it at the end of the war, if Frederick William would recognise the French annexation of Genoa and give him a free hand in Italy. Frederick William's answer reached the Emperor on the 22nd of August. The King was quite ready to take over Hanover; but, seeking as usual an impossible neutrality, he desired explanations as to Napoleon's dealings with Hanover, Italy, and Switzerland. The Emperor stood by his terms, and answered plainly that unless Prussia threatened Austria, she should not have Hanover. Meanwhile Austria likewise urged Frederick William to join with her; and the Tsar, to whom Prussia was bound by treaty, pressed him in exceedingly firm language to enter the coalition, or at any rate to allow Russian troops to pass his frontier, hinting not obscurely that these concessions, if not freely granted, might be extorted by force. Simultaneously General Duroc arrived at Berlin, as envoy from Napoleon, to propose an active alliance. Embarrassed and bewildered, sure only that he wanted everything and would give nothing, the King on the 7th of September put his army on a footing of war; warning the Tsar that any act of violence would drive him into the arms of France, but at the same time intimating to Duroc that Prussia could

Aug. 22.

Sept. 7.

1805. hardly preserve neutrality without the occupation of Hanover. The rival powers then became keener in their competition for Frederick William's help. On the
Sept. 15. 15th of September the Tsar sent a polite ultimatum, again claiming the alliance of Prussia, and passage
Sept. 17. for his troops through her territory; and on the 17th Duroc, under Napoleon's orders, became more than ever importunate for Prussia's alliance with France, since one of the French columns was going, freely or by force, to march through country which was under Prussian protection. The King once more declared that he would maintain strict neutrality, and sent a reproachful letter to the Tsar, asking for an interview, which missive arrived just in time to avert a forcible entry of the Russian troops into his dominions. Count Hardenberg, who by his own account had done his best to urge Frederick William to break definitely with France, became much agitated over the situation and professed impatience to see a British force disembark in Hanover. His hope was that his master, when he realised that Napoleon could not give him the province, would at last throw in his lot with the coalition.

All this happened at the end of September. On the
Sept. 27. 27th of that month the Tsar wrote again to Frederick William politely asking him to hasten the moment for Russian troops to pass the Prussian frontier, and promising a subsidy of a million and a quarter sterling from England for every hundred thousand Prussians put into the field. The King still stuck to his neutrality, and Hardenberg was in despair; but
Oct. 6. fortunately on the 6th of October, Frederick William learned that the French troops, by their passage through Anspach, had violated his own sacred territory. Then the weak man, becoming suddenly violent, wished to send the French envoys their passports on the spot, and to invite the Russians to cross his boundaries immediately. Hardenberg averted this folly; but
Oct. 7. on the next day it was decided in Berlin, first, to inform Napoleon that Prussia considered herself

absolved from all obligation to France, next, to 1805. summon Alexander over the frontier, and finally—a thoroughly characteristic move—to occupy Hanover. The matter seemed so far settled that, on the 15th of Oct. 15. October, the shrewdest head in Europe, Metternich, who was in Berlin at the time, reckoned on seeing the Prussian and Russian troops united on the Bohemian frontier in a few weeks. But on that same day the news of Ney's victory at Elchingen on the 14th reached Berlin, and the King began again to waver. He summoned Count Haugwitz, the advocate of peace, to share the Foreign Office with Hardenberg, the advocate of war, and wished not only to close his boundaries to the Russians but to evade his interview with the Tsar. Alexander thereupon announced that he would come to Berlin in person, and arriving at Potsdam on the 25th of October, soon revived the Prussian monarch's Oct. 25. drooping spirits. Duroc took his leave with threats; and after enormous persuasion Frederick William was induced to send Count Haugwitz to Napoleon. This envoy was instructed to offer the Emperor the basis of negotiations laid down in the Anglo-Russian treaty of the 11th of April, to give him until the 15th of December to accept or refuse it, and, in the event of his refusal, to intimate that Prussia would join the Coalition with one hundred and eighty thousand men. Metternich tried hard to reduce the period of grace to forty-eight hours, lest the Allies should be devoured piecemeal, but in vain. The agreement was signed on the 3rd of November; Haugwitz departed on his Nov. 3. mission on the 14th; and Frederick William relapsed Nov. 14. into misery over the fact that he had actually committed himself to a decision.

Such and so abject was the man upon whom the fate of Europe at this crisis depended; and such the course of events at his Court during the momentous months of the autumn of 1805. It is now necessary to turn to Pitt's dealings with him. Whether Hardenberg's saying as to a landing of the British in Hanover

1805. reached their ears or not, it is certain that early in October Pitt and his colleagues were considering the possibility of rousing and supporting an insurrection in that province. They had at first some idea of landing troops at Stralsund, and marching into it from that quarter. Negotiations had been going forward through Mr. Pierrepont, our Minister at Stockholm, since the beginning of 1805 for the defence, through the help of British subsidies, of Swedish Pomerania by a joint force of Swedes and Russians. The task of concluding a convention between these two powers was of enormous difficulty, for the mad King of Sweden haggled incessantly for absolute control of all the forces, which, though his own contingent formed but one-third of the whole, he was to command in person. However, in February 1805 the agreement was signed. The Tsar was to send from forty to fifty thousand troops, and King Gustavus twenty to twenty-five thousand; the British Government was to provide £50,000 to place Pomerania in a state of defence; and it was arranged that the treaty should take active effect whenever the French in Hanover should move either towards Oldenburg, Mecklenburg, or Holstein.

Then followed months of wrangling over the subsidy to be paid to the Swedish troops by England, and new difficulties over the landing of the Russian force in Pomerania; for it is ill negotiating with any lunatic and worst of all with a royal lunatic. However, at last all obstacles were overcome, and at the

Sept. end of September a treaty of alliance was signed whereby Sweden engaged to furnish ten thousand men for defence of Pomerania, but to call them twelve thousand; England on her part agreeing to pay for the latter number at the rate of £12 : 10s. a man. At the same time the Russian troops, twenty thousand strong[1] under Count Tolstoy, disembarked at

[1] Infantry 15,836; Cavalry 1705, with 1615 horses; Artillery 1749, with 590 horses. Total (including the train), 19,348 and 3205 horses.

Stralsund on the 5th of October, so that matters showed 1805.
signs of real progress. A few days later, on the 14th Oct. 14.
of October, news reached the Swedish Court of Prussia's changed attitude towards France, in consequence of the violation of her dominions in Anspach. This infused new life into the preparations. Pierrepont urged the King of Sweden to advance into Hanover at once, before Prussia could offer to do so; and simultaneously the British Foreign Office pressed Tolstoy to take the same course. The King of Sweden did not love Prussia and had returned to Berlin his Order of the Black Eagle, on hearing that Frederick William had accepted the insignia of the Legion of Honour. He was likely therefore to seize any opportunity of making himself disagreeable to his brother potentate; and altogether all indications pointed to an early recovery of Hanover.[1]

In England the Ministry had meanwhile resolved to send a force to aid in the reconquest of the province.
On the 10th of October orders were issued for six Oct. 10.
thousand men of the King's German Legion to embark for foreign service under the command of Lieutenant-general Don, who was to proceed to Berlin in advance of his force in order to ascertain the feelings of that Court towards the landing of a British force in North Germany. The plan of operations was sketched by Brigadier van der Decken, a Hanoverian officer who had been prominent in raising the first corps of the King's German Legion. He urged that the force should not be of smaller strength than twenty-five thousand men, so as to enable it to advance into Hanover with confidence and without delay. Napoleon, as he pointed out, could constantly detach troops to overwhelm any British army that landed in North Germany; and between November and March such an

[1] F.O. Sweden, 33. Pierrepont to Sec. of State, 13th Jan., 7th, 15th Feb., 20th March, 8th, 26th April, 9th July, 25th Aug., 1st Sept., 4th, 14th Oct.; Sec. of State to Pierrepont, 25th June, 18th Oct. 1805.

1805. army could not re-embark, if hard pressed, but must cross the Elbe, which might be a hazardous operation, and retire eastward into Lauenburg. Owing to the approach of winter and the prospect of navigation being obstructed by ice, the detachment of the King's German Legion ought to sail at once, without waiting for the result of Don's mission to Berlin, disembark at Glückstadt on the Elbe, occupy and fortify Stade, and establish magazines at Cuxhaven and Bremerlehe. These two last should be the places of disembarkation for the rest of the troops, since the dearth of provisions and horses in the country was such that it would be imprudent to land the entire force at one spot. The British contingent should be concentrated at Verden on the Weser and should advance towards Nienburg, while the Swedes and Russians moved towards Lüneburg, Zell, and Hanover. The French were concentrated at Nienburg, at Hameln, and at Fort St. George, over against Hameln, on the west bank of the Weser; but Hameln was the only place which was really formidable and would require a regular siege.[1]

Oct. 16. Decken's advice bore immediate fruit. On the 16th Don was informed that nearly eleven thousand men[2] would be embarked at once for the Elbe in order to expel the French, now under four thousand strong, from Hanover, and that five thousand more would be held in readiness in the Downs. Meanwhile he himself was to go out at once to Berlin. His original instructions bade him sound the dispositions of Prussia towards the projected enterprise, and discover if she had an understanding with either France or Russia as to the occupation of Hanover; though it was not to be supposed that on any ground she could object to King George's reoccupation of his own dominions. He was also to ascertain the views of Denmark in case a

[1] Sec. of State to C.-in-C., 10th, 14th Oct.; Don to Sec. of State, 14th Oct.; Decken to Sec. of State, 16th Oct. 1805.

[2] K.G.L. 4808; 4 cos. 95th Rifles, 400; Brigade of Guards, 2000; 1st Regt. Caval. K.G.L. 575; 4th, 14th, 23rd Foot, 2800; 2 brigades of Artillery, 300.

retreat of the British troops through Holstein should 1805. be necessary, and those of the Duke of Mecklenburg, in the event of their wishing to advance through his territory upon Stralsund. As regards the operations, he was not to land nor advance into the interior unless assured of the safety of his force, nor to remain in the country after the harbours were frozen unless certain of a safe retreat; and his chief business would be to collect the army of the Hanoverians.

These orders were due to intense and rightful distrust of Frederick William; but on the 18th the news Oct. 18. of that sovereign's fury against Napoleon over the affair of Anspach set many misgivings at rest. Then Ministers suddenly woke to the idea that, with the concert of Prussia, it would be possible to recover not only Hanover but Holland. For a moment there was some idea of a descent upon Walcheren; and on the 24th Oct. 24. orders were sent to Don not to put to sea until further directions should reach him. It seems, however, that the military officers discouraged the project by urging the possible difficulties of a re-embarkation during the depth of winter; and on the 25th Don was finally Oct. 25. directed to sail with the first detachment of troops to the Elbe, Lord Harrowby having been appointed to take his place on a special mission to Berlin.[1]

By the 29th the first division was embarked; and Oct. 29. three days later van der Decken sailed forward in advance to collect supplies and transport. Arriving on the 8th of November, he sent home a report to the Nov. 8. following effect. Both Swedes and Russians were advancing westward. Prussian troops had actually entered Hanover and taken up positions on the Ems, securing the chief passages into the Netherlands by the occupation of Bentheim, and meanwhile living on the country with extreme hardship to the inhabitants. The people rejoiced greatly over the arrival of the British troops; but between the exactions of the

[1] Sec. of State to Don, 16th, 17th, 19th, 25th, 28th Oct.; to Lord Keith, 24th Oct. 1805.

1805. French and of the Prussians the province was much exhausted, and horses would be difficult to procure. The whole of the French force had been withdrawn into Hameln, where it was blockaded without hostilities by a Prussian detachment. The Prussian Commander-in-chief, the Duke of Brunswick, was very anxious for his men to be relieved in all their present stations by the troops of the Allies. For the advance into Holland Brunswick would detach fifteen thousand of his own troops to co-operate with the British, distributing the rest of the force between the middle Rhine and Moselle to keep up communications between his main army and that of the Allies. Finally, on pretext of guarding his magazines, the Duke wished to keep two battalions in Bremen; and this van der Decken evidently considered an extremely suspicious circumstance.[1]

Nov. 17. A few days later, on the 17th, General Don, after long detention by foul winds, anchored at Cuxhaven, and, pursuant to instructions from Harrowby, prepared for immediate disembarkation. But affairs were not going happily with the allied force. The King of Sweden, upon landing in Stralsund, found that Tolstoy had rushed off to Berlin to see the Tsar, leaving no report concerning his army, nor so much as an officer to receive His Majesty. This was unmannerly in any case, and Gustavus was one who was quick to construe discourtesy as insult. He was already greatly incensed that Frederick William had ordered Prussian troops to Hanover without informing him; and he instantly sent orders to halt his advanced guard, which had already reached Lauenberg on its march westward, vowing that he would return home. Pierrepont hastily intervened. It was his function to keep his Swedish Majesty in good temper, and he stood by Gustavus as a man stands at the head of a nervous horse, watching for every motion of eye and ear, and lavishing soft words and caresses. Tolstoy returned hurriedly from Berlin with apologies,

[1] Decken to Sec. of State, 12th November 1805.

though he did not conceal that he disliked the imposition of any man as commander over his head; and the incensed Gustavus, having thrown everything into confusion for several days, at last consented that his troops should cross the Elbe.[1] 1805.

Having made his peace, Tolstoy hastened to Lüneburg, summoning Don thither to go with him to the Duke of Brunswick's head-quarters at Hildesheim, some thirty miles south of Hanover; and there at last some definite arrangements were made. The British troops were for the present to occupy a line on the Lower Weser with their right at Blumenthal, their left at Verden, and advanced posts pushed forward on the river Hunte; while Tolstoy's right division should occupy the Weser from Hoya towards Minden and its left should blockade Hameln. In these positions the two commanders hoped in the course of a few weeks to be able to find horses and drivers for their artillery, and to mobilise their forces generally for an advance into Holland, towards which French reinforcements were already said to be marching. How any one could expect for a moment that a mixed force, in great measure dependent on the wills of such men as the Kings of Sweden and Prussia, could operate successfully against such a master of energy and action as Napoleon, it is difficult to see. The British Government did in fact lose patience, and, after urging upon Don an immediate descent on Holland, decided to embark twelve thousand additional troops without waiting longer to hear of the intentions of King Frederick William. This reinforcement increased the British contingent to twenty-five thousand men, of which Lord Cathcart was appointed Commander-in-chief. He was directed to disembark it in the Ems; Ministers expecting that, by the time of its arrival, Don and Tolstoy would already have advanced from the Weser to the Yssel. But meanwhile Tolstoy had come to the conclusion that the reduction of Hameln by a strict

[1] Pierrepont to Sec. of State, 28th Oct., 3rd, 9th Nov. 1805.

1805. blockade was a very important object; and that this operation, requiring as it would nine thousand men, would leave too few for an invasion of Holland. He was ready, if the British Government pressed him, to leave a corps to observe Hameln and to advance at once to the Yssel; but he and Don agreed that it would be better to delay a forward movement until the Swedes should have come up and Prussia should have finally declared against France. Then with their armies mobilised and a frost to make the waters passable, invasion of Holland would be an easy matter.[1]

The British Ministers bowed to the inevitable. The Allied Army in Hanover, having neither transport nor supplies, was plainly unable to move; and Cathcart's division was ordered to disembark, as Don's had done, in the Weser. Cathcart himself was to sail at once, and the mission of his force was explained to be not only to recover Holland, but to assure the Allies of the British on the Continent of England's firm determination to aid them not only by liberal subsidies but by active operations. All, however (such was the purport of his instructions), must depend upon Prussia. Harrowby's latest reports left no doubt that she would remain neutral; but it was certain that she had sent an ultimatum by the hand of Haugwitz to Napoleon, and there was every hope that Napoleon would reject it. In this case Prussia would be committed to war, and intelligence of the event ought to reach the Weser by the 15th of December. It was understood that Frederick William was desirous of the recapture of Holland from France, and he would probably be strengthened in his zeal by Harrowby's representations of England's readiness to assist him in this object. In fact, a main purpose of sending the British contingent of troops was to enable Prussia to march a force into

[1] Don to Sec. of State, 19th, 25th, 28th Nov.; Sec. of State to Don, 19th, 27th Nov.; to Lord Harrowby, 27th Nov.; E. Cooke to H.M. Consul, Embden, 26th Nov. 1805.

Holland without unduly weakening her strength in 1805. Franconia and Lower Saxony. But it was possible that, if the King of Sweden advanced with all his troops, they, together with the Russians and British, might well suffice to reduce all Holland north of the Meuse and Rhine; and, if Gustavus did actually take command of the Swedes and of the Russians whom the Tsar had placed under his orders, then Cathcart was, as a provisional arrangement, to obey directions from him likewise. Finally the British troops were not to advance into Holland on any ill-concerted errand, as a mere diversion; but it was hoped that no such idea would be in contemplation, for the British Ministers were specially anxious to recover Holland during 1805, and would deeply lament the necessity of deferring the operation to another year.[1]

Meanwhile Haugwitz was on his way to Napoleon charged with the momentous ultimatum which, as the Allies hoped, would throw Prussia into their arms. He journeyed slowly, being delayed partly by his own inclination and partly by Napoleon's orders; but at last on the 28th of November he was permitted to Nov. 28. reach Brünn and was received with icy coldness by the Emperor. He put forward Prussia's scheme of mediation none the less, and Napoleon accepted it, upon the condition that no troops, Russian, Swedish, or British, should pass the frontier of Holland. Haugwitz readily consented to this, thereby light-heartedly upsetting the whole of England's combinations and all the elaborate arrangements that Harrowby and Hardenberg were debating at Berlin. Napoleon then sent him to Vienna to confer with Talleyrand. The Emperor was on the eve of a great battle; he understood thoroughly that Prussia would turn upon him if he were beaten, and he did not forget her intrusion upon him at so critical a moment. Four days later, as Dec. 2. has been told, he fought and won the battle of

[1] Instructions to Cathcart, Nov.; 5th Dec.; Sec. of State to Harrowby, 7th Dec. 1805.

1805. Austerlitz; on the 6th was concluded the armistice
Dec. 6. which eliminated Austria from the struggle; and on
Dec. 14. the 14th Napoleon sent for Haugwitz to vent upon him his rage against Prussia. The interview was a stormy one, and the Emperor closed it with the ominous words that in a few days peace between France and Austria would be signed, and that he would not say what his relations with Prussia might then be. He was, however, still anxious to conclude an alliance with Frederick William if it were possible; wherefore summoning Haugwitz once more to his presence, he warned him that, if his King forced France into war, Hanover should never belong to Prussia. He then offered him a treaty of offensive and defensive alliance upon the following among other terms—that Prussia should take Hanover, should give Anspach to Bavaria, should cede Neufchatel and Cleves to Napoleon himself, should guarantee to France her present dominions and all future gains in Italy, and should further guarantee to Bavaria and Würtemberg such new possessions as might be dealt out to them by himself as reward for their services to France. Haugwitz duly accepted this
Dec. 15 offer; and on the 15th of December the Treaty was
Dec. 20. signed at Schönbrunn. On the 20th Haugwitz was given to understand that the article concerning Italy included Naples, and that Hardenberg must be dismissed from King Frederick William's councils. Therewith he was suffered to take his departure to Berlin.

During the interval the British Cabinet awaited in anxious suspense the issue of Haugwitz's mission. Pitt had gone to Bath, a dying man, though as yet he knew it not; and Mulgrave and Hawkesbury had gone with him. Harrowby's letters gave none but unsatisfactory accounts of the attitude of the Court of Berlin. Frederick William was evidently waiting upon events; and the Prussian Staff was opposed to a direct attack upon Holland as a permanent operation, though favouring the advance of a small detachment towards it to make a diversion. Anxious, however, to show 1805. zeal and good-will, Ministers ordered eight more British battalions and some German cavalry to sail for the Weser on the 10th of December, with the melancholy Dec. 10. result that the transports were at once dispersed by a heavy gale and part of them cast away. Cathcart, arriving at Cuxhaven on the 15th, was met by the news Dec. 15. of Austerlitz and by an intimation from Harrowby that, in consequence of the armistice between Austria and France, the Prussian Staff deprecated any movement towards Holland. He therefore detained all his transports so as to be ready for re-embarkation. A day or two later came a strange rumour, which found its way even to England, that the Russians and Austrians had fought a second action against Napoleon and had driven him back upon Vienna. The Ministers in London therefore ordered yet more troops to sail for the Weser, and continued to urge Prussia to come to a decision as to her policy and her plan of campaign. They also condescended to explain that England had made enormous efforts to give the Allies solid support upon the Continent, that she was running great risks by sending men to North Germany at a season when they might be unable to re-embark, and that foul winds and ignorance of Prussia's intentions were really accountable for the delay in the appearance of her troops. Cathcart was further apprised that the position of the British on the Weser was now becoming a matter of substantive importance in itself, for the French troops were reported to be collecting in Holland, and there was always the chance that Napoleon might direct a force upon Hanover from the south and east. The Cabinet was anxious to protect the unfortunate province in order alike to save it from a renewal of harsh treatment, to ensure the recruiting of the German Legion, to secure the British magazines on the Elbe and Weser, and to maintain easy communication between England and North Germany. Finally a long and confused statement of the disposition of the Prussian armies was

1805. enclosed to the British General to show that operations of some kind were still possible.[1]

Dec. 29. On the 29th of December, however, the British Ministers in London received unmistakable news, long delayed by foul winds, of the disaster of Austerlitz and of the armistice between Austria and France. Being unable in the absence of Pitt to give Cathcart further instructions, they merely sent him additional transports to bring off his troops, which in the circumstances was the wisest thing that they could do. Affairs were steadily going from bad to worse. The King of Sweden, after allowing part of his troops to march as far as the Elbe, and even moving himself some way westward, declared that he would not act while the attitude of Prussia was so uncertain, though the first shot fired from a Prussian gun would be the signal for him to advance in force. The Tsar, however, after retiring in deep depression to St. Petersburg upon the defeat of Austerlitz, had placed Tolstoy's detachment under the orders of the King of Prussia; and King Gustavus very naturally refused to make himself in any way dependent upon the commands of Frederick William, whom he rightly held in utter detestation and contempt. The position of Cathcart was very difficult. Additional British troops continued to arrive; but many transports were missing, and comparatively few of his battalions were complete in consequence.[2] The French force to west

[1] Sec. of State to C.-in-C., 19th Dec.; to Harrowby (private), 21st Dec.; to Cathcart, 23rd Dec. 1805.

[2] Troops of the second division arrived on the Weser on or before 1st Jan. 1806:

Major-general Sir Arthur Wellesley's Brigade .	3rd Foot,	590
" " " .	8th "	447
" " " .	36th "	657
Major-general Fraser's Brigade . . .	26th "	438
" " . . .	28th "	968
" " . . .	91st "	508
Major-general Sherbrooke's Brigade . .	5th "	480
" " . . .	27th "	251
" " . . .	34th "	402

Royal Artillery, 3 companies, with horses; R.E. detachment.

of the Yssel under Louis Bonaparte was increasing; 1806.
and another force under Augereau was menacing Hanover on the south from Frankfort on Main. The behaviour of Prussia was growing more and more equivocal; her preparations for war were backward; and her army, owing to the age and apathy of its generals, was deficient in the discipline which constituted its sole strength. Nevertheless, evacuation of North Germany by the British would, in Cathcart's judgment, certainly precipitate Prussia towards a disastrous peace, whereas the presence of a British force might hearten her to stand firm until the Russians had recovered themselves. On the other hand a frost might at any moment make re-embarkation impossible, and then there would be no retreat except into Prussian territory and on to the Prussian armies. This retreat King Frederick William refused to grant unless the British troops on the Weser retired in rear of the Prussians, so as to ensure that there should be no provocative action towards Holland, and unless the blockade of Hameln were relaxed so as to give some relief to the French garrison. The whole state of affairs was so uncertain that Cathcart could only arrange a temporary disposition of his troops in concert with the Prussian General Kalkreuth, and then await orders. The British therefore occupied Bremen and Verden, and the Russians Hoya and Nienburg. The Swedes were perforce left on the Elbe to act as a reserve, if they should consent to act at all; and the Prussian contingent remained in observation on the line of the Ems, ready, if need were, to lean its right upon Minden so as to cover the British left and keep up communication with Magdeburg.[1]

Such, however, was Cathcart's distrust of Prussia that he made every preparation to collect and embark the recruits which had been gathered for the King's German Legion, lest King Frederick William's officers

[1] Sec. of State to Cathcart, 29th Dec. 1805; Cathcart to Sec. of State, 1st (with enclosure), 2nd, 6th Jan. 1806.

1806. should try to take them from him. At length, on the
Jan. 7. 7th of January 1806, Hardenberg informed Harrowby that there was every prospect of his master's coming to an arrangement with Napoleon to occupy Hanover, until peace should be concluded between Britain and France. He added that hostilities between Prussia and France were most improbable, that the King was about to recall Tolstoy's troops from North Germany, and that he saw no advantage in any continuance of the British troops in that quarter. Harrowby took his leave on the same day, first sending a letter to inform Cathcart of his departure, which message, however, did not
Jan. 21. reach that General until the 21st. Cathcart without delay sought Tolstoy, who had always been frank and open with him, and learned that fifty thousand Prussians were on the march to occupy Hanover in force. A few days later he received a copy of Haugwitz's treaty of the 15th of December, with an intimation from the British Minister in Berlin that it had been ratified (which was not strictly correct), and would be carried into effect at once. Almost immediately afterwards he received orders from England to re-embark his force, which was now over twenty-six thousand strong,[1] for the King's German Legion had increased by one-
Feb. 13. third during its stay in Germany. By the 13th of
Feb. 15. February all was ready, and on the 15th the army sailed with a fair wind, leaving Hanover to the tender mercies of Prussia, possibly with a hope, and most

[1] *British.*—1/ Coldstream Guards; 1/3rd Guards; 1/3rd, 1/4th, 1/5th,† 1/8th, 1/9th, 1/14th, 1/23rd, 1/26th,† 2/27th,‡ 1/28th, 1/30th,† 2/34th, 1/36th, 1/89th, 1/91st, 1/95th,* R.A.; R.E. Waggon Train.

(† 5 companies only arrived; ‡ 6 companies only arrived; * only 4 companies sent.)

Germans.—1st and 2nd Heavy Dragoons; 1st and 3rd Light Dragoons; 1st and 2nd Light Battalions; 1st to 7th Line Battalions; Regiment of Artillery.

Total: British	510 officers;	14,058 N.C.O.'s and men.	
„ German	382 „	11,693 „ „	
	892	25,751	

certainly with an ardent wish, that Prussia might pay dearly for it. 1806.

Such was the end of the expedition to the Weser, not a small expedition measured by the standard of that day, and not destined, as was thought, to play an unimportant part. It proved to be an egregious farce; but at this distance of time it is perhaps difficult to judge of it aright. The general idea of operating upon Napoleon's flank and rear was no doubt sound; but for success the whole plan depended necessarily on Prussia. The King of Sweden was so uncertain and his force so small that his help was of little moment; but the Russian contingent was an important matter, and these troops could not obtain access to the sphere of action without leave from Prussia; nor in truth could any important operation be undertaken without the actual aid of Prussian regiments. Was Prussia a power to be counted upon at such a crisis? To this question all previous experience since the French Revolution answered emphatically in the negative. Blindness, timidity, self-seeking and double-dealing had from the first been the special characteristics of the Court of Berlin; and, while Frederick William remained in power, it was hopeless to look for change or improvement. It may of course be urged, probably with some correctness, that Cathcart's army was intended to play a diplomatic part, partly tempting and partly forcing Prussia to join the Coalition. But was it likely that a man who would not keep his engagements with his dearest friend and most powerful patron, Alexander of Russia, but compelled him almost to extort the fulfilment of them by armed strength—was it likely that such a man would learn strength of purpose and common honesty from an unskilful negotiator such as Harrowby, backed by a handful of British soldiers? There was therefore some further motive to prompt the dispatch of this futile expedition; and this was almost certainly the anxiety of the British Government to have a British force in Holland when the overthrow

1806. of Napoleon should be accomplished. This idea of eternal petty expeditions to the Netherlands was a mania with Pitt, which he most unfortunately bequeathed to his successors. The ultimate destiny of Holland was no doubt of overwhelming importance to England; but it was idle to suppose that England's part in the shaping of that destiny would be determined by a small party of red-coats on the spot, rather than by the successful operations of a strong British force against France in another quarter. Yet such seems to have been the fixed idea of Pitt and his colleagues. They appear to have argued that the expedition to the Weser might simultaneously answer a number of ends. It might cause Prussia to declare against Napoleon, in which case it might lead to the recovery of Holland; at all events it would collect recruits for the King's German Legion, and show the earnestness of the British intentions. But, if Napoleon won a great victory over the Russians, the whole enterprise fell to the ground, for every one in Europe knew that Prussia would side with the conqueror. On the other hand, if Cathcart's troops had been thrown into Italy together with Craig's, then, no matter what the action of Prussia, no matter what the success or failure of Austria and Russia, the diversion was bound to tell. Such employment of an army for a definite military purpose was, however, outside the scope of Pitt's intelligence. That military and diplomatic operations can go hand in hand, each seconding and abetting the other, no man understood better than Napoleon; and his perfect mastery of the art of combining the two constitutes one of his greatest claims to supreme genius in the conduct of war. Pitt had some inkling of the advantages of this art, but lamentable ignorance of its practice. For this reason again and again he sent generals to different quarters of Europe with vague orders to do something, no great matter what, but at any rate something, which would show that England was an active ally. Such was the

purport of the instructions which Abercromby carried 1806.
to Holland in 1799, Craig to the Mediterranean, and Cathcart to North Germany in 1805, with results that are too well known to us. By this purposeless distribution of troops the armed force of England was frittered away in paltry and useless detachments; for, if an expedition is to do nothing in particular, there is no reason why it should consist of forty thousand men rather than four thousand. The practice was infinitely mischievous. It demoralised the men; it discouraged the officers; it took the heart out of the Generals. More than any other cause it brought about that readiness to re-embark and to abandon enterprises which made the British Army the laughing-stock alike of its own nation and of Europe.

Before Cathcart returned Pitt was dead, worn out Jan. 23.
by disease, anxiety, and overwork. Wholly unsuccessful as he was as a Minister of War, it were ill to dismiss so great a man with no eye but for his military failures. The story of his genius as an administrator during ten years of peace must be left to others to tell, but that of his leadership of England through a time of supreme peril must not be set aside without brief commemoration in a military history. It was well that at a time when many were dazzled by the spectacle of a great people uprising in blind fury to conquer what it hoped might be its liberty, the forces of order should have found such a champion as Pitt. It is true that, as such, he was bound to join or to seek as allies rulers so abject as the Bourbons of Naples and Sicily, so contemptible as Frederick William of Prussia, so insane as Paul of Russia and Gustavus of Sweden, so weak as the Emperor Francis; but that was the misfortune of his time, not the demerit of his cause. For the crusade of the Revolution as initiated by the Girondists, continued by the Convention and the Directory, and finally prosecuted to its death by Napoleon, was a crusade not of liberty but of enslavement. It was against this that Pitt stood forth, as a man who had learned the nature of

1806. freedom not from the writings of sentimental dreamers, but from the history and the wisdom of his own countrymen, and was aware that it is a "plant of slow growth," which has its roots in patience, charity, and self-respect, and cannot be forced into blossom by violence, intolerance, and spoliation. Amid reptile Bourbons, cringing Hohenzollerns, and irresolute Hapsburgs, the figure of Pitt towers aloft gigantic; and gigantic not from the meanness of their stature only. For this was a man of such singleness of purpose, such immovable integrity, such dauntless courage, such lofty patriotism, that he could not but exalt and purify any cause that he embraced. To Englishmen he was the incarnation of uprightness, and he was trusted by them accordingly. He could not be infallible, and he was frequently deceived. At a time when the world was agitated by forces which seemed to be beyond the range of human experience, the insight and calculations of the ablest statesman might easily be at fault. But the people felt certain that he would take the course which he thought best and most worthy for the country, and would pursue it with perfect contempt of possible disadvantage or danger to himself, so only his honour should be safe. Napoleon ascribed the extraordinary ascendancy of his great rival to his eloquence, and envied him his gift of oratory. He was mistaken. Pitt's strength lay in his perfect straight-forwardness and unblemished character, without which his speeches, in these days unreadable, might have seemed wearisome even to his contemporaries. So great an example was not lost upon his successors, even the least of whom faced Napoleon with a boldness which modern French historians survey with astonished admiration; and in truth England's part in the struggle was dignified to the very end by the commanding nobility of William Pitt.

CHAPTER X

THE Ministry which succeeded to power upon the death of Pitt was that known by the name of All the Talents; and the array of great names was such as to justify the title. Lord Grenville was Prime Minister; Fox was at the Foreign Office; Charles Grey, later Lord Howick and Earl Grey of the Reform Bill, at the Admiralty; Lord Moira at the Office of Ordnance; and William Windham in charge of the department of War and the Colonies. This last appointment was significant, for Windham had been the most bitter critic of the military measures of Addington and Pitt, and there could be little doubt that he would introduce drastic reforms. Nor were reforms unnecessary, for the "Twenty Pound Act," as Pitt's Additional Force Act had been nicknamed, was conclusively proved to be an utter failure. Attempts had been made at the end of 1805 to galvanise it into life by increasing the reward to the parochial officials for every recruit that they might levy, and by sending military officers round the country to instruct them in their duties. Nor had these efforts been wholly unsuccessful. In all some thirteen thousand men had been attested under the Act; and Pitt's supporters maintained that, since the beginning of 1806, it had furnished on an average three hundred recruits a week. But these figures were fallacious. Of the thirteen thousand enlisted, nearly three thousand had deserted; and investigation showed that the remainder had for the most part been purchased from crimps, which was the thing that Pitt had been 1806.

1806. specially anxious to avoid. The fate of the Act was therefore certain. The one thing uncertain was the nature of the new plan that should follow upon its repeal.

April 3. On the 3rd of April Windham in a speech to the Commons set all doubts upon the subject at rest. After a long preliminary discussion of the methods employed for raising men in the past, he laid it down that voluntary enlistment alone was possible to recruit the Army for service abroad, and that, to make voluntary enlistment a success, the Army must be rendered an eligible calling. This object could be easily accomplished by an increase of pay; but such a resource was economically impossible. Much might nevertheless be done by encouragements and rewards, and by limiting military service to a term of years instead of extending it, as heretofore, for life. He proposed therefore to allow every two years' service in the West Indies to count as three; to increase the scale of pensions; and to allow men to enlist in future for a short period, at the end of which they could engage for a second term, with a slight increase of wages, and again for a third term with a further increase. At the end of the second term they would be entitled to a pension roughly equivalent to half pay; and at the end of the third term they would finally retire on little less than full pay. The three periods of service for infantry were to be each of seven years; for cavalry, ten, seven, and seven years; for artillery, twelve, five, and five years. By this arrangement he confidently believed that the ranks of the Regular Army would be kept permanently filled.

The proposition was bold and startling, but it was not novel; and it seems tolerably certain that Windham really borrowed it from Robert Craufurd, who had repeatedly declared his belief in short service. To sound the feeling of the Army upon the subject, the Duke of York had in 1804 called for the opinions of fourteen prominent General Officers, seven of whom,

including Lord Moira, were in favour of the change, 1806.
six were against it, and one was doubtful. It was, however, remarkable that General Hewett, the Inspector-general of Recruiting, was strongly opposed to it, and that Sir John Moore wrote an impatient answer, as though the proposition were hardly worth discussing. In his view it was idle to talk of keeping the Army full except by some form of compulsion, in which case service ought certainly to be limited in point of time; but no change in the terms of enlistment would procure men who could not be obtained without it. "If," he argued with much force, "limited service and enormous bounties could tempt men to enlist, would the Army of Reserve and the Permanent Additional Force created by Mr. Pitt's Act be incomplete?" However, the House was very willing to give Windham's plan a fair trial; and the necessary legislation was easily effected by a few changes in the schedules of the Mutiny Act. On the other hand, Windham guarded himself against possible danger from the total failure of the system by a second measure, which permitted fifteen in every hundred men of the Irish Militia to enlist in the Army every year, thereby assuring a supply of from three to four thousand recruits from this service annually. Pitt's Act was repealed; the fines, amounting to £1,800,000, which were due from defaulting parishes, were remitted; and the traditions of military policy inherited from Pitt, so far as they concerned the Regular Army, were definitely abandoned.

Nor did Windham shrink from making an equal break with the past in respect of the rest of the land-forces. The ballot was suspended for two years, until the strength of the Regular Militia should be reduced to the establishment of 1802; and Windham did not conceal his hope that in future the ranks of that force might be filled by voluntary enlistment for a reasonable bounty. Finally he turned upon the Volunteers, whom he had always condemned as a costly encumbrance, and announced his intentions of gradually taking away

1806. all their allowances, and of withdrawing privileges and exemptions of every kind from all corps which accepted more from Government than their arms and accoutrements. To create a force which should take their place, he introduced and passed an Act which, after repealing the First Defence Act and the Levy en Masse Act, provided for the training of all the men in the country who were liable to service in the Militia. Two hundred thousand of them, chosen by ballot, were to be called out every year and trained for not more than twenty-four days, with wages of one shilling for each day, and at no greater distance than five miles from their homes. Substitutes were forbidden, but exemption from one year's service could be purchased by a fine of £10; and every man who had undergone one year's training was exempt from the ballot for two years. No provision was made for the organisation of the men into companies or battalions, though the King was empowered to appoint officers and non-commissioned officers to instruct them; but, in case of invasion, the trained men could either be formed into new corps or embodied with old corps; and it was Windham's firm intention that, at any crisis of national danger, the trained men should be drafted into regiments of the Line.

Thus at last some effort was made to exercise the manhood of the country in arms for its defence, a step which ought to have been taken by Pitt in 1794. But, though the principle of the measure was right and sound, the details were crude and, as the sequel showed, insufficient. Windham's idea, apparently, was so to instruct the nation in the use of weapons that, after augmenting the Regular battalions to the greatest strength compatible with efficiency, the citizens should group themselves into bands under local leaders, and carry on a harassing warfare after the fashion of La Vendée. There was and there is very much to be said for such warfare against an invading enemy. Indeed the lesson cannot be too strongly impressed upon the

body of the people that, if a foreign force should land 1806.
on their shores, every citizen who kills, captures or, to use the modern phrase, puts out of action even a single man of the enemy, has rendered a national service. When every straggler, every messenger, every unwary sentry, every weak patrol and every small party is taken, shot, or knocked on the head, war speedily becomes a weariness to the invaders, as the French discovered in Spain from 1808 to 1813, the Germans in France in the winter of 1870, and as we ourselves have learned from more than one experience. But, though Windham's Act professed to train the nation to the use of arms, its author had only the haziest notions as to the manner in which instruction should be imparted ; and it seems that for this most important matter he relied upon the parish-constables. These functionaries were required to be present at all exercise of the men ballotted under the Act, in order to arrest any who should be guilty of misconduct and bring them before a magistrate, who could punish them by fine, or by imprisonment in default of payment. The House of Commons, while giving those enactments the force of law, was greatly disposed, and with very good reason, to treat them as a joke. Nevertheless in due time a man arose who was able, as shall be seen, to take what was good in Windham's Act and turn it to useful account.

Meanwhile the state of the Army for the moment was by no means unsatisfactory. In March the Regular force at home, which had been recruited for general service, numbered, including the King's German Legion, twenty-two thousand cavalry, sixty thousand infantry, and ten thousand artillery. There was no danger of invasion, so that from thirty to forty thousand men were at disposal for offensive operations. Moreover, the year had opened well with the news, which arrived at the end of February, that the expedition to the Cape of Good Hope had been completely successful. It will be convenient, before going further, to give a brief account of this campaign.

1805. Baird's force, as has already been told, was a part of that which had been embarked at Cork for despatch to Jamaica in 1805, upon the alarm of Villeneuve's raid in the West Indies. It consisted of rather more than six thousand men,[1] two hundred of which were cavalry; and Baird was ordered, immediately after fulfilling the object of his mission, to send the Thirty-eighth, Fifty-ninth, and Twentieth Light Dragoons to India. The convoy, consisting of sixty-one transports escorted by nine men-of-war under Commodore Sir Home Popham,
Aug. 31. sailed from Cork on the 31st of August, reached Funchal in Madeira on the 28th of September, and, sailing again on the 3rd of October, put into Bahia
Nov. 10. on the 10th of November. A transport and a store-ship were wrecked while working into the bay, and Brigadier Yorke, who was in command of the artillery, was drowned, together with two men. After making good defects, the ships again sailed on the 26th of
1806. December, made the land in the neighbourhood of
Jan. 4. Table Bay on the morning of the 4th of January 1806, and on the evening of the same day came to anchor between Robben Island and the Blueberg. Baird had intended to land next morning at an inlet in the coast to the north of Melkbosel Point and within sixteen miles of Capetown; but during the night a gale set in and, though one brigade was actually ordered into the boats, the surf was too heavy to allow a landing. He
Jan. 5. therefore, on the night of the 5th, detached Beresford with the Thirty-eighth and his few mounted men to Saldanha Bay, sending a frigate in advance to take

[1]

3 cos. R.A.	285	1/83rd	701
Royal Staff Corps	20	1/93rd	622
1/24th Foot	493	1/59th	906
1/38th	913	Detachments	149
1/71st	764	20th L.D.	200
1/72nd	599		
		Total	5652 rank and file.
Add one-eighth for officers and sergeants			708
			6360

possession of the port and secure, if possible, horses and cattle. He himself had intended to follow with the rest of the army on the morrow; but on the morning of the 6th the surf had so far abated as to make disembarkation possible; and accordingly the Highland Brigade[1] was ordered into the boats under command of Brigadier Ferguson, who had previously made careful reconnaissance of the coast. There was no force to oppose a landing except a single company of burgher militia, which was kept at a respectful distance by the guns of four ships; and the chief danger arose from the surf, which was still violent. A small transport was run aground to act as a breakwater, and thanks to this precaution and to the skill of the bluejackets, one boat only, containing thirty-six men of the Ninety-third, was swamped. Every one of the unlucky Highlanders was drowned; and these together with another man killed, two officers and two more men wounded by the bullets of the burghers, constituted the only casualties of the disembarkation. The rest of the force with some artillery and supplies was landed next day; and the first and greatest difficulty of the expedition was overcome.

1806. Jan. 6. Jan. 7.

It seems surprising that the Dutch commander, General Janssens, having had full forty-eight hours' warning, should have made no better preparations for resistance; but in truth every circumstance was adverse to him. By the use of signal guns he alarmed the whole country within fifty leagues of Capetown; but the wheat was threshing; the grapes were ripening; the farmers were in the midst of their busiest season; and the heat was such that journeys could only be undertaken by night. Apart from the burghers, the resources of Janssens were small. He had one battalion of Waldeck mercenaries four hundred strong; a second of half that number, consisting of sharp-shooters recruited from all nations; and a third—the Twenty-second regiment of the Dutch line—besides a few dragoons and artillery, making up a total of twelve

[1] 71st, 72nd, 93rd.

1806. hundred regular troops. In addition to these he had two hundred and forty French sailors, between three and four hundred coloured artillerymen and infantry, and rather over two hundred burghers, the whole composing a heterogeneous and ill-assorted force such as is seldom brought together. However, he collected it for what it might be worth, in all about two thousand men with sixteen guns, and at one o'clock
Jan. 8. on the morning of the 8th he marched out towards the Blueberg to meet the British.

On the same morning and at nearly the same hour Baird likewise began his march upon Capetown with over four thousand men, two howitzers and six light guns, and seized the heights of the Blueberg before Janssens could reach them. From thence discerning the Dutch General in the act of forming line of battle to encounter him, he divided his force into two columns; the Highland Brigade advancing straight on the road to Capetown, and the remaining brigade[1] turning off to the right. Arriving within cannon-shot, Baird opened fire from his artillery and was answered by the Dutch guns; but, at the sight of a few round shot falling near them, the Waldeckers turned and ran. The Dutch Twenty-second thereupon also gave way, and, after rallying for a moment under Janssens in person, fled again at the sight of the Highlanders advancing and could not be stopped. They had suffered little, for the Highland Brigade had committed the fault, rare in British troops, of firing a volley at long range before closing with the bayonet; and indeed the behaviour of this Dutch Twenty-second and the Waldeckers was the more discreditable since the rest of Janssens' troops, French, Dutch, and negroes, regulars and irregulars, stood and fought with great gallantry. However, with his line thus weakened, Janssens had no alternative but to fall back. At Rietvlei he was able to collect what was left of his force, when he sent the Waldeckers to Capetown in disgrace, and led the rest, with the

[1] 24th, 59th, 83rd.

exception of the French sailors, into the mountains of 1806. Hottentot Holland. His losses appear to have somewhat exceeded two hundred killed and wounded. Those of the British were one officer and fourteen men killed, nine officers and one hundred and eighty-eight men killed, wounded, and missing. Five-sixths of the casualties occurred in the three Highland battalions, the remaining brigade having been but little engaged. It is worthy of note that Baird reported Janssens' force to be five thousand instead of two thousand strong, and yet contrived that only the Highland Brigade should be employed in the fight. Such proceedings long have been, and still are, far too common among our Scottish Generals.

On the evening of the action Baird bivouacked at Rietvlei, in much anxiety as to the possibility of obtaining provisions from the fleet. Popham, however, by great exertions contrived to throw a small quantity ashore; and on the 9th the army pushed forward to Jan. 9. Capetown over arid sand, taking up a position at Salt River, about a mile and a half north of the town, where the General hoped to ensure communication with the fleet and, if necessary, to land his siege-train. Here Beresford and his detachment joined the army, and here Baird received overtures for a suspension of arms from the Commandant at Capetown; with the result that within twenty-four hours a capitulation was signed and the town was occupied by the British. Janssens still Jan. 10. remained to be dealt with, but his force was fast dwindling owing to desertion; and Baird, while making his dispositions to attack and cut him off, endeavoured to end matters by a letter complimenting him upon his gallantry, urging the fruitlessness of resistance, and offering honourable terms for the surrender of the colony. After a little hesitation these were accepted, and on the 18th of January was signed the final Jan. 18. capitulation which delivered Cape Colony to the British.[1]

[1] R.O. Cape of Good Hope. *Military Transactions*, i. pp. 104-142; Theal's *History of South Africa*, i. 138-150.

1806. So far all had gone well. The capture of the Cape, of course, signified the locking up of from three to four thousand men in a distant garrison, but this was no great price to pay for the safety of India. There was little to be feared from the inhabitants. The Dutch and French troops, which had formed the bulk of Janssens' army, were sent back to Europe under the treaty of surrender; and the enlistment of the Waldeckers from the Dutch into the British service more than made good the casualties of Baird's short campaign. An additional stroke of luck came soon after. The Dutch colours were kept flying in Table Bay for some time after the country had passed into British hands; and a French frigate, deceived by this wile, sailed into the anchorage and was at once taken. She proved to have on board several companies of the Second and Fifty-fourth British regiments, which she had captured in transports at the mouth of the Channel, and was carrying to Mauritius. These men were homeward bound from the Mediterranean, so that they were isolated from their battalions, but at all events they were recovered, and were no unwelcome addition to the garrison at the moment. Unfortunately, however, Baird chose to turn this windfall to the worst possible account.

Sir Home Popham, the commander of the fleet which had escorted Baird, was a restless officer of insinuating manners, who had early in his career gained favour in high places. In 1793 and 1794 he had been entrusted with the charge of gun-boats, pontoons, and similar matters under the Duke of York, and had acquitted himself always with credit. Running backwards and forwards between the Low Countries and England with despatches, he had been seen and consulted by Ministers, and, being always ready with a decided opinion upon any enterprise, enjoyed, in a quiet way, considerable influence with them. He was by no means without ability. He had devised and was constantly improving a code of naval signals; and in the matter of embarking and disembarking troops in an enemy's country he was full of skill and resource. He had worked so much with the Army that he thoroughly understood the service, and would spare no pains to ensure the health and comfort of any troops with which he was concerned. In the Navy also he was popular, for he looked carefully to the interest of the men and officers under his immediate command, particularly in the matter of prize-money, which was frequently the main object of his operations. This, indeed, was his weakest point. Constant employment in more or less independent stations had given him an opportunity of dabbling in mercantile transactions which, in the opinion of his contemporaries, were by no means to his credit. The same cause had led him to persuade himself that he was a great diplomatist and administrator; and in his distant command at the Cape he thought that he saw an opportunity for adding both to his wealth and to his importance. 1806.

Already, in previous volumes of this history, the reader has encountered the name of Miranda, in connection with revolutionary movements in the Spanish colonies of South America. Miranda was a Venezuelan of Caracas, who in 1782 had been dismissed from the Spanish service under an accusation of complicity in illicit trading with North America and of corrupt delivery of the plans of the fortifications of Havana to the British Government. From that time onwards he never ceased his efforts to drag the British Government into countenancing and supporting a revolution in South America. In 1783 he put forward a complete plan for the emancipation of the Spanish Colonies with the help of England, but was repulsed by Fox and North. In 1790, at the time of the dispute over Nootka Sound, he brought the same plan before Pitt and, though cordially received, was foiled by the pacific settlement of the controversy. Failing then to obtain a pension from Pitt, he entered the service of the French Republic and fought under Dumouriez. In 1796, upon the outbreak

1806. of war between England and Spain, he again sought Pitt, and so far commended his scheme to the Ministry and its advisers that, as we have seen, an expedition was actually prepared, and only abandoned with the greatest reluctance and regret. On this occasion he contrived to enlist the sympathy not only of Henry Dundas and Popham but even of so sober a person as Lord Grenville. When he found that England had her hands already overfull, he returned in 1801 to France to try his fortune there. As, however, he could obtain nothing from Bonaparte, he came once again to England in 1802, when Addington gave him encouragement and countenance, though shrinking from the final step of equipping a ship for him. But, when Pitt returned to office, Miranda and Popham, having already gained over Lord Melville[1] at the Admiralty, urged their views upon the Prime Minister with increased vehemence; and matters went so far that Popham on the 16th of October 1804 produced a long memorandum, working out the details of an expedition to South America. Sir Arthur Wellesley, at the request of Ministers, likewise compiled similar particulars for a descent upon the Orinoco.

Nothing however came of this, though Popham afterwards affirmed that, from his recollection of what had passed, the Ministry had given him a free hand to make a descent upon Buenos Ayres. It is possible that both Pitt and Melville were guilty of some indiscretion in their frequent conversations with Popham, for the enterprise was exactly of a nature to captivate their unmilitary minds. Popham averred that the imports from South America into Spain in produce and specie were worth some twenty millions annually, that two-thirds of this sum passed into the hands of France and that, unless the British anticipated him, Bonaparte would shortly send expeditions to Vera Cruz, Mexico, Brazil, and Rio de la Plata. How Napoleon was to send so large a force over the sea with a navy so inferior

[1] This of course was the Henry Dundas above mentioned.

to England's Popham did not pause to explain nor the Ministers to inquire. Lord Grenville, on the other hand, had taken a truer measure of Miranda than his late colleagues and, whatever he may have thought of him in 1796, was unwilling to trust him in 1804; but, being in opposition during Pitt's administration, he was of course without influence with the party in power. The truth is that Miranda was simply a shallow, unscrupulous adventurer, not wholly innocent of knavery, and that Popham's character at bottom perhaps differed not very greatly from that of Miranda.[1] 1806.

The result of all these discussions as to seconding a revolutionary movement in South America was that Popham, finding himself at the Cape with a fairly strong squadron and no immediate work to be done, thought the opportunity a good one to make a sensational stroke for his own hand. He therefore besought Baird to trust him with a battalion, in order to make a beginning by the capture of Buenos Ayres and of the province now known by the name of Argentina. It says much for his powers of address that he could persuade Baird even to listen, for that General was hard, rough, difficult, and jealous of his own authority. But a Scot is rarely loth to perpetrate a job for his own countrymen. The General therefore told the Commander that if he chose to take his own regiment, the Seventy-first, he might do so, but that he should have no other. Popham gladly accepted the offer. The Seventy-first was embarked under the command of Colonel Beresford, the future marshal of Portugal, together with a few artillerymen, four guns, and a handful of dragoons;[2]

[1] *Athenæum*, April 19, 1902, *Pitt and General Miranda*, by Hubert Hall; Popham's memo. of 16th Oct. 1804 in Popham to Sec. of State of 30th April 1806; *Dropmore Papers*.

[2] R.A., 3 officers, 33 n.c.o. and men, 4 guns (2 complete with horses and drivers)

20th L.D. 1 officer, 6 men.

71st Foot. 32 „ 883 „

Total 36 *officers*, 922 *men*. Also 60 women (6 to each company) and 40 children.

1806. and the Colonel received instructions intimating that, in Baird's opinion, a force of less than a thousand men, with a few seamen and marines, was sufficient to master the Spanish possessions on Rio de la Plata—a country half as large as Europe, with a capital containing seventy thousand souls. In case of failure, continued the instructions, Beresford was to return at once with all his troops to the Cape. This clause was very necessary; for Popham was quite capable of making a long marauding voyage round the Spanish settlements after the Elizabethan fashion. The Commodore then ordered the whole of his squadron to get under way, leaving not a single ship upon the station; and on
April 14. the 14th of April the armament, much envied by the rest of the garrison, sailed away to the west.[1]

For a week the voyage was prosperous; but on the
April 21. 21st one of the transports with two hundred men on board parted company and disappeared, diminishing the military force so seriously that Popham thought it prudent to bear up for St. Helena. From thence he and Beresford wrote to England on the 30th to report what they had done; Popham with long and elaborate explanations which betrayed his consciousness of having acted amiss; Beresford with a short but urgent appeal for instructions as to his dealings with the inhabitants. Popham then contrived to wheedle the Governor of St. Helena into granting him a reinforcement of nearly four hundred men[2] from the garrison of the island; and on
May 21. the 21st of May the armament resumed its voyage to Rio de la Plata. After a long and tedious passage Cape St. Mary, which marks the northern side of the entrance
June 8. to the river, was sighted on the 8th of June; Popham himself together with an officer of engineers having gone forward in a frigate on the 27th of May to explore the navigation of the channel and reconnoitre the country.

[1] Baird to Sec. of State, 14th April 1806; "Recollections of the British Army," in Colburne's *Military Magazine*, June 1836.

[2] Artillery: 1 officer, 101 n.c.o. and men. St. Helena Infantry: 8 officers, 278 n.c.o. and men.

Owing to fogs and baffling winds the convoy did not 1806.
overtake this frigate until the 14th of June; and then June 14.
the two commanders decided that the point to be attacked must be the open town of Buenos Ayres.

This, it must be remarked, was a serious deviation from Popham's original plans. Monte Video was the place which he had at first intended to occupy, for he trusted, upon extremely slender information, that its fortifications were in ruins and that it would surrender without firing a shot. His design had then been to send the few Spanish regular troops in the country to Europe, and by repairing the defences of the city to give the British a place of arms from which they would not be easily dislodged, or where, at worst, they could have some chance of a safe re-embarkation. The reason alleged for his change of plan was that the bread-stuffs of the troops were exhausted, that none could be spared from the men-of war, and that there was greater certainty of collecting supplies at Buenos Ayres than at Monte Video. The cogency of such arguments must be admitted; but with our knowledge of Popham's antecedents and character, it may also be suspected that the Commodore doubted the success of an attack upon Monte Video, and that he therefore declared for an immediate movement on Buenos Ayres, where he could be sure of finding the object of which he was really in search, namely prize-money.[1]

Accordingly such troops as were in the line-of-battle ships were transferred to transports of lighter draught;
and on the 16th the vessels moved up the river, groping June 16.
their way slowly owing to fogs and difficulty of navigation. At length on the night of the 24th of June they June 24.
lay off Buenos Ayres, and next morning reached Point June 25.
de Quilmes, some eight miles below the city. The disembarkation was accomplished without mishap or opposition in the course of the afternoon and night, though a hostile force was visible two miles away upon

[1] Popham to Sec. of State, 30th April; Beresford to Sec. of State, 30th April; to Baird, 2nd July 1806.

1806. a slight eminence at the village of Reduction.[1] At eleven
June 26. o'clock on the next morning Beresford moved off. The space between his camping ground and Reduction was a level plain which the rains of winter would presently convert into a swamp, but which was at the moment passable even by guns. The enemy numbered about two thousand men, chiefly undisciplined cavalry, with eight guns; and, as the open character of the ground forbade any attempt at a turning movement, Beresford formed the bulk of his force into a single line, with two six-pounders upon either flank and two howitzers in the centre, holding only the St. Helena Infantry with two more field-guns at a short distance in rear, in case the Spanish cavalry should menace his flanks. On coming within range of the enemy the advance was checked by a tongue of swamp, and Beresford halted his line to enable the guns to pass round it. The forward movement was then resumed, and the Spanish cannon opened a well-aimed fire. Beresford's troops therefore quickened step, found themselves plunging into another swamp, which brought the guns to a standstill, but hastened on in spite of all difficulties to the foot of the hill occupied by the Spaniards. The enemy's artillery, being ill-served, did small damage after the first few minutes; their infantry retired when the British reached the foot of the hill; and a few volleys from the crest scattered the whole force in precipitate flight. Four guns were the trophies of this insignificant combat, and Beresford halted for two hours to find the means of

[1] Force disembarked—

Staff . . .	7 officers		3 horses.	
R.E. . . .	1 "	2 n.c.o. and men.		
R.A. . . .	3 "	33 "	" 13 "	four 6 prs.
St. Helena Artillery .	1 "	101	"	two 5½-in.
20th L.D. . .	1 "	6 "	"	howitzers.
71st . . .	31 "	833 "	"	
St. Helena Infantry .	7 "	175 "	"	
Marines . .	9 "	331 "	"	
Seamen . .	10 "	90 "	"	two light 3 prs
Total . .	70 off., 1571 men, 16 horses, 8 guns.			

moving them, and also to extricate his own pieces from the morass. This done, he marched at once to secure the one bridge over the Rio Chuelo, a small stream about thirty yards wide which lay about eight miles from Reduction, barring the way to Buenos Ayres. Before he could reach it he perceived that the bridge was in flames, and, though he pushed forward a small detachment in the hope of saving at least a part of it, he found that he was too late. The enemy could be heard through the darkness moving guns down for the defence of the passage; and Beresford therefore called the detachment back to the main body, a mile from the river, where he bivouacked for the night. 1806.

At dawn of the next morning reconnaissance showed that the enemy was in position on the further bank, sheltered by houses, hedges, and shipping, whereas the hither bank offered no cover nor shelter of any kind. Beresford at once brought forward to the water's edge the light company of the Seventy-first together with his eleven guns, and was received by a wild and ill-aimed fire of all arms. His artillery soon silenced that of the Spaniards, and the passage of a few British troops in rafts and boats brought the enemy's feeble resistance to an end. By eleven o'clock the whole British force had passed the river; no enemy was to be seen in the three miles that separated the stream from Buenos Ayres; and Beresford sent a summons to the Governor to surrender. After a short parley the terms were agreed upon; Beresford granting to the garrison the honours of war and to the people protection of private property, with continuance of the existing municipal and judicial authority, and restoration of captured coasting vessels to their owners. Upon these conditions, and at a cost of one man killed and a dozen wounded, Beresford's handful of troops obtained possession of a town of seventy thousand inhabitants with fortifications containing eighty-six guns of all calibres.[1] June 27.

So far Popham's audacious stroke was crowned with

[1] Beresford to Sec. of State, 11th July 1806.

1806. success, and success of the kind which was dearest to his heart, for Beresford sent home nearly eleven hundred thousand dollars of prize-money. But the situation of the British was critical, and Beresford was fully aware of it. There remained in the Colony about two thousand Spanish infantry, of poor quality indeed but still regular troops, besides four to five thousand irregulars, which could assemble at need; and it was tolerably certain that these would fall upon the invaders with overwhelming strength upon the first appearance of weakness or misfortune. It was possible to conciliate the population of the city itself, but not that of the entire country; and to reduce it to submission Beresford needed a strong force of cavalry, which he did not possess. Moreover, the coming of the British had thrown everything into disorder. The viceroy had fled into the interior; and the inhabitants, while seizing the moment to shake off the yoke of Spain, had not yet yielded to their new masters. All therefore was unstable and unsettled. The one thing certain was that the Colonists were deeply ashamed of having surrendered to so puny a force, and not less alarmed at having no greater protection to count upon in case of an attack by an expedition from Spain. Their position was thus both unfair and intolerable. Beresford, while seeking to remove the most conspicuous of their grievances, rightly refused to commit the British Government to any definite line of policy. It was only natural, therefore, that the Colonists should regard his forcible intrusion upon them and his confiscation of the King of Spain's property as little better than an act of piracy. Popham might represent the proceedings as intended to further the cause of emancipation in South America; but the Colonists were to be excused if they considered a British occupation of their capital as a strange and unwelcome form of liberty.

Matters at Buenos Ayres had reached this point when, at the end of July, the letters of Beresford and Popham from St. Helena reached Downing Street. The enterprise having been undertaken without the knowledge or sanction of the Government, and its issue being still unknown, Windham was unable to give Beresford further instructions than to maintain himself if he could, to avoid all share in any revolutionary enterprises, and to interfere generally with the inhabitants as little as possible. If he found that he could not hold his own, then he was to send the troops back to the Cape and return home on leave. In any case, however, a reinforcement of two thousand men under Sir Samuel Auchmuty, together with supplies and stores, would be sent out to La Plata immediately.[1] 1806.

It is difficult to see what more, in the circumstances, the Government could have done; for Popham, as it turned out, had chosen a singularly inopportune moment for his wild adventure. The victory of Austerlitz and the change of Government in England had led to rapid and startling results in Europe, to meet which the Ministry of all the Talents had need of all the resources of England. Austerlitz at a single stroke had driven Austria from the Coalition, wrecked the Holy Roman Empire, confirmed Prussia in a trembling neutrality, decided the fate of Naples, and incidentally clouded the victory of Trafalgar with the dust that rose from the collapse of Pitt's pygmy combinations in the Mediterranean. Napoleon's first act had been to reward his German allies by the grant
of higher titles and the promise of large tracts of 1805.
Austrian territory. These promises the Treaty of Dec. 26.
Pressburg enabled him to fulfil. Thereby Austria yielded to Baden and Würtemberg sundry petty fiefs; to Bavaria, Tirol and Vorarlberg; and to France every inch of territory that she had gained at Campo Formio; recognising Napoleon also as King of Italy, and retaining on the Adriatic no more than Trieste. On the same day Napoleon ordered St. Cyr to march
upon Naples; on the 27th he decreed that the Dec. 27.
Bourbons had ceased to reign in that kingdom; and
on the 31st he nominated his brother Joseph to carry Dec. 31.

[1] Sec. of State to Beresford, 24th July 1806.

1805. his decree into effect. Months before, he had incorporated the Ligurian Republic into the French Empire, and he now designed to make Holland, which was already a department of France, into a kingdom for his brother Louis.

None the less, when the Emperor returned to Paris on the 24th of January 1806, his further plans for the reconstitution of Germany were not yet feasible, and his situation was still an anxious one. The Tsar, despondent for the moment after Austerlitz, recovered himself and resumed his defiant attitude when he reached St. Petersburg. In the Mediterranean the British and Russians had been driven from Naples, but not yet from Sicily. Lastly there was always uncertainty as to the intentions of Prussia. It is true that Napoleon had extorted a favourable treaty from Haugwitz at Schönbrunn on the 15th of December, but it remained to be seen whether Frederick William would ratify it. As a matter of fact Haugwitz, returning triumphantly with his treaty, was extremely ill-received. Frederick William hated any definite arrangement which he could not evade; and Haugwitz had brought him back an alliance with France. The weak King again became violent for a time, and assured the Russian envoy that he would never divide his fate from that of the Tsar. Then he subsided into abjection and resolved to ratify the treaty with modifications. He would have the alliance with France to be purely defensive; he would guarantee Venetia only, among the new acquisitions of France in Italy; and he would hear of no guarantee for Naples until England sanctioned the transfer of Hanover to Prussia. He then again assured the Tsar of his unalterable friendship, ordered his troops to occupy Hanover —the one thing which he was sure that he wanted—and sent Haugwitz to Paris with the treaty thus amended. The man's only idea of honour was a graduated scale of deceit, of which he reserved the lower degrees for his friends and the intenser for his enemies.

Haugwitz reached Paris on the 1st of February, 1806. and on the 3rd was received by Talleyrand with alarming coldness. On the 4th Napoleon heard the Feb. 4. news of Pitt's death and of the accession of Fox to the Foreign Office, and at once conceived the idea of detaching England from the Coalition, or at any rate of paralysing her for a time by negotiations. Fox gave him an opening by warning him of a plot for his assassination; and the overture was joyfully welcomed. But first it was necessary to come to decisive conclusions with Prussia; which was duly effected on the 5th of February. On that day Talleyrand informed Feb. 5. Haugwitz that the treaty of the 15th of December, not having been ratified, was void; and ten days later he Feb. 15. peremptorily submitted to him a new treaty to the following effect. Prussia was to take over all the dominions of King George the Third in Germany, and in return was to yield Neufchatel to France, Cleves to a nominee of Napoleon, and Anspach to Bavaria; and the several parties were to enter into possession of the territories thus transferred within five days of the ratification of the treaty. Prussia was further to close Lübeck and all ports and rivers in the Baltic to British shipping, to guarantee the French Empire, including Venetia and Naples, as also the integrity of Turkey, Bavaria, Würtemberg, and Baden.

Rightly thinking that rejection of this treaty would mean war, Haugwitz signed it and sent it on to Berlin. There also Hardenberg perceived that the only alternative to ratification was war, and King Frederick William accordingly confirmed the agreement on the 26th of February. He was well advised; for Feb. 26. Napoleon, finding that Prussian troops had already occupied Hanover, took possession of Anspach, Neufchatel, and Cleves without waiting to hear of the fate of the new treaty at Berlin. However, this point of friction between the two powers, though ominous for the future, did not disturb the most important condition which had been accepted by Frederick William—the

1806. closing of the Baltic ports to British trade. This stroke against England was followed up by open declarations of Napoleon to his Legislative Chamber
Mar. 2, 5. on the 2nd and 5th of March that Italy, Belgium, and Holland were thenceforward essential parts of his Empire, subject to his immediate direction, and therefore, as a necessary consequence, barred to British commerce.

The object of the Emperor's policy was now comparatively plain. He had, as he hoped, tied Prussia hand and foot by his last treaty. It remained for him to come to an agreement either with Russia or with England, in full confidence that the secession of either power from the Coalition would force the other to come to terms. But this was no such easy matter. In the first place, the restrictions laid by his late measures upon British trade were evidently designed to dragoon rather than to persuade England towards a peaceful settlement. In the second, Fox was resolute to prosecute no negotiations except in concert with Russia. In the third, no arrangement with England could be final unless it decided the fate of Hanover, which country Napoleon had already promised to Prussia; and, until the question of Hanover was determined, the Emperor could not carry out the final reconstitution of Germany which was to take shape shortly in the Confederation of the Rhine. Lastly, the darling wish of Napoleon's heart was to turn the Mediterranean into a French lake; and this of necessity involved the attainment of two preliminary ends, namely, predominance of French influence with the Ottoman Porte, and, still more important, the possession of Sicily. All circumstances combined to create a diplomatic situation of extraordinary intricacy, which was not simplified by the fact that all parties were striving eagerly to second their diplomacy by some telling strategic blow.

The negotiations with England were informally opened by Talleyrand with Lord Yarmouth, one of the travelling Englishmen who had been detained in

France by Napoleon's decree at the opening of the war. Yarmouth declined to enter into any discussion of the subject except on the preliminary condition that Hanover should be restored to its rightful sovereign. To this Talleyrand raised no objection; though the article which was most vital to Prussia in the recent treaty was thereby very seriously imperilled. The effrontery of Talleyrand's action was sufficiently cynical, and yet it was not unjustifiable, for Frederick William the Little had been as careless of his obligations as Napoleon the Great. No sooner, in fact, had the King of Prussia signed his treaty with France than he sent the Duke of Brunswick to St. Petersburg to report it to the Tsar; with the result that, within six weeks of binding himself by an alliance with France against Russia, he concluded a secret agreement to ally himself with Russia against France. Every precaution was of course taken to lull Napoleon into false security while this trickery was going forward; but Frederick William had deceived too many parties to escape betrayal by some one of them. The British Ministry, indignant over the occupation of Hanover by Prussian troops, made public the papers concerning Lord Harrowby's negotiations at Berlin, which showed that it was not from goodwill towards France that Prussia had refused to join the Coalition. Napoleon, after reading these, published in the *Moniteur* so furious an attack upon Hardenberg that Frederick William hastened to dismiss that Minister ostensibly, though not actually, from office, in order to allay the Emperor's wrath. But the British nation was not less angry than Napoleon over these revelations, particularly when Prussia added injury to insult by closing her ports to British trade. The British Government promptly retorted by laying an embargo on all Prussian vessels in British ports, and declaring the Ems and Weser in a state of blockade; and these measures were finally clinched on the 21st of April by a Royal message to Parliament declaring war against Prussia by sea. In

[Margin notes: 1806. — Mar. 21. — Mar. 29. — April 1. — Apr. 4-5. — April 21.]

1806. both Houses members seized the opportunity to state as pointedly as possible their opinions of King Frederick William and of his policy; and, if that monarch failed to awake to a sense of his own contemptibility, it was certainly not the fault of the debaters at Westminster. The lesson was enforced by the sweeping of the Prussian flag off the seas in the course of the next few weeks; and yet this invective and these reprisals were directed at one who really clung with desperate though dissembled tenacity to England's most valuable ally, the Tsar Alexander. Never was there a more grotesque political situation.

Throughout this time Fox was pursuing active negotiations with Russia, with the special object of thwarting Napoleon's designs in the Mediterranean. Throughout the long diplomatic game with Russia the French Emperor's great card had been Turkey, which he was equally ready to dismember in order to conciliate the Tsar, or to champion in order to embarrass him. The Eastern question had become more urgent since the Peace of Pressburg; for by the acquisition of Dalmatia the French Empire was extended to the marches of the Ottoman. The partition of the Sultan's dominions having long been a favourite project with Russia, the Tsar embraced the opportunity to press it upon England; and Fox, though unprepared to go to such extreme lengths as this, nevertheless assured the Russian Ambassador that, in case of need, England was prepared to occupy Alexandria. The point must be borne in mind, for, as shall be seen, this arrangement for upholding Russian influence at Constantinople, whatever the cost, was actually carried out within twelve months.

At the time, however, Napoleon was checked in Eastern Europe by the intrigues of Russia with the Montenegrins concerning Cattaro. This place under the Treaty of Pressburg should have been delivered up to France; but, as no French commissioners arrived at the time to take it over, Russian agents persuaded the inhabitants that they might yield the place to whom they chose. The Montenegrins at once rose in insurrection, compelled the small Austrian garrison to surrender the fortress, and transferred it to the Russians, who hastened to occupy it in force. Napoleon was furious. He suspended the march of his army from the German states into France, and declared his intention of holding Braunau on the Inn until Cattaro should be delivered up to him. He had hoped to close the eastern coast of the Adriatic altogether to British ships; and it enraged him to see its most important port still open to them. However, he characteristically indemnified himself by seizing Ragusa, neutral territory against which he had neither quarrel nor grievance; which done, he proceeded to develop his further plans alike for excluding the British from the Mediterranean, and for bringing fresh pressure to bear upon Russia by skilful manipulation of Turkey. On the 9th of June,[1] he ordered Sebastiani to repair to Constantinople, there to assure the Sultan of his firm friendship and support against all enemies and in particular against Russia, while he himself prepared to assemble a force in Dalmatia in order to second Sebastiani's mission by threats. 1806. June 9.

During this time the Emperor's negotiations with England continued, but made little progress, the two parties being steadily at variance over two principal points. The first of these, as has already been mentioned, was Fox's refusal to treat except in concert with Russia; the second was the cession of Sicily to France, which Napoleon persistently demanded, and Fox as persistently refused. The Emperor designedly protracted the business, hoping always that the capture of Sicily by Joseph Bonaparte might give him the upper hand in dictating conditions of peace; but, as we shall see, his expectations upon this head were doomed to something more than disappointment. None the less, the dexterity which he showed in the

[1] *Corres. de Napoléon*, 10,339.

1806. diplomatic struggle was extraordinary. After much discussion, he deferred to Fox's determination not to treat apart from Russia ; but he did so only to seek reconciliation with Russia apart from England. The Tsar, as it happened, was willing, though rather in the hope of gaining time than of coming to an understanding, to open informal negotiations, for which purpose he despatched M. d'Oubril to Paris, ostensibly upon some business of exchange of prisoners. Delaying d'Oubril's arrival on various pretexts lest he should meet and take counsel with Yarmouth, Napoleon made a last effort to break down the resolution of the English nobleman. Finding persuasion to be useless, Talleyrand did not scruple to threaten that France would seize Spain and Portugal, shut their ports against the British, and so force England to come to terms. The menace failed to move Yarmouth ; and d'Oubril was then admitted to the capital. The Russian proved to be clay in Talleyrand's hands; and in a few days he was beguiled
July 20. into signing a treaty whereby, among other matters, Russia recognised the cession of Cattaro and Dalmatia to France, and of Sicily to Joseph Bonaparte as King of Naples. Having obtained this, Napoleon flourished it in the face of Yarmouth in the hope that it would scare him into accepting the terms of France, which concession would in its turn compel the Tsar to ratify d'Oubril's treaty. He offered also to restore to England the sovereignty of Hanover and to confirm her in possession of Malta, requiring in return that she should acknowledge Joseph as King of the Two Sicilies. Since Fox had lately shown signs of relenting upon
July 26. the article of Sicily, Yarmouth upon the 26th of July agreed to cede that island to France ; and Napoleon felt with some confidence that he had at last brought both Russia and England to the point of signing peace.

Without delay therefore he proclaimed the dissolution of the Holy Roman Empire, and the reconstitution of Germany under the Confederation of the Rhine. The Confederation consisted of sixteen states : two kingdoms—Bavaria and Würtemberg; three grand duchies—Baden, Darmstadt, and Berg; one ecclesiastical principality—Frankfurt; and ten secular principalities, over which presided two princes of Nassau, two of Hohenzollern, two of Salm, and one each of Isenburg, Arenberg, Lichtenstein, and de Leyen. The whole were under Napoleon's protection, and were bound to provide him with sixty-three thousand troops when called upon. Berg, it may be added, was given to Murat under Napoleon's new system of appanages, even as Holland had been given in June to his brother Louis, and Naples to Joseph. Austria was pressed to accept this new model of Germany under threats; and Prussia was tempted to accede to it by the insinuation that Hanover should be assured to her and that Frederick William might shortly look for an imperial crown. Unfortunately, however, Yarmouth in his cups betrayed to Lucchesini, the Prussian Ambassador at Paris, that Napoleon had already promised Hanover to England; and this fact was promptly reported to Berlin. Nevertheless the Emperor continued to believe in the prospect of a speedy peace with England, for on the 5th of August a formal negotiator from Fox arrived in Paris in the person of Lord Lauderdale. But in the meanwhile the intelligence of d'Oubril's treaty had reached London and raised a storm of indignation, which was heightened by the news of the Confederation of the Rhine, signifying as it did further restrictions upon England's commerce. Lauderdale, moreover, had been directed after all to insist that Sicily should not be abandoned to France; and indeed had Fox known at the moment, as Napoleon did know, what had lately passed in Calabria between the British and French troops, his instructions would no doubt have been even firmer upon this point than they were. However, Lauderdale was resolute enough as to Sicily, and, finding Napoleon equally determined to the contrary, on the 9th of August demanded his passports. Day after day Napoleon excused himself from granting

1806. Aug. 5. Aug. 9.

1806. them, hoping that time would work in his favour. Francis of Austria, in obedience to his mandate, had renounced the title of Emperor of Germany and had recognised Joseph as King of the Two Sicilies; and any day might bring the Tsar's ratification of d'Oubril's treaty from St. Petersburg. Then England, forsaken both by Russia and Austria, would, as the Emperor reckoned, be thankful to close with his conditions.

But at this point, to the general surprise, the whole of Napoleon's combinations were upset by a sudden revolt on the part of Prussia. When the Confederation of the Rhine was first reported at Berlin, Frederick William received the news with satisfaction, giving out that he would himself form a similar confederation of Northern Germany, with Prussia, enriched by the possession of Hanover, at its head. But presently he realised that thereby he would commit himself completely to Napoleon's side against Austria and Russia; and the bare thought of this caused the greatest indignation among the many Prussians who felt ashamed of their Sovereign's ignoble truckling to the Corsican adventurer. A few days later there arrived at Berlin Lucchesini's report that Napoleon had actually offered Hanover to England; and certain suspicious movements of French troops, added to other unpleasant circumstances, brought matters to a crisis. The miserable King completely lost his head. Public feeling in his capital had passed hopelessly out of his control; the moment of trial which he had so long evaded was at hand; and at this perilous moment, his trusted friend the Tsar had, as he thought,
Aug. 9. made his peace with Napoleon. He indited a humble letter to Alexander begging for help; and on the next day he ordered his army to be mobilised, remaining in despicable and trembling suspense until a courier from St. Petersburg should apprise him of his fate. On the
Aug. 26. 26th the answer arrived. Alexander had declined to ratify d'Oubril's treaty, and had disgraced d'Oubril himself. The clamour of the Prussian army for war was at once redoubled; and Frederick William saw

that the die was cast. The occasion was one in which 1806. even a Bourbon of that period might have risen, if only for a moment, to the height that is worthy of a patriot, if not of a King. But of this Hohenzollern it had been written, " Upon thy belly shalt thou go, and dust shalt thou eat." He wrote frantic letters to all the neighbours whom he had swindled and deceived, with abject promises to do anything that they wished. He would freely grant Bavaria to Austria, nay, if need were, he would share Germany with the Emperor Francis; he had never intended to keep Hanover against the wish of England, and he would gladly defer the final settlement of the question until the close of the war upon which he was about to enter. No doubt at the moment he was sincere, for he was sincerely frightened; but he had sown abroad too many lies to reap any but a goodly harvest of contempt.

Napoleon's answer to all these preparations was an order to Berthier to countermand the return of his troops to France, to concentrate at Bamberg, and to send officers to reconnoitre the country between Bamberg and Berlin.[1] He had no intention of refusing Prussia's challenge, though the situation for him was serious. Here, within less than a year of Ulm and Austerlitz, was a new coalition of England, Russia, and Prussia leagued against him; and a defeat would bring all Europe upon his back. Above all, there were bad signs in Italy, where since July things had gone but ill with Joseph Bonaparte and his arms. It is now time to look into Italian affairs more closely.

[1] *Corres. de Napoléon*, 10,730, 10,744, 3rd, 5th Sept. 1806.

CHAPTER XI

1806. Our last sight of Sicily was in February 1806, when by the firmness of Craig, in spite of Mr. Elliot's protests, the small British force in the Mediterranean was brought into the harbour of Messina after the evacuation of Naples. Upon the flight of the Neapolitan Court to Sicily, the help of these troops was hastily
Feb. 16. invoked for defence of the island; and on the 16th of February they began their disembarkation at Messina. On the same day Craig, worn down with illness and anxiety, wrote to ask leave to resign his command, since he felt himself no longer equal to the burden. It was in truth no light one. The people of Messina from the highest to the lowest welcomed the British as protectors; but the Neapolitan army, which should have seconded their efforts, did not exist. By the Queen's command, her reigning favourite, M. de Damas, and the Hereditary Prince of Naples were left behind with some six or seven thousand men to bar the entrance to Calabria. These were attacked by a much smaller body of French and scattered to the four winds by the first shot. About a thousand of them, chiefly mounted troops, fled after the Prince to Reggio, from whence they were carried by British transports into Sicily. The French
Mar. 24. followed close upon them; and on the 24th of March French posts and picquets were lining the northern shore of the Straits of Messina. But for the presence of the British, they would have passed the sea at the same time—almost in the same boats, to use Sir John

Stuart's own phrase,—with the fugitives. So truly 1806.
were vindicated Craig's foresight and resolution.[1]

This defeat of Damas, for he and not the Hereditary Prince was in truth the commanding officer, proved to be a blessing in disguise. Though the mishap was probably no fault of his, he was of course held responsible for it. He was, therefore, dismissed from all his offices to make room for the return of old Sir John Acton, who, until sacrificed to the wish of Napoleon, had for many years been King Ferdinand's principal adviser. By Acton's counsel, the feeble old monarch was induced to come alone to Messina, nominally to issue orders for defence of the country, but really in order that he might be withdrawn from the influence of the treacherous Queen and of her party. In fact, it was little help that the Neapolitan Government could afford, for even the most important fortresses were destitute of guns and stores; and the only national garrison consisted of some seven thousand worthless troops in and about Palermo. Practically, therefore, the whole weight of the defence was laid upon the British; and Craig was compelled to summon the Eighty-first regiment from Malta to Sicily, which he did very unwillingly, for the garrison of Valetta contained, in his opinion, far too large a proportion of untrustworthy foreign troops.
Shortly afterwards, at the beginning of April, Craig April.
sailed for England, so ill that he was not expected to reach it alive, and the command in the Mediterranean devolved upon Major-general Sir John Stuart.

Meanwhile a conviction was growing in the British Cabinet that the general theatre of the war was moving eastward, and that the British force in the Mediterranean might play an important part in it. The controversy over Cattaro had turned Windham's attention to the eastern shore of the Adriatic; and on the 10th of May he wrote privately to Craig lamenting the weakness of his little army, but authorising him, if he could do so

[1] Craig to Sec. of State, 12th, 16th Feb.; Sir J. Stuart to Mr. Cooke, 19th Feb.; to Sec. of State, 26th May 1806.

1806. without endangering Sicily, to send troops to occupy some of the ports in Dalmatia. As it happened, even while Windham was writing, Craig was on his way from Plymouth to London, with his health much restored by the voyage, and hence with full ability to give information and advice exactly when it was most wanted. Windham's design of frittering away his troops in Adriatic ports arose from an idea that Napoleon, having once established himself in Dalmatia, would carry the war into Hungary, the Turkish provinces, and ultimately into Russia. Craig gently set his foot both on the design and on the reasoning. The occupation of Adriatic ports by the British would, he said, be useless in itself and would cause extreme jealousy in the Russians. As to Napoleon's advancing from Dalmatia into Russia, such a notion was highly speculative; for a country without roads, population, or supplies was ill-calculated for operations against so powerful an enemy as the Russians; while an advance of the French upon Constantinople would certainly bring the Austrians down at once upon their flank and rear. Napoleon's assembly of troops was in fact, as we have seen, simply a device for strengthening Sebastiani's diplomacy with the Porte. Instead therefore of wasting men and money on visionary schemes, Craig recommended rather the despatch of heavy guns and carriages for the fortification of Syracuse, Agosta, and Milazzo, and of light field-pieces which could be carried on the backs of mules for the defence of the interior of Sicily.[1]

This advice Windham wisely took to heart. Already roused by the negotiations to a sense of the importance of Sicily, he had directed Collingwood to detach a squadron for its protection, and ordered two more battalions, the Seventy-eighth[2] and Eighty-ninth, to reinforce the garrison. Moreover, Stuart, upon the spot, was energetic in self-help. In April King Ferdinand

[1] Craig to Sec. of State, 8th, 28th May, 7th June; Windham to Craig, 10th May 1806.

[2] 2/78th.

placed under his command, unasked, the line of defence 1806. from Milazzo to Cape Passaro, though the Neapolitan force which was allotted to this charge amounted to fewer than four thousand bad and discouraged men. The Militia was, indeed, placed at the General's disposal, but, as it consisted merely of a list of names, was of little profit. Stuart, therefore, obtained leave from the Court to raise a corps of five hundred Sicilian Fencibles, drawing British pay and wearing the British uniform; and men were readily found to fill its ranks. At the same time a flotilla of small craft was organised for the defence of the straits, the men being chiefly mariners of Sicily and the Lipari Islands, under the direction of a few officers of the British Army. It is curious that the crews of these vessels declined to come forward until General Stuart permitted them to serve under the British flag, for they refused utterly to fight under that of King Ferdinand. Thus by the end of May the British force, increased to seven and eight May. thousand men, lay ensconced with its left fortified at Milazzo and with outposts on its right extending towards Taormina; the flotilla scouring the straits, and a few vessels of war lying at anchor before Messina.[1] Altogether the situation was greatly improved, and would have been promising but for the defects of the military and naval commanders.

Stuart, whom we have already seen in Egypt, was not without brains and energy; but he was vain, flighty, and superficial, and therefore incapable either of projecting or executing any sound or far-seeing plan of operations. Sidney Smith, the naval commander, though brave and restlessly active, was quite as superficial as Stuart and a great deal vainer. He had rendered a very conspicuous service at Acre, and took good care that all the world should know it. As a partisan leader he had unquestionably great gifts of daring, readiness, and resource; but for the higher operations of war he was absolutely unfitted, having

[1] Stuart to Sec. of State, 26th May 1806; Bunbury, 227-229.

1806. neither depth nor foresight nor fixity of purpose. He could talk of no subject but himself; he worked chiefly if not exclusively for his own hand and his own distinction; he would flaunt himself like a peacock in any company; he had a pestilent love of displaying his name and exploits in the newspapers; and, worst of all, he was docile even to servility when concerned with crowned heads. In a word, he was utterly unfit for supreme command.

The French, on the other hand, were little more fortunate than ourselves. Joseph Bonaparte was timid, irresolute, and querulous, and as a general absolutely incapable. Subordinates, indeed, he had many, to the extent of two marshals and twenty-seven generals for a force of fifty-two thousand men. Massena, the ablest of them, joined to the highest military gifts a low character and an avarice so insatiable as to swallow up all principles of honesty.[1] Reynier, the most prominent of the rest, was a fairly good officer, but pompous and fatally conceited. The entire army was spoiled by easy successes. The regimental officers, though undoubtedly brave and probably able, were careless to the last degree, negligent of the elementary rules of their profession, and content, from a sense of their own and their army's superiority, to accept any risk rather than be troubled to take the simplest precautions.[2] Their first advance into Neapolitan territory had been practically unopposed; and Napoleon had never ceased to urge Joseph to press on to Sicily at once, being the more anxious to possess it for the hold that it would have given him over the British in the current negotiations. But there was one Neapolitan General who was ready to fight and could make his men fight, the Prince of Hesse-Philipstadt, who held the sea-girt fortress of Gaeta in defiance of the new King of Naples and all his men. Gaeta was a terrible thorn in Joseph's side.

[1] See, for Napoleon's opinion of him, *Nap. Corres.* 10,311; one among many such judgments of the man.

[2] See the letters of Paul Louis Courier.

Throughout the month of March Napoleon was urging 1806. his brother to besiege it ; and, though at last at the beginning of April the operations were begun, they made no progress until by Napoleon's positive order the direction was given in June to Massena.[1] Another sore trial to Joseph was a tendency of the Calabrese to rise in insurrection, obedient to the agents sent among them by the Queen of Naples. His brother adjured him to be severe and merciless, not wholly without effect ;[2] but these troubles caused him to scatter his troops at wide intervals over the country. This, as Napoleon early pointed out, was a perilous arrangement when his enemy was master of the sea, and able at any moment to land a force which could sever his communications.[3]

Sidney Smith, to his credit, soon perceived the opportunities offered to his squadron by the conformation of the Italian peninsula. He had arrived on the 21st of April at Palermo, from whence he presently April 21. sailed to the true centre of operations, Gaeta. The fortress was exceedingly strong ; though blockaded by the French on the side of the land, it was always open from the sea ; and so long as Gaeta held out, Joseph's hold upon Neapolitan territory was precarious. Smith threw a much-needed supply of ammunition into the place, and left a part of his naval force to second a sortie of the garrison on the 15th of May, which was May 15. attended by complete success. This was good and essential service, but it did not suit Smith's vanity to mix himself up in any operations in which he had not supreme command. He therefore turned aside to attack Capri. This island was by no means unimportant, since it covered the maritime communications of the French to southward ; but on the other hand every insular post thus seized signified the locking up not only of troops but of ships for its protection ; and this was doubly true of Capri because of its vicinity to a

[1] *Nap. Corres.* 10,296. [2] *Ibid.* 10,131.
[3] *Ibid.* 10,085-6.

1806. strong French force at Naples. Smith, however, was a man who looked no further than to the issue of the next Gazette. He could master Capri with the resources of the squadron alone, and would be able to write a pompous despatch upon the subject. He attacked the
May 12. island accordingly on the 12th of May, took it with little difficulty, wrote his pompous despatch, and asked Stuart to provide his conquest with a garrison. Stuart thereupon sent five companies of Corsicans under an excellent officer, whose reputation still lies crushed under a mountain of slanders, Captain Hudson Lowe.
June. At the beginning of June Smith returned to Messina, where he requested of Stuart the loan of a few troops to make raids and destroy batteries on the Neapolitan coast. Stuart rightly refused to squander detachments of soldiers upon objects so trivial, but offered to supply a large force for operations on a greater scale, and suggested a descent upon Calabria. Smith assented, and sailed away to Palermo to ensure the assistance of the Neapolitan Court.

A descent upon Calabria, that is to say, a mere raid with no ulterior object, was, it will be observed, the highest enterprise which these two vain and jealous men could set before themselves. It was a painful contrast to the wise and far-seeing designs which Charles Stuart had thought out when he sailed to Messina eight years before. Moreover, Smith and Stuart, as it happened, had founded their plans upon false information. They reckoned that Joseph had but thirty thousand instead of fifty thousand men in all, and that five thousand of these were in lower Calabria under General Reynier, scattered and isolated, and therefore easily to be dispersed with the help of the Calabrese insurgents. As a matter of fact about fifteen thousand men were with Massena round Gaeta; three thousand more were holding Naples; about twelve thousand under St. Cyr were occupied in subduing Apulia; and the troops in Calabria under Generals Verdier and Reynier counted ten thousand. And these numbers represented effective men, Joseph's original army having been reduced by casualties and sickness from fifty to forty thousand. However, an offensive movement founded upon false intelligence was far better than no offensive movement at all; and Stuart even carried his projects so far as to hope, vaguely, that upon his landing the partial insurrection of the Calabrese would become general, and that without further exertion upon his part Massena would be forced to raise the siege of Gaeta. He therefore made his preparations quietly and stealthily, embarked the necessary stores by degrees and without ostentation, sent his transports to various little ports, and kept his troops marching from quarter to quarter as though to occupy a more extended line of defence; whereby he was able at once to bring the men into condition and to conceal his real designs. With all his defects, Stuart was by no means without ability of a certain kind. 1806.

Meanwhile Smith sailed, as has been said, to Palermo, where his servile instincts and portentous vanity made him a ready tool of the Queen. The King, Queen, and Royal family, to his intense delight, accepted hospitality from him on board his flag-ship, the *Pompée*; and he obtained from them a decree, dated on the 28th of June, investing him with unlimited authority, by land as well as by sea, within the Neapolitan dominions. By this instrument he became in fact the King's vicegerent for the recovery of his kingdom; and he was fully authorised to take command of any Neapolitan troops or subjects without reference to Stuart. It need hardly be said that he was careful not to consult the General before accepting this office; and it is superfluous to add that this accession to his importance inflated his conceit to bursting point. Basking in the moonshine of the royal smiles, Smith omitted all further communication with Stuart concerning the projected expedition, until on the 23rd of June the General lost patience, June 23.
and announced that, unless the Admiral appeared before the 27th, he would sail without him to the Bay of St. Euphemia, under the escort of the senior naval officer

1806. at Messina. The time, Stuart added, was propitious; for the French had enraged the Calabrian peasants by attempting a forced levy of them for military service, and the whole population was ripe for insurrection. Smith answered with the air of a man who had more important matters to attend to. The Prince of Hesse had written that Gaeta was in distress for supplies; the Admiral had therefore sent two Neapolitan men-of-war with troops to his assistance, and was himself about to fly to the succour of the place. In the circumstances he recommended Stuart to cruise along shore, menace Policastro, Salerno, and the Bay of Naples, then by a "night-run" relieve Gaeta from immediate pressure, land in some unexplained and mysterious fashion on both sides of the besieging army, "make a clean sweep of the besieger," fill up Gaeta with stores, and return to profit by the alarm which would be spread by the appearance of his armament on the coast. In fact, Smith scribbled down every wild idea that occurred to him at the moment, in singularly incoherent, ungrammatical, and unintelligible English.[1]

Meanwhile, without waiting for this precious missive
June 25. to arrive, on the night of the 25th Stuart had called his transports alongside the quays to take in the guns and horses. The men likewise had received their orders to march to their appointed places and embark at daybreak. The duty was performed with perfect order and secrecy; not a soul had an idea of the object of the expedition except the General and two of his staff; and altogether it must be said that this part of the proceedings was admirably managed. The troops consisted of seven battalions besides artillery, numbering in all about five thousand five hundred of all ranks, and were organised into an advanced corps and three brigades.[2] Two of these battalions were composed,

[1] Sidney Smith to Stuart, 26th June 1806. Enclosed in Stuart's narrative.

[2] Stuart's embarkation-return, forwarded in his despatch of 6th July, gives the strength of the force, artillery included, at 4795

according to the accepted but vicious practice, of flank-companies. Indeed Craig had so far extended the principle of forming the choicest men into special corps, as to take the best shots from the battalion-companies also and set them apart, with the name of "flankers," as sharp-shooters under picked officers. The "flankers" of the Thirty-fifth only accompanied the expedition, and, added to the flank-companies, must have represented the cream of the regiment. The flank-companies generally, excepting those of the Eighty-first, were, to use Bunbury's expression, hard, biting old soldiers; and the battalion-companies of the Twentieth and Twenty-seventh were of the same quality. The three remaining battalions were young and had never seen a shot fired. Of cavalry, Stuart, for want of horse-transports, had none, except sixteen of the Twentieth Light Dragoons to act as orderlies. The Brigadiers were, taken together, a far abler lot of officers than were generally to be found in a British force; Cole, Kempt, Oswald, and Ross being all men who made their mark later in the Peninsula. Any one of the four would have made a better commander than Stuart. 1806.

Sailing on the 26th under the escort of the *Apollo* frigate and of two more ships of war, the expedition June 26.

rank and file. Adding one-eighth for officers and for the sergeants, we get a total of 5400. The returns given by Mr. Oman, *Journal of the Royal Artillery*, March 1908, show a total of 251 officers and 5280 non-commissioned officers and men.

Advanced Corps: or *L.I. Brigade*.	Colonel Kempt. Light Companies of 20th, 1/27th, 1/35th, 1/58th, 1/61st, 1/81st, and of Watteville's regiment. "Flankers" of 1/35th. 2 companies of Corsican Rangers. 1 company of Sicilians. 2 four-pounder guns.
1st Brigade.	Cole. 1/27th (8 companies). Grenadier-Companies of 20th, 1/27th, 1/36th, 1/58th, 1/81st, and Watteville's. 3 four-pounder guns.
2nd Brigade.	Acland. 2/78th (10 companies), 1/81st (8 companies). 3 four-pounder guns.
3rd Brigade.	Oswald. 1/58th, and Watteville's (each 8 companies). 3 four-pounder guns.

20th Foot (8 companies) detached to make a diversion.

1806. June 30. reached the Bay of St. Euphemia on the 30th of June, Colonel Ross with the Twentieth being left to make a feint of attacking Reggio and Scilla, with orders to follow the main body as soon as the purpose of making a diversion should have been fulfilled. The transport which carried Kempt and his Light Infantry had lagged astern; wherefore Colonel Oswald was appointed to lead the debarkation at dawn

July 1. of the next day with seven flank-companies and the Corsican Rangers. No enemy appeared on the beach; and this first division was safely landed a mile below the village of St. Euphemia itself. As the boats returned to shore with a second load of men, Oswald pushed his party forward in extended order towards the village, the ground being covered with trees and scrub. Very soon they were met by a sharp fire in their front, and the Corsican Rangers were driven in upon their supports by a sudden rush of the enemy. Oswald, however, speedily restored the fight, and, seeing that the second division of troops was now on the beach, advanced rapidly, charging his opponents on both flanks and routing them completely, with the loss of ten officers and some eighty men killed and taken. They proved to be three companies of Poles from the French post at Monteleone; and it was fortunate that their commander was so ill-advised as to make his resistance after, instead of during, the disembarkation of the British.

Following up his success, Oswald pushed forward and occupied St. Euphemia; and by the evening of

July 1. the 1st of July every man, gun, and animal had been disembarked. The engineers were then set to work to form lines of defence with sandbags on the beach, using an old ruined tower as a centre, so as to cover the re-embarkation in case of disaster; while the Advanced Corps moved on to Nicastro, five miles inland, where they were joined by two hundred armed Calabrese, described by one of Stuart's officers as ruffians

July 2. of the lowest type. On the 2nd there came to Stuart

a letter from Smith, written off Amantea, on the coast 1806. about fifteen miles north of St. Euphemia. Smith was careful to mention that he had been long delayed by the presence of the royal family of Naples on board his ship, that he had been further detained by the necessity of arranging for a diversion in Sardinia and for throwing stores into Gaeta, and that consequently he had not been able to leave Palermo until the 29th. He added that he had received no news of Stuart at Milazzo on the previous night, and could perceive no sign of him at daylight on the 1st; that he did not like to go into St. Euphemia's Bay, in case he should not find the General there and might not be able to get out again; and that he was therefore cannonading Amantea as a diversion in his favour. Finally he announced that he had circulated the Royal Decree, which appointed him Commander-in-chief, to the insurgent leaders, and had much pleasure in authorising Stuart himself to give orders to them and to the natives at large. The General, though consumed with inward wrath at the patronising tone of this letter, dissembled his feelings and replied quietly by begging Smith not to distress the adjoining coast, as it would only turn friends into enemies. He intimated further that he had already issued a proclamation to the inhabitants as Commander-in-chief of King George's army, and could see no necessity for authorisation of his proceedings by King Ferdinand or his deputy. This statement was only too true, for Stuart had gone so far as to call upon the inhabitants to rise, giving them an indefinite promise of assistance from England; a proceeding which was beyond his powers and instructions, and which rightly brought upon him the censure of the Government.[1] However, the immediate point for us is that the two commanders were already within measurable distance of a quarrel.

Throughout that day and the next Stuart remained July 3. stationary. His landing had been a complete surprise;

[1] Sec. of State to Stuart, 15th Sept. 1806.

1806. and, to turn this advantage to full profit, it was obviously his policy to advance at once, and to fall upon Reynier's troops while they were still dispersed. Unfortunately a heavy surf rose on the beach on the night of the 1st of July, which made the landing of provisions, reserve-ammunition, and baggage-animals a slow, difficult, and dangerous matter; and it is hard to blame the General for refusing to take the risk of marching until he was sure of his supplies and stores. None the less, the delay enabled Reynier to collect a superior force and to move at once against his opponent. As a matter of fact, the bulk of the French General's troops were immediately under his hand at Reggio or within a day's march of it; and the detachments which held his line of communications could all be picked up on the way as he marched northward upon St. Euphemia. Starting accordingly, with four thousand men, upon the first intelligence of Stuart's departure from Messina, Reynier gathered up in succession three battalions at Palmi, Tropea, and Monteleone, and in three days covered the eighty miles from Reggio to Maida, where he arrived on the night of the 2nd to 3rd of July. The force then with him included about fifty-seven hundred infantry in nine battalions, rather over three hundred sabres of cavalry, and one battery of horse artillery, with close upon four hundred gunners and engineers, making in all just under six thousand four hundred of all ranks.[1] The infantry was organised

[1] The exact figures, for which we have to thank the industry and research of Mr. Oman, are :—

6 French battalions	4123
1 Swiss battalion	630
2 Polish battalions	937
Cavalry	328
Artillery and Engineers	373
Total . .	6391

Mr. Oman, and apparently Reynier's return, make the total 6440, which does not tally with the sum of the details; but the difference is trifling.

into two brigades under Generals Compère and Digonet, 1806. Compère's consisting of the 1st Light Infantry and 42nd of the Line, each of two battalions, Digonet's of the two battalions of the 23rd Light Infantry and the three battalions of Poles and Swiss.

On the morning of the 3rd Stuart received positive July 3. intelligence that Reynier was encamped by the river Lamato, below San Pietro di Maida ; but the reports as to his numbers were extremely contradictory, some stating them at six thousand, others at three thousand, with the commentary that more troops were expected from Reggio but were not yet come up. Stuart therefore rode out in the afternoon with his staff, escorted by a company of Grenadiers, and reconnoitring the French position from a height over against it, decided that it must be turned by its left flank ; for its entire front was covered by the Lamato, which though fordable was an impediment, and its flanks, especially on the right, were protected by dense underwood. The country being much broken by olive-yards and thick brushwood, he reconnoitred also the edges of the forest of St. Euphemia, gave special directions as to the outposts, and rode back, little suspecting that Reynier, with a small escort of cavalry, had been in the wood at the same time as himself, observing the British position, and had only missed him by a few minutes. That night Stuart issued his orders that the troops should march at daybreak next morning to attack the French position. Four companies of Watteville's with artillerymen and three field-guns, altogether about three hundred and thirty men, were appointed to hold the entrenchment on the beach ; leaving something under forty-three hundred of all ranks (for Ross's battalion-companies of the Twentieth Foot had not yet appeared), with three field-guns and eight mountain-guns, to enter the line of battle. In sanguine confidence Stuart had accepted the lowest estimate of the French army, and felt sure of numerical superiority.

Accordingly at daylight on the 4th of July the July 4.

1806. July 4. British troops moved southward along the shingly beach and the marshy pastures that adjoined it, upon the river Lamato, from whence they were to strike inland upon the left of Reynier's position. The march was made in two parallel columns; Kempt's brigade leading the left or inland column, with Cole's in rear, and Acland's the right column, with Oswald's in rear. Two light mountain-guns, carried by mules, were attached to each brigade; three slightly heavier field-guns followed Acland's column; and the *Apollo* with two smaller vessels sailed parallel to the army by sea, to protect it in case the French should fall upon its flank. The march was slow and fatiguing, the marshes being in many places deep and the sand on the shore so heavy that the field-guns could only with difficulty be brought forward. The sun rose intensely hot before the few miles along the beach had been traversed, and the men were already jaded when they reached the Lamato, where the columns wheeled inland to their left and entered the plain of Maida. It was now a quarter to nine. The patrols of the French cavalry, which so far had followed the march of the British, fell back; and Reynier's army was seen filing by its right from its bivouacking ground and descending into the upper portion of the same plain. Reynier likewise was advancing confidently to the attack, though he believed himself to be inferior in numbers. Five thousand men, he said, were enough to drive six or seven thousand English into the sea; and the great Emperor himself had written less than a month before that with nine thousand picked troops of Joseph's army he would undertake to beat thirty thousand English.[1] Reynier, who had tested the quality of the red-coats in Egypt, ought to have known better than this; but he, in common with the whole of the French army, was demoralised by easy successes.

Upon wheeling eastward into the plain the British columns had to thread their way through the marshes of the lower Lamato and through belts of coppice; upon

[1] *Corres. de Napoléon*, 10,325.

emerging from which Stuart formed them into order of battle and continued the advance in echelon of brigades from his right. Kempt's Light Infantry led the way with its right skirting the thickets that bordered the Lamato; next to it came Acland's brigade, and next to Acland's that of Cole. Oswald with his twelve companies and three field-guns formed a reserve in rear of the centre. Meanwhile the French cavalry and horse-artillery manœuvred in the front, raising much dust, which, added to the haze of a burning day, obscured the movements of their infantry. Their guns and the British field-pieces exchanged shots during the advance; and on reaching the French huts by the Lamato, Kempt deployed his light companies and detached the Corsican Rangers, supported by the light company of the Twentieth, across the thread of water and bed of shingle which represented the Lamato, to clear some thickets on the further side. The Corsicans had hardly entered the wood when a sharp fire and a charge from two companies of sharp-shooters, which had been concealed there by Compère, drove them back in confusion upon their supports. The company of the Twentieth was hard pressed and its captain was killed, but it stood its ground until the "flankers" of the Thirty-fifth came to its help and drove the French back in disorder. The Corsicans, rallying, followed them up, and the British companies doubled back to their places on the right of Kempt's brigade.

1806. July 4.

And now the French cavalry galloped away towards the British left; the dust subsided; the French infantry was seen advancing rapidly to the attack; and the British officers could not fail to notice that it was considerably superior in numbers to their own. Reynier's plan, as he reported after the action, was to make "a vigorous charge which should break up a section of the enemy's force, so that the remainder should not be able to embark, and would be obliged to surrender, especially the part which had been turning the French left." On his left was Compère's brigade,

1806. July 4. namely the 1st Light Infantry and the 42nd of the Line, veteran regiments of deserved reputation and counting over twenty-eight hundred bayonets. Next to Compère's, and intended either to support it or to form the centre of the line, was Peyri's brigade of one Swiss and two Polish battalions, altogether fifteen hundred bayonets. Finally on the right was Digonet's brigade, which included twelve hundred and fifty bayonets of the 23rd Light, besides the cavalry and guns. Since the French camp faced to north, and Reynier's line of battle was to face westward, the French army had to begin by changing front to the left. Hence it necessarily followed that Compère's brigade, which formed the left of Reynier's line, was the first to come into position, Peyri's and Digonet's having to make a wider circuit to take up their new alignment. The consequence was that Reynier's advance, like that of Stuart, was made in echelon of brigades, but from the left instead of from the right; both armies refusing, as was natural, the flank which was unsupported. From this again it followed that the heads of the two echelons, namely the brigades of Compère and Kempt, were bound to be the first that should come into collision.

Both armies were formed in line, the British two deep, the French three deep; and they approached each other in perfect silence, which was broken only by the occasional boom of the guns upon either side. The French shot, however, flew high, doing little or no damage, whereas the British struck true into the enemy's advancing array. Compère's brigade appears to have been formed in echelon of battalions from the left; and the front of the leading battalion of the 1st Light did not exceed one hundred and seventy to one hundred and eighty yards, whereas Kempt's line, his men being formed only two deep, had a front of fully two hundred and twenty yards. The red and blue lines strode on until they were separated by less than a hundred yards, when the leading French battalion halted and fired a

volley. Kempt likewise halted and returned the fire, 1806.
and the two lines exchanged some two or three rounds, July 4.
after which Kempt resumed the advance with trailed arms. In this duel of musketry the British must evidently have gained the upper hand, for Kempt, observing that his men were encumbered by their greatcoats, which they wore bandolier-wise, actually halted them, when they must have been within no more than seventy yards of their opponents, and bade them throw their coats down. The front rank turned about to help the rear rank to obey the order; and the French mistook the movement for the beginning of a retreat. Their men, evidently relieved by this happy prospect, began to cry out, "Forward! Charge!" and Compère galloped to the front, shouting "Cease fire! Cease fire! Charge!" Kempt kept his men slowly moving forward, with the words, "Steady, Light Infantry! Wait for the word. Let them come close." Biding his time till the French were within thirty yards, he gave the order "Fire! Charge bayonets!"; and before the British could pass through the smoke of their volley, the foremost of the French turned and fled, carrying away with them the rear battalion of the 1st Light. Compère, though struck by two bullets, did indeed ride into the British ranks, gesticulating wildly with his unwounded arm and swearing with the strength of seven devils; but his gallantry was of no avail. A few brave men alone followed him, and were speedily overcome with the bayonet. For the rest, the fugitives fled headlong up the hill towards their camp, with the red-coats dashing savagely after them. Through the camp and along the hill-side for more than a mile the pursuit continued, until at last, at the village of Maida, Kempt succeeded in halting and rallying his men. By that time the 1st Light had lost nearly nine hundred men in killed, wounded, and prisoners, whereas Kempt had hardly lost fifty. None the less, for the future purpose of the battle, Kempt's brigade was useless and out of action.

Meanwhile the next echelons on either side had

1806. July 4. come into collision, namely the 42nd of the French Line on the right of Compère's brigade, and the Seventy-eighth and Eighty-first of Acland's brigade. Here again the French were the first to fire, doing little damage, whereas the British counter-volley was telling and destructive. The British artillery—four four-pounders upon Acland's right—was also far more effective than the French; and, in fact, two volleys from Acland's brigade sufficed to defeat the 42nd, which gave way and ran before the bayonets could reach them. They rallied, however, after a time, and took up a position from which they could either support Reynier's right wing or cover the retreat of his left. Meanwhile Reynier brought up the next echelon, Peyri's brigade of Poles and Swiss, which had been on the right rear of Compère, to check the progress of Acland. The Poles behaved very ill and gave way before the Eighty-first directly; but the Swiss, who wore red coats, were mistaken by the Highlanders for Watteville's men, and were allowed to approach unharmed within very close range and to pour in a damaging volley. Once undeceived, the Seventy-eithth took up the challenge vigorously. After a sharp duel of musketry, the Swiss fell back; and Acland's brigade strode on triumphant with the Highlanders in advance.

Observing that Acland's battalions were now in the air, Reynier galloped away to the 23rd Light upon his right, with the idea of turning them against Acland's left flank. But Cole's brigade was coming up too quickly upon Acland's left to make such a manœuvre possible; and the French commander was fain to hold Acland in check as best he could by demonstrations with his mounted chasseurs and horse-artillery. Acland himself, realising that the Seventy-eighth was too far ahead, sent an order to the battalion to halt until the Eighty-first should come up into line with it. The order was misdelivered or misconstrued into a command to retire; and the Seventy-eighth fell back in

some confusion, though it was quickly rallied, the 1806.
chasseurs having been driven off by the fire of the July 4.
field-guns. By this time Cole's brigade was coming up on the extreme British left, having been much delayed at the outset by the first manœuvres of the French cavalry and horse-artillery, which had compelled the infantry more than once to form square. Reynier had nothing to oppose to it but the 23rd Light, which, together with his mounted troops and their guns, were the only unshaken troops left to him to secure his retreat. Forming the 23rd upon slightly rising ground he stood on the defensive, threatening every movement of Cole's with a charge of cavalry, and detaching his light companies to harass the British battalions from the brushwood on Cole's left flank. Cole threw back the left of the Twenty-seventh to repel this attack; but he could do no more than hold his own, for ammunition was running short, and the men were growing exhausted under the intense heat of the sun. Oswald presently brought up his reserve on Cole's right, which improved matters; and just at the critical moment a staff-officer galloped up to report that Ross had landed with the Twentieth Foot and was hurrying forward in double quick time. Sidney Smith had arrived in St. Euphemia that morning, and, seeing Ross's transports coming in, had happily advised that the troops should be landed at once at the mouth of the Lamato. During the disembarkation Ross heard the firing begin, and, the progress of the boats being slow owing to a heavy surf, he did not wait for the last loads but ran with all speed to the scene of action. He was met by Bunbury, who briefly explained the state of affairs; when, promptly grasping the situation, Ross plunged into the brushwood on Cole's left, drove out the sharpshooters, poured a volley into the French squadrons, which sent them into the rear in confusion, and then wheeling to the right opened a shattering fire upon the flank of Digonet's battalions. This decided the action. After a feeble attempt to hold his ground Reynier drew

1806. July 4. off his troops towards the 42nd, which had rallied some distance in rear, and, skilfully covering his retreat by his cavalry and sharp-shooters, retired rapidly towards Catanzaro. Had the British possessed but two or three squadrons of cavalry, hardly a man of Reynier's army could have escaped.

The action, as has been seen, was fought in three sections by each of the three British brigades independently, from which it might be surmised that the Commander-in-chief had been killed. But it was not so. Stuart was cantering about all over the field, heedless of personal danger, enjoying himself keenly as a spectator, but giving not a thought to the direction of the battle. From the moment when Kempt's brigade had routed that of Compère, Stuart's head was completely turned by the glamour of present success and visions of a glorious future. His staff, unable to obtain any orders from him, gave information as to what was passing to the Brigadiers, who carried on the action practically by themselves. When, however, all was over, Stuart was obliged to say whether there should or should not be a pursuit, and he decided that there should not. The men were indeed jaded by the march and the fight, and choking with thirst; water was only to be found in the Lamato ; and there was no means of bringing forward supplies. But the action after all had lasted only an hour and a half ; it had been brilliantly successful, and victory will carry troops far. Moreover, Ross's regiment was fresh and Kempt's brigade was well forward—indeed was actually marching for some time parallel with the retreating French—though in the absence of orders from Stuart, Kempt dared not take the initiative. After a while therefore he halted, only detaching the Light Company of the Twentieth under Captain Colborne—the future Lord Seaton—to keep touch with the enemy. Kempt's brigade did not return to camp till next morning ; and Colborne, as was to be expected from so good an officer, hung closely to Reynier's skirts

as far as Borgia, within ten miles of Catanzaro, 1806.
when finding himself unsupported he was fain to July 4.
return.

Meanwhile Stuart ordered the rest of his army back to the beach for repose; and each of the brigades received permission in turn to bathe in the sea. Cole's brigade was enjoying this privilege when a staff-officer, deluded by the dust raised by some frightened buffaloes, came galloping down, crying aloud that the French cavalry was approaching. Then followed a scene which has no parallel in the history of the army. The Grenadiers and Twenty-seventh rushed out of the water, seized their belts and muskets and fell into line with ordered arms, ready to fight and give a good account of themselves without a shred of clothing.[1] The staff-officer, who has fortunately preserved the scene for us, treats only of its ludicrous aspect; but to us it gives also some insight into the discipline and spirit of the old soldiers of the past. It is only unfortunate that Colonel Bunbury did not set down the judgment passed by these men, in their own language, upon the hapless but imbecile officer who gave the false alarm.

Stuart for his part was subjected to a trial which must have been inexpressibly galling to him. Still intoxicated by his success and troubled only by nervous anxiety to give proper expression to it in his despatch, he found on his return to the shore that the *Pompée* was at anchor in the bay with Sir Sidney Smith on board. On that very morning a letter had reached the General from that illustrious sailor, explaining at great length the reasons why he, as King Ferdinand's vicegerent, had thought right to delegate certain authorities to his military colleague, and adding that, since Stuart was content with the naval assistance already at his disposal, he should go with his flag-ship to northward. Yet there the Admiral was, and, worse than this, he accounted for his presence by saying that he had fully

[1] Bunbury, pp. 249-50.

1806. July 4. expected the army to be beaten, and had resolved to run the *Apollo* ashore with her broadside to the beach to cover the flight of the red-coats. However, he was full of compliments and hospitality, invited Stuart and his staff on board the flag-ship, talked a great deal about himself and the siege of Acre, instructed Stuart in the art of folding a turban on a lady's head, and incidentally asked him how he could best serve him. "By going northward," said Stuart, with such emphasis as can be guessed. "Everything to southward is now
July 5. in the power of the army." Next morning came news that Reynier was endeavouring to rally his army at Catanzaro; and at daybreak the General returned ashore, after receiving once again Sidney Smith's assurance that he would sail to the north, or in plain words to Gaeta.

There was in fact a great opportunity open to these two commanders. By hastening at once to Gaeta with a thousand troops and the news of the victory, Sidney Smith could have put new life into the garrison; and if at the same time Stuart, after leaving a small force to secure Lower Calabria, had carried the rest by sea to threaten Naples, the French must not only have raised the siege but evacuated both the Calabrias in order to save the capital. The insurrection might then have gained formidable headway; the French hold upon the Neapolitan dominions would have become extremely precarious, and Italian affairs might have marred Napoleon's plans on the eve of his quarrel with Prussia. But General and Admiral alike were impostors, and the favourable moment was allowed to pass. For forty-eight hours the army was left "kicking its heels and eating grapes," to borrow Colonel Bunbury's picturesque phrase, while the General laboured in travail with his despatch. So absorbed was he in the task of adorning his exploits with an appropriate setting, that he could spare no attention for the movements of the army—so eaten up with self-esteem that he could find no time for duty.

In truth the action of Maida was an extremely

brilliant and creditable little affair. Five thousand two 1806.
hundred British troops had met six thousand four July 4.
hundred French in the open field, with no advantage of circumstances or position, and had inflicted upon them so crushing a defeat as to amount very nearly to a disaster. Reynier's losses, considering that the British had not a mounted man in the field, were almost incredibly severe, and Stuart's as incredibly small. Of the British there fell in all three hundred and twenty-seven, of whom one officer and forty-four men were killed, eleven officers and two hundred and seventy-one men wounded. The heaviest casualties fell upon the Seventy-eighth and Eighty-first, though in each of these two battalions they were fewer than one hundred. On the French side Reynier acknowledged a loss of thirteen hundred killed, wounded, and prisoners; but the true figure was probably over two thousand. The number of the killed was abnormally great. According to Stuart's despatch, over seven hundred bodies were buried on the field; according to his Quartermaster-general, who is more probably correct, over five hundred. The prisoners, wounded and unwounded, exceeded a thousand, and the wounded who were not captured cannot have fallen far short of another thousand. The British were lucky in the contempt with which their opponents treated them, and still more lucky in the timely arrival of Ross and his regiment on the field; but nothing can detract from the credit of their victory. The conduct of all the men was good, and that of the old soldiers admirable.

The action has long been celebrated because, according to Stuart's despatch, the British and French crossed bayonets. The fact is at best doubtful; and the true interest of the fight lies really in exactly the opposite direction. Maida was a soldiers' battle, and was won solely by the superiority of the British training in missile tactics. In the first place, the British musket threw a heavier bullet than the French—sixteen bullets to the pound as compared with twenty-two to the

1806. pound—which gave it a greater power of disabling a man. In the second place, the British soldier being by nature cooler in action as well as carefully taught and strictly disciplined, loaded his piece better, ramming charge and bullet well home, so that there was smaller loss of velocity through windage. Thirdly, the British fought in double and the French in triple rank, which signified not only that every British musket was brought into action, but that the British presented a greater front of fire. If a battalion of six hundred British, to give a concrete example, occupied a front of, say, two hundred yards, a battalion of six hundred French covered only one hundred and thirty-five yards; so that the British array overlapped the French by at least thirty yards, and was able to shatter its flanks as well as its front. Moreover, the same round shot, tearing through the ranks of the French, would disable three men, and of the British only two. Add to these advantages the special characteristic of British infantry since the days of the archers—cool, steady marksmanship—and combine with it perfect readiness to close with the bayonet; and it is not difficult to understand how Maida was won.

To return now to the course of the operations, Stuart, after a prolonged struggle of forty-eight hours
July 6. with his despatches, wrote to Sidney Smith on the 6th of July that he should detach a brigade under Colonel Oswald to Monteleone, with orders to capture all the posts upon the west coast on his way southward, and that he himself should lead his main body over the mountains to Catanzaro. Smith answered on the same day that he should use every effort to give the General a naval force on the Adriatic, adding in his usual inflated style, "I hope to electrify the people of Terra di Lavoro by our pressure on the enemy at Gaeta." Satisfied with this assurance, Stuart, after a most unjustifiable delay of three days, pushed Oswald's Light
July 7. Brigade forward on the evening of the 7th to Monteleone. The garrison of three hundred and

seventy of all ranks at once surrendered; but Stuart, 1806.
on entering the place, learned to his amazement that July 7.
Sidney Smith was still on the south coast, renewing the capitulations of all the places that had already yielded to the army on shore, and that he had even despatched a naval officer, in advance of Oswald, to summon Monteleone in his own name. Thus the Admiral, in the face of his promise, had left Gaeta to its fate, and was following the track of the General in order to steal his poor laurels from him. Stuart's vanity was unfortunately wounded more deeply than his sense of military honour. Without a thought for Gaeta, he deliberately halted for four days at Monteleone to write a tale of complaints to Mr. Elliot.[1] This letter ran to the effect that he could not continue to expose the lives and reputation of his victorious troops for the re-establishment of the Kingdom of Naples, so long as King Ferdinand's decree, instead of inculcating confidence in the army, directed public obedience and attention to "another channel," or in other words to Sir Sidney Smith. He had, he continued, advanced as far as Borgia in pursuit of Reynier, when he perceived that the said decree paralysed his efforts to direct the country. He therefore trusted to Elliot "to impress upon the Court of Naples the magnitude of his army's services and their great importance to the future security of the Kingdom of Naples."[2]

Practically therefore this man of small mind renounced all the few profits still to be gathered from his victory owing to sheer sulkiness over the proceedings of his still smaller colleague. In fact he confessed to Mr. Elliot a few days later that it was Sidney Smith's

[1] Bunbury says that he employed these days in polishing still further his despatch concerning Maida, which in fact was not sent to England (though a vessel was ready to take it) until a fortnight after the action. No doubt this is partly true; but Bunbury either did not know, or loyally concealed, the bitterness of Stuart's feeling against Smith.

[2] Stuart to Elliot, 10th July 1806; enclosed in his general narrative.

1806. assumption of supreme command, and the medley of control resulting from it, that had arrested his pursuit of Reynier.[1] But it was really true that Sidney Smith had enormously increased Stuart's difficulties. That volatile officer, completely under the influence of the infamous Queen of Naples, had been flitting about the coast, scattering arms and proclamations among the refuse of the population and inciting them to insurrection. These people, generically known as the *Masse*, quickly formed themselves into bands under leaders termed the *Capitani delle Masse*, and laid themselves out for a carnival of brigandage. No confidence could be reposed in these ruffians, whom Smith, in his shallow ignorance, had chosen to dignify as patriots. The *Capitani* would forsake their commands at the mere rumour of the approach of the French, and were more likely to join than to oppose them if the French were victorious; and meanwhile they turned their arms against their wealthier compatriots and confounded the whole of Calabria with cruelty, murder, and rapine.[2] Stuart restored order so far as his strength permitted;
July 12. but before the 12th he learned, while still at Monteleone, that the insurrection had produced at least one weighty result. The insurgents had hoisted the royal standard at Cosenza; General Verdier, his ammunition being exhausted, had been compelled to retreat with some loss by forced marches from thence northward;[3] and, more important still, Reynier's direct retreat was now cut off, and the only line left open to him was the road that followed the windings of the eastern coast. Yet Stuart in reporting these facts to England could find nothing to present with them but a request that a medal might be granted to his army for Maida.[4] He appears never to have thought of the

[1] Stuart to Elliot, 19th July 1806.
[2] Gen. Fox to Sec. of State, 31st Aug. 1806.
[3] Intercepted letter from Verdier to Reynier, 15th July, in Fox to Sec. of State, 2nd Aug. 1806.
[4] Stuart to Sec. of State, 12th July 1806.

effect that Verdier's retreat would produce on Reynier, 1806.
who still lingered at Catanzaro, trying to restore order and spirit in his demoralised army. It seems never to have occurred to him that he might himself have marched to Cosenza and effected by design what had now come about by happy chance.

Within the paltry sphere of operations to which he had limited himself, all was going as well as possible. His faithful naval helper, Captain Fellowes of the *Apollo*, was moving steadily down the coast and gathering in the isolated French posts one after another, his first capture being that of one hundred prisoners at Tropea on the 7th. Brigadier Brodrick, again, July 7.
who had been left in command at Sicily, grasping at once the true significance of the victory at Maida, had collected twelve hundred British and Neapolitans, and with the co-operation of Captain Hoste of the *Amphion*, had crossed the straits to Reggio. Surrounding the place before the garrison could escape, he received its surrender, together with that of some six hundred prisoners, after two days' investment. The news of this success reached Stuart on the 14th at Palmi, to July 14.
which he had at last moved after his long delay at Monteleone. But additional news accompanied it, which only made the General the more anxious to return to Sicily. It now appeared that Sidney Smith, under pretext of sailing to Gaeta, had but disguised another determined effort to wrest from the General the credit of the military successes. Instead of sailing to Gaeta he had hurried round to Scilla, had landed his marines, and was actually besieging the fortress according to his own peculiar military ideas. Meanwhile he had sent to Sicily pompous accounts of the naval operations and of his share in the success of Maida, which were duly published in the Messina Gazette. He claimed to have taken four hundred prisoners at Amantea, a piece of news which somehow never reached the army while the *Pompée* lay in the Bay of St. Euphemia. He averred that Stuart had landed under

1806. the fire of the *Apollo*, which was not only untrue but absurd, for there was nothing for the *Apollo* to fire at. He informed the Queen of Naples, in language of almost incredible bombast and absurdity, that the success of the recent operations was due to the vesting of the superior direction in himself.[1] Nothing could be more false; and, as a matter of fact, the King of Naples, in reply to Elliot's remonstrances, incontinently cancelled the decree under which the Admiral had acted, declaring that it had been turned to a use for which it had never been intended. But this was not the worst
July 19. of Sidney Smith's shortcomings. On the 19th of July he wrote again to the Queen of Naples that the reaction caused by recent measures had made itself felt at Gaeta, and that, on the 9th, three thousand French troops had been seen by a British naval officer marching from the trenches upon Naples. But, in
July 18. truth, on the 18th, even before he had written the words, Gaeta had surrendered.

This disaster, for it was nothing less, was due wholly to Sidney Smith's egoism; and by a righteous nemesis, it occurred in circumstances which deprived him of an extraordinary opportunity of gaining distinction. Smith's leading motives in avoiding Gaeta had

[1] I give here the text of the letter, slightly abridged. Impostors of Sidney Smith's type are always among us; and it is well that a brand should be set upon any one of them who is detected. "The advantage of the concentration of authority is already manifest. He who can speak as supreme commander can accomplish *coups de maître*. It is this unity of plan and action which gives Bonaparte his success. Now this unity of power is vested in me. Let it remain in me, and I will dare to do more than he will dare to imagine. If Italy can dispute no longer the empire of the world with France, she can at least preserve her independence. Stuart has done what he promised me. He beat Reynier in a masterly fashion. One more battle, and both Calabrias are ours. We have already Further Calabria except a few ports which I am now engaged in reducing." Yet upon Stuart's complaint of Smith's delegation of authority to him, the Admiral had written (2nd July) that the powers given to him by the Court of Naples were much greater than he had thought, and that he considered it his duty to the General to remove any possible difficulty.

been two, jealousy of the Prince of Hesse-Philipstadt, 1806.
to whom would justly have been awarded the chief credit for a successful defence; and jealousy of Stuart, over whom he claimed to hold command. It so happened that the gallant old Prince was wounded; and, released from the pressure of his strong hand, the Neapolitan officers of the garrison at once bethought them of surrender. On the 14th, news July 14.
reached Capri that affairs in Gaeta were going amiss, whereupon Captain Rowley of the Royal Navy resolved to proceed there at once, taking with him the naval force at his command and an officer of engineers, lent to him by the military commandant. Hudson Lowe was, indeed, eager to go himself; and was only restrained by the fact that Rowley's withdrawal left Capri exposed to the attack of a superior naval force at Naples. The British officers inspected the works of Gaeta and, finding them still tenable, ordered repairs to be made, taking the Governor with them to explain what should be done. To their surprise, the Governor had never even seen the batteries of the fortress, much less Massena's lines; but for all that he refused to deliver up his command to a British officer. The utmost that could be extorted from him was, that he would consult his officers before thinking of surrender, and that at worst he would ask for an armistice of three days. The British captains went back to their ships, but, hearing that a flag of truce had been sent to Massena, relanded to find that the Neapolitan chiefs were drawing up a capitulation. Breaking in upon them, they read the articles, which seemed to be honourable. The Neapolitans also pledged themselves to fight to the death if their terms were refused, and to take no final step without communication with their allies. Satisfied by these assurances, the British officers retired for the night. A few hours later they heard that the best of the Neapolitans had deserted to the enemy, and that the rest had signed a disgraceful surrender. Treachery, July 18.
of course, underlay the whole transaction; but if Sidney

1806. Smith had arrived there with, or even without, a thousand men on the day after Maida, the whole garrison would have been heartened; and, after the disablement of the Prince of Hesse, Smith would certainly have secured command and could have added a second really fine and useful service to his defence of Acre.

As things fell out, he not only missed the glory of Gaeta, but was ignominiously repulsed from Scilla, which by a delightful irony became the trophy of the army. The French commandant made a most gallant defence, and the walls of the fortress were so thick that the British could make no impression upon them until they brought up their siege-artillery. With heavy guns, however, Colonel Oswald speedily reduced it to sur-
July 24. render, and made its garrison of nearly three hundred men prisoners of war. Sidney Smith had already disappeared, on the 18th, bound at last for Gaeta; but meeting the news of the surrender on the way, he turned aside to carry on a little warfare of his own in the Gulf of Policastro. Deprived of the command-in-chief, of which he had made such parade, and threatened with the prospect that the name of Gaeta might be thrown in his teeth, he doubtless thought it prudent to hide himself away. Stuart, on the other hand, embarked his troops at Reggio, leaving garrisons there and at Scilla, and returned to Sicily. He expressed some compunction at leaving the *Masse*, who had now committed themselves deeply against France; but the insurrection was the work of Sidney Smith, for which, in consequence, he did not feel responsible. He hoped nevertheless to second and encourage them by demonstrations upon the coast, for which purpose he sent General Acland with the Fifty-eighth and Eighty-first to cruise off Salerno and the Bay of Naples. As regards Reynier, Stuart was content to send one battalion, the Seventy-eighth, by sea to Catanzaro with Captain Hoste of the *Amphion*. Surrounded as the French General was on all sides by insurgents.

Stuart thought that he would find it difficult to escape so long as Gaeta held out, for on the 27th of July he had not yet heard of the fall of that fortress. There were, however, unpleasant reports from Palermo that Massena was marching with ten thousand men to the rescue of his colleague, and therefore, in Stuart's opinion, it was necessary to act with caution.[1] No one would dream from his despatches that he considered either Gaeta or Reynier's army to be any concern of his. He had won a brilliant action in the open field, and that sufficed him. 1806. July 27.

Fortunately Hoste and Colonel Macleod of the Seventy-eighth were men of a different stamp. Sailing from Reggio on the evening of the 25th, they caught sight of part of the French army next morning in full retreat upon Cotrone. The road ran nearly parallel to the beach and within gunshot of the sea, being bounded to the landward by a chain of mountains, on which Macleod had entreated the *Masse* to assemble, in order to harass the enemy's flank. Macleod at once sailed ahead of the French column, and made a demonstration of landing. The column halted, and changed direction towards the mountains, whereupon Hoste opened fire on its centre and rear and dispersed it; and, had the insurgents but been present to do their part, they might have inflicted very heavy loss. But not a man appeared. The leaders upon whom Sidney Smith had lavished arms and flattery, disbanded their followers upon the mere rumour of a French advance; and a great opportunity was thus lost. Hoste's cannonade killed and wounded fifty or sixty men; and the fleet then sailed to Cotrone where it anchored, after exchanging a few shots with the citadel late in the evening. On the following morning Hoste allowed the French to take up a position within range of his guns, when he stood in and again drove them to the mountains. Several deserters came to the British that evening, who reported their comrades to be much harassed and discontented and their leaders

July 26.

July 27.

[1] Stuart to Sec. of State, 26th July 1806.

1806. July 28. much perplexed; but after a day's halt the column resumed its retreat northward on the 28th, wreaking savage vengeance on the villages that lay in its path. Unable to ascertain by what route they were moving, Macleod urged the peasants to pursue and harry them; and after receiving the capitulation of Cotrone, returned to Messina. He brought with him five hundred prisoners, half of them wounded, from the hospital at Cotrone. It is difficult to avoid the conclusion that by a little more vigour immediately after Maida Reynier's army might have been almost totally destroyed.[1]

Stuart meanwhile returned to Messina to exhibit his laurels, as his chief staff-officer expressed it. In truth, in spite of his failings, he had done some solid work. He had fought an action which had shaken the reputation of the French and enhanced that of the British; he had destroyed five hundred of their best troops, and taken from two to three thousand prisoners; he had driven the enemy from both Calabrias, capturing all the stores, guns, and boats that they had collected for the invasion of Sicily; and by the occupation of the ports on the north of the straits he had averted, for a time at least, all danger of such an invasion. But on the other hand Gaeta had fallen, and not all his petty successes could counterbalance this great failure. Naples, which, by a little attention to his duty, Stuart might have made a distraction to Napoleon for another twelve months, perhaps even to the wrecking of the Emperor's plans in Germany, was now firmly established in French hands; and, while this was so, Sicily could not be considered safe. It is true that Sidney Smith was far more responsible for this state of affairs than was Stuart, for the Admiral had actually given the General to understand that he would sail to the relief of Gaeta. No language of reprehension can be too strong for his behaviour. But Stuart also was greatly to blame for

[1] Macleod to Fox, 27th, 29th July; in Fox to Sec. of State, 3rd Aug. 1806.

his general inefficiency; and happily he met with his reward. 1806.

On arriving at Reggio he heard that General Fox had been appointed to command in the Mediterranean, and that large reinforcements were on their way to him. This in itself was nothing very mortifying. Fox was high up on the list of Lieutenant-generals, though by reason of his age, health, and mediocrity, he was by no means the man who should have been appointed to the post, which, in fact, he owed to the interest of his brother Charles James. Having much of his brother's generosity and sweet temper, Fox nominated Stuart to command in the two Calabrias, sought his advice, and did everything that a courteous gentleman could do to uphold his subordinate's honour and importance. All this was pleasant enough for the victor of Maida; but together with Fox the Government very wisely sent out Sir John Moore, to be actually though not nominally Commander-in-chief. Now this was the rival of whom above all others Stuart was most jealous. Moore was not only his senior in the service, but of far greater reputation, a man of clear insight into the heart of things, of high disdain for charlatans, and of a critical faculty which was but too keen. Good-natured old Fox might be cajoled; but Moore was a man who would put hard questions with a bright searching eye, and would combat hollow arguments with unsparing contempt. Stuart shrank from the ordeal, and obtained leave to go to Malta until he could take a passage to England. He was rewarded with the ribbon of the Bath, which he ill deserved, and his chief subordinates with a medal for Maida, which they had most justly earned. We shall see Stuart again in the Mediterranean, and shall find him unchanged.

Fox arrived in Sicily on the 22nd of July, and July 22. within a fortnight the situation had become anything but satisfactory. Sidney Smith's wild proceedings and the belated despatch of Acland to Salerno had done great mischief. Several leaders on the coast about

1806. July. Naples and Salerno had called their followers out to insurrection prematurely, only to find French columns descending upon them directly after the fall of Gaeta. The *Masse* made no attempt to withstand the enemy by uniting their bands, nor even to impede them by occupying the passes. It served the purpose of their leaders much better to use the arms, which Smith had given them, for forcible plunder of their own towns and villages. With great difficulty Hudson Lowe persuaded many leading persons in the Principato to remain quiet; and it was well for them that they did so, for the French took signal vengeance on the native villages of the worst offenders, and shot all men taken with arms in their hands. Meanwhile refugees in inconveniently large numbers were crowding into Capri; and the French were steadily advancing southward. The British consul for the Ionian islands had applied to the Russian commander at Corfu to spare some portion of his eight ships of the line and twenty-nine armed vessels for a demonstration on the coast of Puglia and Abruzzi; but the request was refused on the ground that the security of Cattaro forbade compliance. Furthermore, when the news reached Palermo of d'Oubril's treaty with Napoleon and of his cession of Cattaro, the Court of Naples at once veered round towards friendship with France; the Queen's party regained the ascendency; Acton was dismissed from office, and Circello, Her Majesty's reigning favourite, was installed in his place. Altogether the outlook was extremely disquieting, and Fox very wisely sent Moore in a vessel up the western coast to inquire and to report.

Moore sailed accordingly, and fell in with Sidney Smith in the Bay of Policastro, with his flag-ship seriously damaged and a long list of killed and wounded, the result of cannonading a tower armed with one gun and garrisoned by thirty Corsicans, who were only waiting for the Admiral to cease fire in order to desert from the French service to the British.[1] Having

[1] Bunbury, pp. 267-8. Sidney Smith of course said nothing of

satisfied himself that Smith was doing far more harm 1806. than good by indiscriminate distribution of arms and Aug. incitement to rebellion, Moore sent Acland and his two battalions back to Messina, in order to give no countenance to further risings. Before the fall of Gaeta such demonstrations might have been of service, but they were so no longer. Every day in fact showed that, by their fatal neglect of that one essential point, Smith and Stuart had ruined all favourable prospects in the Mediterranean. The force in Sicily, though augmented by the arrival of three new battalions[1] to a strength of between twelve and thirteen thousand men, was none the less compelled to stand on the defensive, for the entire French army was now released for active operations in the field. At the beginning of September Sept. Reynier began again to push his patrols towards Monteleone. The few Neapolitan troops that held the place, being unsupported by the Calabrese, fell back before them; and the French General finally fixed his headquarters at Mileto, from whence his advanced posts were thrust forward towards Palmi. Meanwhile he made every preparation against the arrival of reinforcements, which should enable him to reoccupy the entire coast of Lower Calabria.

It may seem strange that Fox, with Moore at his elbow, made no attempt to beat up Reynier's quarters; but there were two strong reasons against such action. In the first place, both the Generals on the spot and the Government at home were rightly averse from raising false hopes among the Neapolitans by petty raids which were of no permanent value. In the second, after the signature of d'Oubril's treaty, Fox was firmly persuaded, having no information to the contrary, that France and

this in his despatches, and merged the casualties into those of several weeks of petty operations.

[1] These appear to have landed on July 26th, and were the 1/21st, 2/27th, 2/35th. They all came from England. The two second battalions were very weak, and composed of the indifferent material which had been collected under the Army of Reserve Act.

1806. Russia had come to an agreement, and that England, being now isolated in Europe, must most carefully husband her resources. He was strengthened in this conviction by the fact that further reinforcements promised to him from England had not appeared. The truth was that the British Cabinet, in consequence of Talleyrand's threats against Portugal, was urging the Court of Lisbon to emigrate to Brazil with its fleet and
Aug. 6. army; and on the 6th of August had resolved to support its diplomacy by the despatch of an armament to the Tagus. A force of nine battalions[1] was therefore embarked under the command of Lieutenant-general Simcoe, though it could only be completed by intercepting the reinforcements that had been designed for the Mediterranean and South America. The plan was however abandoned; and in the middle of September the Government decided to forward these troops to
Dec. their original destinations. In December, therefore, after a long voyage of three months, nearly five thousand men[2] were added to the force in Sicily, increasing it to a total of nearly nineteen thousand of all ranks.

But meanwhile the storm in Germany had burst, and all the hopes of the Coalition had been dashed to the
Sept. 12. ground. On the 12th of September Napoleon called upon Prussia to disarm, and, receiving only defiance
Oct. 6. in reply, took up the challenge, and on the 6th of

[1] 1 and 3/1st Guards, 1/13th, 1/40th, 1/45th, 1/52nd, 1/62nd, 1/87th; 8 cos.* /95th.

The Brigadiers were Wynyard, Paget, Brent Spencer, and Sir S. Auchmuty.

[2]

1 and 3/1st Guards	2559	rank and file.
1/52nd	961	" "
1/62nd	498	" "
	4018	
2 companies R.A.	250	

Sec. of State to Fox, 15th Sept. 1806. Return in Bunbury, p. 459.

* These appear to have been 3 cos. of 1/95th and 5 cos. of 2/95th. Cope's *History of the Rifle Brigade*, p. 17. But this portion of Cope's book is extremely slovenly and inaccurate.

October declared war. All Europe was high in hope 1806.
that deliverance was come at last. Godoy, impatient of the control of Spain by France, opened negotiations with England; and Italy, fired by the successes of Maida and Capri, was ready, as in 1799, to turn upon the French. In three weeks all was over. On the 14th of October were fought the battles of Jena and Oct. 14.
Auerstadt, and by the 31st Prussia's boasted army had ceased to exist and her power was shattered to fragments. Her collapse was not only complete but ignominious, and excited little pity though great dismay. Russia still remained in arms; but Alexander had chosen this most inopportune moment for a quarrel with the Turks. England's part was above all things to give him assistance; but the chances of a successful offensive in Italy had been wasted by Sidney Smith and Stuart, and unfortunately British troops, which should have been employed in Europe, were diverted far over sea by the avarice and self-seeking of Smith's brother charlatan, Home Popham. It is necessary, therefore, now to return once more to events in South America.[1]

[1] The authorities for the operations in the Mediterranean are the official records in the Record Office. W.O. Mediterranean, Vols. 142 *seq.*, and the Secretary of State's Entry Books, W.O. Vols. 52 *seq.* Bunbury's *Great War with France* is also invaluable as well as admirably written; and there is useful information also in Boothby's *Under England's Flag*, and the *Life of Lord Seaton*. Mr. Oman in his study of Maida (*Journal of the Royal Artillery*, March, 1908) has collected most valuable statistics and facts from the French archives. The inimitable letters of Paul Louis Courier are of the greatest interest and worth on the French side.

CHAPTER XII

1806. IMMEDIATELY upon his occupation of Buenos Ayres,
as has been told, Beresford wrote to Baird an urgent
appeal for reinforcements. Sir David promptly re-
sponded by despatching to him two battalions, three
squadrons, and other small detachments to the number
of about twenty-two hundred of all ranks,[1] which sailed
Aug. 29. from the Cape on the 29th of August. Sir Home Pop-
ham, for his part, took the extraordinary step of sending
a circular round to the leading merchants of London,
reporting that he had opened a gigantic market for
their goods and inviting them to take advantage of it.
Nevertheless Beresford was not deceived as to the
danger of his position ; and very soon the Spanish
colonists awoke to a shameful sense of the surrender
which they had made to a handful of men. By the
third week in July Beresford was aware that a rising
against him was in preparation, and that the leaders of
the movement were two men, Captain Liniers of the

[1]

R.A.	6	
1/38th	811	
47th	685	
1 company /54th	103	
2 squadrons /20th L.D.	191	
1 squadron /21st L.D.	140	
	1936	rank and file.
Add one-eighth for officers, sergeants, and drummers	244	
	2180	

Spanish Navy, and Puerridon, one of the municipal officers of Buenos Ayres, who had at first been most friendly towards him. These two began to collect forces on both sides of the river, Liniers at Monte Video, and Puerridon at Pedriel, about twenty miles outside Buenos Ayres. Leaving Popham to check Liniers, Beresford marched at two o'clock on the morning of the 1st of August upon Pedriel, with five hundred and fifty men and six guns. Misled by his guides, he did not reach his destination until eight o'clock, when he found about two thousand hostile troops drawn up in a good position with ten guns. Twenty minutes sufficed to disperse them and to capture all their cannon; and Beresford returned to Buenos Ayres the same night, having lost five of his own men wounded, against a loss to the enemy of about one hundred killed, wounded, and taken. 1806. Aug. 1.

Beresford counted upon this success to secure him at least until reinforcements should arrive; but on the night of the 3rd Liniers successfully crossed the river with twenty-eight vessels, unobserved by Popham's squadron, and landed at Las Conchas, twenty-one miles from Buenos Ayres. Gales and torrents of rain prevented Liniers from moving and Beresford from marching out to attack him, as he desired; but at length, on the 10th, Liniers, having been joined by several thousand raw levies from Buenos Ayres, began his advance upon the city, sending forward a summons to Beresford to surrender. The latter replied by a defiance; and shortly afterwards one of his outlying guards was surprised and attacked at the north end of the town. Sallying forth to rescue this party, he found himself too late; whereupon taking up a defensive position in front of the fort, he resolved, if there were yet time, to retreat. On the 11th accordingly he ordered the sick, the women and the children to be embarked during the night, and arranged a signal with Popham which would intimate to the Commodore that the troops had evacuated the fort and were marching to Enseñada to Aug. 3. Aug. 10. Aug. 11.

1806. re-embark. Throughout the 10th and 11th, however, a constant fire was maintained upon his men from the houses adjoining their position; and on the morning Aug. 12. of the 12th it was evident that the whole population had turned out to the attack. Beresford's chosen refuge was in the square directly in front of the fort, an open space about one hundred yards across, and divided almost in half by a long colonnaded building. Two streets entered it from the rear on each side of the fort and were protected by its guns; two more debouched into it from each flank opposite to the ends of the central building; and two more again met at each of the further angles. In the building itself was stationed the Seventy-first; the St. Helena infantry was posted so as to enfilade the rear entrances; and the marines and seamen were drawn up in front. Guns were also brought up to close the approaches on the flanks, and the principal houses in the square were likewise occupied.

At about half-past nine the enemy delivered their attack upon Beresford's front and both flanks, directing their artillery chiefly against his front. In the streets the assailants were easily beaten off and three of their guns taken; but a galling fire from the tops of the buildings, that commanded the fort and square, worked havoc among the British. Towards noon Beresford, having lost one hundred and sixty-five men [1] and being unwilling to sacrifice more to no purpose, ceased firing and hoisted the white flag. The tumultuous levies opposed to him showed no respect to the flag; and it was some time before Liniers could check their further aggression, towards which, as is usual in such cases, the absence of any danger prodigiously emboldened them. After a short parley with Liniers, a capitulation was drawn up and signed by the two commanders, to the effect that British property should be respected, and that Beres-

[1] 2 officers and 46 n.c.o. and men killed.
8 officers and 99 n.c.o. and men wounded.
10 " " " missing.

ford and his people should become prisoners; but that 1806. they should be immediately exchanged for the prisoners captured by him at Buenos Ayres, and should be shipped to England. There can be little doubt that Liniers intended faithfully to observe this treaty, for he sent his own aide-de-camp to Popham with orders to bring up the transports for embarkation of the troops; but circumstances were too strong for him. Popham's raid had caused an insurrection against the authority of the Spanish Government; the Viceroy had been driven out, and revolutionary leaders had usurped his power. Such folk, especially if they are of southern blood, do not boggle at trifles. The colonists had lost six or seven hundred killed and wounded in the attack, and their chiefs had some excuse for feeling vindictive against the British. They therefore repudiated the treaty, confiscated all British property, and carried Beresford and his men away prisoners some hundreds of miles into the interior.

Here then closed the first act of this little drama. Popham, and later on Beresford, inveighed bitterly against the treachery of the colonists, who had turned against them after swearing allegiance to King George. Such outcry was ridiculous. If the British had offered the inhabitants deliverance and protection from Old Spain, they would have been received with open arms; but there was no reason why the colonists should expose themselves to the vengeance of their mother-country simply to satisfy the cupidity of a British Commodore. Most unfortunately Popham was safe on board his ship in the river, so that the colonists had no chance of hanging him as he deserved. However, it was no pleasing task for him to report the disastrous issue of his raid, which he endeavoured to palliate by alleging that at least it had done material damage to Spain.[1] But, long before his letters reached home, Spain was negotiating for alliance with England; and when that

[1] Popham to Admiralty, 25th Aug.; to Duke of York, 6th Sept. 1806.

1806. alliance was finally made two years later, the memory of this attack, being naturally though wrongly ascribed to the British Government, still rankled in the minds of good Spaniards. However, the mischief was done; and Popham could only withdraw his ships, having first embarked a few small British detachments which were still ashore, and drop down the river to a safer anchorage.

Sept. 13. A month later, on the 13th of September, Beresford's report of his original capture of Buenos Ayres arrived in England, and was received by the nation at large with transports of delight. Visions of new markets, boundless wealth and relief from the terrible burden of taxation rose before the eyes of all; and merchants and speculators hastened to ship off large cargoes to La Plata in response to the imprudent circular from Popham. Only the unfortunate Cabinet which, with its hands already over-full, had to provide for a new and unforeseen demand for troops, was touched by doubt or dismay. At least one of its members, the Prime Minister Lord Grenville, was extremely angry; and it was, I suspect, mainly at his instance that the decision was taken to recall Baird, the Governor of St. Helena, and Popham, and to try the last-named by court-martial. But, most regrettably, no effort was made to repudiate the Commodore's action. We have seen that a force had already been appointed to sail for Rio de la Plata under Sir Samuel Auchmuty, and had been countermanded in order to furnish troops for the Portuguese expedition in August. The latter enterprise having been abandoned, there was no reason why the reinforcements should not proceed to South America; and Auchmuty

Sept. 22. received instructions to that effect on the 22nd of September. His troops numbered in all rather over four thousand of all ranks,[1] and his orders bade him

[1] Auchmuty's force—

1/40th	1000
1/87th	826
3 cos. /95th	300

place himself under Beresford's command. In case 1806.
Beresford should be in difficulties or should have surrendered, he was to endeavour to repair the loss and to obtain a footing which should enable him to hold his own, pending the arrival of a further reinforcement of three thousand men, which would sail three weeks after him. If this task should appear hopeless, he was to return to the Cape. In any case, the further reinforcement above mentioned was required elsewhere, and was not to be detained longer than was demanded for the relief of Beresford or the recovery of a station on the coast.

To Beresford himself Ministers wrote with a certain grimness, which showed their embarrassment and misgiving. "You are not accountable for the expedition," they said in effect, "and your conduct is approved. We have for long been restrained from invading Spanish South America by the fear of exciting a revolt against Spain, which could only be controlled by a British force of superior strength. It is with this view, as much as with that of securing valuable possessions, that your force has been so much increased. Use your judgment and your troops principally to avert the evil of such a revolt as we have mentioned, making none but inevitable changes in the Government. Above all, avoid pledging the King's Government to conditions which it might not be able to make good. We can only assure the inhabitants of protection so long as our troops are there; and our desire is that they shall never suffer from their amicable disposition to us."[1] From such scanty information as was before them

1 co. /R.A. with drivers	170
17th L.D.	700 (dismounted)
	2996 rank and file.

(Sec. of State to Auchmuty, 22nd Sept.). *Military Transactions*, i. 20, adds the 9th L.D., and calls the total 3400 r. and f. But the 9th had not sailed in November. *Courts and Cabinets of George III.*, iv. 95.

[1] Sec. of State to Beresford, 21st Sept. 1806.

1806. Ministers could hardly have written more fairly than this. Beresford, upon the first hasty view, had reported that the inhabitants were friendly, and that a reinforcement of two thousand infantry and six hundred cavalry would be sufficient to hold the country. Moreover it was true that Ministers had refused to invade South America, Lord Grenville having declined to listen to the most insinuating arguments of Miranda; and their unwillingness to incite an insurrection, which they could not support, had doubtless been heightened not only by the memories of La Vendée, but by Sidney Smith's recent follies in Calabria. Why then did they direct Auchmuty to make good or to supplement Beresford's work by the employment of force? The only explanation is that they yielded to the pressure of the merchants and to the outburst of vulgar enthusiasm with which England is apt to greet those self-seeking adventurers who, under pretext of wreaking an old national grudge, force their country into war for their private advantage. Moreover, it must be granted that the temptation to undertake the venture was strong. Napoleon's great plan for excluding British commerce from the Continent of Europe could be laughed at if the whole of South America were thrown open as a new market; and there was promise of further advantage in the interception of the gold which flowed through the channel of Spain into the Emperor's treasury. Still, piratical raids of the kind, from Cromwell's attack upon St. Domingo onward, have never prospered when countenanced by Government; and it would have been a good warning to adventurers of later generations if Popham's action had been repudiated and Popham himself disgraced.

Oct. 9. Auchmuty sailed on the 9th of October; and four
Oct. 13. days later Baird's reinforcements from the Cape entered Rio de la Plata, to learn with blank amazement that Beresford and the whole of his men were prisoners. Lieutenant-colonel Backhouse of the Forty-seventh thus found himself in command of some two thousand

men in a strange land, with no orders and no means 1806. of divining what the Government might wish him to do. However, after consultation with Popham, he determined to land and take up a position on shore. Disembarking accordingly on the 29th with four hundred Oct. 29. men of the Thirty-eighth off Maldonado, he swept away with the bayonet some six hundred colonists, who tried to protect the place, and duly installed himself, having captured their two guns. On the following day the Oct. 30. island of Goretti, which secured the harbour, as well as batteries mounting thirty-two guns, were surrendered to him ; and thus both ships and men were completely provided for at a cost to the British of six men, and to the colonists of fifty men, killed and wounded. After this brief encounter no enemy came within ten miles of Maldonado for some time ; and this was fortunate, for it was an open town and so situated as to be untenable by a small force. However, since Backhouse did not discover that fact, he was not uneasy ; and as Popham had obtained a good anchorage, which was all that he wanted, he was careful not to point out the defects of the position, even if (as was very improbable) he perceived them. Moreover, Backhouse was able at first to procure horses for his cavalry, and to bring in supplies with little difficulty or danger. There he remained, therefore, for over three months, unmolested indeed, but wholly isolated from the world until in due time Auchmuty arrived in the river.

But meanwhile popular pressure or infection by popular sentiment had enlarged the Government's ambition with regard to South America ; and in the course of October Windham evolved one of the most astonishing plans that ever emanated from the brain even of a British Minister of War. Robert Craufurd, a Colonel low down on the list, was, to the great indignation of his superior officers,[1] the instrument selected to carry this out. His instructions began by

[1] *An Authentic Narration of the Proceedings of the Expedition under Brig.-Gen. Craufurd* (London, 1808).

1806. premising that the fame of the superiority of British over Spanish rule must no doubt have crossed the Andes, and that it was therefore intended to send four thousand men,[1] escorted by a sufficient squadron, to gain a footing upon the west coast of South America. The reduction of the province of Chile was to be the ultimate purpose, and the capture of a strong military post on the west coast the primary object, of the expedition. If Craufurd should succeed in conquering Chile, or any part of it, he was to preserve peace and order. He was not to encourage revolt in the neighbouring provinces, and not to pledge England to give protection longer than her troops should remain on the spot ; but at the same time he was to be most careful to announce and to prove that protection and not booty was the purpose of the enterprise. If he should obtain possession of Valparaiso, he was to lose no time in informing Beresford, " and in concerting with him the means of securing by a chain of posts, or in any other adequate manner, an uninterrupted communication both military and commercial between Chile and Buenos Ayres." [2]

This last brilliant suggestion for carrying a chain of posts across the Andes along a line, as the crow flies, of nine hundred miles—the distance, roughly speaking, from Madrid to Amsterdam—is added to the draft of the despatch in Windham's own handwriting. How it was to be effected, and how at the same time Valparaiso, Buenos Ayres, and Monte Video were to be occupied by a total force of six thousand men, the Minister did not explain. Nor is it obvious how an invading General

[1] The force originally appointed for him consisted of:—1/5th, 678 ; 1/36th, 900 ; 1/45th, 661 ; 1/88th, 762 ; 5 cos./95th, 500 ; 2 cos. R.A., 250 ; deserters, 250. Total, 4001 r. and f., say 4500 of all ranks. But a subsequent return (S.S. to Whitelocke, 5th March 1807) stated it as follows:—2 sq./6th D.G., 299 ; R.A., 243 ; 1/5th, 836 ; 1/36th, 822 ; 1/45th, 850 ; 1/88th, 798 ; 5 cos./95th, 364. Total, 4212 r. and f., say 4800 of all ranks. The deserters above mentioned were probably men enlisted from among the French prisoners of war,—a most dangerous and foolish practice if the recruits were of French nationality.

[2] Sec. of State to Craufurd (secret), 30th Oct. 1806 (two letters).

could proclaim, especially in the face of Popham's raid, that he came to afford protection and not to take booty, and at the same time give no assurances to the population that the protection would be more than temporary. Military officers by incapacity and misjudgment have frequently placed Ministers in situations of cruel difficulty, but it may be doubted whether any General has ever set them a task quite so impossible as that prescribed, not in the doubt and turmoil of a campaign but in the tranquillity of the closet, by Windham to Craufurd. 1806.

However, this expedition to Chile by no means exhausted the projects of the Ministry for South America. Lord Grenville, of all men, who had so far maintained his sobriety, came forward at about this same time with a plan for an attack upon Mexico from both sides; from the east with six thousand European and half as many black troops; from the west by a thousand Europeans and four thousand Sepoys from India, who should first attack Manilla and thence proceed to Acapulco. "The objection obviously is," he wrote with a candid self-criticism that is infinitely ludicrous, "that these two attacks cannot correspond exactly in point of time"; but none the less he was inclined to risk the eastern expedition alone rather than delay it. Accordingly Sir Arthur Wellesley was directed in November to report upon the matter and to draw up plans of operations, which he duly did at great length,[1] discussing further the feasibility of an attack upon Venezuela. The irony of the whole situation was heightened by the fact that in June Miranda had returned to the British West Indies from an abortive attempt to excite a revolution at Caracas, and had begged men, arms, and ammunition from General Bowyer at Barbados. Bowyer very properly refused to have anything to do with him; but Miranda, who was nothing if not persistent, contrived to make his way again to Caracas, where he published on the 2nd of August

[1] Wellington, *Suppl. Desp.* vi. pp. 35-61.

1806. an impudent proclamation that he had come to fight "for the independence of the Venezuelans under the auspices and protection of the British fleet." This done, he wrote to Sir Eyre Coote at Jamaica for any assistance that could be afforded. Coote, like Bowyer, declined to send him anything, and in November the Secretary of State wrote to approve of Coote's action.[1] To judge by appearances, therefore, the audacious greed of a Commodore had sufficed to throw the entire Ministry off its balance, so that it swayed to and fro, in hopeless vacillation, between the expediency either of devoting all the strength of England to the conquest of South America, or of leaving that continent wholly untouched.

Fortunately Grenville's wild idea was abandoned; though Craufurd's force, after long delay, sailed from Falmouth amid much curiosity as to its destination. Some of the troops had already been embarked for months, but by the care of their officers they were in good health; and Craufurd before sailing examined every ship minutely himself, giving liberal orders for all articles that could contribute to the comfort of the men. The whole convoy numbered forty sail of transports and merchantmen,[2] and was escorted by four ships of the line and as many smaller vessels under Commodore Stopford; but this squadron was to be replaced before the end of the voyage by a fleet under Admiral Murray, who was the naval commander-in-
Dec. 14. chief of the expedition. On the 14th of December the fleet anchored at Porto Praya in the Cape de Verde Islands, to await the arrival of Murray. Three
1807. weeks passed without a sign of the Admiral; and on
Jan. 6. the 6th of January Craufurd, pursuant to his orders, sent off the Ninth Light Dragoons, under convoy of a
Jan. 7. frigate, to Rio de la Plata. On the following day he represented to the Commodore that Government had

[1] Bowyer to Sec. of State, 20th June; Coote to Sec. of State, 26th August; Sec. of State to Coote, 6th Nov. 1806.

[2] The 9th L.D. sailed with this convoy.

particularly urged haste upon him, and proposed that, 1807.
unless Murray should come in by the 11th, Stopford should escort him on to the Cape of Good Hope.[1] Stopford agreed; and accordingly on the 11th the squadron, less two ships of the line which returned Jan. 11.
home, weighed anchor, and on the 23rd of February reached Table Bay. Feb. 23.
Here Admiral Murray, who had left Porto Praya after Craufurd's departure, was already expecting his arrival impatiently; for new orders had just come in from England. Vague reports of the recapture of Buenos Ayres had penetrated to London by way of Lisbon on the 2nd of January; and a swift sailing vessel had been sent forward to the Cape to direct Murray and Craufurd to proceed straight to Rio de la Plata. To Auchmuty[2] likewise were now sent definite orders to recover the territory of Buenos Ayres, and, only after that object had been accomplished, to despatch Craufurd to fulfil his original mission.

Meanwhile Auchmuty himself after a weary voyage had at last reached Maldonado on the 5th of January. Jan. 5.
His transports being bad sailers, he had been obliged to put into Rio Janeiro for water; and, having there heard of the recapture of Buenos Ayres and of the occupation of Maldonado by a force of unknown strength, he was prepared for the possibility of unpleasant news on his arrival. Nothing, however, was yet amiss with Backhouse, though his provisions were becoming scanty and the difficulty of obtaining them was very seriously increased. The enemy kept four hundred horse perpetually hovering round Maldonado, and these troops had become extremely troublesome. They were armed with musket and sword, and their methods of warfare were such that the English dragoons, whose natural bulk added to a cumbrous equipment was far too heavy for the native horses, were powerless against them. "They ride up," wrote Auchmuty, "dismount, fire over the backs of

[1] Craufurd to Sec. of State, 11th Jan. 1807.
[2] Sec. of State to Auchmuty, 3rd Jan. 1807.

1807. their horses, mount and gallop off. All the inhabitants are accustomed to this sort of warfare, and every inhabitant is an enemy."[1] The prospect was not cheering. Feeling himself too weak to attempt Buenos Ayres, Auchmuty, after consultation with Admiral Stirling, who had come out with him to supersede Popham,[2] decided that the only possible enterprise was an attack upon Monte Video. This, however, was no easy matter. Four twenty-five pounders had indeed been sent with him, but no battering-train, no ammunition, no sappers, no military artificers, very few entrenching tools, and only one subaltern of engineers. All material for a siege had to be drawn from the ships; and Popham's squadron had already expended much of its powder. But there was
Jan. 13. no help for it. Auchmuty on the 13th evacuated Maldonado, leaving a small garrison on the island of Goretti; and sailing up the river landed on the morn-
Jan. 16. ing of the 16th in a little bay, west of the Caretas rocks, about nine miles below Monte Video. The Spaniards, though assembled in force and with guns in position, made little attempt to oppose the disembarkation, few being bold enough to face the fire of the ships. Auchmuty was thus able to post his army strongly about a mile from the shore in order to cover the landing of supplies and stores; and on
Jan. 19. the 19th he advanced upon the city. A force of four thousand mounted men offered a feeble resistance to him, but was speedily brushed away; and the fugitives seem to have carried panic with them, for on the same evening the suburbs of Monte Video were evacuated. Auchmuty, while halting his main body for the night two miles from the citadel, pushed his advanced posts forward almost to the walls. In

[1] Auchmuty to Sec. of State, 7th Feb. 1807.

[2] The Admiralty, which did not love Popham, carried its resentment against him so far as to leave him to pay for his own passage home in a merchant brig. Colburne's *Military Magazine*, August 1836, p. 491.

this position he was attacked next morning by a force 1807. of six thousand men with several guns. They advanced Jan. 20. in two columns, the right consisting of cavalry, which threatened to turn his left flank; while the left, made up of infantry, assailed his left centre. The infantry was checked by a picquet of four hundred men, which held its own until reinforced by three companies of the Fortieth. But the Spanish foot refused to yield to a charge of this little body until the Rifles and Light companies fell upon their flank, when they gave way and were pursued with great slaughter into the town. From two to three hundred Spaniards were killed and as many taken; and the cavalry, seeing the fate of their comrades, at once retired, leaving Auchmuty free to invest the city without the slightest further molestation.

Monte Video stands on a rocky ridge of distinct formation from the land around it, and at that time covered no more than a peninsula measuring about a mile north and south by a mile and a half east and west. Surrounded by water on three sides, it was fortified upon those sides with a series of thirteen very heavy seaward batteries, which were built to suit the configuration of the ground and were connected by a covered way. All were difficult of approach owing to the rocky nature of the shore; the most important of them were covered by a small enclosed fort, called after St. Philip, at the north-western angle of the peninsula; and the only landing-place was on the northern front, at a stone pier within the harbour. On the east or landward side the city receded from the water on each flank in such manner as to form a great salient angle, of which the southern face was about a thousand yards long, and the northern about twelve hundred. The landward front had been originally protected only by a stone wall some four feet thick and fifteen feet high, but to this had been added, at the point of the salient angle, a square fort with four bastions, whereof the face towards the country was further covered by a ditch and a small ravelin. The whole was revetted with brick,

1807. and possessed no entrance except from within the town over a small drawbridge. On each flank of this fort were two demi-bastions, mounting heavy ordnance; and beyond these again, at a distance of about three hundred yards, stood two more demi-bastions, that on the north side mounting fourteen, and that on the south side seven guns. The entrances to the town were two: the north gate between the citadel and the fourteen-gun battery; and the south gate, about one hundred yards from the river, being strongly protected not only by the cannon of the seven-gun battery but by two heavy guns in a round tower near the water. Altogether the defences of Monte Video showed one hundred and thirteen pieces of artillery, twenty-four of them in the citadel, and over forty more on the landward face. The works, contrary to the information furnished to Auchmuty, were in excellent repair; and in their vicinity the rock was so close to the surface that ordinary entrenching tools were useless. The garrison numbered six thousand brave but imperfectly trained men. Auchmuty's numbers were slightly superior, but his troops were by no means all of the first class. The Forty-seventh was in indifferent order; the company of the Seventy-first consisted of mere children; and Auchmuty could only describe the Eighty-seventh as fine boys. The Thirty-eighth, Fortieth, and Seventeenth Light Dragoons were, however, excellent; and it was on them, together with the seamen and marines, that Auchmuty depended chiefly for success in a hazardous enterprise.[1]

[1] Auchmuty to C.-in C., 6th Feb. 1807.

The force was brigaded as follows:—

Cavalry Brigade. Col. Lloyd, 17th L.D.; 17th, 20th, 21st L.D. 959 sabres.

1st Infantry Brigade. Col. Browne, 40th; 38th, 40th, 87th, and 3 cos. of 95th.

2nd Infantry Brigade. Brig.-gen. Lumley; 47th, 1 co./71st, naval batt. (800) L.I. cos. of infantry regiments.

R.A. 123 men with 6 guns.

Total. 5632 r. and f., say 6300 of all ranks.

Admiral Stirling had generally 1400 men ashore, and his flag-ship

The General's first task was to land his own heavy guns and several others borrowed from the broadsides of the fleet, the latter of which, owing to the small size of their wheels, were a source of much trouble. Meanwhile the scattered buildings outside the northern front were cleared away, the largest only being left standing in order to cover the erection of the first batteries, namely one of four twenty-four pounders and another of two mortars, against the citadel. On the 23rd an additional battery of two guns was constructed with the object (which was not attained) of preventing the enemy's gunboats from bringing stores, supplies, and even water into the town from the other side of the harbour. On the 25th the four-gun and mortar batteries opened fire, while the smaller vessels stood in to cannonade the town; but the attack produced no appreciable effect either on the works or on the spirit of the inhabitants. On the 28th, therefore, another battery of six guns was established against the citadel, which soon knocked the parapet to pieces, but left the ramparts little injured. The supply of powder now began to run short, and Auchmuty, as a last resource, threw up another battery of six guns within six hundred yards of the works, in the hope of breaching the wall close to the south gate. By the 2nd of February the breach was reported to be practicable, and since a hostile force of four thousand men was said to be approaching, Auchmuty summoned the Governor to surrender. He was answered by defiance, and resolved to assault before dawn on the morrow. The forlorn hope consisted chiefly of men of the Fifty-fourth under a sergeant of the Thirty-eighth and Lieutenant Everard of the Queen's, who, though attached to the Thirty-eighth, claimed the privilege as belonging to the senior regiment. Two companies of Rifles, the flank-battalions, and Thirty-eighth were to follow them, with the Fortieth in support. One company of Rifles

1807. Jan. 23. Jan. 25. Jan. 28. Feb. 2.

was frequently left with only thirty men aboard. Stirling to Admiralty, 8th Feb. 1807.

1807. and the Eighty-seventh were posted by the north gate, which was to be opened for them by the other column. The remainder of the troops were held in reserve against the possible arrival of a relieving force from without.

Feb. 3. At three o'clock, in extreme darkness, the attacking column stole out towards the breach, arriving close to it before it was discovered. The first discharge of the enemy's guns struck down only one man, but the second laid low twenty-five men out of thirty who were following in immediate support; and the leaders, on arriving at the breach, mistook it for the untouched wall and passed it by. In truth the enemy had so cunningly barricaded it by vast piles of hides, laid one upon another, that it was hardly practicable. For fifteen minutes the column wandered about under a very heavy fire, until at last Captain Renny of the light company of the Fortieth found the breach, and fell as he mounted it. With great difficulty, for the passage would admit but three men abreast, his soldiers forced their way to the summit and dropped from it twelve feet into the body of the place. Some then dashed into the town, while others turned to their left and carried in succession all the batteries round the place as far as Fort St. Philip. Even so, however, the Fortieth, which followed in support, also missed the breach, and passed twice under the fire of the batteries before they found it. Meanwhile the second column by the north gate grew impatient, and some of the Rifles, scaling the wall, forced the gate open to admit their comrades. The streets, which were laid out regularly at right angles, were defended by field-guns unlimbered at their heads ; but these were speedily captured and the town was cleared with the bayonet. The citadel still made a show of resistance, but some riflemen ascending the towers of the cathedral, which commanded the works, speedily made an end of it. At half-past eight the place surrendered at discretion ; and after some slight disorder, which was easily repressed, the troops were so thoroughly under control that within a few hours the 1807. inhabitants were walking as usual about the streets.

The enemy's loss in the assault was very heavy. About eight hundred were killed, five hundred wounded, and two thousand taken prisoners, the remainder escaping across the harbour in boats, unmolested by the British squadron. The British casualties also were not light—six officers and one hundred and ten men killed; twenty-one officers and two hundred and fifty-eight men wounded. The Light Battalion, with sixty-three killed and eighty-four wounded out of four or five companies, suffered most heavily, and next to them the Thirty-eighth with twenty-seven killed and one hundred and twenty-one wounded. In this regiment alone nine officers were struck down, three of them by mortal hurts. It was noticed that, in the case of wounds of the lower extremities, tetanus invariably supervened, with fatal results; and to this cause were due the deaths of Colonel Brownrigg and Colonel Vassall, the excellent commanding officers of the Light Battalion and Thirty-eighth. Altogether the action was creditable to Auchmuty and to his troops, for the cross-fire upon the breach from the uninjured batteries on each flank was terrific, and would have daunted any but good and resolute soldiers. In fact, but that the shortness of the range prevented the enemy's grape-shot and canister from scattering,[1] the attack would very probably have failed.

The losses of the British during the siege had been trifling, and those in the preliminary operations had not amounted to one hundred and fifty; but Auchmuty, none the less, felt powerless to do more until Craufurd's detachment should arrive. On the 6th a welcome Feb. 6. reinforcement appeared in the shape of the Ninth Light Dragoons, which had been sent forward, as has been already related, from Porto Praya; but this in itself was insufficient. The population was to all appearance inveterately hostile; and the only operation which

[1] Colburne's *Military Magazine, loc. citat.*

1807. might possibly alter its attitude was the capture of Buenos Ayres. But even if this were successfully accomplished, six thousand men were too few at once to hold Monte Video and to occupy a capital of sixty to seventy thousand inhabitants. The province, moreover, continued to be unquiet. In Buenos Ayres the revolutionary party had installed General Liniers as Governor; and the Spanish Viceroy, who was hovering near Monte Video with a small force and watching Auchmuty's movements, was seized by emissaries of this party and carried prisoner to the capital. Convinced by this that the inhabitants, however hostile to the British, were still more hostile to Spain, the General was about to invite them to throw off Spanish rule and accept that of King George, when he was surprised by the sudden appearance of Beresford and Pack who, by the help of two South American gentlemen, had contrived to escape, while travelling inland towards their appointed place of confinement. Beresford declined to take the command from Auchmuty, and prepared to go home; but he was able first to assure him that, though the party which was friendly to England was strong, it looked, none the less, above all things for independence, and would not accept British rule except with a proviso that the country should not be handed back to Spain upon a peace. This being the one pledge that Auchmuty was unable to give, his overtures naturally came to nothing. To strengthen his position, therefore, he occupied Colonia del Sacramento on the north shore over against Buenos Ayres, kept small columns in movement around Monte Video to preserve order and bring in supplies, and possessed his soul in patience until reinforcements should arrive.[1]

Meanwhile the British Cabinet, looking to the diversion of Craufurd's force to Rio de la Plata and to the steady accumulation of troops in that quarter from England and the Cape, decided to send out a senior officer to take command of the whole. One member at

[1] Auchmuty to Sec. of State, 6th, 20th March 1807.

least of the Cabinet would have been content to leave 1807.
Auchmuty in charge of the entire army;[1] but it was always possible that Beresford might have been released through Auchmuty's operations, in which case the supreme direction would have fallen to him. Upon the whole, therefore, Windham was probably right to send out a new commander-in-chief; for Beresford, whether or not through his own fault, had not been very successful, and nothing was yet known of Auchmuty's acquittal of himself in this his first independent command. The choice fell upon Lieutenant-general John Whitelocke, an officer who was last seen by us at St. Domingo in 1794, and who had since been Inspector-general of Recruiting. The reasons for this selection are not very obvious. Windham personally wished to appoint either Sir John Stuart, who was just returned clothed in the glory of Maida, or Robert Craufurd; but the Duke of York very properly objected to both, Stuart being such a man as we know, and Craufurd so junior an officer that he could not have passed over Auchmuty's head. Lord Grenville proposed Sir George Prevost, who had shown most admirable spirit and resource in Dominica on the occasion of Villeneuve's raid in 1805. Finally Lord Granville Leveson-Gower, who was not in the Cabinet, suggested Whitelocke,[2] possibly with a view to gaining the appointment of a kinsman as his second in command; and Whitelocke was finally chosen. It is not easy, after the misfortunes that subsequently befell the man, to form an opinion as to Whitelocke's ability; but he had certainly done good service in the West Indies, and was not without knowledge of his profession. His most objectionable characteristic seems to have been arrogant but spasmodic self-confidence, with an affectation of coarse speech and manners which he conceived to be soldier-like bluntness, but which often degenerated into mere rudeness towards some of his inferiors and familiar obscenity of language towards others. He

[1] *Courts and Cabinets of Geo. III.*, iv. 123.
[2] Windham's *Diary*, p. 497.

1807. stooped to court the favour of the rank and file by affected use of their phrases, with the inevitable result that he earned only their thorough contempt.[1] The inference is that he sought popularity with the lower ranks of the Army because he was unable to gain the respect of the higher. Such an officer is wholly unfit for any command.

The only additional force sent out with Whitelocke was a single battalion—the Eighty-ninth—a draft of five hundred recruits, and one battery of Horse-Artillery, altogether about eighteen hundred men of all ranks. His instructions directed him simply to reduce the province of Buenos Ayres; but the object of his enterprise was defined to be, not so much to annoy or distress the enemy, as to occupy such stations or territory as could most easily be captured and would not require a larger garrison than eight thousand men. It was still uncertain whether Craufurd had received his orders to sail to Rio de la Plata; but Auchmuty's troops, added to the eighteen hundred men now despatched with Whitelocke, were considered sufficient to capture Buenos Ayres and to enforce the recovery of Beresford and of his fellow-prisoners. Finally it was intimated to Whitelocke that he might raise native troops, if he thought proper, and that if Buenos Ayres were mastered, he was to be civil Governor of the province, with a salary of £4000 a year from the provincial revenues.[2]

The General sailed accordingly in the *Thisbe* frigate at the end of March, and reached Monte Video on the
May 10. 10th of May after a voyage of nine weeks. He found all well with Auchmuty. An attempt had been made
April 22. on the 22nd of April to surprise Pack's detachment at Colonia, but this had been foiled with trifling loss, and all was quiet. On the other hand, neither Craufurd nor the reinforcements from England had arrived; and Whitelocke decided to await their coming before attacking Buenos Ayres, devoting himself meanwhile to

[1] Colburne's *Military Magazine*, *loc. citat.*
[2] Windham to Whitelocke (secret), 6th March 1807.

preparations for an advance. These were not easily accomplished. In spite of all exertions, horses enough could not be procured for the guns and cavalry. Such as were obtained were unbroken, and soon sank under the burden of unwonted work and insufficient food; for it was midwinter south of the line, when the native grass contained little nourishment and no other description of forage was obtainable. At last, on the 30th of May, Craufurd's detachment was reported to be off the mouth of the river. On arriving at Table Bay on the 23rd of March, he had agreed with Admiral Murray to sail in ten days, as soon as the transports should have been victualled and watered; and in fact the armament actually sailed on the 6th of April, reached St. Helena on the 21st, and, after taking in water, set off again on the 26th. But even on the 30th of May Craufurd's voyage was not nearly over. Fogs and contrary winds delayed him in the river, and not till the 14th of June did the whole of the transports reach Monte Video. By that time some of the troops had been on board ship for nine full months.

1807. May 30. June 14.

Meanwhile the enemy was collecting reinforcements to cut off or attack Pack's isolated troops at Colonia; and Whitelocke had found it necessary to reinforce the post to a strength of some fifteen hundred men. On the evening of the 6th Pack received intelligence of a body of the enemy encamped at San Pedro, some twelve miles away, under the command of General Elio, an officer lately arrived from Spain. Starting at three o'clock on the next morning with a force of about eleven hundred men of all ranks[1] Pack came upon Elio at seven o'clock, and found him securely posted on rising ground, with a deep and marshy stream covering his front and both flanks, and the only ford defended by four field-guns and two howitzers. He decided to attack at once. The troops therefore crossed the ford

June 6. June 7.

[1] 9th L.D., 54; R.A., 31; 40th, 481; 95th, 200; Light companies, 247. The detachment at Colonia consisted of 9th L.D., 40th, 3 cos. /95th, 3 cos. L.I.

1807. June 7. on a very narrow front, waist deep in water, formed up on the further side, always under heavy fire of artillery, and advanced to the attack without firing a shot. The enemy's cavalry fled at once, but the infantry stood until the British were within a few paces, when they suddenly broke and were pursued with heavy slaughter. They left on the field one hundred and twenty dead, as many wounded, over one hundred prisoners and eight guns, while Pack's casualties did not exceed forty-eight, nearly one-third of which were due to the accidental explosion of an ammunition-waggon.

Now, therefore, it was for Whitelocke to determine upon his plan of campaign; and in order to do so he had first to decide some very difficult questions. That his first object must be to capture Buenos Ayres there was no doubt; and there was equally no doubt that the brunt of the work must fall upon the Army, for the river near the shore was so shallow that the men-of-war could not approach nearer than to within six to eight miles of the city. First, therefore, a place of disembarkation must be selected; and the investigations of the Navy soon narrowed the choice down to a single point. Above Buenos Ayres the navigation was too difficult and intricate for a fleet of transports; below it there was but one place where an army could be disembarked under cover of the ships of war, namely Enseñada de Barragon, some twenty-four miles below the city. If the protection of the fleet during the disembarkation were dispensed with, there was the Point of Quilmes, where Beresford had landed, which possessed the advantage of lying within eight miles, as the crow flies, from Buenos Ayres; but reconnaissance showed that a battery had been erected to command the passage through the marsh, and so to foil any future attempts similar to Beresford's. It was therefore no reproach to Whitelocke that he fixed upon Enseñada for his landing-place.

Next, how was the march from the strand to the city to be accomplished? The shore from Enseñada to

Buenos Ayres to a distance of two to four miles inland 1807. is but two feet above the level of the river, and in the rainy season was almost entirely under water.[1] Beyond this marshy ground the land rises gradually to a height of twelve or fifteen feet; and this higher tract extends westward, broken only by a multitude of little streams, as far as the village of Reduction, where another wet level, running far up the country, is interposed between that village and the capital. Through this level runs the little river Chuelo, over which the wooden bridge, which had been destroyed on the occasion of Beresford's landing, had been replaced. Little, however, was known or could be learned of the country, except of that portion of it which had been traversed by Beresford between Point Quilmes and Buenos Ayres. The few colonists of Monte Video friendly to the British knew nothing of the opposite shore over one hundred miles away; and little more was to be learned at Colonia, which lies indeed over against Buenos Ayres, but rather remoter from it than is Calais from Dover. Such vague information as could be collected amounted to this. From Enseñada to Reduction the distance was twenty miles; and from Reduction to the capital nine miles more. There were three different roads—one on the sands, a second through the marsh, and a third, which was the best, on the heights. To reach this last some marshy ground must be passed, which was reported to be always practicable for a coach, and to be commonly traversed by the waggons of the country; but, the heights once gained, the road was firm and good. From Reduction the high road crossed the Chuelo by the bridge; but by making a detour the head of the river could be turned. There were few farm-houses on the road, and the troops could expect little shelter short of the suburbs of Buenos Ayres. As to fuel, it was not to be found except in human dwellings, for there was not a tree to be seen for miles. With regard to supplies, the plain swarmed with cattle, which

[1] *An Authentic Narrative*, etc., p. 183.

1807. could be caught by the native lasso-men, but there could be no certainty of finding bread-stuffs in any quantity until Buenos Ayres was reached. Such details as the extent and condition of the swamps behind Enseñada and the obstacles, excepting the Chuelo, that lay on the road, were utterly unknown. It may be urged that Whitelocke should have sent an officer to explore the route; but it is extremely doubtful whether this would have been possible. The population was bitterly hostile. There were indeed a few British officers who could speak Spanish, but probably not one who could have successfully disguised himself. Had such an one travelled alone the country, the people would have made little of cutting his throat;[1] had he taken an escort, it would have been quickly surrounded by superior numbers and overpowered. Possibly it might have been practicable to bribe a priest to go as travelling companion with a reconnoitring officer, but even then it would not have been safe to trust the priest. At any rate no such thing was done, and no reconnaissance of the landing-place or line of march was made.

Then came the question of transport. Horses, as has been told, were difficult to procure; and those that had been obtained were for the most part unbroken and in any case too weak for any but the lightest work. In a campaign where cavalry was all-important and where the equivalent of three strong regiments of British dragoons was on the spot, Whitelocke found it impossible to mount more than two squadrons. It was therefore evident that the men must carry rations for three days upon their backs, and that, upon the occupation of Reduction, communication with the fleet must be opened at Point Quilmes in order to draw fresh supplies from the ships. So entirely was this necessity accepted by Whitelocke that he gave no orders to the commissariat to provide animals for purposes of transport. The only means of carriage that were provided,

[1] *An Authentic Narrative*, p. 189.

therefore, consisted of half-a-dozen small mule-carts to 1807.
bear supplies from the water's edge to any chosen depôt; and it was not until the ships actually anchored before Enseñada that the Commissary, according to his own account, realised that the army was to be landed not five miles, but more nearly thirty miles, from Buenos Ayres.

Next arose the question of the time for the attack, which was most difficult to decide. The rainy season was immediately at hand and, though implying no such deluge as the monsoon in India, signified none the less a heavy though intermittent rainfall, which would cause much sickness among the men if they were long exposed to the weather, with great gales which would impede the operations of small craft in the river. Good fortune might or might not delay the rains until the army reached Buenos Ayres; but it was only reasonable to expect that, if Whitelocke deferred his operations until the rains ceased, the enemy would take advantage of the respite to convert Buenos Ayres from an open into a fortified town. On the other hand, Craufurd's detachment, which constituted fully one-half of the effective force, had been on board ship for quite nine months, and some of the corps for even longer; and it was certain that these men, after being cooped up and lowered by marine diet and lime-juice, would be weak, an easy prey to sickness, and wholly unfit to undergo immediately the hardships of a campaign. Colonel Denis Pack, who had been in the country for a year, was strongly of opinion that the operations should be delayed, but Whitelocke never consulted him upon the point, and Pack therefore kept his ideas to himself.[1] If, however, the army remained on the left bank of the river, Whitelocke was apprehensive lest he should be unable to feed during the winter so large a force as that which he commanded; and for this and other reasons he decided to open the attack at once.[2] In support of this view of Whitelocke's, Leveson-Gower wrote to Windham on July 9 that

[1] C.-M., p. 423.

[2] *Ibid.* p. 23.

1807. the army on arrival, though not positively pressed for victuals, was so short of flour that, in order to provide twenty-one days' bread, it was necessary to use a ship-load of flour sent from the Cape at Auchmuty's request. This difficulty, however, could probably have been overcome; for Auchmuty had twice written to England for flour, on the 7th of February and 20th of March, so that a supply was to be expected from thence very shortly.

There remained one minor point to be settled before the campaign was opened. Should Colonia be held as well as Monte Video, and converted into an advanced base of operations and a second fortified station upon the river La Plata; or should it be abandoned? Whitelocke seems to have left the determination of this matter to Leveson-Gower, who was sent to Colonia with discretionary orders to hold the place, if it could be safely retained with a diminished garrison, or to evacuate it. Auchmuty and Pack were in favour of keeping a garrison in Colonia, since, among other advantages, it would have facilitated the collection of a supply of cattle for the army; but they were not consulted.[1] Leveson-Gower, after a short survey, destroyed the guns of the place and withdrew the troops from it to the main army. It seems that Whitelocke had some idea of transporting his main body to Colonia and keeping it there embarked until an advanced column should have occupied Reduction, and enabled Point Quilmes to be used as a place of disembarkation. This would have been a sensible plan; but it was promptly negatived by Leveson-Gower.

Meanwhile the army was formed into four brigades[2] under Auchmuty, Lumley, Craufurd, and Mahon; and a garrison of thirteen hundred rank and file was set

[1] C.-M., pp. 198, 205.

[2] Brig.-Gen. Sir S. Auchmuty's brigade: 5th, 38th, 87th.
Brig.-Gen. Craufurd's brigade: 9 cos. L.I., 95th (8 cos.).
Brig.-Gen. Lumley's brigade: 17th L.D., 36th, 88th.
Col. Mahon's brigade: 2 sq. 6th D.G., 9th L.D. (both dismounted), 40th, 45th.

apart for Monte Video, consisting of two companies of 1807. the Thirty-eighth, the Forty-seventh, the detachments of the Twentieth and Twenty-first Light Dragoons, some Marines and a Local Militia. Here may be seen the signs of an unpractical mind in the Commander-in-chief. The Forty-seventh, as Auchmuty had reported, was not in the best order, and its commander not the most brilliant of officers, but at least it was in condition for marching and had experience of active service. The Thirty-eighth, again, was an admirable corps; and it was mere waste of good material to relegate two of its companies to idleness; indeed, the proceeding was at the time ascribed to the Commander-in-chief's spite against an officer of that regiment.[1] The Twentieth and Twenty-first Light Dragoons had also been for some time in the country and were ready for work. On the other hand, the rank and file of the Eighty-eighth, though good, were very young; and this regiment, with its travelling companions the Thirty-sixth and the four troops of Carabiniers, was certain to suffer greatly from fatigue after nine months on board ship. Nevertheless these were chosen for the attack on Buenos Ayres; and the Carabiniers, encumbered with their white leather breeches and jack-boots, were provided with muskets to convert them into infantry, while the seasoned and hardened corps which had been for months in the country were left to walk about Monte Video. Lastly, Leveson-Gower had contrived to quarrel bitterly with the cavalry by ordering wholesale and quite unnecessary destruction of all the spare clothes and equipment that the regiments had in store;[2] and altogether the force was not in the best of tempers when it started upon its campaign.

[1] This officer, Lord Muskerry, was the one person in the army who knew something of the country between Enseñada and Buenos Ayres; and he had declared that no one but a madman would land at Enseñada in midwinter. Whitelocke, therefore, left two companies of his regiment at Monte Video, and put Lord Muskerry in command of them. Colburne's *Military Magazine*, October 1836, p. 213.

[2] C.-M., pp. 162, 165.

CHAPTER XIII

1807. CONTRARY winds delayed the departure of the troops
from Monte Video; and the first division was not under
way until the 17th of June, nor anchored off Colonia
June 24. until the 24th. Gower joined this corps in the evening
and hurried Pack's garrison on board its transports; but
June 26. fog prevented the convoy from sailing until the 26th,
when it met the remainder of the army standing up the
June 27. river for Enseñada. On the following day the gunboats
of the fleet were each of them armed with an eighteen-pounder at the bows; the Light Brigade under Craufurd
was transferred to vessels of light draught; and orders
were issued verbally, but not in writing, for the troops
to be ready to disembark on the next morning, every
June 28. man with cooked rations for three days. Accordingly at daylight on Sunday the 28th of June the disembarkation began. A long bar of sand obstructed the approach to the shore, and the Light Brigade was compelled to wade for some distance to reach it; but later on a passage through the bar was found, which enabled the rest of the troops to be landed perfectly dry. No resistance was made to the disembarkation which, owing to the narrowness of the channel of access, was not completed until dark; and no sign of an enemy was seen. Gower had received orders to push inland, with an advanced corps consisting of Craufurd's brigade, the Thirty-eighth and Eighty-seventh, to the heights about four miles distant, which he duly did, arriving on his ground at one o'clock in the afternoon. This, it may be added, was the beginning of a general

derangement of all the organisation prescribed a few days before. Four of the eight companies of the Ninety-fifth were taken from Craufurd and transferred to the main body under Whitelocke; and Auchmuty was left disconsolate on the shore with one battalion only of his brigade, namely, the Fifth, which though in excellent order had, even as the four[1] companies of the Ninety-fifth, only just been released from three-quarters of a year on board ship. 1807.

On the following day the main body advanced from the shore, and then the chapter of surprises was opened in earnest. Between the strand and the heights lay a swamp, nowhere less than two feet deep in water, which extended for a distance of fully two miles. Gower on the previous day had found what was pointed out to him as the usual road through it, and in attempting to discover a better track had several times experienced the greatest difficulty in extricating his horse from the slough. Moreover, the foundation, being not of sand but of earth, grew steadily worse with the trampling of many feet; and the passage was far more difficult for the rear of his column than it had been for the van. Into this sea of black liquid mud the six thousand men of the main body now plunged in a narrow column, and floundered forward, tripping over reeds and aquatic plants, and reeling over the treacherous bottom as best they could. It was trying and fatiguing work; but all ranks seem to have accepted it as a good joke, and to have taken care by judicious splashing that no man should emerge in a less filthy condition than his neighbour. But a great deal of the food carried by the men was rendered uneatable by water; the guns stuck fast; and the defects of the commissariat were found out within an hour. June 29.

Whitelocke had ordered his Commissary to land three days' rations of biscuit and spirits, which was done

[1] Five companies of the 95th came with Craufurd. They had been for *eleven* months on board ship, and one at least of them must have remained with the advanced party.

1807. on the same day; but neither General nor staff had taken the trouble to inform the Commissary that sixty pack-saddles had been brought forward to transport these supplies, and that, if need were, sixty men of the Seventeenth Light Dragoons would be dismounted to furnish the necessary horses. The Commissary, by no means in an unruffled spirit,[1] applied to Colonel Bourke, the Quartermaster-general, for means of carriage; the
June 30. pack-saddles and horses were landed on the same day; and on the morrow the work of loading began. At once there ensued a scene of wild confusion. The unbroken horses not unnaturally would not endure the saddles, but kicked and plunged in all directions. Several broke away and were never seen again; others dashed off with their saddles only, but without their load; and, altogether, of some eight tons of biscuit disembarked, about one ton was forwarded to the army, a small quantity was re-embarked, but the greater proportion was lost or ruined in the swamp. Attempts to bring forward the rum in the mule-carts were equally fruitless. The wheels stuck fast and could not be moved; and the Commissary was fain to stave in the casks where they lay, and to abandon their contents also to the all-devouring swamp.

Meanwhile the guns, although drawn each by six instead of the usual team of four horses, had remained in the swamp until late on the 29th, when most of them were extricated by some hundreds of seamen and soldiers. Sixteen in all had been landed, and of these five light pieces captured from the Spaniards were
June 29. spiked and abandoned. Whitelocke, on joining Gower that morning, gave him the Thirty-sixth and Eighty-eighth, which had just struggled through the swamp, in lieu of the Thirty-eighth and Eighty-seventh.[2] He then sent him forward for a few miles with these regiments, added to Craufurd's brigade, four six-pounders,

[1] The bitterness of Commissary Bullock against Whitelocke can be read between the lines of his evidence.

[2] C.-M., pp. 168, 192.

two three-pounders, and a handful of mounted men of 1807. the Seventeenth Light Dragoons; while the main body halted on the ground that Gower had occupied on the preceding night. Gower for his part so arranged his order of march that Lumley's brigade should always be three or four miles in rear of Craufurd's; the object being that the troops should find fuel and, to some extent, shelter at the few farm-houses that lay on the route to Buenos Ayres. The enemy, after the first day, hovered about the columns unceasingly, not daring to attack, but pouncing constantly upon every isolated man; and the mounted troops with the British force were so few, and grew daily so much fewer, owing to the collapse or escape of the native horses, that communication between the different bodies was impossible. What Leveson-Gower did in detail for his own division, Whitelocke, doubtless under his subordinate's advice, did for the whole army, with the result that the advanced corps led the way in two distinct bodies, and the main body followed likewise in two or three distinct corps, all without cohesion and without communication, and of course without power of mutual support. Strangely enough, though Popham, the greatest authority upon signalling in the Navy, had worked so long with the Army, no military officer had bethought him of introducing a code of visual signals for service in the field.

Gower, then, plodded forward to his appointed place, with directions not to advance further until the main body should come up; and Whitelocke, the swamp having been passed, gave orders for his own division to march at nine o'clock on the morning of the 30th. But now arose the awkward question of June 30. victuals. Owing to the procrastination of the General and the faulty work of his staff, many of the troops had never received the order to carry three days' provisions with them; owing to the march waist-deep through the swamp, much that the men had with them had been destroyed; and in any case the village of

1807. June 30. Reduction, where supplies could be again obtained from the fleet, was still two days' march distant. There was therefore every prospect that the force would be without food for at least one day and, if overtaken by any mishap, would be in a state of starvation. Auchmuty imparted his anxiety upon this head to Whitelocke who, after anathematising his chief supply-officer, complained that he was obliged to do the work of commissary and store-keeper as well as of General. "If a General does not himself attend to the supply of his troops, Sir," said Auchmuty, "they will often want provisions."

As it happened, a flock of sheep was discovered and driven in that morning; and Whitelocke delayed the time of marching, already fixed for the late hour of nine, in order that the men might take advantage of this windfall. But there was confusion and delay in the distribution. Many of the men received no meat; none had time to cook it; and the only real advantage of the delay was, that it enabled half a ration of biscuit to be served out from the scanty remnant which had been saved by the Commissary from the swamp. Then at last the army marched, leaving Mahon with a very few mounted and a great many dismounted men of the Seventeenth Light Dragoons, besides four companies of the Fortieth, to form a rear-guard and an escort for the artillery. Auchmuty's brigade led the main body, which halted at a farm a little before sunset; and Auchmuty was then sent forward for three or four miles, according to the fashion approved by Gower, with the Forty-fifth, Ninth Light Dragoons, Carabiniers, and four companies of the Ninety-fifth. These last two corps, it will be remembered, had arrived with Craufurd, so that there was every necessity to spare them any additional exertion. But such reasoning did not appeal to Whitelocke. He would dismount and march with the men, trying to exchange the slang of the barrack-room with them and receiving little response; but he was incapable of the incessant watchfulness over their comfort and the incessant care to save them unnecessary fatigue, which really endears a General to his troops. Had he given them a full ration that morning and promised them enough to eat on that night, the men would have known and trusted him to be their friend. 1807. June 30.

On overtaking Gower in the evening, Whitelocke urged him to make an effort to reach Reduction that night. Gower promised to do his best. The marches had been neither long nor severe, the ground on the heights being firm, with the exception of some small but deep streams with boggy bottoms, which from time to time crossed the line of march and immersed the men waist-deep. But want of food, and still more want of condition, had told heavily upon Lumley's brigade; and the folly of placing these unseasoned and immature troops in the advanced corps was now apparent. Whitelocke was eager to occupy Reduction in order to obtain supplies. If, in the first instance, he had given Lumley the troops which had been left behind at Monte Video, and if he had ordered Gower in the morning to make a bold push for Reduction at any cost, Gower would probably have reached it without difficulty, and all might have been well. But starting upon a night march, unfed after a long halt, Lumley's brigade simply collapsed; and after traversing three or four miles Gower halted, reporting to Whitelocke that if he went further he should be obliged to leave the whole of the Thirty-sixth and Eighty-eighth behind. Whitelocke approved of his action, and riding forward next morning was so much struck with the exhausted July 1. condition of the Eighty-eighth that he ordered the whole army to leave their blankets behind and to march on with their great-coats only. None the less he called upon them to make a great effort in order to go beyond Reduction towards the Chuelo, presumably with the object of securing the bridge. Lumley had taken the precaution to bring with him from Monte Video native lasso-men, who produced some bullocks on the morning

1807. July 1. of the 1st; but the men had no time to cook the meat, and they had received no bread, so that the young soldiers of the Eighty-eighth started in greater exhaustion than ever. Gower had hoped to pass the Chuelo by a ford on that day, but found it impossible; and the advanced corps, after a march of only fifteen miles, halted three miles beyond Reduction. Gower reported that he believed himself to be still five miles away from the river, and that, having observed a large fire at some distance away, he imagined that the bridge had been destroyed. Meanwhile at a little before sunset the main body moved up to the village of Reduction itself, and there halted for the night.

At last, therefore, the coveted goal was reached. Communication could be resumed with the fleet; but there were still two miles of morass between the village and Point Quilmes over which every ounce of provisions must be carried. Whitelocke in the course of the evening decided to halt during the next day, with the object at once of making a personal reconnaissance of the fords of the Chuelo, of procuring bread and spirits from the fleet, and of allowing Mahon to bring forward the artillery which was still in the rear. Thereupon parties were actually directed to go down to Point Quilmes to bring up supplies. A rest would have been very welcome, for the troops were much exhausted, not so much by the distance which they had traversed as by want of food and by unnecessary and injudicious halts during the march. At 2 o'clock on
July 2. the morning of the 2nd, however, Whitelocke altered his mind and dictated a letter to Gower, ordering him to proceed with the advanced corps, pass the Chuelo at the first ford which he should find practicable above the bridge, take up a position on the northern [1] suburbs of Buenos Ayres, open communication with the fleet, and send a summons to the Spanish commander to

[1] He called it the western side, but he meant the northern; the orientation of Buenos Ayres being incorrectly given in the contemporary maps.

surrender. The reason given by Whitelocke for this 1807.
sudden change of plan was that he was anxious to put July 2.
his troops into cantonments, a consideration which was perhaps pressed upon him by a heavy fall of rain during the night of the 1st. Bourke, his Quartermaster-general, protested against the decision, urging his extreme ignorance of the country and the necessity for reconnoitring the river; but Whitelocke was peremptory, and Bourke rode forward with the letter himself.

On receipt of the order Gower showed dissatisfaction, and not without reason. The Thirty-sixth was much fatigued and the Eighty-eighth, as he alleged, not only exhausted but unsteady. In fact the horsemen, which had hovered around him throughout his march, had become bolder than usual on the previous day, and had annoyed him much during the night. Bourke advised him to ride back and to state his objections to Whitelocke in person; but Gower answered that he had received a peremptory order and should obey it, though he still evinced great uneasiness as to the consequences. Bourke promised to report his misgivings to Whitelocke, adding that probably the advanced corps would be supported by the entire army, and thereupon rode back towards Reduction. Auchmuty had already approached Whitelocke that morning to represent the necessity of allowing the troops to rest at least for the day, pointing out that his own brigade was much fatigued, and that the advanced guard, judging by the number of stragglers left by Lumley's battalions in Reduction, was in a still worse plight. The General replied that his decision would depend upon a letter from Gower. Bourke in due time appeared and was greeted by the General with the question, "Well, does General Gower seem pleased with his orders?" Bourke presented Gower's letter, the chief point of which was an intimation of his resolve to keep to the high ground and cross the Chuelo either by marching round its source or by some practicable ford high up the stream; since

1807. July 2. by all reports the Paso Chico, which was the ford indicated by Whitelocke, was impracticable. Bourke then urged that, looking to the condition of the Eighty-eighth, some support should be given to the advanced corps, whereupon Whitelocke agreed to send Gower a battalion. Shortly afterwards, to the general astonishment, he ordered the entire army to march at once. Some oxen had been procured and slaughtered, and the meat was about to be cut up and distributed; but the men were commanded to leave it on the ground, and were not allowed to carry the pieces in their haversacks. Auchmuty remarked to the General that the troops had no provisions. "Don't you see that it is going to rain?" was the only reply; and at ten o'clock the starving army moved away.

Gower, for his part, had marched an hour earlier, so that his rear must have been at least four miles ahead of the main body. By this time his force was seriously diminished. The Light Battalion numbered under nine hundred men, and the Thirty-sixth and Eighty-eighth were reduced, owing to the multitude of men unable to march, to no more than one thousand bayonets jointly. The mounted troopers with him, who had never exceeded sixty, had shrunk to a mere handful in consequence of the break-down of the horses; and Gower was obliged to mount his two orderlies upon his own spare chargers. Experience had shown that, in the midst of the enemy's irregular horsemen, communication between the different divisions of the army was unsafe unless ensured by a force of the strength of a company. One of Gower's aide-de-camps had been captured while carrying his orders between the two advanced brigades, and another had been stabbed within three hundred yards of the line.[1] Gower had no information of the enemy's dispositions, except that they had erected powerful batteries to defend the

[1] Gower to Windham, 9th July 1807. Gower, however, omitted to mention that his two brigades were habitually four or five miles apart.

passage of the bridge on the Chuelo; and it was pretty 1807.
evident that Whitelocke intended him to turn the July 2.
defences of the river. But where he should discover a ford, what forces he might find opposed to him as he approached Buenos Ayres, and whether the main body was to remain halted or follow to support him—all these things were hidden from him. After a short time signs of the enemy could be seen on the other side of the Chuelo, and, after two or three hours, Whitelocke's division was also visible in the rear, apparently pursuing the same route as the advanced corps. The question of a ford by which to pass the Chuelo was, however, not so easily decided. The nearest was known as the Paso Chico, but this was represented to be very difficult; and Gower, as we have seen, had intimated to Bourke that he should seek another ford higher up the stream. Craufurd, whose brigade was as usual far ahead of Lumley's, after passing a brook called the Masiel, saw in his front a body of the enemy's horse which retired before him, and in its retirement appeared to have crossed the Chuelo. Gower therefore decided to follow them and found the Paso Chico open to him. The water was indeed more than waist-deep for the tallest man, but having a sound bottom, presented no difficulties which could not be overcome by care. Thus the principal obstacle in the way of the march to Buenos Ayres was passed with ease and safety.

Lumley's brigade reached the ford between two and three o'clock, just as Craufurd's left it. His two regiments were in a miserable state. The men had shown signs of exhaustion very shortly after they marched, and soon they were straggling in all directions, unable to keep up; yet even so Gower assigned to them the heavy work of taking four guns across the ford. Craufurd presently observing a body of the enemy in motion as if to take up a position upon the heights opposite the ford, asked Gower's permission to forestall them. He received for answer that he might

1807. July 2. go on and act as he thought best, and that Gower would support him with Lumley's brigade. Craufurd advanced accordingly, gained the heights unopposed, and marking signs of wavering in the enemy, decided to take advantage of their hesitation and move straight upon the town. Twice Gower sent him orders to halt, but Craufurd answered that in his opinion it was very desirable to proceed ; and proceed he did. He had arrived at a house, known to those concerned in the operations as White's house, about a mile outside the town on the west side, when Gower came in person to the head of the Light Brigade. The ground was extremely blind and intricate, covered with gardens, orchards, and high fences, so that the enemy, though suspected to be near at hand, was invisible. The brigade entered the angle of a large space, which was in fact the Corral or slaughter-yard of Buenos Ayres, and halted to allow its few field-pieces to come up. Many of the men were resting themselves by leaning against the house, when suddenly they were startled by the report of a single gun, followed by a heavy discharge of grape and round shot from all parts of the yard. For a moment the troops huddled themselves together. Gower spoke a few words to Craufurd, who, whatever their intent, interpreted them as an order to attack ; and the Light Brigade rushed forward with a cheer, in the form of a crescent, straight upon the guns. The Spaniards in dismay left their batteries and fled. Their infantry, which was lining the hedges, fled likewise, and the brigade pursued them hotly into the town, bayonetting several of the fugitives, until an order arrived from Gower, directing Craufurd to return to the Corral. The Brigadier answered by a message that he thought it would be advantageous to continue the pursuit into the town, and begged permission to do so. Gower replied by a second and peremptory order to return to the Corral, adding that the wounded men, who did not exceed forty, were liable to be cut off by straggling parties of the enemy. Reluctantly Craufurd obeyed.

Craufurd himself was of opinion that if he had been left alone he would have captured the town then and there. The enemy was in fact completely surprised. Their leaders had in the first place massed nine thousand men with over fifty guns to guard the bridge over the Chuelo, but, finding that Gower was avoiding the bridge, had sent about three thousand men to hold a ford below the Paso Chico, and a second column to observe the Paso Chico itself. Upon discovering that the British had crossed the river, the first column, led by General Liniers in person, was ordered to retire to the Corral, where it was routed by Craufurd; the second, afraid of being cut off, took a circuitous route to the south-western angle of the town; and the remainder, which had been left at the bridge, were subsequently called in, after spiking or destroying several guns which they were unable to bring away with them. Moreover, any preparations which had been made for defence of the town had been designed to meet an attack upon the northern face. From this it is evident that Whitelocke's plans were known to the Spaniards; for it will be remembered that he had given Gower orders to occupy the northern suburbs, intending himself to march round the northern side of the town and resume his communication with the fleet. Gower, however, was not without justification for his caution, quite apart from his rather absurd plea concerning the wounded men; for Lumley's brigade, which should have been close at hand, had vanished and was nowhere to be found.

1807. July 2.

Very soon after crossing the ford Lumley lost sight of the Light Brigade, and was obliged to follow it as best he could by conjecture. The men were lagging terribly, and, when the sound of firing was heard, they were unable to respond to their Brigadier's appeal to hurry on. Many dropped down on the road; and Lumley, seeing that he must leave half of his force behind him, hardened his heart and pushed on with as many men as could keep up. For a time he guided

1807. July 2. himself by the footprints of Craufurd's companies and by the sound of the firing; but the light began to fail, and presently he lost all trace of them. For an hour he wandered about, without an idea where to find his comrades, until, growing apprehensive of the danger that might await a crowd of weary men in a maze of narrow lanes, he wheeled his two regiments northward and by good fortune stumbled upon Craufurd's brigade just as it was about to retire. He then left outposts on the ground which Craufurd had occupied, and withdrew with him to the Corral, where both brigades bivouacked for the night.

But the disappearance of Lumley's brigade affected Gower far less than the fact that there was no sign of the main body of the army. Considering that he stood upon not the best of terms with Whitelocke, it is likely enough that Gower imputed to his chief that night a deliberate design to entangle him in difficulties. The suspicion was doubtless undeserved, though circumstances might seem to colour it. Whitelocke had duly marched at ten o'clock; he had sent a message to the Admiral to take the fleet as close as he could to the northern end of the town; and he had despatched orders to Mahon, who was on his way to Reduction, to follow him early on the next day. His guide had told him that he would find a good ford over the Chuelo six miles to south-westward, and had provided him with a peasant to show him the way, so that he felt easy and confident. Towards noon Gower's column was in sight about three miles away, moving in a direction at right angles to the march of the main body; but the guide, being consulted, declared that Whitelocke's column would take the same direction as soon as it had crossed the Masiel, and indicated the landmarks which showed the position of the ford. Whitelocke's troops accordingly passed the Masiel, and arrived between half-past two and three at two farm-houses. The advanced column was now out of sight. Whitelocke afterwards explained that, reckoning upon Gower's avoidance of the Paso Chico, he had made sure of overtaking the 1807. rear of his column; but that, having lost all trace of July 2. it and seeing no possibility of crossing the river that night, he turned to his Quartermaster-general and proposed to halt where he stood for the day. Bourke demurred, stating that unless orders were sent to Gower to halt also, the advanced corps would certainly proceed, pursuant to its instructions, to the northern suburbs of Buenos Ayres. Whitelocke hesitated, and as soon as Auchmuty came up, referred the question to him. Auchmuty, who wished to give his men food and rest, and for that reason had opposed the march of the morning, strongly advised a halt, pointing out that there were plenty of sheep close by and fuel wherewith to cook the meat. He was, it should be added, under the impression, which seems to have been shared by the army generally, that Gower's mission extended no further than to win the passage of the Chuelo;[1] and he knew nothing of Colonel Bourke's protest against leaving him unsupported. Whitelocke therefore sent a message back to Mahon, directing him to remain with the rear-guard at Reduction, and halted for the day. Towards evening he heard the sound of a cannonade near the city, but took no notice of it; and the army, which had been exhausted rather by bad management than by hard work, was left to enjoy the comforts of an early halt and a sufficiency of meat and fuel.

A little before daybreak on the 3rd, Whitelocke's July 3. division moved off, and reached a safe but exceedingly narrow ford over the Chuelo between nine and ten o'clock. The water being armpit-deep, it was one o'clock before every man had made the passage; but a mile and a half beyond the ford an officer from Gower met Whitelocke; and in another hour the entire force, with the exception of Mahon's detachment, was united on the west side of the town. Gower, in the morning, had sent a summons to Liniers to surrender Buenos

[1] C.-M., p. 202.

1807. July 3. Ayres, which had been defiantly rejected; and the British outposts had been engaged for most of the day, though with no incidents of any importance. It was true that the advanced corps had not taken up its position in the northern suburbs, as Whitelocke had directed, in order to open communication with the fleet; but it was too late to correct this fault at so late an hour of the afternoon. Rain fell in torrents as soon as the main body came in; and Whitelocke simply aligned his troops upon Gower's, further directing the whole line to fall back in rear of the Corral, in the hope of drawing the enemy, who had never ceased firing at the picquets, into the open ground. The movement, however, failed of its object, and the troops took shelter in houses for the night, receiving rations both of bread and liquor, which Gower had collected in the suburbs.

In the evening Whitelocke asked Gower whether, having been in the suburbs for twenty-four hours, he had thought of any design for the attack of the town. Gower answered in the affirmative, and produced his plan; whereupon, after further consideration, Whitelocke decided to abandon his own idea of attack and adopt that of his subordinate. The officers commanding regiments and brigades were accordingly summoned

July 4. to headquarters at nine the next morning, where Gower was ready to expound his scheme to them. It was abundantly simple. The army was to enter the town in thirteen different columns along as many different streets. One of these was to seize the Plaza de Toros, a fairly commanding position at the north-east angle of the city; the remainder were to push on to the last row of houses overlooking the river, capture them, and form up on the roofs. After this explanation Whitelocke dismissed all but the Brigadiers, and announced his intention of attacking at noon. Auchmuty, who had arrived late at the conference, remarked that his officers were wholly unacquainted with the intended attack, that they would hardly have time to examine their ground in order to make the necessary arrangements, and that broad noon was not the best time for a hostile advance into a populous city. Gower concurred in this reasoning, and the attack was deferred until daylight of the following morning. It does not appear that any of the officers present brought forward any objection to the plan, though Colonel Pack, who by reason of his acquaintance with the town of Buenos Ayres was admitted to the conference of Generals, hinted at strong disapprobation of it. Whitelocke, however, evaded further discussion with him; and Pack said no more, though he noted that the Commander-in-chief had the air of a man who was acting against his better judgment.[1]

1807. July 4.

Pack had guessed aright. Upon his first arrival at Monte Video Whitelocke had pointed out to Craufurd the peculiar construction of the houses, their flat roofs surrounded by parapets, and other circumstances which adapted them admirably for purposes of defence. He had added that he would never expose his troops to so unfair a trial as a fight in the streets of a large town like Buenos Ayres, composed entirely of such houses; and Craufurd had heartily agreed with him. So strong indeed was the General's feeling upon the subject that he seems to have set down his opinions in writing, with a corollary that such a mode of attack as he had just accepted from Gower would not be resorted to, even under more favourable conditions than the present. Moreover, his own plan was known, in general terms, to be that he should rest the left of his army upon the La Plata, land his heavy guns, and in conjunction with the gunboats of the fleet batter the town till it surrendered. The reasons which he alleged for the necessity of an immediate assault were the fatigue of the troops, the inclemency of the weather, and the want of provisions.[2] The difficulty of feeding his army was in fact the source of all his troubles during his brief campaign; and it is evident that, whether through incapacity or neglect, he had never set himself from

[1] C.-M., p. 410.

[2] *Ibid.* p. 170.

1807. July 4. the first to grapple with it. With a general sense of his own incompetence and of the awkward situation in which it had placed him, he appealed to Gower on the afternoon of the 4th to testify to the soundness of his orders and dispositions throughout. Gower pleaded the inability of an inferior officer to judge of the acts of his superior, whereupon Whitelocke declared that he regarded his second in command as an avowed enemy and would supersede him in his appointment.

Meanwhile the Quartermaster-general in the course of the afternoon endeavoured to point out to the Brigadiers the streets which were to be followed by the troops of each brigade. He found the task to be no easy one. Gower had made all his dispositions in reliance upon a Spanish map of the city, but this was found to differ considerably from the actual conformation of the ground; and Bourke reported to Gower that the columns could not be placed as he wished and expected. He indicated further that if the troops advanced, as Gower had ordered, from west to east direct upon the river, the enemy would probably retire into the streets north and south, close in upon the columns, and cut them off from any support outside the town. Gower made light of these objections; and the plan was left unaltered. Efforts were made to collect crowbars and other tools to break in the doors of houses that might be barricaded; and a few, though not nearly sufficient, were brought together and distributed chiefly to Craufurd's brigade. The reason for this allotment of the tools will be made clear by a detailed account of Gower's dispositions.

The town of Buenos Ayres was laid out in regular rectangular blocks, each about one hundred and thirty yards square, its eastern face abutting upon the river. It measured, roughly speaking, about two miles from north to south by one mile from east to west, the ground sloping gently upwards from the river inland, so that the Corral, upon which the British army was

encamped, overlooked the whole of the buildings down 1807.
to the water's edge. As was natural, the principal July 4.
edifices were all close to the shore; the fort forming the centre of those along the eastern front. This was described as a "square work of about one hundred paces on the exterior polygon, and flanked with small bastions." The walls were about fifteen feet high from the level of the interior to the top of the parapet, which rose not more than four feet above the rampart, the guns being mounted *en barbette* upon field-carriages; and there was no ditch except on the side that faced the town. It was commanded, as Beresford had discovered to his cost, by several houses in the vicinity, and altogether was wholly insignificant. Its western face abutted on the Plaza Mayor, or Great Square, the scene of Beresford's unsuccessful defence, divided, as will be remembered, by an arcade, with a parapetted roof. On the north-western face of the square stood the Cathedral, with a lofty dome and parapet. Nearly a mile to northward of the Great Square lay another and more important open space, situated on rising ground close to the river at the north-eastern angle of the town. This was the Plaza de Toros, in which stood the amphitheatre for the exhibition of bull-fights, with the artillery-barracks and arsenal lying beyond it. It was separated from the town by a little ravine, of which it occupied the higher side. Below it towards the river there was a flat unoccupied space, where an enclosed battery had lately been erected to flank any approach to the eastern face of the town along the beach. Southward of the Great Square, and four blocks distant from it, was another small open space, having on the west side the convent of St. Domingo, the largest ecclesiastical building in Buenos Ayres next to the Cathedral. Yet further south, almost at the south-eastern angle of the town, stood a large building, originally designed for a royal hospital, called the Residencia, standing within an irregular quadrilateral space of which one-third was open and the rest

1807. July 4. occupied by buildings. This space was enclosed partly by the buildings themselves, which presented a lofty blind wall to the streets on both sides, partly by a slighter wall some ten feet high; and the Residencia as a whole offered the advantage that its roof was not commanded by the top of any adjacent houses. It stood back about two or three hundred yards from the river; and if this building, the fort, and the Plaza de Toros were occupied, there was free communication between them, unimpeded by any houses along the shore. On the other hand, in advancing from west to east the troops would descend steadily from higher to lower ground; and all the loftiest buildings in the town stood at the eastern extremity near the river.

The dispositions for the attack were as follows. On the left or northern side Auchmuty was to detach the Thirty-eighth, complete, to seize the Plaza de Toros with the ground adjacent to it, and there to take post. Next to the Thirty-eighth, in succession came the Eighty-seventh, the Fifth, the Thirty-sixth, and Eighty-eighth; which, each of them divided into two wings, were appointed to advance down eight parallel streets to southward of the Thirty-eighth. Auchmuty accompanied the right wing of the Eighty-seventh; Lumley the right wing of the Thirty-sixth. Next to these came the Eighty-eighth in two wings, this battalion forming the extreme right of the left attack. The four central streets were left vacant,[1] except that the street which ran directly from Whitelocke's headquarters to the fort was to be occupied, but not traversed, by the Carabiniers with two guns, who were to make a false attack.[2] The first street to southward of the four central streets was assigned to a part of the Light Brigade under Pack, the second to the remainder of that brigade under Craufurd, each column taking with it one three-pounder. The two wings of the Forty-fifth were to move parallel with them down the two

[1] C.-M., p. 550. [2] *Ibid.* p. 77.

next streets. The whole were to march to the last 1807. square of houses on the river, as has been said, and to July 4. form on the tops of the buildings.[1] If any failed to penetrate so far, they were to lodge themselves at the furthest point to which they were able to advance. As a general instruction, it was ordained that in all cases of doubt the detachments were to incline outwards; that is to say, Auchmuty's and Lumley's brigades, which formed the left wing, were to bear to their left, the remainder, which formed the right wing, to their right; but the command to this effect was conveyed in language so loose and obscure that Craufurd's staff-officer, in making his transcript of the orders, very pardonably omitted it.[2] This initial mistake augured no good for the success of the attack.

[1] In the plan I have attempted, as I trust with success, to show the street traversed by each party of troops, by the light not of Gower's orders but of sundry hints which appear in the evidence given at Whitelocke's court-martial. But the task has been one of great difficulty.

[2] The order ran thus :—" Each officer commanding a division of the left wing, which is from the 88th to the 87th inclusively, to take care that he does not incline to his right of the right wing, that is Light Brigade and 45th to the left." The order is printed thus both in *Military Transactions* and in the Minutes of the Court-Martial, and as it stands is mere gibberish. If it be punctuated as follows :—" Each officer commanding a division of the left wing, which is from the 88th to the 87th inclusively, to take care that he does not incline to his right; of the right wing, that is Light Brigade and 45th, to the left," it can, by considerable effort, be construed into sense. Its true meaning, judging by Whitelocke's defence, is that which I have given in the text, viz. the columns of the left wing if they could not follow the streets assigned to them, were to bear to their left; the columns of the right wing, namely, the Light Brigade and 45th, in the like case were to bear to their right; and the reason was that, by converging on the centre, they might come under the fire of the guns in charge of the Carabiniers. Strangely enough, no member of the court-martial seems to have taken exception to the wording of this ridiculous clause, so it is possible that the orders were written in two parallel lines, and the missing verbs and particles filled up by the words *ditto ditto*, etc. The credit for the discovery that this clause was not transcribed by Craufurd's staff-officer belongs to Capt. Lewis Butler, *U.S. Magazine*, Aug. 1905.

1807. Meanwhile the enemy had recovered themselves and made every preparation for a stubborn defence; for the Spaniards, as they had proved at Numantia and were shortly to prove again at Zaragoza, are never so formidable as in street fighting. On the evening of the 2nd their troops had been utterly demoralised. Their leader Liniers was missing, and for some time he was actually within the line of the British outposts, his retreat having been intercepted by the rapid advance of the Light Brigade. He escaped, however, in the course of the night, and, taking advantage of Whitelocke's inactivity on the 3rd, vigorously incited the people to resistance. Cannon were stationed at the outlets of the streets whose westward end was held by the British, and additional ordnance was brought to the fort to cover the approach by river. Trenches were cut in the principal streets near the Great Square, and guns were placed to flank them. The houses were stoutly barricaded and provided with every description of missile to be hurled upon the British columns. The clergy had used all their influence and oratory to rouse patriotic enthusiasm; and every soul, men, women, and children, was ready to play his part, the very slaves being armed with rude pikes. In all, the defenders seem to have consisted of some nine thousand men, regulars, militia, and volunteers, with more or less of discipline and organisation, and some six thousand others in irregular but not leaderless groups. Of these about five thousand, including all the best marksmen, occupied the houses, with a store of provisions and an ample supply of ammunition; about two thousand more occupied the Bull-ring and its neighbourhood, while others were distributed in and about the fort to be employed as circumstances should require. The rest of the population seconded them as best they could, which they might do effectively in a city where every house was a fortress.

July 5. Before dawn on the 5th the British troops took up their positions for the attack, in all about forty-five hundred bayonets.[1] Mahon's detachment was still in Reduction; scores and indeed hundreds of exhausted soldiers had also been left there; and, through foolish and unnecessary exposure of the men at the advanced posts during some sharp skirmishing on the 4th, a good many, both officers and privates, had fallen. Punctually at half-past six the firing of a cannon gave the signal to advance, and the columns entered their appointed streets. Every British officer noticed the deathlike stillness of the town, for the very dogs in the houses had been tied up; and it was not until the columns had advanced for some distance that any of them met with opposition. But, as Whitelocke had decreed that his army should be divided into tiny isolated detachments, it will be necessary to follow the fortunes of each one of them separately.

1807. July 5.

Auchmuty on the left with the two wings of the Eighty-seventh was the first to come into action. He had advanced for more than a mile without meeting the slightest resistance, when suddenly two guns opened a destructive fire of grape directly before his front. The regiment pushed on, and presently the cannonade was supplemented by a heavy fire of musketry upon his left front. The head of the right wing came to a halt; the rear loaded and began to fire wildly; and soon the whole of the column wavered and ran back. The Colonel, Sir Edward Butler, and the officers rallied the men; and Auchmuty ordered them to break into a garden on his right, in order to find a way into the next street to southward. They succeeded in doing so, and discovering a deep water-course in the centre of the street, which sheltered them from the fire, followed

[1] Returns from *Milit. Trans.*

R.A.	190
Light Brigade	1160
1st	1950
2nd	1060
3rd	1320
	5680 r. and f.

But of these 1100 men were held in reserve, 600 of them to act if need were, and the remainder to guard the sick and prisoners. The force which penetrated into the town was about 4500 bayonets, say 5000 of all ranks. C.-M., p. 504.

1807. July 5. it down to the river, where Auchmuty occupied a large house and collected the remains of his column. The left wing of the Eighty-seventh presently joined him, having suffered as severely as the right, and having been likewise driven out of its course. In spite of its temporary unsteadiness the Eighty-seventh had done well, having killed several of the enemy, and captured about one hundred prisoners and three guns.

There then Auchmuty waited, learning to his surprise that the fire of musketry which had checked his advance had issued from the Plaza de Toros which, according to the map given him by Gower, ought to have been three streets to his left instead of directly to his front. But meanwhile the Fifth Foot, next to southward of him, had also advanced. The right wing reached the banks of the river at a quarter past seven without encountering the slightest opposition, hoisted the King's colours on the top of a house, and occupied a neighbouring church. The left wing under Major King charged bayonets as soon as it entered the town, moved rapidly down the street and came upon four Spanish guns retiring from its left. The Spanish gunners promptly shot their teams, spiked the cannon and ran away, leaving King to pursue his path to the river unmolested. Arrived there, the Major took possession of a house, and displayed the regimental colours on the roof, which assured Auchmuty that his eastern flank was safe. Very soon, however, a galling fire was opened from the Plaza de Toros, which commanded the house that King occupied; but he maintained his position until, between half-past nine and ten o'clock, the firing from the Plaza ceased.

There was indeed good reason why it should cease. On the extreme left the Thirty-eighth under Colonel Nugent, after about twenty minutes' march, found itself in a narrow lane leading to the Plaza de Toros, at the head of which was a large house occupied by the enemy. The lane was so deep in mire that many both of the officers and the men had their shoes drawn off their feet; but the regiment hurried on, leaving a party to force the doors of the house, and found itself exposed to a concentric fire of artillery from several guns stationed at different points in the open ground round the Bull-ring. The Ring itself, a brick building of twelve sides, presented nothing but a blank wall with a gallery above, from which the Spanish sharp-shooters could fire without danger to themselves. Nugent, after losing several men in a vain attempt to storm the batteries, withdrew his battalion and sent two companies round to his left to occupy a house on the cliff by the enemy's extreme right, in the hope of turning their flank. The house at the end of the lane was first forced, and a single grenadier of the Thirty-eighth, one of the worst characters in the regiment, dashed in by himself and made his way straight to the roof. There he encountered fifteen men, of whom he bayonetted two instantly; whereupon several of the rest feigned death, but a group of four retired into a corner to make a concerted attack upon him. Still single-handed, he rushed at these, bayonetted one, and had driven another to leap from the house, when his comrades arrived and made a speedy end of the survivors. Shortly afterwards the second house by the cliff was forced, and the British opened a galling fire from the roof upon the enemy's gunners. These presently spiked their guns and retreated into the Bull-ring; but there remained still a closed battery to be dealt with, and this was captured by a sudden and unexpected rush of the Thirty-eighth from the back door of the house. The gunners, some sixty in number, unable to reach the Bull-ring, took refuge in a barrack, but were so closely pursued that the British entered with them, and after a short but savage encounter in the barrack-rooms, put every one of the sixty to death.[1] The rest of the Thirty-eighth meanwhile seized the guns, and finding a twelve-pounder unspiked, turned it upon the Bull-ring. At this stage Auchmuty appeared on the scene

1807. July 5.

[1] Colburne's *Military Magazine*, Dec. 1836.

1807. July 5. with some of the Eighty-seventh, and surrounded the building completely. After a few shots, parties of the enemy came rushing out, only to find their retreat cut off; and presently those that remained in the building hung out the white flag and surrendered at discretion.

So far, then, all had gone fairly well on the northern side, in spite of Gower's hasty dispositions. It seems certain that both the Thirty-eighth and the Eighty-seventh, though carefully following Gower's orders, went where he had no intention that they should go; but at any rate the Plaza de Toros, the most commanding position in the city, had been taken; and Auchmuty had also captured about a thousand prisoners and thirty-two guns. On the other hand, the Thirty-eighth and Eighty-seventh had suffered so severely that Auchmuty dared not reckon his brigade that night above the strength of twelve hundred men. The Eighty-seventh alone, out of fewer than seven hundred of all ranks, had lost fourteen officers and one hundred and seventy-one men killed and wounded.

To southward of Auchmuty, Lumley's brigade of the Thirty-sixth and Eighty-eighth was more hardly tried. The Thirty-sixth took the two streets next adjoining those traversed by the Fifth, Lumley himself accompanying the right half-battalion. The roads had been broken up, which made progress slow; and firing began from various directions upon the columns almost as soon as they entered the town. None the less the regiment penetrated to the cross-street next adjoining the river, and forcing open some houses in the last two blocks to eastward, hoisted its colours upon a tall building that overlooked the beach. The enemy in the fort and in the Great Square thereupon opened fire from seven guns, with great precision, upon the house whereon the colours were flying, at the same time sweeping the cross-streets with showers of grape. Simultaneously a hail of bullets poured upon the Thirty-sixth from marksmen concealed behind the parapets of adjoining houses; and Lumley, though he could maintain his position, was absolutely powerless to do more. The Eighty-eighth fared even worse. The left-hand column under Major Vandeleur had not marched one-third of the distance to the beach when fire was opened upon it from windows and house-tops on every side. Vandeleur ordered his men to advance at the double, which they did with cheers, under an increasing shower of musketry, hand-grenades, stink-pots, brickbats, and every description of missile. Two guns opened upon them from the bottom of the street, and two more enfiladed them from the Great Square, as they passed by the cross-streets which led into it; but none the less the men pressed on to the very end of the road, scrambled over a breastwork of sand-bags and a ditch beyond it, and found to their dismay that they were in a trap. There was no outlet from the street to the beach but by a narrow ramp, which was enfiladed by the guns of the fort at a range of two hundred yards. Vandeleur with great difficulty forced his way into the nearest house, but found it impossible to occupy the roof, because every man was at once shot down. He tried next to hold another house over against the first; but his men were immediately driven from the roof by the guns of the fort. The hours passed away without a sign of support from any side; and at a quarter past eleven Vandeleur, having lost great numbers of his men killed or wounded, hoisted the white flag, and was escorted with his few surviving soldiers into the fort.

1807. July 5.

The right wing of the Eighty-eighth, under Colonel Duff, was so weak when it paraded for the attack that the commanding officer left the colours behind and sent a message to request that two companies, which were detained at headquarters, might be allowed to join him. The companies arrived in due time with their muskets unfit for service, General Gower having directed the flints to be removed. There was some delay while spare flints were collecting from such men as could give them; and the right half-battalion then advanced to a

1807. July 5. church which had been pointed out to Duff by Lumley as his objective—apparently the church of La Merced in the second block of buildings westward from the beach. Strangely enough not a shot was discharged at the column until it reached the gateway of this building, when a tremendous fire of musketry was poured upon it from the adjacent houses. The door of the church was strongly barricaded; it was found impossible to break it down; and Duff, after losing many men, was fain to abandon the attempt and plunge further into the city towards the citadel. The firing pursued him wherever he went, and finding that half of his men had fallen, he turned back, took possession of three houses, and formed on the roof such soldiers as were left to him. Here he held out for some hours, but his men dropped fast under the enemy's fire; and at a quarter before noon, seeing no prospect of support from any side, he too hoisted the white flag and was escorted into the citadel.

Here he met Vandeleur, his companion in misfortune, who had surrendered half an hour earlier. Duff's battalion had gone into action about five hundred strong, and had lost fifteen officers and one hundred and eighty-three men killed and wounded. A few men of the Eighty-eighth escaped over the house-tops and reported to Lumley the disaster which had overtaken their regiment; but the Spaniards had already revealed the fact by turning all their strength against the Thirty-sixth. Twice they summoned Lumley to surrender, and twice he refused; whereupon they brought forward their guns on the beach, escorted by some seven hundred men, in order to shatter the houses held by the British to pieces about their ears. It was a rash movement. Colonel Burne of the Thirty-sixth with fifty men flew at this escort at once, drove it headlong before him under the walls of the fort, spiked the guns, and hurried his gallant little party under shelter of a wall before the cannon of the fort could open upon them. Meanwhile, one of Lumley's officers had contrived to make his 1807. way to Auchmuty, and to send back a message from July 5. the General, recommending that the Thirty-sixth should join him at the Plaza de Toros. Lumley answered by a request for support; but his message never reached its destination. However, at two o'clock the Brigadier collected his men, including a party of the Fifth which had opened communication with him, and retiring along the beach under a heavy fire from the fort, joined Auchmuty, not without some additional loss, before three o'clock. His brigade had been sacrificed to no purpose whatsoever.

Such were the fortunes of the left wing, to northward of the four central streets: it remains now to follow those of the right wing to south of them. On the extreme right, the Forty-fifth advanced in two columns, the right under Colonel Guard, the left under Major Nichols, upon the Residencia, which had been prescribed by word of mouth as the object of its attack. This was evidently a verbal variation from the written orders; and the result was that the Forty-fifth moved by two streets a long way to south of those originally assigned to them. The place was reached, taken, and occupied with trifling loss within an hour; and thus a very strong position on the south-eastern flank of the city was secured, assuring easy communication with the fleet. Some distance to the left of Nichols, the Light Brigade moved off in two columns; the left column consisting of four companies of the Ninety-fifth and five light companies—in all about six hundred bayonets—under the independent command of Colonel Pack; the right column of four more companies of the Ninety-fifth and four light companies, under the personal direction of Craufurd. Both columns passed through the town to the beach unmolested except by a few cannon-shot from the Great Square; and Craufurd, finding the fort to be within five hundred yards of him, determined to advance upon it by the beach, sending orders to Guard to follow him

1807. July 5. with the Forty-fifth in support. No intimation, it must be observed, had been given to Craufurd that Guard was to occupy the Residencia, nor had any hint of this intention appeared in general orders.

Meanwhile Pack, having divided his column into two and given the command of half of it to Colonel Cadogan, turned northward, along two parallel streets, two blocks apart, conceiving, as had Craufurd, that the Great Square and the fort were the points where he was intended to attack. This movement brought him near the Franciscan Church, where in a moment half of his men were struck down, and he himself was wounded by the fire of an invisible enemy. Hastily retreating to the street along which he had originally advanced, he found Cadogan's party also retiring, having suffered the like maltreatment. Cadogan had led his men with little loss to the gateway of the Jesuits' College, when every man of his leading company and every horse and man attached to his single field-gun had been in an instant shot down. About half of his men had followed him into one house; the rest had dispersed themselves to seek shelter wherever they could find an open door. Cadogan himself was in great distress, declaring that he and his men had done their duty, but that success was impossible.

Profoundly impressed with the hopelessness of the enterprise, Pack made known to Cadogan his intention of withdrawing to the Residencia. Cadogan deprecated this idea; and Pack agreed to stay where he was until he should see Craufurd. That General soon appeared at the back of the Convent of St. Domingo, and was presently joined by Guard, who had come with his grenadier-company from the Residencia to open communication with the Light Brigade. Pack urged upon Craufurd the impracticability of the task entrusted to him, and pressed him strongly to retire to the Residencia. Craufurd hesitated, representing the expediency of occupying the Convent of St. Domingo; and Pack reluctantly gave way. The door of the convent was blown open by the second field-gun attached to the 1807. Light Brigade; the building was occupied; and the July 5. captured colours of the Seventy-first, being found within, were hoisted above it. No sooner did the British troops appear on the roof than a considerable fire was opened upon them from the adjoining houses; but there was no reason for anxiety until noon, when a Spanish officer appeared with a flag of truce. Not doubting but that the messenger bore a proposal from Liniers to capitulate, Craufurd was staggered when he was met on the contrary by the news that the Eighty-eighth had surrendered, and that Liniers called upon him also to surrender. Craufurd dismissed the flag at once with a curt refusal; but, shortly afterwards, a large body of the enemy marched into the street by the entrance to the convent and prepared to seize the field-gun, which, being too wide to be brought into the building, had been left outside. Then realising how critical was his position, Craufurd hauled down the colours which he had hoisted, and made ready to retire to the Residencia. Guard with his grenadier-company made a rush at the gun, and swept away the hostile column which threatened it; but in three minutes forty of his men were killed or wounded by the fire from the adjacent houses; and Craufurd, seeing that the evacuation of the convent was impossible, ordered the men back to their posts and resumed the defence. Presently all firing ceased except in his own immediate neighbourhood, which sign he interpreted to mean that the attack had failed at all points; and at half-past three, judging that assistance or relief was hopeless, he surrendered. Cadogan, having lost ninety-seven men out of one hundred and forty, besides five officers, had surrendered some time before.

Thus this curious and disjointed action came to an end. Throughout its duration Whitelocke had been pacing up and down near his headquarters in deep anxiety. No reports reached him. So slovenly was the work of his staff that, though he never changed

1807. July 5. his position throughout the day, not one of his Generals knew, except by conjecture, where he was to be found. But this was of small importance, for no messenger from any one of the columns could have reached him alive. At nine o'clock he sent a staff-officer down one of the central streets to ascertain what was going forward; but the morning was too hazy to allow anything to be distinctly seen even from the house-tops; and he therefore directed the column of the Carabiniers and Ninth Light Dragoons to advance towards the Great Square. The Dragoons moved forward accordingly, but were presently checked by a destructive fire, and after heavy losses fell back to a place of safety, and halted. Whitelocke then sent one of his aides-de-camp to try to find out the position of the attacking columns; and he, after climbing to the top of the highest house open to him, was able to report at half-past eleven that British colours were flying on the left and on the right centre. Subsequent attempts of this officer to penetrate further into the town were fruitless; and the endeavours of another officer to make his way towards the Residencia with a few mounted dragoons were likewise foiled. At last, between two and three o'clock, Whitelocke asked if any officer would volunteer to obtain news of Auchmuty. Thereupon Captain Whittingham, afterwards well known as one of our military agents in Spain, took an escort of about fifty mounted and dismounted men and, after much skirmishing with scattered bodies of the enemy, made his way to the Plaza de Toros. Having heard Auchmuty's report, he galloped back with the dragoons alone, and at half-past four was able to give the General the first information that he had received of the day's work, namely, that Auchmuty had been successful, and that the Eighty-eighth had been captured. Of the fate of Craufurd nothing was known. In fact, with the exception of some motley bands of Spaniards which attempted a feeble attack upon the baggage-guard from the rear, Whitelocke had seen nothing either of the enemy or of his own troops during the day.

Auchmuty had asked him through Whittingham to shift his headquarters to the Plaza de Toros at once; but the General decided not to move, hoping that further intelligence might reach him during the night. 1807.

At half-past six on the following morning Whittingham was despatched with an escort of forty mounted and dismounted men to find the Reserve under Colonel Mahon, and to order him to move at once to the Corral. Mahon, pursuant to his directions, had marched from Reduction on the previous day, and finding the bridge over the Chuelo intact, had crossed that river at five in the evening, and encamped on the northern bank within two miles of the Residencia. Having delivered the message to him, Whittingham turned next to the Residencia itself, where he found Major Nichols of the Forty-fifth entirely confident of his power to hold his own, but unable to give any news of Craufurd. As if to verify Nichols's words, the Spaniards actually brought up cannon to batter the Residencia while Whittingham was there, whereupon the Major sallied out with a party of the Forty-fifth, drove them away with a single charge, and brought off two howitzers in triumph. But meanwhile, very soon after daylight, a letter had reached Whitelocke from General Liniers. The Spanish commander, after stating that he had captured General Craufurd and considerably over a thousand prisoners, offered to restore them and all the British soldiers captured since Beresford's first embarkation, if Whitelocke would withdraw all his troops from the province; adding that if the offer were refused he would not, in view of the exasperation of the populace, be answerable for the safety of the prisoners. Whitelocke rejected the proposal, but suggested a truce of twenty-four hours for collection of the wounded; after which he and Gower rode down to join Auchmuty at the Plaza de Toros. July 6.

There the three Generals consulted together upon the situation. Whitelocke reckoned his losses in killed,

1807. July 6. wounded, and prisoners at twenty-five hundred men; but he was below the mark. The killed numbered four hundred and one of all ranks; the wounded six hundred and forty-nine; the prisoners, several of whom were hurt, nineteen hundred and twenty-four, making a total of very nearly three thousand casualties,[1] or more than half of the force engaged. On the other hand, the British had captured over a thousand prisoners and more than thirty guns; they were in occupation of strong posts on each flank of the city; and they had still an effective force of over six thousand of all ranks ready for further operations. But the troops had lost confidence in their commander; and, apart from this significant fact, it was evident alike to Whitelocke, Gower, and Auchmuty that the conquest of the province was impossible. Moreover, even if Buenos Ayres were captured, it could only be held by a garrison of such strength as England could not dream of sparing. Gower was therefore sent to Liniers with instructions to obtain, if possible, an extension of time for the evacuation, and facilities for the British traders to dispose of their goods. A suspension of hostilities was proclaimed in the course of the afternoon; and on
July 7. the 7th a definite agreement was signed, to the effect that all prisoners on both sides were to be restored, and that the British should evacuate the province within ten days. Monte Video was excepted from this last provision, it being arranged that the place should be held by the British for two months, and then given back to the Spaniards uninjured and with its artillery intact. A proposal that liberty of commerce should be granted to British traders for four months was utterly rejected.

Beyond all question the decision of Whitelocke was wise, the one instance indeed of wisdom that he had

[1] | | | | |
|---|---|---|---|
| *Killed* . | 15 officers, | 386 | n.c.o. and men. |
| *Wounded* . | 57 ,, | 592 | ,, ,, |
| *Taken* . | 94 ,, | 1831 | ,, ,, |

About 250 of the prisoners were wounded.

manifested during the campaign. But the troops, sore 1807. at their maltreatment by an enemy whom they knew to be contemptible in the field, were furious with rage. "General Whitelocke is a coward or a traitor or both," were the words in which they wrote their opinion of him on the walls of Buenos Ayres; and the harsh phrase was eagerly caught up by the multitude when the bad news reached London. The English at home indeed had more than usual cause for exasperation. So humiliating a defeat, following so close upon the victory of Maida, was in itself hard to bear; but the pecuniary loss which accompanied it was unendurable. There had been frantic speculation in the new market which Popham, in his vanity, had proclaimed to be open in South America. Not prosperous merchants only, but large numbers of the needy, the rapacious, and the impecunious had staked their all, or their neighbours' all, in the great venture; and, as is usual in such cases, tons of rubbish, which could find no sale in any other quarter, had been shipped over to Buenos Ayres. Now it was seen that the long and perilous voyage had been undertaken in vain, and that the whole of the goods exported, whether valuable or worthless, would be returned upon their owners' hands. There were loud calls for an inquiry, and Whitelocke was put on his trial by court-martial. The Court was a strong one. General Medows of East Indian fame was President; and among the nineteen remaining members were Lake, Harris, Moore, Cathcart, David Dundas, and Henry Fox. It sat for thirty-one days. The charges were four in number: First, that Whitelocke had exasperated the spirit of resistance in the people of Buenos Ayres, by making excessive demands upon them when they seemed likely to come to terms; secondly, that he had mishandled the whole of the military operations, particularly in attacking Buenos Ayres with unloaded arms; thirdly, that he had made no effectual attempt to control or support the different columns during the attack; and fourthly, that, when still in

1807. a position to have taken Buenos Ayres, in spite of the heavy losses in the assault, he had deliberately preferred to evacuate the country. He was found guilty upon all the charges, except that of prohibiting all firing during the attack, and was sentenced to be "cashiered and declared totally unfit and unworthy to serve His Majesty in any military capacity whatever."

The finding shows the strength of public feeling at the moment. The first charge may be dismissed as absurd: the Spanish colonies on the Plate would have accepted a British occupation on no terms except those which Whitelocke was expressly instructed to decline—independence under British protection. The remaining charges cannot so lightly be passed over, but it must be admitted that the General's difficulties were enormous. Attention has already been called to the initial problem which was presented to him for solution, namely, whether he should attack at once or wait until September, as also to the unfortunate but inevitable delay in the ascent of the river by the transports of Craufurd's division. Allusion has also been made to the virtual impossibility of reconnoitring the country and obtaining intelligence, and especially to the obstacles which beset all arrangements for transport and supply. Whitelocke was fortunate in effecting his debarkation unmolested; but the risk which he encountered was so great as to be justifiable only by the result. Had he refused, as very reasonably he might have done, to incur the hazard, the alternative was to disembark far away from the city and to make a long march by land, in which case it is hard to see how he could have fed his army. The fleet was indeed in the river, but the river was practically an inland sea, very shallow near the shore, yet dangerous for small craft in rough weather, and with few safe inlets to shelter them. No operation could seem simpler upon paper than that the Army should have marched parallel to the shore, drawing its supplies from the fleet, which

should have moved on a level with it; but none was 1807.
in actual fact more impracticable.

On the other hand, it must also be admitted that the man did not make the best of his very difficult task. He seems on this occasion to have had no self-reliance, and to have leaned wholly upon Gower, who, it is abundantly evident, was as conceited as he was unpractical, and as overbearing as he was incompetent. Gower has been rightly called the evil genius of the expedition; but a strong and able Commander-in-chief would have left him at Monte Video, in defiance of the fact that he had been specially appointed by the Secretary of State for War.[1] Far from that, Whitelocke seems to have been torn by doubts whether to bully or to court him, with the result that Gower obtained his own way on every point, and mismanaged everything. The marches were contrived so as to harass the men to the utmost, and the final attack upon Buenos Ayres was simply fatuous. The avowed intention was to seize two strong positions upon the flank of the city, which indeed was actually effected; but why the men should have been marched through the streets in thirteen small columns upon these two points is absolutely inexplicable. Whitelocke was sensible enough to see the danger of such a proceeding, but not strong enough to steer clear of it. For reasons best known to himself, he yielded to Gower; and Gower, as usual, did his worst for his chief. Great outcry was raised against Whitelocke for not accompanying his army in the attack and for renouncing all control of it. He replied that at his headquarters he was as accessible to the army at large as at any other place; and this was undeniable, for if a commander deliberately divides his force into thirteen parts, and thrusts each of these into a blind alley from which its retreat can easily be cut off, the chances are decidedly in favour of his losing

[1] Gower thought himself specially beholden to Windham for his appointment, and went so far as to write to him an apology for the failure of the campaign. Gower to Windham, 9th July 1807.

1807. all communication with at least twelve of them. This might have been foreseen, and provision might have been made in orders for the contingency. Some code of signals could have been arranged; and, above all, Mahon's reserve might have been brought up under the Commander-in-chief's hand to act at any point where its assistance was needed. But Gower was purblind and incapable, and Whitelocke was helpless to correct him. The written orders were meagre and obscure; and Gower worse confounded the confusion that he made, by issuing supplementary verbal orders to certain individual leaders without imparting them to the rest. The comment of a Spanish General upon the assault and the defence is the hardest condemnation to be found of Whitelocke's conduct. "Half the number of troops which attacked this capital would make themselves masters of it, supposing the same defenders, equally armed and disciplined. . . . I will rather say that ten thousand English sheep came to present their throats to the knife."[1]

It is interesting to note that Whitelocke threw the blame of the main disaster upon Craufurd and Pack, who, instead of wheeling outwards in pursuance of their orders, deliberately wheeled inward upon the fort. Craufurd, for his part, retorted upon Whitelocke the accusation that the Commander-in-chief had abandoned him. There was some ground for complaint on both sides. Mention has already been made of the omission of an important but unintelligible clause from Craufurd's copy of the orders; but, apart from this, Robert Craufurd was not remarkable at any period of his career for excessive deference to the commands of his superiors. Again, his rejection of Pack's advice to retire to the Residencia, after the failure of Pack's own preliminary attack, was extremely characteristic of the man. On the other hand, Auchmuty had equally disobeyed the written orders; and, since Craufurd had penetrated to the river unopposed, it was reasonable

[1] *Castlereagh Desp.* vii. 402.

for him to assume that Whitelocke required more of 1807.
him than merely to take refuge at the Residencia. The enemy's force was supposed to be concentrated about the Great Square. Presumably Whitelocke intended to attack it from both flanks; otherwise why had columns been sent through all the streets, and why had not the Light Brigade been sent direct together with the Forty-fifth to the Residencia? If the British gunboats were intended to co-operate in the final attack, the guns of the fort must first have been silenced by the army, for they could not be reached, owing to shallow water, by the cannon of the fleet. Craufurd in fact argued as if Whitelocke, or Gower in Whitelocke's stead, had actually formed a plan of operations; whereas, as a matter of fact, they had formed none. They simply directed the columns to enter the town, expecting little resistance, and left the rest to chance. In brief, they made the mistake, which, though old as human nature, seems unhappily to enjoy perpetual youth, of undervaluing their enemy.

As to the question of renewing the attack on the 6th or 7th, in conjunction with the fleet and with the help of guns landed from it, there seems to be no reasonable doubt that the operation was feasible and would have ensured the capture of Buenos Ayres. Indeed, according to the Spanish General already quoted, if the British had merely maintained and fortified themselves in the positions which they had already mastered, the inhabitants must have laid down their arms within four days from lack of provisions.[1] But, even if the city had been taken, either by bombardment or by blockade, the fact would hardly have reconciled the Spaniards to British rule. Moreover, even when captured, it would have been, at best, difficult of defence against a hostile population. All supplies except from the river would have been cut off; the entire country would have been closed to the British; and, in case of a retreat, re-embarkation would have been extremely difficult and

[1] *Castlereagh Desp.* vii. 400.

1807. hazardous, for no channels or docks had been dredged out for Buenos Ayres in those days, and consequently there were no quays. The troops must therefore have evacuated the city in boats; and those boats could not have been covered by the guns of the fleet, for the men-of-war could not safely lie nearer than four or five miles from the shore. A re-embarkation from Point Quilmes would have been still more difficult, and the retreat thither from the city most dangerous. Beyond all doubt, therefore, Whitelocke did right to come early to terms with Liniers; and, though it may well be that his sagacity in coming to this decision was quickened by discouragement, it must be remembered that he had served for long in St. Domingo, and had observed the failure of an expedition, conducted upon much the same principles, in that quarter. From the military point of view, the only satisfactory feature in the campaign was the good behaviour of the troops in the assault.

It remains to pass judgment upon the Ministers who sent Whitelocke away upon his mad and impossible errand. Enough has already been said to show that they acted in complete ignorance or misconception of the true condition of affairs on the Rio de la Plata. No ignorance or misconception, however, can excuse the absurdity of the orders originally given to Craufurd, nor the contradictory injunctions addressed to Whitelocke. He was to reduce the province of Buenos Ayres by force of arms and exile the authors of the insurrection which had overthrown Beresford; and yet he was to consider that his main object was not to distress or annoy the enemy but only to occupy a portion of his territory. Again, he was to attach the inhabitants to British rule, but was forbidden to give them assurance of British protection against the vengeance of Old Spain after the conclusion of peace. These astonishing orders emanated from the Ministry of all the Talents; and one is tempted to imagine the wit and sarcasm with which they would have been criticised by Windham if they had been addressed to him by Whitelocke instead of to Whitelocke by his accomplished self. Nevertheless, the extreme difficulties of Ministers must not be overlooked. It should be remembered that Popham had committed them, without their knowledge or consent, to the extravagant venture against Buenos Ayres. They duly recalled Popham in disgrace, as we have seen, and tried him by court-martial; but the Commodore escaped with a severe reprimand, and was almost immediately employed again upon an important service. This was utterly wrong, for he ought to have been dismissed the Navy. But Popham had succeeded in enlisting the cupidity of England in his favour; the pressure of public opinion was difficult to resist; and, as has already been said, the temptation to neutralise Napoleon's Continental blockade by opening new markets in South America was extremely strong. Glory, popularity, and prosperity all seemed bound to follow upon success; and the enterprise commended itself heartily to the gambling spirit of the nation. But gambling should not have been confounded with statesmanship. 1807.

Again, if Ministers were resolved to play a game in which the chances, on the mere showing of common sense, lay very heavily on the side of failure, they might at least have shunned the additional risk of appointing an untried commander. Far from doing so, they actually displaced the capable Auchmuty in favour of the incapable Whitelocke; thus proving themselves to be not only bad administrators but bad gamblers. Nevertheless, by the irony of fate, their mismanagement was the salvation of England. It was worth the humiliation, the loss of brave men and the expense of money to be freed once for all from the fatal entanglement of a permanent and precarious occupation on the Rio de la Plata. If the indignant shade of Whitelocke still broods over the fortune of many British Generals who, though no less deserving of disgrace than himself, have escaped court-martial and cashierment, it may at least

1807. find consolation in the thought that the evacuation of South America after his defeat was a wise, true, and courageous service to his country, worthy to rank with Thomas Maitland's happy evacuation of St. Domingo.

Authorities.—The reports of Whitelocke's court-martial constitute the principal authority for the expedition to Buenos Ayres; that of Gurney (2 vols. 1808) is preferable to that of Blanchard, and Ramsay (1 vol. 1808), being rather fuller and containing far better maps. Any statement for which I have quoted no authority may be accepted as based upon these reports. My references are to Blanchard's edition, which is the more easily accessible, and are indicated by the letters C. M. The official despatches (W. O. Orig. Corres. 161, 162) contain little of importance that is unprinted. There is useful material in *An Authentic Narrative of the Proceedings of the Expedition under Brig.-Gen. Craufurd* (1 vol. 1808, Lond.), and in the numbers of Colburne's *Military Magazine*, April to December 1836. There are also a few details in the *Life of Sir Samuel Whittingham*, and in the *Journal of a Soldier of the Seventy-first* (Edinburgh, 1819). The best extant account of the expedition as a whole is to be found in Captain Lewis Butler's article in the *United Service Magazine* for June, July, and August 1905. Though I do not always endorse the opinions therein advanced, I have found the narrative to be of great value; and I must gratefully acknowledge also the advantage which I have derived from oral discussion of the campaign with the author.

END OF VOL. V

Printed in Great Britain
by Amazon

55806648R00271